Social Work and Social Order

RUTH HUTCHINSON CROCKER

Social Work and Social Order

The Settlement Movement in Two Industrial Cities, 1889–1930

UNIVERSITY OF ILLINOIS PRESS
Urbana and Chicago

For Malcolm

Publication of this work was made possible in part by a grant from the Auburn University Humanities Fund.

© 1992 by the Board of Trustees of the University of Illinois
Manufactured in the United States of America
C 5 4 3 2 1

This book is printed on acid-free paper.

Library of Congress Cataloging-in-Publication Data

Crocker, Ruth.
  Social work and social order : the settlement movement in two industrial cities, 1889–1930 / Ruth Hutchinson Crocker.
      p.   cm.
  Includes bibliographical references and index.
  ISBN 0-252-01790-0
  1. Social settlements—Indiana—Indianapolis—History. 2. Social settlements—Indiana—Gary—History. 3. Social control.
  I. Title.
HV4196.I53C76   1992
362.5'57'0977252—dc20   91-2450
                                                               CIP

Contents

Acknowledgments

It is a pleasure to acknowledge the many debts, intellectual and otherwise, that I have incurred while writing this book. My interest in the settlement movement was first engaged by Allen F. Davis's *Spearheads for Reform: The Social Settlements and the Progressive Movement, 1890–1914* (1967); this book attempts to answer some of the questions raised by his important study. I built on the foundations laid by social-work historians, but, as the endnotes to this volume show, I owe an intellectual debt also to many historians whose focus was not primarily on the settlements or on social work at all, but whose research was nevertheless full of significance for my own. My goal was to write a history of the settlements that integrated new insights and theories in what, for lack of a better term, can be called social history. I therefore acknowledge here the contributions of many in social history, labor history, the history of African-Americans, of women, and of immigration and ethnicity; also the contributions of those brave and brilliant few who wrote interpretations of the wider shifts in the modern political economy—E. P. Thompson, Herbert Gutman, David Montgomery, David F. Noble, and others. I want especially to thank Nancy Cott, Elizabeth Fox-Genovese, Linda Gordon, Alice Kessler-Harris, Mary Ryan, and Katherine Sklar, representatives of an extraordinarily creative generation of women historians and historians of women, for the inspiration they have provided.

I owe a special debt of gratitude to Harold D. Woodman, a fine historian and mentor whose love of history inspired my own. He encouraged this project in its early stages, guided it in its previous life as a dissertation, and always forced me to challenge my material with difficult questions. I am grateful for his encouragement.

Several other good historians at Purdue provided advice and encouragement that helped me to nurse and nudge this manuscript through its early stages. Philip R. Vander Meer, Lester H. Cohen, and Linda Levy Peck all offered quite different insights.

Earlier versions of parts of this book were delivered as papers at meetings of the American Historical Association, the Organization of American Historians, the Berkshire Conference on the History of Women, and the Social

Science History Association, where they were perceptively criticized by Stuart Brandes, Clarke A. Chambers, Allen F. Davis, Stephen Meyer, Elizabeth Israels Perry, and Arnold H. Taylor, among others.

For comments on chapters of this manuscript presented in other forms and forums I am grateful to Ron Cohen, Allen F. Davis, Larry G. Gerber, Darlene Clark Hine, Allen W. Jones, Ralph E. Luker, Robert McDaniel, Brian Price, Linda Reed, Arvarh E. Strickland, William F. Trimble, and to anonymous readers for the *Journal of American History* and for the *Indiana Magazine of History*.

When I began to write about Gary, historians Ray Mohl, Neil Betten, Ron Cohen, and Jim Lane had already written important studies of the city and region. Their work exemplified the best of social history; I have tried to continue in their footsteps.

I also wish to thank the many other historians, librarians, and archivists who aided my research: Ron Cohen and Jim Lane at Indiana University Northwest; archivists Stephen McShane and Robert Moran at the Calumet Regional Archives; and Jean Isaacs and her staff at the Gary Public Library. Others who answered research inquiries included Linda Dunn, Lake County Librarian; Lance Trusty at Purdue University, Calumet; Peg Schoon at the Archives of Purdue University, Calumet; and James J. Divita of Marion College. In Indianapolis, I must thank the staff of the Indiana State Library and also Eric Pumroy and the staff of the Indiana Historical Society Library. At Indiana University-Purdue University in Indianapolis (IUPUI), archivist Jeanette Matthew shared her expert knowledge of Indianapolis history.

Several people with firsthand knowledge of the settlements were kind enough to talk to me or send me materials. They included Mr. Ray Spencer, director of Christamore between 1955 and 1965 and Rev. James Cis of Hammond, Indiana, director of the Gary-Alerding Settlement from 1943 to 1953. Also useful were phone conversations with Dr. William E. Clark, who lived in Gary between 1932 and 1954, and was on the board of both Campbell House and Stewart House. Mrs. Charlene Pettit at the Chancery of the Catholic Diocese of Fort Wayne-South Bend helped me to trace the history of the founding of Gary-Alerding Settlement. And at the East Chicago Historical Society in Indiana Harbor, Mrs. Evaline Johnson and Mrs. Gertrude Webber shared their impressive collection of materials on the history of the Calumet Region. At Hawthorne Social Service Center (not included in the present study), Mrs. Alma Lemen allowed me to read Rev. Clarence Baker's manuscript, "History of Haughville, West Indianapolis."

Christamore, American Settlement—now named Mary Rigg Center—and Flanner House are still working settlements, or neighborhood centers, to use the current term. The directors of these settlements politely hid their surprise that I should be interested in such antediluvian matters as the history of their agencies before 1930. They allowed me access to what remained of the settlements' early papers. I wish to express my gratitude to Dorothy F. Unger of Indianapolis Settlements, Inc., Mr. Glenn S. White and Sarah Kimbrough of Flanner House; and to Mr. Clark Miller of Mary Rigg Center.

My research took me to the archives of two religious denominations. At the Archives of Indiana Methodism at DePauw University, Greencastle, Indiana, an efficient staff facilitated my use of materials on Gary Methodism; while in Indianapolis Mr. Wade Rubick of UCMS (United Christian Missionary Society) allowed me to use materials on the home-missions movement. I would also like to thank Dr. Grant Loavenbruck at the national headquarters of the United Neighborhood Houses of America, Inc. (successor to the National Federation of Settlements) in New York City.

The research for this book was completed with the help of two consecutive David Ross Fellowships from the Graduate School of Purdue University. A Dissertation Fellowship from the Indiana Historical Society allowed me to complete the writing, free from the hectic pleasures of teaching. Katie Alliston at Purdue and Patrice Benson at Auburn were expert typists. Support for typing the revised manuscript was provided by a grant from the Auburn University Humanities Fund. The Humanities Fund also provided a generous subvention toward the publication of the final manuscript; I am very grateful for this support.

I am very grateful to the Chancery of the Archdiocese of Fort Wayne–South Bend for giving me permission to quote from the letters of Bishop Alerding. I would also like to thank James Madison, editor of the *Indiana Magazine of History*, for permission to reprint a version of my earlier article "Christamore: An Indiana Settlement House from Private Dream to Public Agency," 88 (1987): 113–40; and James B. Lane and Edward J. Escobar for permission to use portions of my essay "Gary Mexicans and 'Christian Americanization': A Study in Cultural Conflict," which appeared in their *Forging a Community: The Latino Experience in Northwest Indiana, 1919–1975*. Vol. 2, Calumet Regional Studies Series (Chicago: Cattails Press, 1987), pp. 115–34. Finally, I would like to thank Richard Wentworth and Karen Hewitt at the University of Illinois Press for their efficient guidance and my copy editor, Janice Feldstein, for her careful and expert work.

The problem of social work and social order has preoccupied me for some years and in many settings. It came with me to the gritty wastes of Northwest Indiana and along the broad avenues of Indianapolis; it accompanied me during a baking summer in Grenoble; it dogged my footsteps during a sabbatical to Australia, the continent at once most urbanized and most empty—English, American, and ancient all at once. And even in England, in green, leafy Surrey or at Weymouth, by the seaside, it was never completely forgotten. I finished rewriting in East Central Alabama, where outdoors the scent of hot sunshine on dry pine needles makes work almost impossible unless one retreats to some air-conditioned "room of one's own." Fortunately I had such a room.

In Penelope Lively's wonderful novel *Moon Tiger* (London: Penguin, 1987), the fictional heroine, famous historian Claudia Hampton, old and near death, muses on her great project—"A history of the world, yes, / And in the process, my own" (p. 1). All histories are also the history of their author. Readers will judge whether the fact that the author of this book has been an immigrant and an outsider has enriched or vitiated this study of American reform. My admiration for the settlement workers who went to live among the poor in the early twentieth century is tempered by my sober reassessment of what they were able to achieve. I share their guilt, admire their romantic gesture, but know intellectually that the gesture was not enough.

The support of colleagues at Purdue and Auburn and the love of friends and family have helped me through the research and writing of this book. They enabled me to bring this project to completion, though its shortcomings are mine alone. My daughters, Anne and Elizabeth, have been helpers, intellectual companions, and friends. My mother, Jessie Barton Hutchinson, taught me to love the English language; she is responsible for whatever there is of readability in this book, though she has not yet read it. My father, the late Robert Peter Hutchinson, showed me how much can be accomplished by one energetic and creative individual. Finally, my husband, Malcolm, will greet the completion of this book with pleasure and relief. But because he has always supported my work in every way, my book is dedicated to him in love and gratitude.

Abbreviations

ACA	Association of Collegiate Alumnae Papers, Sophia Smith Collection, Smith College, Northampton, Mass.
AL	Bishop Alerding Correspondence, Chancery of the Diocese of Fort Wayne, Ind.
Ch.H.S.	Chicago Historical Society
CRA	Calumet Regional Archives, Indiana University Northwest, Gary, Ind.
CSA	College Settlement Association Papers, Vassar College, Poughkeepsie, N.Y.
DePauw	Archives of Indiana Methodism, DePauw University, Greencastle, Ind.
E.Ch.H.S.	East Chicago Historical Society
GPL	Gary Public Library, Gary, Ind.
IHS	Indiana Historical Society, Indianapolis, Ind.
II	International Institute Papers, Calumet Regional Archives, Gary, Ind.
ISL	Indiana State Library, Indianapolis, Ind.
IUPUI	Social Service Collection, Blake Street Library, Indiana University-Purdue University at Indianapolis
NCCC	Proceedings, National Conference of Charities and Corrections
NCSW	Proceedings, National Conference of Social Work
UCMS	United Christian Missionary Society Library, Indianapolis, Ind.
UNH	United Neighborhood Houses of America, Inc., New York City

Introduction

While most aspects of Progressive-era reform have undergone searching reappraisal by historians, the settlement-house movement has seemed to occupy a privileged place in Progressive historiography as the central drama of the era's crusade for social justice. As middle-class reformers who "settled" in the slums to share and improve the lives of the poor, the settlement workers seemed to embody the best side of the Progressive impulse to humanize industrial society: they were the quintessential Progressives. Thus, historians Arthur S. Link and Richard L. McCormick in their survey *Progressivism* (1983) characterized the settlement workers as "social progressives," in the vanguard of social reform, and contrasted them with other Progressives whose goal was "to restrain and direct the unruly masses." Similarly, in his 1983 study, *Poverty and Policy in American History*, Michael B. Katz described the settlement workers as "the most humane and progressive" reformers of the period.[1]

To a surprising extent, our account of the settlements has continued to rest on the narratives of those who participated in them, the first settlement workers. These pioneer reformers—Jane Addams, Lillian Wald, Alice Hamilton, Florence Kelley, Graham Taylor, Vida Scudder, and others—wrote such vivid accounts of their struggles on the urban frontier and penned such admiring biographies of settlement friends and associates that their personalities and battles have come to represent the settlement movement as a whole. Their collective biography became a portrait of a humanitarian crusade against social and industrial evils, their battles, a heroic campaign to persuade government to pay the social costs of industrialization.[2]

The heroic nature of the movement and the central role in it of the Boston, New York, and Chicago settlements were thoroughly documented in Allen F. Davis's important study, *Spearheads for Reform: The Social Settlements and the Progressive Movement, 1890–1914* (1967). Focusing on the activist, nationally known settlement workers, Davis showed how the settlements spearheaded reform in recreation, education, health care, and living and industrial conditions. The settlement movement seemed, to all intents and purposes, an early-twentieth-century rehearsal for the Great Society programs of the 1960s.[3]

The parallel was in some ways accurate. Settlement workers were in the vanguard of the social-justice movement of the Progressive era, just as the Peace Corps and VISTA volunteers were in that of the 1960s. In the traditional account, the social-justice movement was a broad coalition including social-gospel ministers, charity experts, economists, and sociologists, new and esoteric specialists like playground experts who promised to remake childhood through scientifically designed playgrounds, model-tenement promoters, and temperance crusaders, all with their own panaceas. At their elbow were journalists like Jacob Riis with *How the Other Half Lives* and dozens of other authors of muckraking exposés who succeeded because they appealed to a middle-class readership eager for news of a working class from which it had become socially and spatially alienated.[4]

If the settlement workers' preoccupation with the evils of urban society was a common anxiety of their age and class, their approach to the problems of poverty, ignorance, and class conflict was novel, even daring: let those with wealth and education go and live among the poor. By "settling" among the less fortunate, they would practice a true charity, sharing the day-to-day existence of the poor while showing them better standards of life and culture. Settlement workers went into the slums partly to understand how the other half lived, and partly to help them to live better.[5]

In the years following the founding of the first American settlement house in 1886, dozens of college-educated men and women became settlement workers, entering the slums and tenement districts with the same spirit of sacrifice and adventure that others of their generation took to the mission fields of India and China. They founded university settlements in Chicago, New York, and Philadelphia; Hull House and Chicago Commons, Boston's South End House, and New York's Nurses' Settlement. Soon, settlement workers found themselves moving beyond their neighborhoods to seek legislative reform at the state and federal levels. Making the settlements their base, Jane Addams, Lillian Wald, Julia Lathrop, Florence Kelley, Robert Hunter, Graham Taylor, Grace and Edith Abbott, Alice Hamilton, and others launched careers in public service that made the names of their settlement houses synonymous with Progressive reform.[6]

The list of reforms that they promoted was impressive. Pressure from settlement workers led to the Labor Department's Investigation of the Conditions of Women and Child Wage Workers in 1906. Florence Kelley, Robert Hunter, J. G. Phelps Stokes, and others led campaigns for state laws regulating child labor. Kelley, Wald, and Addams were successful in persuading Congress to establish a Federal Children's Bureau in 1910, and Julia Lathrop was its first director.[7] Settlement residents Mary Kenny O'Sullivan and William English Walling helped set up the Women's Trade Union League in 1903 to protect working women.[8] At the neighborhood level, residents of Hull House and of the University of Chicago settlement battled the corruption of Chicago ward politicians, demanding that municipal government provide services for the health and safety of city-dwellers. On a larger scale, the ambitious Pittsburgh Survey, directed by settlement-resident Paul Kellogg, was the first full-scale, systematic investigation of the impact of industrialization on the life of an entire region. Other settlement residents called attention to the plight of black Americans: Mary White Ovington, Henry Moskowitz, Florence Kelley, and Lillian Wald organized the conference that resulted in the founding of the NAACP in 1909. In addition, settlement workers established a variety of other reform organizations such as the National Conference on City Planning, the National Playground Association, and the American Civil Liberties Union.[9]

The contribution of the settlements to reform did not end with the eclipse of the Progressive movement in 1914, for the settlement houses, with their mission of humanizing the industrial order, were nurseries for the reforms of the New Deal. If the 1920s was a period of dormancy, a "seedtime for reform," the harvest came in the 1930s when many "graduates" of the Progressive-era settlements played a role in formulating and administering the programs of the New Deal.[10]

The traditional account of the Progressive-era settlements as "spearheads for reform" was a convincing, even an inspiring, one. After all, it described the movement as the settlement leaders had described it themselves. And this interpretation proved to be remarkably resilient. Whenever historians drew distinctions between the protective and coercive "wings" of Progressivism, they put the settlements on the protective side. For example, Paul Boyer in *Urban Masses and Moral Order in America* (1978) contrasted the settlement workers' campaigns to transform city neighborhoods with the "coercive crusades" waged by missions and temperance societies for the moral reform of individuals.[11]

The generally positive view of the settlements survived several distinct historiographical challenges in the 1960s and 1970s. First, there was the rise of the new social history. With its sympathetic portrayal of the lives of the working class, the poor, blacks, and immigrants, and its insistence that historians try to recover the experience of these groups, the new social history called for a history of social work from the point of view of the clients, not the providers, of social services.[12] The new social history also led historians to question the benevolence and wisdom of middle-class charity among the poor. But although several settlement studies began to reflect this more critical approach, few were able to tell the story of their institutions from the clients' point of view, or to document how poor people reacted to the settlements and their programs.[13]

A second challenge to the Progressive interpretation of the settlements came from the Left. By 1971, some historians were claiming that charities and welfare in the past represented not benevolence but the ambition of philanthropists and their allies to control the poor and the working classes.[14] Historians did not so much deny the existence of benevolence as doubt its usefulness in explaining the mechanisms or outcomes of reform. The rise of the "social welfare as social control" school produced a great deal of writing critical of social welfare and charities in the past but, surprisingly, it did not lead to a reinterpretation of the settlement movement as a whole. However, studies of individual settlements were more critical of the motives of settlement workers, attempted to assess the impact of the settlements on the lives of working-class clients, and began to examine in detail the relation of the settlements with immigrants and blacks.[15]

Meanwhile, historians of women mapped out the history of reform institutions in the Progressive era and claimed settlements like Hull House as the central institutions of female reform. Their interpretation of the settlements thus ran counter to the general revisionism of the "social welfare as social control" school. They saw the settlements as the nurturing institutions of a Progressive-era feminism that facilitated the reform careers of a brilliant generation of female social scientists, reformers, and intellectuals. They were less concerned about how settlements fought poverty than about how settlements sustained women's culture, permitted women reformers public lives, and brought women's issues onto the national agenda. Even as other historians became more critical of the settlements, therefore, historians of women revived the favorable view of the Progressive-era settlements as spearheads for reform.[16]

Recent scholarship on the settlements provides examples of widely differing interpretations. In her 1987 book, *Professionalism and Social Change: From the Settlement House Movement to Neighborhood Centers, 1886 to the Present*, Judith Trolander combined earlier scholarship with research into the post-World War II era to produce an important new history of the settlements. She paid attention to the racial tensions that beset the movement, traced the changing (and declining) roles of women in the settlements, and hypothesized about how professionalization tempered reform activism. However, although she produced significant new evidence about what became of the settlements after 1930, Trolander let stand the "heroic account" of the Progressive-era settlements, arguing that the settlements functioned both as social service and as reform institutions and that they served as a "bridge" between privileged and deprived groups in society. On the other hand, Howard Karger, in a study of the Minneapolis settlement movement, *The Sentinels of Order* (also published in 1987), stressed the social-control aspect of the settlements.[17]

Clearly, new emphases in the historiography of reform and social work have made necessary a reassessment of the settlement movement in United States history. The new social history, by revealing the existence of resilient ethnic and working-class cultures, provides a new perspective on Progressive-era social work which often resembled an all-out assault on such cultures. Studies of the development of the social sciences and of professionalization also have an important bearing on the settlements. But few historians before Trolander considered the settlements in this context. Roy Lubove's 1965 study, *The Professional Altruist: The Emergence of Social Work as a Career*, hardly mentions the settlements.[18] Significant new work on philanthropy, voluntary associations, and the foundations has shown the public significance of private organizations in this period. The settlements pioneered services that were later taken up by cities, counties, and states—but what guided these voluntary agencies in their quasi-public functions? Who set their goals and who imposed limits on their activities?

The "settlement impulse" might have been, in Clarke Chambers's felicitous phrase, "an existential moment," but each settlement occurred in a concrete social setting, taking institutional form amid specific configurations of political and economic power. What happened to the settlement impulse? How were religious reformers, college alumnae, Progressive businessmen—settlement workers and their allies, in other words—deflected from their dreams, whether these were to create a Christian Commonwealth, a revived democracy based on the neighborhood, or a commonwealth of Motherhood? How did they come to be instead (to use Leon Baritz's phrase) the "servants of power," challenging the basic problems of American society, but also by their actions unwittingly aiding the consolidation of a corporate capitalism that rested on wide inequalities of wealth and power? These are the questions that *Social Work and Social Order* seeks to answer.

Historiographical shells have burst all around the settlement movement, altering the landscape of Progressive-era historiography beyond recognition, but what I have called the "heroic account" of the settlements still stands. How accurate was the heroic account? Was it resilient because it answered to a need for a viable reform tradition in the American past, a need now more urgent amid the conservatism of late-twentieth-century America? To be fair, the heroic account was not a portrait of the whole settlement movement, nor did it claim to be. It was the story of the largest and most famous of the over four hundred settlement houses in the United States at the turn of the century. What of the other houses? Were they also spearheads for reform—and who stood to benefit from their reforms? Did their residents fight side by side with working-class allies for higher wages and better conditions; pressure city government; agitate for state laws—even have an impact at the federal level, as Hull House did? Settlement leaders like Jane Addams were articulate and self-conscious about their reform careers: they were expert publicists for the settlements, but what of the other settlement houses? If Hull House and Jane Addams have dominated the historiography of the settlement movement, their prominence was no guarantee of typicality. Perhaps the typical settlement was a smaller, less distinguished Hull House, but then again it might have been altogether different.[20] The point was not to discredit the achievements of the famous settlements. The point was that there was more to tell, and I have tried to tell it.

Jane Addams and Hull House have overshadowed the history of the settlement movement in the United States, but this book is the history of another settlement movement, one less well known but still important for what it reveals about the development of American society in the early years of this century, the years from the Progressive Era to the Great Depression. My reassessment of the settlement movement began with a shift of attention away from the dramatic activities of a few settlement leaders like Jane Addams, to focus on the whole range of reform institutions which called themselves settlements, and especially on the "second tier" settlements, institutions that played an important role in their communities over the forty years of this study but were not headed by nationally prominent reformers.

I went in search of this "Other Settlement Movement" in two midwestern cities not far from Chicago. In Gary, Indiana, and in Indianapolis, seven settlement houses thrived between 1890 and 1930, representing the humanitarian and missionary efforts of a variety of reformers. The heroic version of the settlement movement stressed settlement workers' dedication to a vision of progressive change. Was such a commitment part of the motivation of all settlement workers? Were they, like the settlement workers described by historian John McClymer, technocratic experts with a "vested, professional interest in demonstrating the feasibility of intelligently directed social change"?[21] Did they have a blueprint for a new society, or were they responding pragmatically to needs in their local communities? Did most settlement workers consider themselves part of a national movement, or is the settlement movement itself a historian's construct that throws together a variety of different agencies, founded for many reasons and playing different roles?

Variety characterized these seven settlements. While all of them worked for reform, their agendas differed. Some settlement workers were municipal reformers who defined reform in secular terms as efficiency and honest government; some, using organic metaphors, spoke of the regeneration of neighborhoods; others used a religious language of redemption and salvation. *Christamore* in Indianapolis was founded to reform and uplift a white, working-class neighborhood. The only one of these seven settlements to join the National Federation of Settlements and the only college settlement, Christamore had more in common with the Hull House model than any of the others. Beginning as a college settlement and community of women reformers, Christamore combined the goal of practical neighborhood reform with the vision of a revived Christianity. Christamore's evolution toward a more secular and professional social work by the 1920s reflects important trends in the development of social work in the United States.

Three settlement houses were founded in order to Americanize European immigrants. Two of them were established by Protestant churchwomen. *Neighborhood House* and *Campbell Friendship House* were on Gary's South Side, the teeming immigrant section of a city where half the population was foreign-born. *Immigrants' Aid Association*, later called *American Settlement*, was established by Progressive businessmen to Americanize the Eastern European immigrants of Indianapolis who formed a small but noticeable foreign enclave in the Indiana capital. These three settlements shared a determination to teach the English language along with American values, to help foreigners raise living standards while transcending their ethnic traditions, a process akin to religious conversion, which indeed sometimes accompanied it.

Progressivism, it has been said, was "for whites only." All the more important, then, that two of these seven settlements were black settlement houses. *Flanner House* in Indianapolis and *Stewart House* in Gary were agencies founded for African-Americans by coalitions of white and black reformers. Flanner House was launched by the white Charity Organization Society in 1898, and *Stewart House* was set up by the Methodist Episcopal church with the help of the United States Steel Corporation in 1920. Balancing precipitously between the needs of the black community and the insistence of whites that blacks keep "in their place," these settlements show clearly how racism distorted the reform impulse in the Progressive era. This account will locate the black settlements at the intersection of two historiographical traditions that have previously been separate, namely, black history, and the history of white philanthropy among blacks.

Attention has more often focused on what settlements achieved in the Progressive period than on what became of them afterward. In the 1920s, many settlements were founded or sustained by large corporations, but this aspect of the movement has received little attention. The seventh settlement house of this study, *Gary-Alerding Settlement*, was established in 1923 as a joint venture of the Catholic church and the United States Steel Corporation. Founded during the conservative backlash after the Great Steel Strike of 1919, the Gary-Alerding settlement played a role that contrasts sharply with conventional notions about the settlements as advocates for the poor and powerless. While it brought people spiritual comfort and social services, it was a company-sponsored welfare agency that was an antidote to, not a promoter of, fundamental reform.

Writing the history of seven settlement houses inevitably presented problems of organization. Each of them provided clubs, health clinics, recreation, and the like, but the recital of these almost identical activities seven times would have strained the endurance of both writer and reader. Instead, I chose to emphasize one facet of each settlement house; in each chapter, I developed one theme strongly and merely sketched in the rest. In this way, I hoped to bring out the different aspects of the settlement movement—for American Settlement, Americanization; for Campbell Settlement, religious missionary activity, and so on. This treatment should not, of course, be taken to mean that *only* Campbell House resembled a mission: Gary's other Protestant settlement, Neighborhood House, also had a strongly religious character. But in this case, the availability of sources also determined the study's focus. Rather than examine Neighborhood House as a missionary agency, I focused on its work with immigrant women. Chapter 5, "Give Them Home Life," presented an opportunity to test some generalizations concerning the settlements' role in the Americanization of immigrant women. How did the settlements work with female clients as wives, mothers, and wage workers? What did their prescription of "Progressive Motherhood" imply for immigrant and black women? Were the settlement workers feminists? Did "reform" mean trying to improve the status of wives and mothers as individuals, or did it mean strengthening patriarchal family and community structures? How did race affect the programs and policies of the settlements?

Availability of sources also dictated a differing treatment of the two black settlement houses. Material on the programs at Stewart House was disappointingly scanty, but the external relations of the settlement were well documented. Thus my account of Stewart House in the chapter "Between Church and Mill" describes the web of relationships connecting Stewart House to the black and white elites in Gary, to the steel company, and the Methodist Episcopal church. Settlement houses were not always spontaneous creations of reform idealism, as some older accounts suggest. Some, like Stewart House, were agencies planned and sponsored by employers, where social services went hand in hand with social control. On the other hand, my account of the other black settlement, Flanner House, revolves around an analysis of its programs and policies and attempts to assess the effectiveness of "practical philanthropy along the Color Line."

One theme in this study will be the connections between social work and social order. The philanthropists and reformers who founded these seven settlement houses intended not only to do good but also to supply sources of community cohesion that were lacking. They experienced the growth of the cities in terms of disorder. Poverty, vice, and intemperance were signs of this disorder—evils calling for attention, but also symptoms of a deeper social malaise. Neighborhood organization was to be the means of reestablishing control, winning back the city and binding it once more into a cohesive, well-knit community.[22]

This does not mean that the philanthropists who established settlement houses for the poor were *really* only interested in schemes to manipulate and coerce them. Such cloak-and-dagger explanations are neither convincing nor necessary. They overlook the extent to which the values of the controllers were hegemonic values shared by rich and poor alike. In addition, they overlook how often lower-class and client populations resisted the "controllers" and turned "controlling" institutions to their own ends: they assume that social controllers always achieved the kind and amount of control that they sought.[23]

This account will fully document the intentions of the founders and will assess the impact of the settlements. I have tried to suggest some of the different meanings of a settlement house for the various people who were touched by it. For example, I will argue that Christamore, to the college women who lived there, became a women's institution like Hull House, and to that extent was an empowering institution. However, to its white, working-class female clients, Christamore must have had quite a different meaning, one that I have explored tentatively through the available evidence. Again, to the black women who were excluded from the settlement, Christamore represented a cruel denial of services, services that they obtained, however, from segregated agencies such as Flanner House, and from a variety of black self-help organizations. Thus, I have attempted to explore the meanings of these institutions for their clients as well as their sponsors, for settlement workers as well as for the poor—but I do not mean to imply that the effects of the settlements were always what the founders intended, or that we can "judge motives by assessing the practical effects."[24]

I early abandoned my initial assumption that the settlement workers sought social control. After all, the questions that historians ask determine what answers they receive, and to ask whether settlements were "for" social reform or social control would be to take up a battering-ram where a key would do. The study of these seven settlement houses in two Indiana cities—their programs, their personnel, their funding, their relations with elite groups and with the working class, immigrants, blacks, and women—can provide such a key to understanding how the settlements arose and how they functioned. Ultimately, it should also help us to answer the more important question of why American reform movements have challenged, but have usually been unable to alter, existing structures of economic and political power.

PART I

Indianapolis:
No Heaving, Grimy City

"Not quite so long ago as a generation," wrote Indiana author Booth Tarkington in an affectionate and nostalgic portrait of Indianapolis,

> there was no panting giant here, no heaving, grimy city; there was but a
> pleasant big town of neighborly people who had understanding of one
> another, being, on the whole, much of the same type. It was a leisurely
> and kindly place—"homelike" it was called—and when the visitor had
> been taken through the State Asylum for the Insane and made to appre-
> ciate the view of the cemetery from a little hill, his host's duty of Baede-
> ker was done. The good burghers were given to jogging comfortably about
> in phaetons or surreys for a family drive on Sunday. No one was very rich;
> few were very poor; the air was clean, and there was time to live.[1]

Although Tarkington's good-humored portrait tended to romanticize a
simpler age, the impression it gave of Indiana's capital city was accurate.
Like all American cities, Indianapolis had experienced rapid growth, from a
population of about 75,000 in 1880 to over 233,000 in 1910. The fastest
growth had come between 1860 and 1870 when the Indiana capital experienced a 159 percent population increase. But by the turn of the century,
Indianapolis seemed fairly stable compared to many faster-growing cities.
Tarkington's "pleasant big town of neighborly people" had some basis in
fact. With a quarter of a million inhabitants Indianapolis still gloried in the
title "City of Homes" and retained the look of a provincial capital rather
than a metropolis.[2]

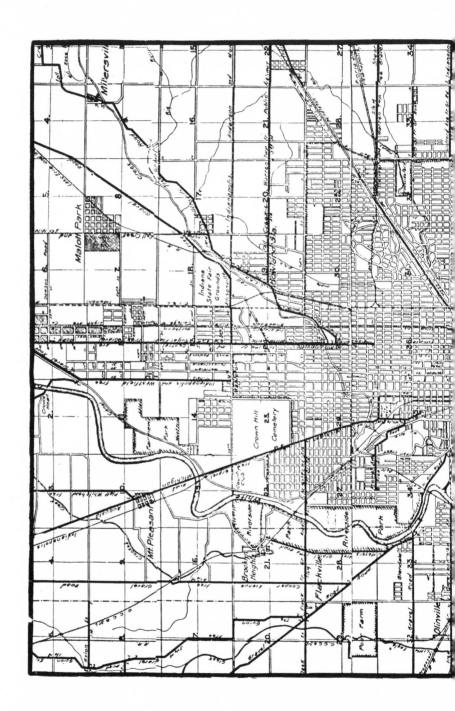

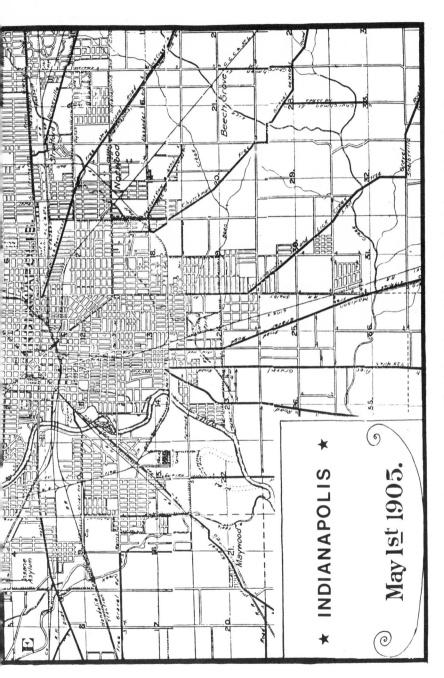

Map 1. Indianapolis, 1905. From "Official Road Map of Marion County, Indiana, May 1, 1905."

As manufacturing and processing industries developed, the physical appearance of the city changed. New public buildings were constructed, housing spread outward, and, because life was not all work, the city fathers planned a system of parks covering over nine hundred acres that was the largest in the nation.[3] Suburbs encroached on the surrounding countryside until the city far outstripped its original one-mile square. Irvington, a planned residential community of winding streets and avenues with Butler University at its center, had an air of prosperity and culture. To the north of the downtown, Woodruff Place, another planned subdivision, epitomized gracious living, and farther out, beyond Fall Creek, was Broad Ripple, named after its amusement park, a harbinger of the even more far-flung subdivisions of the twentieth century. There were industrial suburbs also, such as Mars Hill, an industrial park, and Haughville, west of the White River, with its engineering industries and a mixed population of Irish, Americans, and Slovenians.[4]

The great majority of the people of Indianapolis, 70 percent in 1920, were not foreigners, however, but native-born Americans. Like other cities of the upper South and lower Midwest such as Cincinnati or Louisville, the Indiana capital attracted a steady stream of migrants from rural areas and thousands more who were on their way to larger cities such as Detroit or Chicago where there were jobs or rumors of jobs. These migrants from the South, from Kentucky and Tennessee, and from the Carolinas gave Indianapolis the air of a southern town.[5]

But as early as 1848 an important migration of Germans into Indiana left its mark on the culture and character of Indianapolis with a variety of religious and cultural institutions. In 1920, Germans or the children of German immigrants still formed the largest foreign group in the city. They made up 44 percent of the population, with the Irish coming second at 20 percent.[6] Many other nationalities were present, but most had fewer than 1,000 members, an insignificant fraction of the whole. The "new immigration" was represented by small groups of Slovenians, Russians, Turks, and other Balkan peoples, with the Romanians being the most numerous. The South Europeans settled mainly in the Twelfth Ward, which was promptly called the "Foreign District" to distinguish it from its predominantly American surroundings. Americanization of these foreigners became the urgent task of the settlement houses in the early twentieth century, as we shall see.[7]

Freedmen began settling in Indianapolis in the 1870s, joining an older black community that dated to before the Civil War. By 1910 blacks numbered more than 21,000 and made up 11 percent of the population. Wartime migration increased their numbers until by 1920 the black community numbered 34,000 and formed an important factor in urban life and culture.[8] Their story will be told in Chapter 3.

A significant factor in the growth of Indiana was the development of a diversified industrial economy. In 1880, the $65,000,000 dollars invested in industry in the state was only one-tenth the amount invested in agriculture. But by 1920 the industrial sector had caught up. In this year, two centers of manufacturing, Indianapolis and the Calumet Region (the northwest corner of the state which included Gary), together employed nearly half of all those engaged in manufacturing in Indiana. The industries of the two regions were sharply different, however. While the Calumet Region had technologically advanced, capital-intensive heavy manufacturing centered in a few giant companies, notably U.S. Steel and Standard Oil, Indianapolis had a variety of manufacturing, some of it still small-scale, some, like meat-packing and the manufacture of railroad cars, tending to concentration.[9] The nonmanufacturing sector was larger in Indianapolis than in Gary, 43 percent of the male work force being employed in manufacturing compared to a Gary total of 68 percent. Numbers employed in meat-packing and slaughtering in the Indiana capital grew sharply from 2,085 in 1899 to 4,001 in 1909 and included many first- and second-generation immigrants.[10]

The 1890s saw dramatic growth in the Indianapolis manufacturing economy. Despite the 1893 depression these were the "fat years," when manufacturing increased twice as fast in Indianapolis as in the rest of urban America. The city escaped a severe depression partly because its position at the center of an excellent communications network ensured its continuing dominance as a commercial center, partly because of the rise of the automobile industry. By 1914, the manufacture of automobiles was the third largest industry in Indianapolis.[11]

Despite this, between 1900 and 1910 the rate of growth slowed; shrinking supplies of natural gas ended a period of cheap and apparently inexhaustible power, and between 1910 and 1914 the rate of increase in the city's manufacturing fell to below the national average. At the same time to the north on Lake Michigan, Gary rose to challenge Indianapolis as the state's manufacturing leader. By 1930 the production of Gary's plants was twice that of the Indiana capital.[12]

The 1890s saw not only the expansion of the city's economy but also the emergence of a progressive party in city politics. The Commercial Club, founded in 1890 by William Fortune, announced itself with the declaration that "radical changes in the form of municipal government are necessary before there can be inaugurated an era of the most desirable improvement and change."[13] For the next two decades the Commercial Club was a vocal proponent of reform. Its leaders attacked municipal corruption and the inefficiency of an outdated form of city government, advocating an expansion of municipal services from which all citizens would benefit. After intensive study, the Commercial Club devised a new city charter with a mayor-council organization based on that of Brooklyn, and in 1891, after a struggle, the legislature enacted it into law. The decade following saw a significant increase in the scope and responsibility of city government. Parks and playgrounds, sewage disposal, water supply, lighting, paving, refuse collection, and traffic control all now came to the attention of progressive town government. The city's biographer compared Indianapolis to a youth who had burst his "swaddling clothes" and was now a "lusty adolescent." Businessmen became accustomed to defining what was good for the city; in fact, few challenged the principle that what was good for business was good for Indianapolis.[14]

But beneath the prosperity and growth lay poverty and unemployment. In the depression year of 1873, Kingan's and other packing firms had turned away over 1,000 men a day. The depression of the nineties swamped the private charities and drew no constructive response from "progressive" city government. Inadequate housing, unsafe water supplies, poor schools, and high crime rates were urban problems calling out for action.[15]

The first decade of the twentieth century saw a national awakening to the social problems of industrialization. Reformers experiencing a "Discovery of Poverty" expressed impatience at traditional methods of relief.[16] Some businessmen and reformers spearheaded a campaign to reform and reorganize private charities. In Indianapolis, the Charity Organization Society, founded in 1879 in reaction against the desultory paternalism of the Indianapolis Benevolent Society, stressed efficiency and better management. Led by Rev. Oscar McCulloch, with the backing of a group of business and religious leaders, the COS was innovative in several ways. It attempted to centralize private charity through a clearinghouse and, by introducing bureaucratic methods—thorough investigation of all cases and careful record-keeping—to cut down relief expenditures without hurting the "deserving" poor. The COS also aimed to smooth the relationship between the charities, which served the poor directly, and businessmen who were the major source of funds. The Businessmen's Committee of the society advocated progressive, efficiently run private charity; its endorsement was a guarantee to potential givers that a charitable cause was genuine. It thus anticipated many features of the Community Chests of the 1920s.[17]

The subsequent development of private charities need only be briefly summarized here. The federation of Indianapolis private charities came as a result of World War I. The War Chest, set up in April 1918, authorized a study to be undertaken by the New York-based National Bureau of Municipal Research with the purpose of surveying all agencies and recommending some for financial support, based on efficiency and need. Reform and federation thus proceeded hand in hand. The War Chest became the Community Chest in 1920, and in 1924 the Council of Social Agencies was formed. The ambition of business to direct private giving through one coordinated organization was thus realized just a few years before the Great Depression revealed the inadequacy of private voluntarism and brought the federal government decisively into the relief of poverty and distress.[18]

The development of private charities and the history of the professionalization of social work have been told elsewhere.[19] A more dramatic response to the social problems of industrialization and urban growth began in the 1880s and became a national phenomenon by 1900. This was the establishment of settlement houses. Flanner House, established to work with the black community; Christamore, founded in the Atlas section northeast of downtown; and the Immigrants' Aid Association's "Foreign House" in the Twelfth Ward were Indianapolis settlement houses that reflected a new approach to the poor. A Jewish settlement house that served the needs of Jews from Germany and elsewhere gave a strong example of self-help in the Hoosier capital; however it does not form part of this study.[20]

Rev. Oscar McCulloch, minister of Plymouth Congregational Church, best represented the close connection of the settlements, the social gospel, and the COS in Indianapolis. Under McCulloch's direction, Plymouth Church became an institutional church with a wide range of cultural, educational, and social-service activities in addition to traditional worship services. McCulloch also founded the Indianapolis COS and dominated it until his death in 1891. In McCulloch, the humanitarianism of the social gospel was allied to the businesslike goals of the COS. The minister was not content with a reformed charity: inspired by the vision of Toynbee and Ruskin, he sought an ideal of community and cooperation in place of the atomistic individualism of his time.[21]

In Stanton Coit's ideal of the Neighborhood Guild, McCulloch found the institution that he hoped would restore a sense of community and repair the fragmentation of urban life.[22] The guild house idea evoked an imagined feudal past of social harmony and well-understood obligations, but it was also a blueprint for progressive change. In a speech to the Indianapolis Commercial Club in 1890 McCulloch outlined his idea of a citywide network of settlement houses that would meet some of the material wants of the poor and also uplift them spiritually and morally. McCulloch thus adopted the neighborhood as the basis for urban renewal with the settlement house, a revived medieval guild house, at its center. Quoting the English housing reformer, Octavia Hill, he declared that the two things most lacking in a modern city were order and beauty. "Peoples' Halls"—guild houses or settlements—could supply these. "A simple, attractive house, open by day to women and children, and at night to men and boys, would attract many from the saloon and the street. A reading room, a game and coffee and smoking room, a bath and toilet room—this would make a social center." To reform and uplift the ignorant and needy of Indianapolis, a guild hall should be established for every thousand persons, he declared.[23]

The support of business was crucial to McCulloch's plans. His appeal to business was frankly a commercial one. A settlement was not primarily a religious or missionary organization, he told a meeting of business leaders: improvement of the conditions of working people was in everyone's interests. "Human interest is one with the true commercial interest. In the end, justice is cheapest."[24]

McCulloch's early death at the age of forty-eight cut short his reforming activities. But men who had been active in the Commercial Club and in the COS—Judge Collins, John Holliday, and Frank Flanner—carried on his work. Whereas at the national level the COS and the settlement movement seemed frequently at odds, in Indianapolis they cooperated closely. For example, the settlements provided a convenient base for the friendly visiting that was at the heart of COS practice and that enabled the society to investigate cases of need.[25] The tensions within this ideal—the visionary idealism of Christian Socialism and the more practical considerations of employers—would create institutions with, at best, an ambiguous mandate. Later, the settlement houses, subtly transmuted into community centers, would turn from McCulloch's visionary reform ideals to concentrate on the more mundane tasks of group work while helping to adjust each new wave of blacks and immigrants to industrial life in America.

But this is to anticipate later developments. In the early twentieth century, the settlement that best reflected the minister's vision of social regeneration was Christamore. Although we cannot say whether the settlement's founders, Anna Stover and Edith Surbey, were directly influenced by McCulloch, Christamore combined perfectly the vision of material betterment and spiritual revival he had boldly advocated.

their separate ways after graduation in 1894. Stover went back to Ladoga, and Surbey attended the Kindergarten and Primary Training School at Irvington (a "normal school" for teacher training), where by 1899 she was a member of the faculty.[18]

In 1900, Edith Surbey, too, underwent a religious conversion while attending the Moody Institute. The experience would determine the future direction of her life, for soon after this she joined Anna Stover to create plans for a settlement house in Indianapolis. The friends became deeply attached. Surbey confided to a private memoir, "My soul was knit to hers in a true 'David and Jonathan' love and friendship." Like Jane Addams and Mary Rozet Smith, or Lillian Wald and Lavinia Dock, Stover and Surbey drew energy for their work from their loving, supportive relationship which would last for almost forty years.[19]

February 1905 saw the two friends installed in a rented room on Roosevelt Avenue in the working-class Atlas District of Indianapolis. "Our recreation at this time was drawing plans for a Settlement House," Stover wrote.[20] They surrounded themselves with other young women who were interested in their scheme—student-teachers from the Normal School, Butler College students and alumnae, and teachers from the nearby Washington Public School. There was no more sign of the depression from which Anna Stover had suffered. Planning the settlement house and managing the physically demanding and often dirty tasks of the first few years were a challenge that drove away thoughts of illness, as organizing Hull House had done for the former invalid Jane Addams.[21]

In May 1905, the two women rented a five-room house on Arsenal Avenue in Indianapolis and launched the settlement house which they called "Christamore."[22] Several years of careful planning had preceded their move. They had the backing of several prominent Indianapolis citizens including Professor Calvin Kendall of the public schools and Eliza Blaker of the Indianapolis Free Kindergarten Association, who had agreed to open a branch of the kindergarten at their settlement.[23] They also secured the support of Charles S. Grout, secretary of the Charity Organization Society, and of Evaline Holliday, socially prominent wife of the former editor of the Indianapolis *News*. Eliza Browning of the Indianapolis Public Library agreed to supply the settlement house with library books.[24]

The location of the house was influenced by the encouragement of the largest employer in the district, Hugh Hanna, whose Atlas Engine Works employed nearly a thousand men.[25] In this area of about one square mile northeast of downtown were, in addition to the Atlas Engine Works at Nineteenth Street and Martindale Avenue, the Indianapolis Stove Works, two lumberyards, planing mills, and a bottling plant.[26] The area contained only a handful of immigrants, but its black population was growing rapidly.

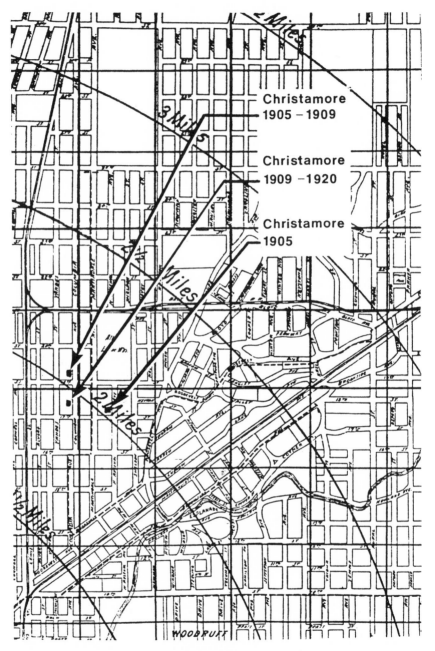

Map 2. Christamore Settlement House, Indianapolis, 1905–20. From R. L. Polk and Co., "City Directory Map of Indianapolis, Indiana, 1909."

There were several white and a few black churches, and a public school, described by a local minister as "one of the smallest and oldest and most poorly equipped school buildings in the city." The streets of the district were all unpaved, and it was estimated that there were between fifteen and twenty saloons.[27]

Housing conditions, though not crowded, left much to be desired. Only about 20 percent of the houses were connected to the city water or sewage systems, and only 5 percent had indoor plumbing. The area was predominantly one of renters, most of them recent arrivals. Unemployment and poverty plagued black families the most, for the Atlas Engine Works employed only white men. But even for whites the economic situation of the district became precarious when the Atlas Works began to reduce its work force; by 1910 it was running only part time.[28]

One settlement house had already been founded and abandoned close by. Its sponsor, the Rev. Carlos Rowlinson, pastor of the Third Christian Church, left a picture of the neighborhood in 1910 which, though overdrawn, illustrates how an urban missionary viewed the challenge of the city.

> The community is not properly housed or fed, it is often cold and hungry, it is often sick and often discouraged, it is without proper employment and proper recreation, it is often drunken and often sinful. A host of the people are down, have lost their money and their friends, . . . do not know how to make money or how to save it, do not know how to cook or how to keep house, and many of them do not care to know these things.[29]

Another observer, sociologist Leander M. Campbell Adams, in a survey of the Christamore district, described conditions as "primitive." Moral dangers went along with ignorance and poverty, Adams found. While the men spent their time loafing in the corner saloons, "poisoned by cheap whiskey, bad beer, impure atmosphere," their wives seemed helpless to maintain good homes. What these people needed was clean recreation and the opportunity for improvement, he concluded.[30]

To Anna Stover and Edith Surbey also, it seemed as if the people of the Atlas neighborhood lacked the skills for urban living and were utterly demoralized. The neighborhood needed a combination of practical help and spiritual uplift, they believed, "not only the outward friendliness and cheer of our work, but the inward change of heart and purpose."[31] Like other settlement workers, they had no trouble imagining a social work that was both "scientific" sociology and religious mission.

Historians have often regarded the settlements as standard bearers of racial equality in a racist era, but a careful study of settlements such as Christamore cannot sustain this view. Christamore's founders had no intention of extending the benefits of the settlement house to their black neighbors; in fact, they interpreted the rather casual intermixing of blacks and whites in the neighborhood as an indication of serious degeneracy. The settlement's mission was to lift the white population to a "higher plane" and to draw the color line more sharply. But by excluding blacks from Christamore, the founders charted a policy that would put the very existence of the settlement house in doubt within ten years.[32]

Between 1905 and 1911 Stover and Surbey developed Christamore into a lively center of neighborhood improvement for its white neighbors. At the same time (though they did not advertise this aspect) Christamore was a practical demonstration of cooperative living for young single women. The settlement attracted a variety of female residents who came and went, some staying only for a summer, others for a year, still others returning each year.[33] Not all the residents had a burning interest in social problems and their solution. Some came because settlement life was a daring adventure. For others, residence at Christamore was a matter of convenience; cheap, respectable lodging for young ladies was difficult to find in Indianapolis as in other cities.[34] A settlement like Christamore, with its atmosphere of female conviviality, heightened by the daring of living in the slums, presented an attractive but still respectable alternative for young women trying to live independent lives. The residents bore up well under the hard physical labor of housework and gardening because of this sense of adventure. In addition, the head residents took an extended vacation each summer, going on long trips that provided themes and material for settlement programs when they returned, refreshed, in September. During these summer breaks, the settlement limped along with a makeshift staff.[35]

Unlike the settlement houses established by a church or business, Christamore operated without an institutional affiliation, although its founders initially sought such a link with Butler College. The decision to terminate Christamore's Butler affiliation illustrates some of the pressures faced by settlement houses. In the spring of 1905, Will Howe, professor of English Literature, and Butler president Garrison accosted Stover at a Butler College chapel service. They questioned her about the projected settlement house and offered to have Butler adopt the settlement. In April 1905, the Butler College Settlement Association was founded to sponsor the venture with a board of directors consisting of professors and alumni. Thus began a brief formal connection between the settlement house and Butler.[36]

As a college settlement, Christamore was to combine investigation with reform, to "investigate and improve existing conditions, and to provide centers for a higher civic, social and religious life."[37] With the first money raised by the board, Stover and Surbey printed leaflets for publicity and rented the cottage at 1918 Arsenal Avenue which became the settlement's first home.

Yet by November 1905, Stover and Surbey had decided that the connection with Butler was an embarrassment. Some potential supporters were lost
because they assumed that Butler College supported the settlement house
financially, others because the "Butler College" label suggested sectarian-
ism. In reality, Christamore was struggling financially; Stover and Surbey
supported it from their private means and by begging donations from friends
and from sympathetic businessmen. In 1906, therefore, they dissolved the
Butler College Settlement Board and in its place organized a board of
twelve citizens headed by Rev. Harry Blunt of the First Congregational
Church. In contrast with the previous board which had been dominated by
the Disciples of Christ, this new board was broadly representative of different churches.[38]

Although the formal connection between Butler and Christamore was
dissolved, the settlement nevertheless continued as a college settlement. Its
director was required to be a college graduate, and Butler students in economics and sociology continued to be residents. An editorial in the *Butler
Collegian*, January 13, 1906, entitled "Our Settlement House," appealed for
students to work at Christamore. "The experience of working for a settlement of this sort is something that no one can afford to miss. You need it
and it needs you, your interests, your contributions. Why not get up a party
of five or six of your friends and see for yourself?"[39]

If the tone of this editorial suggests that some settlement residents were
dilettantes to whom "slumming" was more a diversion than a commitment,
the role of the settlement house in the developing social-work field was
nevertheless important. Before the establishment of university schools of
social work, the training of social workers was improvised at settlement
houses like Christamore.[40] Butler students were required to have practical
experience, or "field work," before graduation, and the city of Indianapolis
was their "social laboratory." As the *College Catalogue* explained in 1905,
"While it does not present the complexity of phenomena to be found in
some larger cities, it is large enough to furnish almost every factor of the
most complicated social life."[41]

A visit or an extended stay at Christamore enabled students in the
"Charities" course at Butler to make a "personal investigation of actual conditions found in the city."[42] For students of Indiana University at Bloomington, some fifty miles south, Christamore was an "urban laboratory" where
those preparing for a career in social work did their field work. By 1910,
Christamore's function in the training of social workers had become so
prominent that the agency was sometimes referred to, not as a settlement,
but as a "Training School for Social Workers."[43]

Settlement residence sometimes led to investigation and reform. In 1910
Indiana University students resident at Christamore compiled data for

Leander M. Campbell Adams's survey of housing and living conditions under the direction of Professor Ulysses G. Weatherley.[44] Like the Hull House residents who compiled *Hull House Maps and Papers*, these Christamore residents tried to get a complete statistical description of their neighborhood. Such surveys were more than an academic exercise. This one provided data for the campaign for a state housing law that passed two years later in 1913.[45]

This relationship between the universities and the settlement house, so quickly established, was soon changed, however. In 1911, Indiana University set up a permanent Department of Social Service in Indianapolis, and this siphoned off many students who might otherwise have entered settlement work. Students now did their practical work and their medical-social research not at the settlement but with the charity patients at the hospital and the city dispensary.[46] Christamore continued to have Butler students as residents and helpers, but the settlement house was no longer crucial to social-work training in Indiana. As in the nation as a whole, the education of professional social workers was no longer dependent on the rather idiosyncratic settlement houses. With the organization of social-work departments in the universities, settlements like Christamore were left shorn of their function of training social workers.[47] But Christamore continued to have an impact on the neighborhood and those who lived there. What was the nature of this impact? What did the settlement mean to the neighborhood?

With the motto "Improvement is the aim, friendship the principle," Anna Stover and Edith Surbey embarked on the first task for any new settlement house, winning acceptance in their neighborhood.[48] Neighborhood visiting and settlement clubs were important to settlements because of their content, of course, but also because they served to establish everyday contact between settlement workers and working-class neighbors that the settlements believed was vital to their mission of breaking down class barriers. Optimistic about the possibility of teaching their values to their poorer neighbors, they hoped that through daily contacts the settlement would begin to regenerate and uplift the whole neighborhood.[49]

Christamore's founders decided to organize a kindergarten for neighborhood children as a practical, needed program that would be welcomed by working mothers. Throughout the nation, settlement workers began kindergartens because of the reforming potential of work with young children. The fact that Stover and Surbey had been trained as teachers and that several of the first settlement residents were kindergarten teachers also made this a natural choice. The Christamore kindergarten was not an isolated effort but part of an older, publicly supported kindergarten system that

Figure 1. Settlement children at Christamore, 1907. Courtesy of the Indiana State Library, Indianapolis.

dated back to the establishment of the Indianapolis Free Kindergarten Association in 1882.[50] In August 1905, Anna Stover moved the settlement house to larger quarters at 1908–10 Columbia Avenue in order to accommodate the kindergarten, which opened in September 1905. The initial enrollment of 45 children had risen to 135 by the following year.[51] In Martha Stewart Carey, kindergarten director from 1907 until her death in 1925, Christamore had a vigorous proponent of this branch of progressive education. Her influence in the life of Christamore was so strong that an account of the settlement house in the 1920s credited her with founding it.[52]

An important part of Christamore's program consisted of club activities with young people. Club work should be "broad, that is religious, industrial, intellectual and social," Anna Stover wrote. She established clubs for all age groups of boys and girls: for the girls, Jewel, Fidelity, Princess, and Loyalty clubs; for the boys, the White Shield Club, the Columbia, and the Young American clubs (see Table 1). Christamore's clubs were designed to produce "real patriotism, a respect for and knowledge of self-government, and cultivation of the spirit of usefulness," one sponsor noted.[53] But

Table 1
Clubs and Classes at Christamore, 1907

Name of Club	Membership	Subjects
Fidelity Club	Girls 9 to 13	Cooking, housekeeping, sewing
Loyalty Club	Young women	Cooking, housekeeping, travel, literature
Young American Club	Boys over 13	Travel, biographies, science, city government
Friendly Neighbors	Women	Cooking, housekeeping, child training, literature
Princess Club	Girls over 12	Cooking, housekeeping, literature
Columbia Club	Boys under 13	Travel, biography, science, city government

Source: *The College Settlement in Indianapolis* (1907), n.p.

housekeeping, rather than government or patriotism, formed the theme of settlement work with girls. The "formula" for their clubs was "alternately cooking and housekeeping with devotional beginnings and social and game endings."[54]

Boys' programs presented problems for most settlement houses: boys could not be ignored, yet they were hard to control, and ideas of proper education for them dictated the use of a gymnasium, which few settlement houses could afford. Boys' programs generally became established only after a settlement had sufficient funds to build a gym and to employ male workers. Wood-carving classes were tried with the boys at Christamore, but even these proved too much for the settlement worker in charge.[55]

Historians influenced by the Hull House model have assumed that settlements were interested in preserving folk and ethnic cultures. But Christamore's founders seem to have had little or no appreciation of the cultural heritage of these rural folk from the Upland South. They judged the homes of their neighbors as sadly lacking in hygiene, order, and regularity. It was up to the settlement workers to teach these migrants from rural Indiana, Kentucky, and Tennessee how to cook, sew, and keep house. They assumed that learning would be one-way.

In fact, the settlement workers ended up learning from their neighbors: living in a poor neighborhood made them more aware of the reality of poverty. After moving into the first house on Columbia Avenue, Stover wrote,

"We shall never perhaps forget the utter physical discomforts of this time."
And in the winter of 1907 she recorded the destitution of people suffering
hard times because of the depression of that year and her inability to enjoy
a missionary tea where missionary women were "serving each other with
needless food, where [sic] those not ten blocks away were suffering for necessary food."[56] The settlement house on Columbia Avenue was in a racially
mixed district; close by was a black church "from which came distracting
shouts at all times of the day and night." And on the other side lived a
"quarrelsome and disreputable" poor white family whose members woke the
settlement residents at four o'clock each morning with shouts and cries.
While Anna Stover remained aware of the gulf that separated college-
trained ladies from Appalachian migrants, she nevertheless tried to draw
near the settlement's neighbors. With well water that had to be boiled for
drinking, no screens on the windows to keep out summer flies and, in winter, stoves that were continually smoky and sometimes dangerous, the settlement residents were overwhelmed with the physical discomforts of slum
life. "It gave to one a real sympathy and concern for all those who labor
under similar conditions," Stover wrote. And as they gradually overcame
harsh living conditions with hard work and a sense of humor the settlement
residents also worked hard to be accepted. "We began to create the sentiment in our neighborhood that for all our learning, we were 'just common
and sociable like'," Anna Stover wrote.[57]

Some of the more famous settlement houses, such as Hull House, established model kitchens and laundries as experiments in cooperative living in
an attempt to reorganize in a more efficient way the unpaid domestic work
that was women's responsibility. But most settlements, like Christamore, remained committed to the ideal of the single-family home with male breadwinner and "Progressive mother," despite the fact that the settlement house
was itself a living demonstration of a community of single females, living
cooperatively.[58]

In order to teach the standards of home life they wanted their neighbors
to adopt, Christamore residents chose a demonstration method: they put
their domestic standards on display at elaborate entertainments to which
the whole neighborhood was invited. One such "entertainment" in 1907,
entitled "The Making of a Home," featured many displays of domestic skills.
The Columbia Boys' Club demonstrated the cooking of vegetable soup, the
Fidelities sweeping, and the Loyalties their prowess at making beds. "But
the washing and ironing by the Jewel Club [girls aged five to nine], with
their tubs and suds and their earnest endeavor, was counted the cleverest of
all," Anna Stover fondly recalled.[59]

Special events like these began to attract neighborhood women to Christamore's clubs and classes. After a discouraging start when the first recruits

to the Friendly Neighbors Club seemed to Anna Stover to be "backward and silent," the group began to be a success. By 1907, meetings of the club were attracting an average attendance of twenty-five. By putting neighborhood women in charge of clothing sales to others in need, the settlement workers tried to involve them in some responsibility at the settlement.[60]

As it became better established, Christamore increasingly became a center for the activity of other welfare organizations and for the promotion of reform. Charity Organization Society workers, for instance, sometimes lived at Christamore, and collectors for the Dime Savings Association were familiar and frequent visitors.[61] Christamore began to act as a clearinghouse for social-service work in its district. The settlement also became a catalyst for reform by playing a role in the progressive campaign to ensure a pure milk supply for Indianapolis.

An increased demand for pure milk in the growing Hoosier capital led to progressive efforts to regulate dairies and retail outlets. The problem was not the quantity of milk available but its quality. Poor distribution meant that milk was often spoiled or dirty when it reached city consumers. The result was a high summer seasonal death rate, especially for children and infants.[62] The Pure Milk Program was set up under the auspices of the Children's Aid Association in cooperation with the City Board of Health, the Kindergarten Association, and the Commercial Club. It was funded by public subscriptions and receipts from the sale of milk.[63] Organized similarly to programs already launched in twenty other cities, the Indianapolis Pure Milk Program provided for the distribution of safe milk, pasteurized at a modern dairy. With five nurses and six physicians in attendance at the distribution stations to examine the babies who were brought there, the program was an important advance for preventive health care. Indeed, the scheme was a great success. By one estimate, in a single year the program had lowered by one-half the seasonal mortality for children under five.[64]

The selection of Christamore as one of five "pure milk stations" strengthened the settlement's position as a community center. There were now opportunities to make contacts with neighborhood people since babies were weighed and information was given to mothers during their visits to the station. In 1911, the work was expanded when a trained nurse was employed at the settlement to make home visits. Nurse Alice Menser was soon making an estimated one hundred calls a week. She did not confine her attention to sickness, but also made the most of her "many opportunities to teach the lessons of thrift, cleanliness, and right living by her presence at the time of sickness."[65]

As the settlement's activities multiplied, its residents began to feel hampered because of lack of space. Consequently, plans were made to build a new settlement house on two lots at 1806 East Columbia Avenue which Anna Stover had purchased for $1,000 in 1907. She had raised the money by asking each board member for $100, and collecting "almost $300, mostly in pennies," from the neighborhood.[66] A building campaign began in earnest early in 1909; funds were collected from well-wishers, and an architect donated his services. Construction was completed in August 1909, and in October 1909 Christamore's residents moved into the new building. Working together with women from the neighborhood, they varnished first all the floors and then all the shabby old furniture in the house, having first visited Eli Lilly's Varnish Works and obtained the necessary materials and "an expert employee to show us how to do the work ourselves." Anna Stover looked back on this exhausting experience with satisfaction, not only because of the improvements to the settlement house, but because she believed that the settlement workers had started a wave of repainting and revarnishing in the Christamore neighborhood.[67]

The new settlement house was an object of pride and satisfaction. "We planned everything so carefully that there is nothing to change," Anna Stover wrote. On the ground floor were the office of the headworker, large rooms for clubs and classes, a sizable hall for the kindergarten, and a gymnasium large enough for basketball games. On the second floor were the apartments of the head worker and a woman assistant director, and more rooms for meetings. Baths for men and women adjoined the gymnasium. "In appearance and attractiveness the settlement serves as a model for the neighborhood," a 1918 report noted. "The neighborhood cannot help to be [sic] better because of the presence of the house."[68]

After the move into Christamore's new facilities, disagreement over the goals, purposes, and programs of the settlement arose between its founders and its board. With the resolution of these disagreements, the settlement house embarked on a new period of maturity, but it did so without the two women who had founded it. As Christamore's activities expanded, the problem of defining its goals became acute. For Anna Stover and Edith Surbey settlement work had been the expression of an inner faith. They had scrubbed floors, importuned businessmen for contributions, ventured down unsavory alleys, all for the sake of an ideal that promised the material and spiritual redemption of their neighborhood—and perhaps of themselves as well. Christamore's emphasis had been on evangelical Protestantism; its social-service work had always been embedded in a missionary purpose. Now the settlement board was urging Stover and Surbey to make the settlement more of a recreation center and to phase out religious programs, a change in policy that the founders could not accept. Their resignation in 1911 was almost certainly caused by this disagreement over philosophy rather than, as they claimed, by ill-health.[69]

After their resignation Christamore completed a transition from religious settlement house to social center. At the same time, the settlement took an important step toward professionalization when it entered the National

Federation of Settlements as a charter member in 1911.[70] As a member house, Christamore was advised to deemphasize religious observance and to adopt the nondenominational stance that was a requirement for affiliation with the national social-work body.[71]

Had Stover and Surbey stayed on at Christamore they would have found much to alarm them in the direction the settlement house took after 1911. By 1918, no religious services were held at the house, signaling the different orientation of Christamore's new leaders.[72] But the two founders persisted in their goal of religious social service. When she left Indianapolis, Anna Stover went on to a career that included founding another "Christamore" settlement house in San Juan, Puerto Rico, a "House of Light" in Los Angeles, a Bible school for Mexican children, and a mission in Mexico City. Her last eleven years were spent in mission work with Russian children in Los Angeles, where she died in 1944. Edith Surbey, her close friend and associate for nearly forty years, died in Los Angeles in 1972 at the age of one hundred.[73]

Settlement reports for 1911 and 1912 show that Christamore was flourishing. With eleven resident workers and seventy-five nonresident and volunteer workers, the house was a hive of activity where about six hundred people attended settlement activities each week. The settlement not only provided educational opportunities to many who otherwise would have been without them, it also supplemented the physical resources of its neighbors; for example, the Christamore baths were in constant use, for only 5 percent of the district's houses had indoor plumbing.[74] When a group of neighborhood people volunteered as collectors in Christamore's fund-raising drive the settlement's new director, Miss Edna Coffing, believed that the neighborhood had begun to identify with the goals of the settlement and to look on it as an asset to the neighborhood. And thanks to larger donations from the business community and college groups, especially from Butler and Irvington benefactors, the settlement enjoyed a few years of freedom from financial worry.[75]

If Christamore's residents had earlier felt as if they were engaged in a lone crusade, they now had the satisfaction of being part of a national movement. Membership in the National Federation of Settlements brought professional recognition. In 1912, Harry Blake Taplin, headworker of Hale House, Boston, and Francis E. McClean of the Russell Sage Foundation visited Christamore. And in 1922, Director Olive Edwards and Martha Stewart Carey traveled to the First International Conference on Settlements in London, the only representatives from Indiana settlements to do so.[76]

Christamore's new leaders understood and accepted the long-term goals of the settlement movement for the neighborhood and the nation. At the neighborhood level, Christamore aimed "to make our's an ideal industrial neighborhood of wholesome, well ordered homes, . . . to build character and self-respect, . . . to produce such men and women as this city and nation may depend on."[77] Evoking a twenty-year tradition of settlement activity that included Toynbee, Denison, Barnett, and Addams, the Christamore leadership reaffirmed their goals for the nation in the words of Jane Addams: "The best result of civilization . . . must be incorporated into our common life and have free mobility through all elements of society if we would have our democracy endure."[78]

Yet this vision of progress was for whites only. And when Olive D. Edwards came to take the position of head resident in August 1915, she almost immediately faced a crisis that threatened to close down the settlement house permanently. Christamore had been founded to serve only whites, but by 1910 blacks made up half the settlement neighborhood. The black ghetto of the Indiana Avenue area was beginning to spread eastward, as blacks seeking betterment moved there from the South. Between 1910 and 1920 the black population of the city as a whole doubled from 15,931 to 34,678.[79] And as the racial composition of its neighborhood changed, Christamore felt the impact of declining attendance; white attendance at the settlement house fell from 4,000 a month in 1913 to only 2,000 by 1919.[80]

For months, Christamore's director and board deliberated. Should they set up a separate branch settlement for blacks, as many other settlements were doing; admit them to the facilities only on certain days; or continue to exclude them and face declining attendance?[81] The decision of Christamore's sponsors to move the settlement rather than integrate it may seem surprising in view of the well-known commitment of settlement leaders such as Jane Addams to racial justice. The move was not untypical, however: as the new institutions of social work emerged in the post–World War I period, they were generally segregated. Only later, when whites had fled the inner-city areas where settlements were located, would they open their doors to blacks.[82]

Wartime pressures and then postwar reconstruction helped push the settlement leadership toward this decision. The War Chest, a business-supported body, had been charged with running both the war charities such as the Red Cross and the city's thirty-five permanent, private civic and philanthropic charities. This new supervisory agency subsequently called in the National Bureau of Municipal Research to conduct a survey with a view to deciding which agencies warranted chest support.[83] The survey report praised Christamore, but pointed out the incongruity of a settlement house located in the middle of a black population that it excluded. The great opportunity for settlement work in Indianapolis was not among whites but among blacks, the report stated. Christamore should consider filling this need. At present its focus was too narrow since its influence was "limited to a group that is fairly competent to help themselves." Christamore must expand its programs to include blacks if it wanted to receive municipal aid from the War Chest, the report concluded.[84]

Christamore's director was inclined to agree. She recommended that the settlement open its facilities to blacks on certain days. But a committee of three appointed in October 1917 to consider the matter dissented. Rather than admit blacks, the settlement house would move.[85]

By 1920, Edwards and the settlement board had decided that Haughville, an industrial district west of the White River with many immigrants but few blacks, should be Christamore's new home. School principals and teachers in the area had agreed to cooperate with the settlement, and so had major employers.[86] In November 1922, the board adopted plans for the new settlement-house building at the corner of Tremont and Michigan Streets in Haughville and launched a campaign to raise $100,000 by subscriptions. Two wings of the building were finished by 1924, and Dr. John Elliott of New York's Hudson Guild presided over the dedication in January 1925. Meanwhile, another campaign raised pledges of $45,000 for a Martha Stewart Carey Wing, which was completed in 1926. Jane Addams was the guest speaker at the ceremony of dedication.[87]

Christamore was endowed with a splendid new building, challenged by a new neighborhood, and recognized by the national leader of the settlement movement. However, new developments in the field of social work in the 1920s—the tendency for voluntary social-welfare agencies to join in federations and to develop closer and more formal relationships with business—presented settlements with a changed climate in which to work. In Indianapolis, the War Chest leadership, originally nominated at a public meeting but henceforth not publicly accountable and self-perpetuating, had become a force with which the city's social workers had to reckon. At the end of the war, the chest had been transformed into a Department of Community Welfare, charged with promoting the "health, education, safety, pleasure, comfort, welfare or convenience" of the citizenry. The Community Chest was able to raise money and make appropriations. It became a quasi-public supplementary health department, education department, charities department, police department, parks-and-playground department, and general welfare department.[88]

Settlement leaders early on had warned that such developments might threaten the spontaneity and activism that had characterized the movement. As settlement workers sought professionalism at the price of moral commitment, settlement work, like other social work, became less a "cause" than a "function."[89] Christamore's Olive Edwards represented this new type of leader, one who expected settlements to take their place within the emerging bureaucratic structures of social work. A college graduate who had trained in several settlement houses in the East, including an Episcopal facility in New York City, she welcomed the opportunity to tie Christamore into the emerging federation of public and private social-service agencies. In a report to the Christamore board of directors she emphasized "the great need of closer cooperation, the importance of the city being districted and a thorough understanding and working together of all social and philanthropic agencies." Not coincidentally, the Indianapolis branch of the American Association of Social Workers was founded in 1923.[90]

Under Edwards's leadership Christamore completed the transition from private voluntary agency to member agency of a citywide federation supported by the Community Chest. In 1917, the settlement had still relied on private donors, raising 30 percent of its income from the Christamore Aid Society and 27 percent from subscriptions. But by 1928, 94 percent of the settlement's funding came through the chest.[91]

It is to Edwards's credit that in a climate of increased professionalism and bureaucracy she nevertheless sought to define the settlement's role in a new and more democratic way. In a frank statement she disowned the settlement tradition of cultural uplift, which had often been indistinguishable from noblesse oblige. Christamore would not be "a place where the rich come to patronize those less well off," nor would its sponsors "offend the people of Haughville with the suggestion that it is a charitable institution, or a school set there to educate them."[92] This new, more democratic emphasis led to the encouragement of community organization in the Christamore neighborhood. The Civic League of Haughville, which met at Christamore during the 1920s, was successful in putting pressure on municipal authorities to improve street paving and lighting and to provide neighborhood playgrounds. And on the eve of the Depression the Christamore board was contemplating the creation of a council of neighborhood people who would have a direct role in the running of the settlement. Unfortunately, this proposal to enlarge the base of the settlement's support was shelved as the agency turned its full attention to meeting the relief emergency.[93]

Despite Olive Edwards's distaste for the notion, however, the settlement was still, when all was said and done, an agency that existed to channel some limited funds from well-to-do groups to a working-class and immigrant constituency in order to raise the standard of living among these groups. As a settlement report of 1925 neatly put it, the objective was "to foster an understanding of American institutions and a desire for the good things in life in the hearts and minds of most of the 15,000 people of Haughville." The result was to be a society undifferentiated by class or ethnic (but not racial) divisions.[94]

Haughville presented a challenge to the settlement different from any it had faced so far—an ethnically mixed population of new immigrants, mostly East Europeans, and an older population of Irish and Germans.

With its move to Haughville, Christamore joined the Americanization crusade in which settlements all over the country were engaged. The settlement was "an isle of happiness, surmounted by the Stars and Stripes," wrote
one newspaper reporter. The settlement's sponsors were able to make a
strong appeal for the support of business; they combined the argument for
efficiency, representing unassimilated aliens as a drag on the city's progress
toward a progressive future, with calls for patriotism. Using an industrial
metaphor that suited the businesslike image Christamore wished to project,
the Indianapolis *Star* called it "a plant whose output is ardent, loyal little
Americans. Into one door is fed little children of foreign parentage . . . out
the other door they rush with gladsome, dancing steps—little Americans."[95]

The settlement's paid staff now consisted of four social workers—Olive
Edwards, head worker; a girls' worker; a boys' worker (male); and a neighborhood visitor—as well as a cook and a janitor. All the regular staff lived
in the house, which made it the city's only "real" settlement. An important
supplement to the regular staff was the Christamore Aid Association, whose
seventy members provided volunteer services for many of the settlement's
activities. The new profession of social work retained a place, lowly but
essential, for the untrained female volunteer.[96]

Support also came from the users of the settlement, for whether or not
working-class people accepted its values, they found its services useful. In
addition to the extensive program of recreation, the settlement house was
continuing to provide regular health clinics, including several dental, prenatal, and baby clinics each week. During 1924 average daily attendance
was 134, and the total attendance during the year was 41,136. By 1928
total annual attendance had risen to over 53,000, by 1931 to over 70,000
(see Table 2).[97]

Was Christamore a success as it entered the thirties? Certainly there
were some success stories: Charles Boswell, who began as a youngster in the
settlement program, became boys' worker at Christamore and later rose to
be mayor of Indianapolis.[98] But in another way, success was impossible to
measure. After all, settlement leaders had defined the settlement in such a
way that they were bound to measure progress by the diminishing number of
things that settlements had to do. On the eve of the Great Depression,
Helen Hart, headworker of Pittsburgh's Kingsley House, surveyed the settlement movement and noted how many programs sponsored by the settlements were beginning to be considered a public responsibility. "One by one
the fields which we occupied alone are being invaded by other organizations—the boys' club, the scout troops, the city recreation center, the
health center, the public bath, the visiting nurses' association, the nursery
school, the library, the public evening school, the vocational guidance bureau," she wrote.[99] At the same time, the 1920s saw a rising standard of

Table 2
Christamore Clubs, 1929

Name of Club	Membership	Object
Men		
Men's Club	27	Athletics
Boys		
Maroons	26	Athletics
Juniors	21	Athletics
Pirates	46	Athletics
M.E.'s	19	Athletics
Eagles	35	Athletics
Cardinals	33	Athletics
Triangles	29	Athletics
Women		
Women's Club	50	Athletics
Girls		
Gloom Dodgers	41	Athletics and Art
Camp Fire Girls	20	Camp Fire Programs
Pollyanna	15	Domestic Art
Priscilla	15	Domestic Art
Busy Workers	15	Basketry
Little Neighbors	15	Dolls Club
Busy Brownies	15	Dolls Club
Monday Club	15	Dolls Club
Loyalty	15	Apron Making
Classes		
Boy Rangers	79	Athletics
Knights	61	Athletics
Cooking	12	
Piano	13	
Music Appreciation	50	
Chorus	45	

Source: Indianapolis Foundation, *The Leisure of a People*, p. 385.

living for better-paid working-class families, which meant that there was less need for the settlement's social-housekeeping role.[100]

By 1930 Christamore had made the transition from settlement to semi-public agency. Anna Stover and Edith Surbey had been the pioneers. Missionaries on the "urban frontier," they had endured present discomforts because they had their eyes on the coming Kingdom. Daring, determined, idealistic young women, they represented a generation whose vision produced the institutions of social welfare and put in place the infrastructure of social work for the next generation. But the postwar federations of voluntary and public agencies had little place for spontaneity or individualism. In an age symbolized by the flapper, the Progressive "social mother" looked quaintly archaic. Extravagant hopes were out of fashion; the new age required social work, not social action.[101]

Developments at Christamore reflected a national trend. While the postwar reorganization of charities strengthened settlements financially by bringing joint fund-raising and coordinated services, it also reduced their independence. A study of the settlement houses during the Great Depression showed the result of settlements taking the hand of business: controversial programs were suspended and democratic policies based on community participation were shelved as settlements deferred to the wishes of conservative sponsors.[102]

One sign of the changed climate in which settlements like Christamore operated as early as the 1920s was the muted optimism of the Intercollegiate Community Service Association, successor to the College Settlements Association. In a report to this body in 1922 social worker Elizabeth Kemper Adams complained that female undergraduates were quite unfamiliar with the unique role and history of the college settlements. The expectation of rapid, dramatic change was no longer there. Idealistic women—and heavens knows there were few of them to be found—busied themselves with "community service," not community transformation.[103] Second-generation settlement workers like Olive Edwards worked for improvement, not for the millennium. Settlement work had become a profession and a lifetime career, and settlements were now just one among a number of other agencies, signaling by their acceptance of the financial support of business that the agenda of reform was no longer incompatible with business goals or a threat to the existing economic order.

CHAPTER TWO

"Adjusting Their Life to Ours": From Foreign House to American Settlement

Down there amidst all the squalid surroundings the lights of Foreigners' House shine out like beacons of hope that guide the poor
aliens to a better life and ambitions.

—Indianapolis *Sunday Star,*
February 21, 1915

For nearly three decades the settlement was practically the sole
agency set to welcome the great body of strangers coming to our
shores, to interpret to them the community at large, to assist
them in adjusting their life to ours.

—Robert A. Woods and Albert J.
Kennedy, *The Settlement Horizon*
(1922)

A mile or so to the east of Christamore, another settlement house was in
operation. At first named Foreign House, then triumphantly renamed
American Settlement in the 1920s, the settlement was an experiment in
Americanization. Settlement houses played an important role in the Americanization movement which was at its height between the 1890s and the
Immigration Restriction Acts of 1920 and 1924; by 1911, nine out of ten
settlements in the United States worked primarily with immigrants.[1] Other
American institutions came into contact with immigrants, of course, but
none were in so frequent or close contact as the settlements. The settlement workers planted themselves in the midst of foreign neighborhoods,
bringing American influences to the newcomers, like colonizers among the
natives.[2] But settlement residents did not always play the role of cultural
imperialists: they were also intermediaries, interpreting the immigrants to
America. Some of them wrote delightful and intelligent portraits of immigrant life, such as Vida Scudder's sketches of the Boston Italians and Lillian
Wald's studies of New York's Russian Jews. Naturally, they also wrote about

assimilation and its problems. Jane Addams's discussion of the strains of assimilation in the ethnically mixed neighborhoods of Hull House, "Immigrants and Their Children," is deservedly the most famous of these.[3]

Impressed by these accounts, historians have usually concluded that the settlement movement was generally benevolent and tolerant toward immigrants. They have portrayed settlement workers as activists in upholding immigrants' rights, yet passive admirers of the flowering of immigrant cultural varieties. Philip Gleason, a careful student of Americanization, wrote that settlements "took a positive view of the cultural contributions [immigrants] could make to American life." Settlement workers were "more sympathetic to cultural diversity than other reformers," agreed Michael Katz. John Higham even asserted that settlement workers "did more to sustain the immigrant's respect for his old culture than to urge him forward into the new one."[4]

But other historians disagreed. They maintained that settlements were agencies of cultural hegemony, where white, middle-class Protestants worked to hasten the abandonment by immigrants of the "old ways"; that settlements were at best paternalistic and at worst contemptuous toward immigrant culture.[5]

One reason for this difference in interpretation was the variety within the settlement movement. Historians faced the problem of typicality: what was a typical settlement? Jane Addams in *The Spirit of Youth and the City Streets* pointed out the dangers of a rapid Americanization that alienated immigrant children from their parents, but her warnings had little effect on the hundreds of settlements across the country working day-by-day to assimilate immigrants to American life—such as the one that is the focus of this chapter. Moreover, even at Hull House, the tolerant attitudes that she expressed in print did not always inform the settlement's programs for immigrants. Further complicating the historian's task of determining the character of settlements' relationships with immigrants is the fact that between 1890 and 1930 the settlements' views of immigrants changed, as did attitudes toward immigrants in the wider society.[6]

By 1912, almost a million immigrants were entering the United States every year, and national attention was beginning to focus upon the immigrant problem. The Progressive party platform of 1912 contained a plank deploring "the fatal policy of indifference and neglect which has left our enormous immigrant population to become the prey of chance and cupidity." It called for federal legislation to effect the immigrants' "assimilation, education and advancement."[7]

The entry of the United States into World War I transformed Americanization into a national priority while eroding its benevolent character. The Americanization campaign led by the U.S. Bureau of Education and the

Committee on Public Information was waged by a variety of institutions. Public schools, night schools, and Y's, visiting homemakers and visiting nurses, all worked to assimilate the foreigners. Settlement workers, who had been quietly helping immigrants for years, suddenly found that their work had become a matter of national urgency and that they were among a plethora of civic and voluntary organizations, all attempting to bring the problem of the unassimilated immigrant to the national attention.[8] Some historians have suggested that, while settlements agreed with other Americanizing agencies about the necessity to end separate ethnic communities, they were protective, not coercive, toward immigrants and had a much more sympathetic approach to immigrants than the crusaders for "one hundred percent Americanism." The history of American Settlement allows us to reexamine settlement work with immigrants at the local level, and to analyze the mixture of protection and coercion that inspired it. What were the changing goals of settlement work with immigrants in the first three decades of the twentieth century, and how far did they coincide with the goals of the immigrants themselves?

Few immigrants found their way to Indiana. The capital, Indianapolis, said one observer, more hopeful than accurate, was "the typical American city which had practically no foreign population and in which the sturdy and liberty-loving New England was blended with the cultured and aristocratic South."

> And if now and then in the newspapers (chiefly in the birth statistics and reports of industrial accidents) we read a name that is neither Lowell nor Bradford, Randolph nor Lee, we pass over it to more agreeable news. But if you were so impolite as to press the subject and ask if we really had no foreigners, we would have to say "Oh yes there are a few hunkies out in Haughville but we don't know anything about them."[9]

But the immigrants came, moving into the tenements and slums, and congregating, a crowded mass of humanity—cheap labor for industry, a headache for health departments, a twinge of conscience for wealthy suburban church members, but little more.

Polk's Indianapolis City Directory of 1910, more concerned with creating a good impression than with accuracy, denied that there was any "foreign problem" in the "City of Homes." There is an "almost total absence of the foreign floating element, and of the disturbances frequently found in the various seaboard and interior parts," the directory noted complacently.[10] The foreign-born made up about 8 percent of the Indianapolis population in 1910. This was a much lower percentage than in cities of the upper Midwest, such as Chicago with 36 percent foreign-born, or Detroit with 34 percent, but it was comparable with other cities of the lower Midwest of similar size, for example, Columbus, Ohio had 9 percent, Cincinnati, 16 percent, and Louisville 8 percent.[11]

Yet by 1910, the city fathers were beginning to be alarmed about the 20,000 foreigners in their midst. One reason was the changed composition of the foreign population. From 1850 to 1900, Indiana's immigrants had been mainly from Germany, Ireland, and the British Isles. But by 1910, half were of the so-called new immigration, Romanians and Serbs, Russians and Turks.[12] Unlike the earlier immigrants, these newcomers were mainly Catholic or Orthodox in religion; most of them were single men who had immigrated without their families and, unlike previous immigrants, they showed little interest in citizenship. In Indianapolis's predominantly German Thirteenth Ward 71 percent of immigrants were naturalized; but in the Twelfth Ward where the new immigrants congregated, only one-third of foreign-born males of voting age were citizens.[13]

The area where the new immigrants settled was fairly well defined. They lived south of Washington Street in the Twelfth and Thirteenth wards. North of Washington Street, they spilled over into the Fifth Ward, where a large black population had settled along Indiana Avenue (see Map 3). The Twelfth Ward, with almost one-third of its inhabitants foreign-born in 1910, formed the heart of the foreign section.[14]

The expanding economy of the Hoosier capital provided plenty of work for these newcomers, although it was very different from what they had been accustomed to in their homelands. Of about five hundred immigrants from southeastern Europe, three-fourths listed their occupation before emigration as farmers, but in Indianapolis most became laborers in the construction, meat-packing, or manufacturing industries. Large railroad-construction projects between 1908 and 1910 drew immigrant laborers to work on track elevation and on the construction of railroads to the west of the city. After the projects were completed, many remained, picking up what work they could.[15] Meat-packing attracted the greatest number of immigrant workers; many of them were employed at Kingan's, the large packinghouse located on Maryland Street. Of 1,361 laborers in meat-packing and slaughtering plants in Indianapolis in 1910, almost three-fourths were foreign-born.[16] A job in slaughtering or packing was often seen as temporary work before an immigrant moved on to something better, but sometimes it proved to be the best there was, as in the following case study, one of a collection of memorable portraits of immigrants compiled by two Indianapolis teachers, Elavina S. Stammel and Charles R. Parks, in 1930.

Stan Stepanoff, a Bulgarian, aged forty-two, lives in an upstairs room with two other Bulgarian men where they "batch," or do all their own work including cooking and mending. Stepanoff was a farmer in Macedonia.

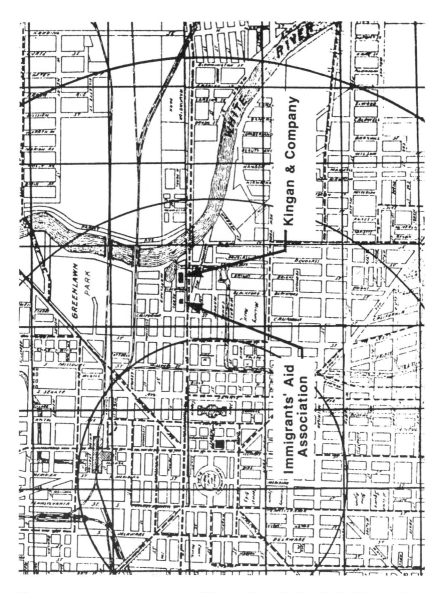

Map 3. Immigrants' Aid Association ("Foreign House"). From R. L. Polk and Co., "City Directory Map of Indianapolis, Indiana, 1909."

When he arrived in Indianapolis, he found work in a packing plant cutting open cows as soon as they were killed. After four years he left the packing house and wandered for three years from one city to another, working foundries, butchering, or doing any other rough labor available. In 1921 he returned to Indianapolis to become a meat cutter in a beef room. He is still employed there.

Stepanoff had only two years education in Macedonia, and, since he has attended no night school in America, he can write little more than his name. He takes no paper and he reads nothing. He was a member of the Eastern Orthodox Church in Macedonia, but he has no relation with any church here. He is not a citizen; neither is he making any effort to become so. He works, eats, sleeps, no more.[17]

Americanizers dreaded the effects on society of thousands of Stepanoffs. They deplored his living conditions, feared the alienation caused by the man's illiteracy and lack of interest in citizenship, wondered at the loss of social control when men who had been brought up an obedient member of a church belonged to no church at all.

In 1909, a group of influential citizens met together and declared the "foreign born" to be the city's most urgent problem. Unless the aliens could be "molded after American ideals," a spokesman wrote in Forward!, the magazine of the Commercial Club, there was "grave danger ahead of us all." The group founded the Immigrants' Aid Society and launched the Americanization movement in Indianapolis, establishing a settlement which they called "the Foreign House" on West Pearl Street in the heart of the foreign section.[18]

The origins of the Foreign House overturn several generally accepted views about the settlement movement. Some historians viewed the movement as having a more enlightened approach to poverty and other urban ills than that associated with the Charity Organization Society (COS). They asserted that the COS led to social control, but that settlements led to reform.[19] The evidence from Indianapolis, however, shows that the differences between the COS and the settlements have been overstated. While the organizers of the Foreign House probably took the idea of a settlement house from the well-known settlements such as Hull House, their affiliations were not to the national settlement movement—the National Federation of Settlements was not even founded until 1911, when hundreds of settlements were already in existence—but to the local COS, the reform-minded Commercial Club, and progressive campaigns such as the public-health movement and the housing-reform campaign. As the following discussion will show, the Foreign House was an outgrowth of COS work among the immigrants, rather than a completely new departure in reform. The settlement would be located in the heart of the immigrant neighborhood, but its preoccupations would be the same as those of the COS, that is, social control as well as social reform.

The Foreign House was the creation of two prominent Indiana progressives, John H. Holliday and James A. Collins. Holliday was founder and editor, until 1892, of the Indianapolis *News* and president of the Union Trust Company of Indianapolis from 1893 to 1899. He was a member of the State Board of Charities and, for fifteen years, president of the city's COS. The settlement's other influential supporter was James A. Collins. As judge of the Indianapolis City Court from 1909 to 1914, Collins urged Progressive reforms in the treatment of criminals, instituted probation for adult offenders, and pioneered work with a juvenile court. Long courtroom experience had convinced him that criminal behavior sprang from environmental causes. He hoped that the Immigrants' Aid Society would help to ameliorate the bad conditions in the Foreign District that bred crime.[20]

When a COS committee headed by Frank Flanner, sponsor of Flanner House, began actively investigating housing conditions in Indianapolis in 1903, there was already a groundswell of support for housing reform that would become a fully fledged housing-reform campaign by 1908. For some years, the COS had been energetically documenting the need for reform in the Foreign District. The results of a COS district-by-district survey in 1906 revealed that the housing problem was also a "foreign problem." "The elements of civilization are lacking in these [immigrant] quarters," declared the COS report of that year, adding uncharitably, "The fortunate side is that there are few children among them."[21]

An investigation of 1910 carried on by Leander M. Campbell Adams (formerly a teaching fellow at Indiana University's Department of Economics and Social Science) showed even more clearly the tangle of substandard housing and living conditions in the "foreign section," identified as an area extending south of New York Street as far as the railroad tracks, west of Capitol Avenue, and east of the White River (see Figure 1). At the heart of this section, Adams found a densely populated area. "It is not over one-half of a square mile in area. But it contains the homes, stores and loafing places of several hundred foreigners, in addition to a packing house and other industrial concerns," he wrote.[22] Eighty percent of the male immigrants were from Romania, Serbia, or Macedonia, and apart from the Romanians, very few had emigrated with wives and children. Adams found evidence of chain migration, with boarding houses and tenements lodging people who were not only of the same nationality, but often from the same town and family in their land of origin. From nine to fifteen men lived in each house, sharing the housekeeping. In the average three-roomed house, one room served as a dining room and kitchen (where the cook slept), and the other two were bedrooms for five or more persons each. One reason for the crowded conditions was the exorbitant rents—the rent for a single room in the Foreign District averaged twice what it was in an American neighborhood, a few blocks south.[23]

Yet instead of being favorably impressed by the strength of immigrant family ties and by the evidence of immigrant resourcefulness, the COS investigators were alarmed at the unhealthy conditions of the immigrant quarters. "No matter how crowded are the conditions under which these people are living, they will always make room for the newcomers. The tie of friendship or blood is far stronger than any theories of healthful living which may be implanted in their minds."[24] And while their sympathies were evidently aroused by the plight of the immigrants, so was their ambition to replace the foreigners' culture with American values and an American standard of living. If immigrants needed protection from those who would exploit them, Americans, too, needed to be on their guard: not only was the Foreign District a health hazard, for "any epidemic which gained a foothold here would spread like fire over the west end of the city," but nameless dangers also lurked there, the dangers (as another settlement worker, slipping easily into the language of public health, wrote) "to our economic, political and moral standards when certain types of newcomers are left to create breeding grounds for much that is incompatible with or hostile to the best values of American life."[25]

In a lengthy paper entitled "The Life of Our Foreign Population" John Holliday presented the case for an agency of Americanization. The new immigrants were quite different from those America had received and assimilated in the past, Holliday argued:

> Unlike the early pioneer who was willing to face the long and dangerous journey across the unknown seas and take up a life of hardship, even of struggle for existence, the immigrant of today is allured by fairy tales to a country unrivalled in its wealth and opportunity to get riches. Unlike the early settler and the previous immigrant who pushed their way, clearing the forest and tilling the soil, the present vast throng settle in the large cities . . . Here they crowd together in the most densely populated districts of the cities and complicate the problems of municipal government.[26]

What disturbed Holliday was the immigrants' separateness—their immunity from the socializing and social control mechanisms that prevailed in society at large. Settling in communities of their own, "ignorant of our language, methods of government and national ideas," the aliens were an unassimilated mass that constituted a political and cultural menace. Hence the need for the Immigrants' Aid Association—an institutional response to "the alarming danger of an uneducated and alien mass of voters in our body

politic, and the menace to our social life and institutions of a class separated by the great gulf of an unknown tongue and the incomprehension of
the ideals that should animate our people in the future, as they have done
in the past."[27]

There was undoubtedly a strain of racism in Holliday's argument. When
he characterized the Macedonians, Bulgarians, Serbians, and Hungarians
as mostly "illiterate peasants . . . who differ greatly in enterprise and intelligence from the average American citizen, take little pride in their appearance and live in dirt and squalor," Holliday seemed to desert his
environmentalist Progressivism for a genetic explanation of immigrant problems, including the suggestion that certain races had a greater capacity for
Americanization than others.[28]

But, in general, such a position did not prove useful to the advocates of
reform: an argument based on race was even a counsel of despair, for if
racial traits alone determined the nature of foreign colonies, then what use
was a settlement, school, or other agency of Americanization? Holliday im-
plicity recognized this fact and rejected the racial argument when he described groups of foreigners in Haughville (across the White River in West
Indianapolis), who had become assimilated and whose standard of living
left nothing to be desired. These immigrants had not come directly from
Europe but from Cleveland, Chicago, and New York. Evidently, it was not
innate "racial traits," but longer exposure to America that counted.[29]

An environmental explanation of the immigrant problem served the reformers much better: treating the immigrants as the victims rather than the
perpetrators of abuses, the settlement's sponsors adopted an optimistic outlook on reform. First they needed facts, and Holliday, former journalist, had
the facts. He documented the "foreign problem" in terms of persons per
room, families per dwelling, rents, wages, and rates of unemployment. He
noted both the "uplifting features" of the neighborhood—churches, schools,
the strength of family and kinship groups—and the pernicious factors such
as greedy landlords and corrupt municipal authorities. Holliday ended on a
note of confidence. Americans *could* help uplift "these strange brethren," he
declared. Indeed, it was in their interest to do so. "Many of these people are
to be our future citizens, what they are to be depends largely upon our attitude toward them. If we impart sympathy and helpful influences they will
become good citizens. If permitted to live in the present manner, they will
be bad citizens.[30]

Neither Holliday nor Adams expected the culture of the immigrants to
retard their adoption of American values. As Americanizers of what historians have called "the Anglo-conformity" school, the settlement's backers
demanded that immigrants abandon their cultural distinctiveness. They did
not imagine that ethnic diversity would enrich the nation's culture—few

Americanizers did. Instead, they expected cultural differences to dissolve once the immigrants had achieved an "American" standard of living. They could not foresee that the virtual ending of European immigration in 1924 would hasten the process, transforming immigrants to ethnics, or that what has been called "the Triumph of Commerce"—the rise of mass entertainment and the consumer culture—would prove a more powerful dissolvent of ethnic separateness than the Americanization campaign itself.[31]

> Consider this mass of people—foreigners of different nationalities, negroes, Americans from a dozen different states and a handful of native citizens of Indianapolis. Could they be expected to mix well in any sort of social organization, or to have many common interests or aims?[32]

Like Holliday, Adams took two approaches to the immigrants, the one immediate and coercive, the other gradualist and voluntaristic. Coercion was necessary, he believed, because the foreigners would soon be, or already were, American citizens:

> If immigration to America is to be open to all nationalities and classes of people without restriction, the people who come here will have a marked effect upon the future generations of American people. Many of their habits and customs will stay with them for generations, changing a little under new conditions, but remaining fundamentally the same. Our customs and traditions will be likewise modified by theirs. These people by naturalization, and their descendants by birth, will be American citizens. Should American citizens be permitted to live under conditions such as these?[33]

Education was too slow a process, its outcome too uncertain, the expert believed. Meanwhile, the childlike immigrants needed a firm hand. "Like young children they should have their actions regulated by authority until they reach a point of understanding." In addition, he called on the city to protect the immigrants by stringent enforcement of the health and housing laws.[34]

The settlement house was a central feature of the Americanizers' plans. The idea was born at the Commercial Club in January 1911, when a group of reformers resolved to approach the immigrants with moral, religious, and practical programs:

> to reach them through Christian laborers of their own race; to ascertain their needs and desires; to strive to attain the best methods of influencing them toward higher thinking and better living; to acquaint them with the principles that make for civic liberty and righteousness, and to foster their growing ideas and extend to them all possible moral and religious aid.[35]

John Kingan supplied the settlement house building at 617 West Pearl Street at a nominal rent. It was a frame building with four small rooms and a large assembly hall on the ground floor. Upstairs were two rooms containing public baths and others designated as classrooms and club rooms.[36]

Because it served a community with few women or children, the "Foreign House," as it was soon called, had a masculine atmosphere which contrasted with the "women's college" ambience of settlements like Christamore—it was more working-men's club or YMCA than (as some settlements were) community of woman reformers. There were smoking and reading rooms, Sunday lectures, and an employment bureau, all planned as an alternative for working-class men in their leisure time to the poolrooms and bars, with their evil and intoxicating influences. During the first winter, Sunday-afternoon meetings at the settlement were addressed by a variety of well-known speakers. Like the Sunday Afternoon Club at Graham Taylor's Chicago Commons settlement, this lecture series dealt with a variety of current and political topics. The response was excellent, with an average attendance of 150 men.[37]

For the goals of the settlement's sponsors were political as well as educational: to change the political environment of the immigrant quarter and to counteract radicalism among the unassimilated aliens. The growing Socialist vote in Indiana and the proliferation of Socialist clubs, with their many immigrant members, caused civic leaders to view the "Foreign Section" as a breeding ground for other kinds of epidemics than public-health ones. Meanwhile, the press applauded the settlement's goals: the Immigrants' Aid Association would help immigrants "escape the pernicious influences and leaders now active among them," an editorial in the Indianapolis *News* noted. The settlement "takes them from the coffee houses and the dirty streets and gives them a glance of the kind of life they can make for themselves," the Indianapolis *Sunday Star* declared approvingly.[38]

Like the more famous settlements, Foreign House also began a campaign for practical reforms in the immigrant quarter, where the nonenforcement of health and housing ordinances was causing a serious situation. The Immigrants' Aid Association had the backing of two health officials: Dr. C. S. Woods, health commissioner of Indianapolis, and Dr. John N. Hurty, secretary of the State Board of Health, a tireless public-health reformer during his twenty-six years in that office. In the wake of the interest aroused by the COS housing surveys, Hurty persuaded the city health department to investigate cases of overcrowding, to condemn unsafe wells, and to supply city water to houses without it. In 1911, the board appointed Alec J. Lupear, a Romanian, as a member of the "sanitary police force." In Lupear, an English-speaking immigrant, the Board of Health had a link with the immigrant community, and the Immigrants' Aid Association had a useful ally. Lupear's efforts led to a cleaning up of the foreign district and improvements in its sanitary arrangements. The picturesque procession of foreign women to and fro in Military Park to draw water for household use from the ornamental fountains, noted with annoyance by the Board of Health in its 1902 report, soon became a thing of the past.[39]

The Immigrants' Aid Association began as an agency protective of a group of citizens who had no other advocate. The first annual report announced its determination to shield immigrants from "the graft and abuse to which the foreigners were subjected by those who could see only a financial return in coming in contact with them." The association investigated the fraudulent "barrel-house savings banks," where immigrants were sometimes tricked into depositing their money. By 1913, the association's legal counsel had recovered more than $1,000 of immigrants' savings from such "banks." The Indianapolis News applauded the association's efforts "to gain the confidence of the Hungarian, or Roumanian laborer, and show him that the proper place in which to put his savings is the American savings bank or trust company," not the corner saloon.[40] Another type of abuse was the so-called straw bondsman who fraudulently extorted bail money from immigrants "arrested" on trumped-up charges. The association's attorney worked to expose this racket and by 1913 was able to claim that the number of these cases of extortion involving foreigners had fallen off sharply.[41]

Housing conditions proved a major challenge. The majority of men in the Foreign District had emigrated without their wives and families; they boarded together, usually with a "boarding boss" in charge and his wife as housekeeper and cook. Reformers considered these boardinghouses both a sanitary and moral menace, but when they approached foreign women with the message of reform they were met with indifference: it was impossible to persuade immigrant women to reform their living conditions when their situation compared so favorably with the lives they had left. As Stammel and Parks explained, "In Roumania, the women work on the farm, and also make all the wearing apparel of both men and women, except the shoes. One woman told us she preferred to cook for twenty-five men, as she is doing, to working as she did in her native land."[42]

The association reached out to these immigrant women, hiring a social worker who began her work in January 1913. During the next year the indefatigable Ellen P. Hanes made 1,580 visits to the homes of foreign women who, a settlement report optimistically put it, were "especially appreciative and . . . desirous of adopting American ways in their domestic life." She organized a club to teach them English and domestic science and in June 1913 started a kindergarten for foreign children. She was, the Indianapolis News commented, "a young women who hears trouble in a dozen different languages and solves them after the American fashion." She also married Alec Lupear, and the couple moved into the residents' quarters above the settlement house.[43]

The marriage raised in symbolic form the question of assimilation: who was being assimilated to whom? Though the original goal of the settlement had been to lessen the "foreignness" of the city's immigrants, conditions produced a different result. For example, meeting the immigrants halfway, the association made a concession when it put the settlement in the charge of an "English-speaking foreigner of ability" and set up an information bureau where immigrants could get help in their own language. The house was put at the disposal of foreign-language groups, and soon many lodges were holding meetings there. In one way the strategy was successful—but plans to Americanize the foreigners fell far short of the organizers' hopes. Despite the sponsorship of influential men like Judge Collins and John Holliday, the agency did not attract the wide support from the Indianapolis citizenry that Christamore did. Even John Kingan, whose packing plant employed thousands of unskilled, poorly paid foreigners, gave only meager support—the house itself (for which he accepted rent), and modest annual subscriptions such as $250 in 1911–12.[44] Without more effective programs for Americanization, the settlement seemed in danger of becoming a "Foreigners' House"—one that served to perpetuate immigrant culture rather than extinguish it. Settlement leaders Robert A. Woods and Albert J. Kennedy would later warn of just such a danger in a revealing discussion of settlements and immigrants entitled "Race and Place." When immigrants and settlement workers became intimately involved together in the life of a neighborhood, they observed, assimilation might sometimes proceed the wrong way. There were some settlement houses, they wrote,

> in which the residents became more or less assimilated to the standards of the immigrant group or groups about it. It is, of course, among the risks of propaganda that the propagandist shall himself suffer conversion. Occasional residents take on the more showy personal qualities of certain European types, adopt less rigid standards with respect to personal relations than those of our country, and incline towards an internationalism based on indiscriminate mixture of peoples.[45]

This passage is remarkable not only for its pejorative description of immigrants, but also for its casual equation of settlement work with propaganda. Woods and Kennedy reduced the culture of the immigrant groups to a set of unflattering comparisons with the American, or Anglo-Saxon, norm. They viewed Americanization not as a cultural exchange with immigrants, but as a one-way learning process, referred to here as "conversion." While it would be tempting to dismiss Woods and Kennedy's description of

the Americanization process as not descriptive of practices in American settlement houses, their portrait of the settlements as agencies of Americanization was a more accurate one than the "Hull House" version.

In contrast with the uncertain success of other parts of the settlement
program, the night school, started in 1911, was an important and successful
Americanizer. It was astonishing to the organizers how many of the men
showed up after a long workday in the meat-packing plants to study subjects
as varied as English, history, geography, citizenship, and arithmetic. Enrollment increased each year between 1911 and 1915 to an average attendance
of fifty-three. In the winter of 1914, the numbers were up to over one hundred every night. Evidently, although some of the Eastern Europeans were
"birds of Passage" who were saving to return to their homelands, others
welcomed the opportunity to learn English at the Foreign House night
school as the first step in upward occupational mobility in America.[46]

The role the night school could play in launching one man toward a new
life as an American can be seen in the case study of Gabriel Potcova, a
Romanian. Stammel and Parks left us this account:

> Potcova began American life operating a sausage stuffing machine. He
> immediately entered a class at the American Settlement and began a sin-
> cere effort to learn English. After three years in the packing house, he
> left, with the hope that he might find work in some downtown business
> house. He tramped from store to store without success. Rather whipped in
> spirit he returned to the packing plant. . . . Two years passed and Pot-
> cova against determined to free himself from the octopus-like hold the
> meat plant had upon him. In the meantime he had left the Eastern Or-
> thodox for the Roumanian Baptist Church. When he saw the minister, a
> young Roumanian from Louisville Theological Seminary, speak so flu-
> ently, Potcova dreamed of the time when he might be a Baptist minister
> also and perhaps return to Roumania to convert his people. He heard of a
> small college in New Jersey where foreigners would be accepted and where
> an opportunity would be given to earn all or part of his expenses. Pot-
> cova left for the college.[47]

Gabriel Potcova's Americanization entailed a dual conversion, religion and
language, Protestantism as well as English.

Religious teaching had meanwhile been added to the programs offered at
Foreign House. Seeking qualified teachers to staff the night school, the settlement turned to teachers from the Disciples of Christ Missionary Training
School. The sponsors of Foreign House followed a national trend when they
added a religious purpose to their Americanization work. Nationally, few
settlement houses were secular, or even nondenominational, and the
founders of Foreign House believed that the uplift of immigrants might involve spiritual conversion as well as raising their standard of living. If the

challenge was (as John Holliday had written) "uplifting these strange brethren by all means possible," including "protection, enlightenment and evangelization of the immigrant population," the settlement might indeed
develop into a missionary institution.[48] Accordingly, in 1911, the Disciples
of Christ, the same Protestant denomination that had supported Christamore and would shortly undertake the entire support of Flanner House,
stepped forward to aid Foreign House.

The role of the Disciples of Christ needs a brief explanation. In 1909,
the national general headquarters, publication offices, and Missionary Training School of the Christian Women's Board of Missions had been established in new quarters at Irvington, a pleasant suburb just east of
Indianapolis. The Missionary Training School prepared students for home
and foreign missions. Like other denominations moved by the social-gospel
spirit, the Disciples of Christ had adopted a social rather than a doctrinal
definition of sin. Turning their attention especially to urban problems, they
began to send out missionaries to the godless masses in America's great cities rather than to the heathen in faraway lands; these missionaries longed to
"save" immigrants who were Catholic or Orthodox, as well as others who
had forsaken the old country's religion but had not yet become attached to
an "American" church.[49] Between 1911 and 1923, then, as professors and
students from the Missionary School became active at Foreign House, the
settlement became part of this missionary effort to win the allegiance of
the immigrants. From being an agency seeking to protect immigrants from
exploitation, Foreign House now added the not entirely compatible goal
of effecting their conversion to Protestantism. The spearhead of municipal
reform was now described as "a valuable laboratory for the College of
Missions."[50]

A new religious tension entered relations between immigrants and the
settlement when the eagerness of the mission students to aid immigrants
was sharpened by their desire to win converts. Now the text used in settlement classes was the Bible. Sunday school was added to the settlement programs, and immigrants were provided with Protestant hymn books and
religious materials in Slovenian and Croatian.[51] H. J. Derthick, superintendent of the training school, reported that tensions ran high between the
religious leaders of the immigrant community and the Protestant helping
agency: "Sometimes the children have to steal through the back alley
through fear of punishment by the priest," he noted. According to the superintendent, immigrants were prepared to brave the disapproval of their
priests because they wanted the services offered by the social agency. In one
case, the intervention of the settlement nurse saved the life of an immigrant woman and her baby. When their priest protested that the family had
sought help from the Protestant agency, the father reportedly told him,

"very curtly," "Those people be Christians. They make my wife and baby well. They be God's people. My children go to Sunday School there. I like to have them. If you don't like it, you go to _____ ."[52]

Such religious rivalry for the allegiance of the immigrant was common in this period. Evidence from the interviews with immigrants conducted by Stammel and Parks suggests that some were persuaded by the Protestant agencies to desert their traditional faith. For immigrants like the Pole Josef Dziechciaruk, moving from one church to another seems an experimental use of a newfound mobility: a move from one religious allegiance to another that paralleled his drift from job to job, always hoping to improve himself.

> He was a laborer for a few weeks in a foundry. He did simple bench work in a machine shop. He hustled freight on a lake boat. Then he returned to the machine shop to run an electric crane. After a year in the shop he found a job as a barber. Dziechciaruk was dissatisfied with his menial employment. He was ambitious, and he entered a business school where he learned to speak English with some skill. Hoping to find greater opportunities, Dziechciaruk moved to Chicago where he worked as a salesman in a department store for six months. Dissatisfied he returned to Milwaukee and traveled for two years for a cutlery and barber supply house. In 1925 the family moved to Indianapolis.
>
> Dziechciaruk hoped to find in Indianapolis a great educational opportunity for . . . [his daughter]. He also wanted to move his family away from the influence of the Polish settlement in Milwaukee. In this city Dziechciaruk secured a position selling vacuum sweepers at L. S. Ayres. He was fairly successful, and he saved enough money to buy a grocery. In less than a year's time he became bankrupt. Then he began working in a barber shop which he ultimately bought and runs today. The Dziechciaruks were Roman Catholics in Poland and during their stay in Milwaukee. They grew increasingly impatient here with clerical domination until finally all church ties were broken. The Dziechciaruks are not atheists, but belong rather to the protestant modernist point of view. Through the influence of Franchizka the family has attended many different protestant churches.[53]

Baptist connections helped John and Anna Pater, whose religious conversion had preceded emigration, to adapt in the new land. They first emigrated from Romania to Akron, Ohio, where many Romanians lived and where John found a job in a coal mine. In this venture and in their subsequent moves, Romanian friends aided their migration and assimilation.

> They saved some money, attended the Roumanian Baptist, and were happy. They had been converted to the Baptist faith back in Transylvania and had learned how wrong it is to dance, to "play cards," or wear jewelry. They were strict prohibitionists. They had learned from their Baptist

ministers to distrust the members of the Eastern Orthodox Church. John's friends in Indianapolis reported that they were prospering. John and Anna moved to this city. . . . They found jobs at a nearby packing plant. John made pressed ham at fifteen dollars a week and Anna "cleaned guts" for link sausage at eleven dollars a week. On these wages they managed to live. They kept their home clean. They dressed neatly but inexpensively. Their food was simple but wholesome. They attended the Roumanian Baptist Church, studied the Bible, and felt that God was smiling upon them. They also saved money.[54]

Vasil Michailoff, a Bulgarian, began work at Kingan's at sixteen and progressed through a variety of unskilled and then white-collar jobs, gradually acquiring an education that allowed him to enter Indiana University in 1928. Stammel and Parks described his religious life as follows:

He is a member of the Eastern Orthodox Church, is intimately acquainted with the priest and the church affairs, but seldom attends the services. He professes to be an agnostic if not an atheist. He characterizes religion as superstition . . . [His] political sympathies are of a radical Socialist character. He has strong leanings toward Communism.[55]

It would be rash to generalize about immigrants' attitudes toward the religious Americanization that the settlement offered from so few examples. Because there was a great deal of anticlerical, agnostic, and even atheistic sentiment among the immigrants, and because the Protestant agency provided needed social services, some foreigners, already alienated from the established churches of their native countries, were tempted to complete their Americanization by becoming members of an American church.[56]

By religious evangelizing among the immigrants, Foreign House worked to erode immigrant culture. But in other ways, the settlement acted as an agency of cultural retention. This was true of music and dancing. The settlement's staff respected these vital elements of the culture immigrants had brought from Europe—Mary Rigg, settlement director in the 1920s, reported with amazement that every immigrant home had a stringed instrument. Music lessons were offered at the settlement, a Romanian choral group rehearsed there, and a Serbian orchestra was organized in 1912. Special entertainments always included musical performances and drew large crowds. Even when immigrants moved out of the district, west of the White River or to outlying suburbs, they came back for these events: a social worker noted "an overflow attendance" at a Christmas performance in 1916. Two to three hundred was the *average* attendance at Foreign House on public holidays.[57]

A reporter from the Indianapolis *Star* who attended one of these settlement entertainments felt as though he had wandered into a foreign country.

"To these temperamental southern Europeans, music is as the breath of life and dancing is the biggest part of any of their festive occasions," he explained to the paper's American readers. "Their folklore is wonderfully rich and their music breathes the spirit of patriotism and joy of life." The dancers wore "gorgeous" costumes, "rich and heavy with gold and embroidery." The music, whether Bulgarian, Serbian, Greek or Romanian, never failed to arouse the group to the pitch of "wildest enthusiasm," he wrote; their dancing was "graceful and abandoned."[58]

Settlement entertainments showed the settlement in the dual role of Americanizer and preserver of immigrant culture. The Washington's Birthday celebration at Foreign House in 1918 illustrated the kind of syncretism that was occurring as the settlement blended immigrant culture with American rituals. First came performances of songs and music by the Serbian orchestra, then followed "patriotic exercises," and to climax the proceedings, a large picture of George Washington was presented to the settlement house.[59]

The powerful example of Hull House has been taken by historians to show that settlements were preservers of immigrant culture, but the organizers of Foreign House seem to have looked on the immigrants' music and dancing as quaint survivals rather than as elements of a viable folk culture. John Holliday commented, "They are fond of dancing, but they are not at all what we would call graceful." To a reporter from the Indianapolis *Sunday Star* who witnessed a celebration at Foreign House, the settlement was like an indulgent parent. He saw the immigrants' music and dance as an expression of a nature that was both childlike and sensual. With crushing condescension, he wrote, "Understanding well the joyous, music-loving life of these aliens in their own land, where on all festive occasions they enter into the . . . folk-dancing like grown-up children, the wise heads that manage the settlement have made it possible for their charges to sing and dance with the same abandon that their ardent natures require."[60] The settlement's "wise heads," he seemed to suggest, only permitted such atavistic displays as a concession to the immigrants, so that they would attend the settlement house and benefit from the programs that were *really* valuable.

As these quotations suggest the settlement had evolved from a men-only institution to one serving the whole immigrant community. But programs for women and children suffered from lack of trained personnel and money, and from the indifference of the intended clients. A brave entry in the Foreign House Yearbook for January 5, 1917, states, "Miss Heath and I organized a Mothers' Club to meet once a month for the purpose of instructing the mothers in proper ways of caring for herself, children, and her home. Five came."[61] A Library Day drew 40 to 50, but a girls' club and a weekly health clinic were both poorly attended, an indication that there were tensions between the settlement's purpose and immigrant goals. One problem was obvious: settlement clubs were the medium for teaching "correct" ideas about a variety of subjects, from the meaning of citizenship to the best way to cook potatoes; thus they always involved the abandonment by immigrant women of traditional ways of doing things. And the old ways died hard: in 1929 the settlement was still trying to stop immigrant women from swaddling their babies.[62]

Although immigrant women and children could have benefited from some aspects of the Americanization program, immigrants, especially immigrant men, resisted the intrusion of the settlement into areas of life that were traditionally private and controlled by the father. The poor response of immigrant women to settlement activities was also a result of the fact that some men simply would not allow their wives and daughters to attend. Italian and Greek men, especially, carried on the traditional obsession about supervising their daughters to protect them from seduction and their wives to assure their fidelity.[63] Eastern European immigrant women traditionally enjoyed leisure activities at home among family and friends; they could not go out independently without causing a scandal. Such patterns were slow to change. What American settlement workers and social workers called "strengthening family life" actually called for restructuring the immigrant family. It involved, according to sociologist Herbert Gans, an attempt "to reduce the segregation between husband and wife, to increase the status of the wife in the family, . . . to bring parents and children closer together, . . . and to reduce the adult-centered focus of the household." By trying to attract immigrant women and children settlements were taking them out from under the control of the father and enhancing the identity of the women as individuals.[64]

The outbreak of the Balkan wars and of World War I drastically affected the settlement house. The foreign population of the district shrank as hundreds of men left to join the armies of their homelands and no immigrants came to replace them.[65] Between 1915 and 1923, Foreign House slipped into a decline. When the National Bureau of Municipal Research surveyed Indianapolis private agencies in 1918 it noted the depopulation of the neighborhood, the dilapidated and dirty condition of the settlement house, and a certain disturbing vagueness about its purpose. "It is obvious that the Immigrants' Aid Society during the years of heavy immigration served an excellent purpose in trying to Americanize the immigrants and to surround them with a desirable social environment," the authors noted. But now the war and the consequent departure of many immigrants "have left the society in a position where it does not feel justified in engaging a competent superintendent, in keeping up the premises or in making the heavy investment necessary to keep the premises in a suitable condition."[66]

The survey recommended against including the settlement in the new federation of city charities: not that Americanization was unimportant—on the contrary, Foreign House was not effective enough. Instead, Americanization should be taken up vigorously by the public schools and by employers, who would soon reap the benefits in increased efficiency and better safety. Compulsory Americanization classes for immigrants would "convert them into loyal citizens and . . . raise their efficiency as producers." As for Foreign House, it should merge with Harley Gibbs Settlement, a Presbyterian mission, or with Christamore, the report concluded.[67]

The wartime emergency had shown up the inadequacy of independent voluntary agencies; now in the postwar social reconstruction the idea of a Community Chest began to emerge. Its forerunner, the "War Chest," was organized in April 1918. In April 1923, after some experimentation with form, membership, and function, its name was changed to the Community Fund and a constitution was adopted. In 1924, the Indianapolis Council of Social Agencies was set up, a new organization which typified the tendency toward rationalization and efficiency of voluntary social services in the 1920s.[68]

Meanwhile, Foreign House had survived the death sentence pronounced by the 1918 survey. In 1923, it joined with a Presbyterian mission working with Romanians and Bulgarians and emerged, refurbished (on paper at least) and triumphantly renamed "American Settlement," as a charter member of the new Community Chest.[69]

But the reality was far different. When Mary Rigg arrived as the new director in 1923, the settlement house stood on Pearl Street, practically abandoned.

> [The] . . . buildings were unkept, in need of repairs and much cleaning. The program of work was practically none. A few were coming to study the English language, but the attendance was so poor, they had decided to close the classes. A Day Nursery was still going on to take care of the children of the working mothers. About six children were coming for music lessons, a general Health Clinic was in operation but was very little used.[70]

The prospect was a depressing one, "not too inspiring to a young college graduate who had made the great decision of choosing Social Work as a profession," she wrote.[71]

Mary Rigg brought both professionalism and enthusiasm to her post. A native of Kansas, she had grown up in Indiana and earned a bachelor's degree. During the war, she was commissioned by the U.S. Department of Labor to do educational and social work. In 1925, she completed a master's degree in social work from Indiana University—her thesis topic, the immigrant people of the American Settlement district. She therefore began her job as settlement director, armed with a thorough knowledge of the settlement neighborhood and its needs. Rule of thumb would be insufficient for this dedicated administrator. Sympathy would be aided by science.

Under its new director, the settlement was completely revived as a neighborhood social center. As a semipublic agency, American Settlement received 73 percent of its funding from the Community Fund, the rest from private donations. A new professionalism was evident: there were three full-time workers in addition to Mary Rigg. And by 1929, the settlement offered a full program of activities and services (see Table 3).[72]

In the 1920s American Settlement operated citizenship classes under the auspices of the public schools, where immigrants learned English and prepared for citizenship.[73] One in four male immigrants surveyed by Stammel and Parks in the 1920s attended such a school. In the case of Pantilimon Panaretoff, who came to America from Macedonia at the age of twelve, the American Settlement night school meant the chance to realize a lifelong ambition.

> Panaretoff spent two years in the grade school completing the eighth grade, and then he enrolled in classes at the American Settlement. For two years he worked during the day at such odd jobs as he could find, but few hours a day were given to the study that was to mean so much to him. Panaretoff early expressed a love for the violin, and his uncle bought a good instrument for him and paid for his first course of lessons. The youth paid from his earnings for those that followed. He studied with several of the best teachers and when he had developed further skill . . . he went to Chicago for a further study with artists of that city. Having completed his work he returned to become a member of the faculty of the leading music school in Indianapolis.[74]

In rare cases, immigrant girls could benefit from the settlement programs as well as their brothers: Franchizka Dziechciaruk, daughter of the Polish family mentioned earlier, entered an Indianapolis night school and learned to write English. She then enrolled in one of the city's high schools and after two years was preparing to enter college. Polish families were much more likely to support a daughter in such a course than Greek or Italian families. Few immigrant women pursued higher education, for most were destined for a career raising children and running a household. Settlements probably attracted the upwardly mobile or otherwise unusual immigrant.[75]

Another area for which the settlement secured cooperation and funds from the city was its playground, created by the demolition of several cottages around the settlement. The city Recreation Department provided equipment and paid two supervisors for summer activities. In the mid-twenties the programs were under the supervision of a young Greek, one of

Table 3
Activities of the American Settlement, 1928–29

Activity	No. Enrolled	No. Sessions	Attendance
Sunday School	38	51	591
Cornet Lessons	6	4	7
Piano	12	3	29
Orchestra	36	13	236
Mothers' Sewing	49	14	262
Girls' Sewing, two groups	60	40 & 33	715
Girl Scouts	53	24	438
Boy Scouts	85	52	760
Boys' Craft	25	38	214
Mothers' Cooking	4	26	59
Daily Vacation Bible School	28	198	3,250
Girls' Gym at Settlement	30	61	457
Girls' Gym at No. 5 School	31	28	319
Boys' Gym at No. 5 School	31	68	499
Basketball at No. 5 School	37	25	325
Playground	62	?	9,466
Comwolei Club	47	38	805
Story Hour Club	26	106	705
Saturday Evening Games Club	20	87	545
Baths		53	372
Motion Pictures		22	4,484
Children for Free Play		243	2,826
Parties and Programs		9	2,020
Practice for Programs		12	264
To Art Institute		1	60
Trips and Hikes		2	87
Clinics—by P.H.N.A.		46	308
Foreign Societies		76	1,699
Day Nursery		359	3,778
Total		1,501	40,384
Total Enrollment for Year			917
Total Different Individuals			460
Families Represented			209

Source: *The Leisure of a People*, pp. 370–71.

sixteen settlement volunteers. The goal of organized play was to change the environment in which immigrant children grew up, to substitute the club-room for the poolroom, the settlement gym for the streets, organized games for the rough and tumble of the gutter, a cosmopolitan group life in the settlement for the ethnically distinct life on street corners and in coffee houses and saloons. That the settlement was partly successful in reorienting leisure is seen from the attendance figures for sports and play activities (see Table 3). But the revolution in leisure, already underway, which would take immigrant children and put them in front of movies and commercialized sports events would be even more far-reaching—and more homogenizing.[76]

In the 1920s, a full-time public-health nurse was employed to visit the homes of foreigners, and one day a week the Public Health Nursing Association held a clinic at the settlement house. But the health work of American Settlement did not survive into the thirties. In a reorganization of public-health nursing in 1932, the association ended its connection with the settlement house. At the national level, the defeat of the bill to extend the Sheppard-Towner Act signaled that American medical care was moving away from a national system of preventive medicine. Subsequently, settlement clinics where the sick and well could come for advice and screening as well as treatment began to decline.[77]

In Indianapolis, as in the nation as a whole, the Red Scare had enormously increased pressures for Americanization. The Federal Bureau of Naturalization called on local communities to adopt "a full, red-blooded American campaign for bringing together the public schools and the adult foreigners to the end that . . . they may make the choice between their present allegiance and allegiance to the United States government." The bureau called on "the best citizens" in every community to carry "the gospel of American citizenship" to the foreign colonies "until foreign colonization groups are only of historical interest—until they are a thing of the past."[78]

Since many Americans associated foreigners with radicalism, settlements in the conservative twenties were forced to operate in an atmosphere of distrust of aliens. American Settlement may have been typical of those that took the offensive in defending foreigners from nativist charges. The settlement had disposed of the "Foreign" label in the 1923 reorganization. Now Mary Rigg tried to combat suspicion of immigrants with understanding: in public statements on behalf of the settlement, she stressed the extent to which immigrants shared American values, worked hard in order to purchase homes, and strove above all for material success.

The Indianapolis press took up this theme in a series of articles on immigrants. "There is no unrest, no red problem at all among these people," the paper told its readers in 1925. "The foreigner comes to us for economic betterment, . . . and therefore work is uppermost in his mind."[79] A writer in 1929 struck the same theme, praising each national group for its special qualities in a catalog of virtues that stood prejudice on its head: the Romanians worked hard in the meat-packing plants, and many of them were proudly sending their children off to college; the Bulgarians had shown their eagerness to become citizens, for half of them had already become naturalized; Greek immigrants were hard-working people who wanted above all to own their own homes, another article explained.[80]

The settlement director approached the immigrants with sympathetic understanding and condemned those who exploited them. "The immigrant does not make the so-called slums," she protested. "He lives here because he is compelled to [and] . . . moves to other sections of the city as soon as his economic condition will permit." Americanization meant improving immigrants' living standards so that all would have "light, sunshine, plumbing, room space and a small plot of ground for a yard." The settlement's task was to help the foreigner find work—"help him secure wages that will maintain high living standards." "Every foreigner is entitled to a living wage and working conditions that do not jeopardize the health of his body or mind," the director declared. "The foreigner is deprived of both of these. The meat packing plants look upon the stranger in our land as the only labor that will do so much work for so little money."[81]

The settlement director's call for fair wages and better treatment was not followed by any organizing activity, however. In the conservative climate of the 1920s the kind of cooperation with organized labor fostered at Hull House in the pre-World War I period was unthinkable. And at a time when immigrants were starting small businesses or moving up from unskilled to skilled work, an attack on the whole wage system seemed as unnecessary as it was unlikely to succeed.

Unlike the early sponsors of Foreign House, Mary Rigg appreciated immigrant cultures and believed that immigrants could make a valuable contribution to American society. She did not see American culture as a fixed entity to which immigrants must conform, but wrote of a culture that was dynamic and capable of receiving the contributions of many peoples. When she used stereotypes, they were flattering ones. For example, the South European, she wrote, "brings much to America. He has much greater appreciation of the arts than the average American. He comes from countries that have known centuries of culture, where men and women have had time to appreciate the beautiful and where the rush and hurry of our industrial society is now known."[82] Such tolerant stereotypes suggest that settlement workers, like Americans generally, had a more relaxed attitude toward American identity than was characteristic of earlier times. But did tolerance also characterize settlement programs in the 1920s? Or was it a strategy to win immigrants' allegiance to some constellation of values and practices called American?

The answer is that at several points tensions between Americanizers and immigrants continued. A major conflict developed over the involvement of many immigrants with selling and distributing illegal liquor. While Mary Rigg understood the cultural importance of drinking in the immigrant community, she knew that family budgets were fragile and that money spent on liquor left less for food. Most immigrants, for their part, viewed the prohibition mentality with incomprehension. "If you no drink, why for you live?" a Slovenian immigrant reportedly asked a social worker.[83]

Religion was another area of potential conflict. While the settlement literature played down religious programming, the settlement continued to conduct a weekly nondenominational Protestant Sunday school on Sunday afternoons, a time when many meetings of foreign societies took place at the house. The settlement's Vacation Bible School was one of the largest in the city, with an enrollment of 198 children of eleven nationalities. In the early years of the century, Americanizers had hoped that Americanization would involve religious conversion; by 1930, the anxiety that pervaded earlier writing about immigrant religion had disappeared, reflecting the trend toward secularization and materialism in the society as a whole.[84]

Religious conversion was still a goal of settlement work with children, however. If settlements had a day nursery, it was not because they approved of mothers going out to work: the settlement ideal was a family wage that would permit every working-class man to support his wife at home. But as long as there were working mothers, the settlement day nursery was a vital service. It was also the cutting edge of the settlement's Americanization program. With immigrant mothers at work (many of them at Kingans) the settlement day nursery was a fine opportunity to Americanize the habits and ideals of immigrant children. A start was made with the children's diets which, one settlement worker reported, contained "strong, pungent seasoning such as garlic or ground red peppers or 'Macedonian corn flakes.' " To counteract such tastes, the settlement staff served the children three meals that were nutritious but bland. Children were also taught "simple but proper table manners." Many had never seen a fork before they came to the settlement.[85]

Settlement classes for immigrant women also concentrated on Americanizing the immigrant diet. While the traditions of the old country were ostensibly preserved, there was at the same time a more or less overt attempt to introduce American ways. Typically, the cooking class began with a discussion of the native dishes of the various countries, but this was just for starters, so to speak. The real purpose of the classes was to teach foreign women "how to prepare the simple American foods, the balanced diet for the pre-school age and school-age child as well as adult." Professionalism and science were arrayed on the side of the Americanizers: the cooking class at American Settlement was conducted by trained dieticians from Riley Hospital and from Indiana Central College.[86]

In another area the best theories of the Americanizers came up against immigrant traditions: sports programs for girls, designed by health reformers to build strong American womanhood, foundered on the refusal of immigrant families to let their daughters participate. But the sports programs for boys were varied and popular.[87]

In the twenty years since John Holliday had called on the citizens of Indianapolis to support a settlement house to Americanize the foreign-born, the attitude of the Americanizers had changed: by 1930 they regarded immigrant religion and culture with indulgence rather than anxiety. Changes in the foreign community were partly the reason. Whereas earlier settlement workers had doubted that these foreigners could ever become Americans, now they were confident that the alchemy of Americanization was working. The settlement's task was still "adjusting their life to ours," but the ultimate attainment of this goal was no longer in doubt because all the evidence pointed to the fact that immigrants shared the values of the Americanizers about hard work, individualism, and the material success that was its reward. A shining example was Alec Lupear, who had been associated with the settlement in its early days and was now owner of the Romanian newspaper, *America*, and an official of an Indianapolis bank.

Stammel and Parks listed the indicators of this assimilation trend among the Eastern Europeans: 81 percent of them took newspapers in English, 61 percent already had their second papers for citizenship; 20 percent had started small businesses. Only 16 percent had made no move toward gaining citizenship. These were not statistics that suggested sullen, unassimilated masses, they were the indicators of upward mobility. The researchers even found it necessary to rebut the charge that these immigrants were "too materialistic." "Few things could be worse than to have a large body of Slavs coming to America who did not desire wealth. Ignorant, uninformed, dirty, stolidly conservative, they would be an infinitely greater menace than the worst of them are now. It is well for us that they desire to rise in the social scale.[88]

Ethnicity still continued to find expression, of course. Eight out of ten households surveyed in 1930 still took a foreign-language newspaper, and ethnic organizations and churches flourished. But sometimes these ethnic associations were themselves an avenue of upward mobility. Accordingly, Americans saw the expression of ethnicity less as a threat than as a quaint survival: American Settlement fostered these survivals, even as the reality behind them slipped away. As mass culture and consumerism marched forward, settlement entertainments were splendid with the costumes of many countries, and at the settlement sewing class, women were encouraged to continue the fine traditional embroidery of their homelands. At young people's clubs, too, a cosmopolitan tolerance was encouraged in programs that focused on the history and culture of the different countries represented there. "World friendship and understanding of each others' racial customs and traditions are stressed," a settlement report stated.[89]

In 1928, a newspaper reporter perceptively summed up the purpose of American settlement:

> On the surface, the work of the settlement house is that of teaching the foreign children and their parents useful and necessary things such as sewing, cooking and the things they do not have a chance to learn in the schools. Beneath the surface, however, one discerns the great underlying purpose of creating from a body of immigrants a class of useful, loyal and intelligent American citizens.[90]

There is no evidence that this was not also the goal of the immigrants themselves.

CHAPTER THREE

Practical Philanthropy along the Color Line: Flanner House, 1898–1930

We shall prosper in proportion as we learn to dignify and glorify common labor and put brains and skill into the common occupations of life.

—Booker T. Washington
Atlanta Exposition Speech, 1895

In 1889, as Jane Addams moved into Hull House and as College Settlement became established among the tenements of New York's Lower East Side, the Charity Organization Society of Indianapolis began visiting the poor in one of the largest black communities north of the Mason-Dixon line. From this work developed Flanner House, which for the next forty years would be one of the city's major social-service agencies for blacks and which continues to serve the Indianapolis black community to this day. The history of Flanner House, for blacks only but controlled by a biracial organization, throws light on white-sponsored philanthropic institutions for blacks in the "Age of Accommodation" and on an aspect of the settlement movement that has received little attention from historians, namely, the black settlement house.

While historians subjected the settlement movement in general to critical scrutiny, they left virtually unexplored the relations between the settlement movement and African-Americans. Historians continued to credit white Progressive-era settlement workers with enlightened policies toward blacks; they pictured settlement workers as among the few white Progressives working to combat racial discrimination and oppression. "Settlement workers were not free of prejudice, of course," Allen Davis wrote, "but many were exceptions in an era that usually thought of the Progressive movement as a program for whites only."[1] This chapter reexamines the relationship between African-Americans and the settlement movement in general, surveys the origins of those social settlements founded especially for blacks and presents a case study of one such black settlement house in Indianapolis, Indiana, revealing the interplay of social reform, social control, and racism that shaped social-welfare institutions among blacks in the Progressive era and after.

The idea that the settlements helped the advancement of blacks originated with the claim of settlement leaders themselves that the "settlement ideal" was one of democracy and racial harmony. Robert Woods and Albert Kennedy, in *The Handbook of Settlements* (1911), wrote an official statement of settlement philosophy, "The typical settlement is one which provides neutral territory traversing all the lines of racial and religious cleavage."[2] Historians still echo this view. "In the struggle for negro freedom the settlement workers stood far above most other so-called progressives," social-welfare historian Walter Trattner wrote in 1979. "In an age of widespread racism and bigotry, many—although certainly not all—advocated the unpopular cause of equality for all Americans, blacks included; they were among the few outstanding pioneers in the fight against racial discrimination."[3]

Another historian who believed that a progressive attitude on racial issues distinguished settlement workers from other reformers was Steven J. Diner. Diner claimed that in contrast with charity-organization reformers, settlement workers were cultural pluralists who accepted the whole range of immigrant and African-American gifts and who understood black poverty to be the result of environment, not racial traits. Diner showed how the writings of Jane Addams reflected her subtle understanding of black culture, her anger at discrimination and injustice.[4] Yet his inference that Addams's views represented mainstream settlement attitudes was unsubstantiated. Other settlement leaders such as Graham Taylor did not share Addams's understanding of racism; in fact, their views resembled the Charity Organization Society position more than historians have recognized.[5]

This is not to deny that some prominent settlement workers were more enlightened on racial issues than their contemporaries. Settlements that combined social work with social investigation were in the forefront of the Progressive-era drive to gather data about urban conditions which produced the first studies of housing, health, and employment among African-Americans in cities of the North.[6] Settlement workers Jane Addams, Mary White Ovington, and Mary McDowell were among the founders of the NAACP in 1909. Jane Addams, as has been mentioned, was an outspoken critic of segregation, who protested the lily-white stance of the Progressive party in 1912.[7]

But the commitment to racial equality on the part of some settlement leaders cannot provide a full and accurate picture of the relationship of the white-led settlement movement as a whole with blacks. While most white settlement workers supported the idea of racial advancement for the Negro, few believed in social equality and few blacks saw it as an achievable goal.

This was a realistic stance in the period that historians of the African-American experience have named "the nadir," when hopes of attaining full constitutional rights seemed at their lowest.[8] Historians have even named disfranchisement and segregation "the seminal 'progressive' reform of the era."[9] Since the Progressive era, previously characterized as a period of democratic reform, is now generally regarded as a period of oppression for blacks, it is necessary to search elsewhere than in the writings and public pronouncements of white settlement leaders for evidence of the real relationship of the settlements to blacks.

A better guide to the black settlements is the *Handbook of Settlements* (1911), and a closer examination of the evidence shows that most settlement houses were founded by and for whites, and few of these even admitted blacks to their programs. Sometimes this was because settlement workers feared that the presence of blacks would deter white attendance. Surveying the movement in 1922, Woods and Kennedy wrote,

> Where the ratio of black to white is slight, the two races usually mix without friction. Large groups of colored people in a neighborhood predominantly white may force a settlement, against its inclination, to choose between the two. In this case the soundest practice is to establish a separate branch, where special forms of work fitted to the needs of colored people are carried on.[10]

Often the exclusion of blacks was achieved simply by locating settlements far from black neighborhoods. Hull House, Northwestern University Settlement, and Chicago Commons, Chicago's most famous settlements, all served immigrant neighborhoods where few blacks lived. Similarly, in a study of Godman House in Columbus, Ohio, and two Cleveland settlements, Alta House and Hiram House, historian David A. Gerber found that although they "did not draw the color line and in fact encouraged black participation," they were all located far from centers of black population and served mainly immigrants.[11] The plight of black Americans was of so little concern to a Kansas City settlement that with unconscious irony it advertised its *inclusiveness* of all immigrant groups by stating, "All but Negroes are received into our classes."[12]

The Indiana settlement movement developed along racially segregated lines. For example, the religious reformers who established Christamore saw their mission as lifting the white population to a "higher plane"—and for them white uplift necessitated black exclusion.[13] When blacks in the Christamore neighborhood began to outnumber whites, Christamore's supporters simply moved the settlement to another location (a neighborhood of European immigrants) in 1920.[14] Gary, Indiana's Protestant settlements also targeted immigrants, and when the Great Migration swelled the black

population, white Methodists set up Stewart House, a separate all-black settlement, with the encouragement and financial support of U.S. Steel (see
Chapter 7).[15]

While most settlements focused on immigrants and working-class whites,
others served only blacks. The *Handbook of Settlements* listed black settlements in New York City, Chicago, Philadelphia, Boston, Baltimore, Minneapolis, Columbus, Ohio, Washington, D.C., Hampton, Virginia,
Englewood, New Jersey, and East Greenwich, Rhode Island—but there were
dozens more, some founded by white philanthropists to aid blacks and others founded by blacks themselves. Because a number of them were religious
institutions, because many were in the South, and also because they tended
to be poor and therefore ephemeral, these black settlements have usually
been ignored in a settlement-house history slanted toward the Midwest and
Northeast, toward secular rather than religious institutions, and toward a
small group of (white) heroines and heroes.[16]

Recently, historians of the African-American experience have begun to
document the role of the black-run settlements in racial reform. Among the
hundreds of institutions established after the Civil War as blacks moved to
cities of the South and later the North, these settlement houses drew on
the talents of educated, energetic race leaders—often women—to provide
vital services to needy people.[17] The Neighborhood Union in Atlanta,
founded in 1908 by Lugenia Burns Hope, organized the talents of philanthropic and educated black women into a reform organization that became
an important catalyst for change in Atlanta's African-American community.[18] As black population shifted to the North, educated blacks continued to provide leadership in such self-help efforts. For example, Locust
Street Settlement in Hampton, Virginia, founded by Janie Porter Barrett,
had as its aim "improving the homes and the moral and social life of that
community." Barrett organized classes, clubs, a night school, and a kindergarten, among a whole range of social, welfare, and educational activities.[19]

Black churches traditionally provided many of the services that in the
white community were associated with settlement houses—job placement,
industrial education, day nurseries, and youth recreation. Later, many of
these functions would also be taken up by the National Urban League. Several variations on this theme occurred; for example, there was Reverdy
Ransom's Institutional Church and Social Settlement, founded in Chicago
in 1901.[20] Another experiment was Rev. Richard Wright's Trinity Mission
and Cultural Center in Chicago's Black Belt. But the mission collapsed
when Wright left in 1905 and was not recorded in the 1911 Woods and
Kennedy *Handbook*. If black-run missions and settlements tended to be un-
stable and to depend on the drive and vision of a single person, it was often
because the black churches already carried a heavy financial burden.[21]

While historians of the African-American experience agree on the important role of such black social-service agencies in racial advancement, they have often dismissed the black settlements established by whites as no more than institutions of social control. But the line between black- and white-controlled institutions should not be drawn too strongly: many black-run settlement houses depended partly on white philanthropy. Both the Wendell Phillips Center and the Frederick Douglass Center counted Julius Rosenwald among their supporters; the Wendell Phillips Center also had the very wealthy Louise de Koven Bowen (treasurer of Hull House) on its board. The influence of Jane Addams, Mary McDowell, and Graham Taylor secured for Reverdy Ransom's settlement financial contributions from Mrs. George Pullman and other wealthy white donors, and Wright's settlement appealed successfully to the enormously wealthy Mrs. Potter Palmer.[22] Without such support, settlements folded quickly for lack of funds. Philpott's study of black settlements in Chicago found that of nine settlements established between 1900 and 1916, only one remained in 1919. Of seven started after the 1919 race riot, again only one was viable by 1930.[23]

White philanthropy did not necessarily mean that blacks derived no benefit from these programs. Nineteenth-century Quaker philanthropy among blacks had generally been benevolent, with policies shaped by a belief in a common Father of all and in the spiritual equality of every person, regardless of race. From 1904 until her death in 1918, Celia Parker Woolley, a white Unitarian minister, made Frederick Douglass Center a symbol of interracial cooperation between black and white middle-class reformers.[24] Wendell Phillips Center, another white-run agency for blacks, was staffed by black social workers and had an interracial board of directors. Its work was entirely with black clients.[25]

Moreover, white philanthropy, whether Quaker or not, did not always mean complete control. In the case of the Philadelphia Institute for Colored Youth, supported by Quakers, historian Linda Perkins found that blacks managed the institution, building it into Philadelphia's major educational force for African-Americans. And an important study of Philadelphia agencies for blacks found that even those funded by municipal government, and thus nominally under white control, nevertheless employed black staff "with the knowledge and experience necessary to formulate a meaningful program of reform."[26]

But Perkins's study stopped in 1903 when the institute was captured by the Tuskegee machine—and Philadelphia might not have been typical of other cities. What happened to such institutions in the early twentieth century when the agents of Tuskegee and their white allies began to dominate local black politics, bringing their ideology of accommodation? Did blacks sit on settlement boards or retain control over settlement programs? Did the settlements develop programs that were a realistic response to poverty and discrimination? Did they become "spearheads for reform" in the black community—and did African-Americans benefit from these reforms?

Social reform and social control are not mutually exclusive. Both explanations are helpful in understanding the origins and development of Flanner House, a black-only settlement house founded in Indianapolis in 1898. The history of this settlement shows how the actions of clients combined with control by elites to shape the social-work institutions of the Progressive era. An examination of its programs and philosophy reveals an institution that in its careful accommodations to whites and its useful but limited programs for blacks typifies "Practical Philosophy along the Color Line."

Flanner House was established as part of the general reorganization of charities carried out by white social-gospel minister Oscar McCulloch of the Plymouth Congregational Church. Previous accounts of the settlement movement have drawn a sharp distinction between the Charity Organization Society (COS) and the settlements. But in Indianapolis the COS, also headed by Reverend McCulloch, was responsible for establishing the first settlement house.[27] A prominent social gospeler and charity organizer, McCulloch was influenced by the ideas of English reformers John Ruskin and Octavia Hill. Between 1879 and 1891 McCulloch transformed Plymouth Church into an institutional church, adding cultural, educational, and social programs to its worship functions. Eventually, he planned for a grand scheme of civic reform—a network of settlement houses that would bring about the moral regeneration and material improvement of the entire city.[28]

McCulloch did not live to see this visionary idea realized for he died in 1891. However, his wishes were carried out in 1897, when the COS launched the Indiana Avenue Neighborhood House on the city's racially mixed northwest side. One founder of the settlement can be identified as Sarah Colton Smith, a white social worker, paid COS agent, and an attendance officer for the public schools.[29] To begin with, the settlement admitted children of both races. But in 1898 the COS decided that it was "inexpedient to have colored and white children attending the same institution." White mortician and COS leader Frank Flanner then donated a building on Rhode Island Street as a settlement house for "the industrial and moral uplift of colored girls and boys," calling it Flanner Guild. The separate building was necessary for the "special needs" of the Negro race, the COS claimed. In fact Flanner Guild would long outlast its parent settlement, for the Indiana Avenue Neighborhood House closed its doors in 1904[30] (see Map 4).

Far from being unusual, this decision to segregate settlement work reflected a national trend toward the establishment of race-specific social-service agencies. Some of the reasons for this development have already

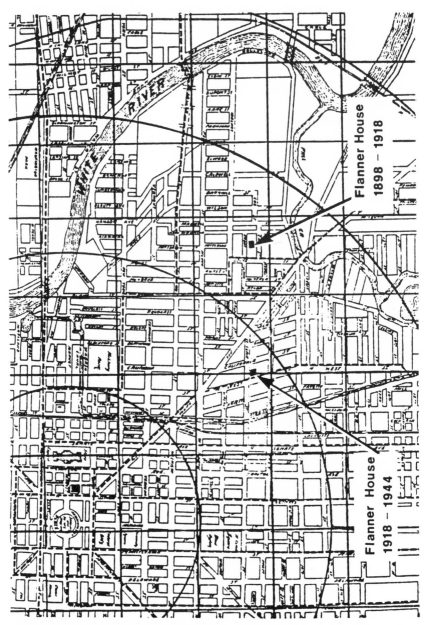

Map 4. Flanner House, Indianapolis, 1898–1944. From R. L. Polk and Co., "City Directory Map of Indianapolis, Indiana, 1909."

been noted. Often black settlements were spun off by established white settlement houses and remained affiliated with them. For example, Robert
Gould Shaw House in Boston was started by settlement workers from the
city's South End House in 1908; Lincoln House in Brooklyn was established
for blacks by the consolidation of a kindergarten, a colored day nursery, and
the Brooklyn Visiting Nurses Service. Blacks excluded from the Minneapolis settlements went instead to the Phyllis Wheatley House.[31] When they
came to sum up the settlement movement in 1922, Woods and Kennedy
described the establishment of such separate branch settlements as "the
soundest practice." Some white social workers believed that the intense racial and economic discrimination experienced by blacks made segregated
agencies advisable.[32]

Ever since the end of the Civil War, Indianapolis had been a destination
for blacks escaping the oppressive race relations and blasted hopes of the
South. The city's small established black community, numbering about
9,000 in 1890, grew steadily until by 1900 Indianapolis had the seventh
largest black community in the urban North. The newcomers found an atmosphere noticeably better than they had left. One black woman, newly
arrived, wrote home to her sister in 1865, "I have sait down to the table
and eat with white folks what I cant do in the South . . . the colored and
Whites are on Equality."[33] But first impressions soon gave way to a more
sober reality, including the competition between blacks and immigrants for
jobs. Indianapolis suffered a major race riot in 1876 when blacks and Irish
fought with staves from a local barrel factory.[34] Despite such outbreaks
black migration continued, keeping pace with the growth of the city as a
whole. Two distinct black residential neighborhoods began to develop to
the north of the downtown. The Fifth Ward was the heart of the black
community. There, blacks formed about one-third of the population in 1910
and two-thirds by 1930.[35]

In response to these newcomers who numbered about 16,000 by 1900, or
9 percent of the population, the County Commissioners began to support
Flanner Guild with an annual appropriation of $500. In addition, Flanner
Guild relied on donations from businesses and individuals, some as large as
$50, others as small as 5¢ or 10¢. Initial support amounted to about $500
in donations from blacks and $1,500 from whites.[36]

The purpose of the agency, its constitution of 1903 stated, was to promote the "social, spiritual, moral and physical welfare of Negroes in Indianapolis, the establishment and maintenance of industrial and other lines of
education."[37] If the name "Guild" recalled the settlement's debt to contemporary English Christian Socialism, a more immediate influence was American—the Tuskegee and Hampton ideal of racial progress through gradual
economic improvement. The blending of these two reform traditions was

Figure 2. Millinery class, Flanner Guild Industrial Neighborhood House, 1904. Courtesy of the Indiana State Library, Indianapolis.

nicely captured when the settlement adopted the name "Flanner Guild Industrial Neighborhood House" in 1904.[38]

Employment was a major concern of the social agency. Facing discrimination from employers and trade unions alike, the newcomers clustered in low-paying, low-status jobs. Only 13 percent of black males found employment in manufacturing (compared with 35 percent of native-born whites and 45 percent of foreign-born whites), while 69 percent of them worked in jobs classified as domestic or personal service. Ninety-two percent of employed black women were in domestic or personal service positions.[39] Declaring that the jobs assigned to blacks were often "unfit for educational and moral advancement," the settlement announced its intention to train them for better paid jobs—"bookkeepers, carpenters, dressmakers, cooks etc." In 1905, the settlement report noted that 150 young women had graduated from millinery classes conducted by the settlement, and that all of them were now self-supporting milliners or teachers of millinery.[40]

But there was little public support for the settlement. In 1903, the Indianapolis *News* complained, "The public has not been at all generous in subscribing to Flanner Guild, as it evidently has not as yet a proper idea of the importance of this work to negroes and whites alike."[41]

More than lack of funds was involved in the settlement's inability to help blacks break through to better jobs. Racism relegated them to the lowliest jobs and denied them the industrial employment that was enabling immigrants to move up. In the face of these realities there was little that reformers could do. One notable exception (which serves to highlight the difference between a black self-help organization and a white-sponsored agency like Flanner House) was achieved by the Indianapolis Women's Improvement Club, an association of upper-class, black women reformers led by Mrs. Lillian T. Fox, which prevailed on the Van Camp Packing Company to staff an entire division of its plant with black female workers. This success would remain an unusual exception until World War II.[42]

In contrast to the achievement of the WIC, Flanner House fell back on a "training program" that was long on exhortation but short on training. The agency did not abandon its efforts to teach blacks work-related skills, but it also relied on the cheaper expedient of teaching good work habits. Every Sunday, the Flanner House auditorium was the scene of "talks and lectures along the line of industry and moral living" given by prominent black and white speakers. Guest speakers in 1905 included several ministers of both races and black businessman George L. Knox, owner of the *Freeman*. White speakers included an ex-mayor, well-known suffragist May Wright Sewall, the superintendent of schools, and the editor of the Indianapolis *News*.[43] The settlement's program of lectures and uplifting talks was evidence of the guild's emphasis on another kind of "industry": on teaching blacks *how to* work. Ignoring the facts of discrimination, white Progressives like Ray Stannard Baker offered work discipline as a panacea: the difference between slavery and freedom, Baker wrote in his discussion of race relations in the North, was simply a new attitude toward work; blacks would never become efficient in the cities of the North until they had internalized the work ethic. Many in the black middle class also agreed that better work habits would lead to better work opportunities.[44]

Flanner Guild programs concentrated on what was practical and possible. To a much greater extent than was true for whites, black women had to find paid employment. Accepting this necessity and recognizing that industrial and white-collar jobs were closed to black women, the settlement adopted the modest but attainable goal of training them as domestic workers. The settlement's Employment Department began in 1904 as a program to aid unwed mothers. It sheltered "fallen, friendless girls" until their babies were born, then tried to find them positions as domestics. The response from both needy black women and potential employers must have been good, for in its first year the guild supplied fifty white families with domestic workers.[45] Linking a domestic ideology with its goal of economic self-sufficiency for wayward girls, the settlement's program typified nineteenth-century "rescue work" which assumed (somewhat optimistically) that the girl's placement in a home ensured her safety and economic maintenance.

The settlement's programs for domestic training reflected a consensus between white and black reformers. Improving the skills and knowledge of the nation's wives and mothers was a goal of the settlement movement nationally and one central to the Progressive agenda of better neighborhood health, recreation, child care, and standards of living. But these goals also coincided with the concerns of the black middle class for whom racial progress meant elevating standards in the home. Agencies to train, place, and protect domestic workers were not unique to settlements but were common to many institutions, including missions, YWCAs, and the Urban League. They were part of racial uplift programs because they promised to solve two urgent problems at once: to provide poor mothers with respectable work and to combine domestic training with uplift. Working in the homes of whites, black domestic workers were to learn higher standards of cleanliness which they would then take back into their own homes. The domestic-help agency also enabled the settlement house to demonstrate its worth to the white community, on whose generosity it largely depended.[46]

But supplying black women with domestic work did little to remove the roots of black poverty or to open opportunities for long-term advancement for African-Americans. Perhaps for this reason the black community was divided in its response to the settlement. Just as in Chicago, Boston, and Cleveland some black leaders fought the establishment of such racially segregated social agencies, so in Indianapolis there was criticism of the settlement's philosophy of accommodation, with its Washingtonian emphasis on economic advancement rather than political rights. The first president of the settlement's board of directors, W. T. B. Williams, was a black Harvard graduate and Indianapolis school principal who would later be closely identified with the Tuskegee machine. Criticism of Flanner Guild may partly have reflected dissatisfaction at the compromises demanded by the disciples of Hampton and Tuskegee in the name of accommodation. One writer in the *Freeman* questioned the settlement's emphasis on manual training: far from being a panacea, as the Washingtonians claimed, he wrote, such "education" was no more than "an easy way to get on with the white race." A settlement history admitted that, from the first, the settlement had been "fought and criticized by the small minds of both races." Indianapolis blacks feared the spread of Jim Crow from the South and correctly recognized in Flanner Guild a harbinger of the new segregated order. They were not impressed with a program of black uplift that aimed to lift blacks to a position decidedly below that of whites.[47]

On the other hand some influential black leaders such as physician Sumner A. Furniss and post office official George W. Cable supported the Tuskegee approach, which historian Louis Harlan has described as "accommodation, at least for a time, to what blacks could not change."[48] The older black elite believed that with hard work, education, and respectability they would accumulate wealth and that political rights would follow. "There are few cities in this country . . . which can boast of more progressive colored men," claimed an optimistic editorial in the *Freeman* in 1888. "Indianapolis takes a front rank in this regard. The colored men share the thrift and enterprise of their white brethren, and they are solving the race problem in a way which redounds to the credit of the race as well as to themselves."[49]

But the deteriorating racial atmosphere after the turn of the century dispelled this mood of optimism. Realists argued that blacks had better fall back on their own resources, not wait for white acceptance in a color-blind society. A writer in the *Freeman* expressed this mood in 1916: "We have learned to forego some rights that are common, because we know the price. We would gain but little in a way if certain places were thrown open to us. We have not insisted that hotels should entertain our race, or the theaters, rights that are clearly ours."[50]

The *Freeman* had begun to reflect these ideas much earlier; it was the time not to agitate questions of political rights or social equality, writers argued, but instead to advance the race in education and economic status. The newspaper thus began to present a more favorable picture of the black settlement house. In a front-page article in 1902, the *Freeman* reversed its previous stand and compared Flanner Guild to Tuskegee, praising its efforts to reach boys and girls who did not attend school and to open new job opportunities for the race. However, controversy evidently still surrounded the black settlement house. Black professionals did not come forward to lead the agency, for when W. T. B. Williams resigned to go to Hampton in 1902, a settlement report frankly described efforts to find his replacement as "a weary, depressing search for a Negro leader with the initiative and vision to take over this seemingly hopeless task."[51] The search ended when Dr. B. J. Morgan, a chiropodist, became head. Morgan had been associated with the Senate Avenue Branch of the YMCA, a black-only "Y" that was to become one of the largest in the nation. When her husband became president of the settlement's board of directors, Mrs. Morgan left her comfortable home to move into the guild "in order that the Institution might be relieved of the expense of hiring a Superintendent."[52]

Another prominent citizen associated with Flanner House was black attorney Robert Lee Brokenburr. Aged twenty-six in 1912, Brokenburr was at the beginning of a long career as a civil-rights advocate. But Brokenburr's term as director of the agency was brief, and other evidence suggests that few blacks wanted to be identified with the white-dominated agency.[53]

It is important that at this low ebb in the settlement's fortunes, black women took charge. In 1902, an association of black schoolteachers with the proud name "the King's Daughters" gathered together the equipment and furnishings for the settlement and set about making Flanner Guild a force for educational and cultural improvement in the black community. They offered literary and cultural clubs for young women, English and woodworking classes for boys. Like most settlements, black and white, Flanner Guild held classes in cooking, sewing, and housewifery. Few charitable or moral-reform movements of the period could have been sustained without the work of middle-class women, and Flanner Guild was no exception. Reform and cultural activities enhanced the self-worth of black women, doubly handicapped by race and gender. Clubs like the King's Daughters or the exclusive Indianapolis Women's Improvement Club spearheaded important reforms. The WIC would subsequently lead the crusade for a hospital for blacks suffering from tuberculosis and would cooperate with the settlement in this work. [54]

In 1906, when black reformer Gertrude Guthrie became Matron, Flanner Guild took on even more the appearance of a "community of women reformers." Guthrie involved herself energetically in all kinds of betterment activities; during 1910 alone her listed activities included the COS Council, the Juvenile Court, the Probation Officers' Association, and the Children's Aid Association. She also attended a national convention of probation officers. [55]

Like the more famous Frederick Douglass Center in Chicago or the Presbyterian missions in Louisville, Flanner Guild represented a joint effort by black and white elites which solicited financial support from both races. [56] Decision making was apparently shared also—although evidence on this admittedly vital point is not available for this early period. The board of directors consisted of five blacks, headed by the settlement director and including Rev. H. L. Herod, of the Second Christian Church. White direction and perhaps control were provided by the five-member board of trustees, a group of prominent professionals including Carleton McCulloch, a doctor and son of Oscar McCulloch. However, at least one black served as trustee between 1905 and 1910. Flanner donated additional property to the guild in 1909, and with donations from the public and a grant of $500 from the county commissioners, the guild erected a new assembly hall to hold two hundred people. Entertainments and musical programs at the settlement confirmed its position as a center of neighborhood culture. [57]

Although it kept the character of a vehicle for white-funded reform in the black community, Flanner Guild also encouraged self-help. The COS supported a Dime Savings and Loan Association based at Flanner Guild; its collectors, described as "a corps of friendly visitors," went into the homes of subscribers to collect savings and often stayed to teach lessons of health, morals, and self-help. By 1907, the 6,000 savers had deposited $25,000. Citing the fact that two-thirds of these savers were black, a settlement report claimed that the guild had been successful in decreasing pauperism and dependency while "educating our people along the line of self-help."[58]

Blacks took the lead in another Flanner Guild program, one to combat juvenile delinquency. With the migrants from the South being blamed for an increase in crime and rowdiness, middle-class blacks used the resources of the settlement to offer constructive alternatives for idle youth. George W. Cable, a black member of the guild's board of directors, was chairman of a group of thirty black volunteer probation officers who worked with the juvenile court of Marion County (the first of its kind in the country). Another effort to prevent delinquency and build character in young men was Flanner Guild Boys' Drill Corps. This program combined training in drill with religious exercises and aimed to produce "tidiness and obedience." But critics claimed that such programs, based on the Hampton pattern, trained blacks for servitude, not citizenship.[59] On the other hand, the Vacant Lots Cultivation scheme, planned and directed by the white COS, was typical of uplift rather than social control. In 1905 the COS donated land and seeds to seventy-five black families through the Flanner Guild. The results were put on display later that year at the Flanner Guild "Fruit, Food and Industrial Exhibit." The COS sponsors were understandably proud of a scheme that produced gardens on waste land while at the same time helping poor people to feed themselves—and so, too, no doubt, were the black families who produced their own food and beautified their yards and neighborhood. But the settlement's claim that the exhibit showed "advancement along the lines of intellect and industry" was far-fetched. The true appeal of these efforts to black and white philanthropists was that they demonstrated self-help in action.

> By securing the use of vacant land in and around the city many Negro families have been encouraged to make gardens thus furnishing healthful and self-respecting occupation for the old or very young members of many Negro families, who otherwise might become public charges.[60]

Black and white sponsors of Flanner Guild had a remarkably similar analysis of the causes of Afro-American "backwardness." To succeed, the race must adopt higher standards, argued Dr. Sumner A. Furniss, the first black physician to be admitted as an intern to the Indianapolis City Hospital. Despite his own struggle to overcome discrimination, the doctor's prescription for working-class blacks was essentially moral. Furniss, who headed the Indianapolis branch of the pro-Washington National Negro Business League, called on successful members of the race to urge others "to more personal cleanliness, insist on a pure home life, and less dissipation and intemperance; to have fewer picnics and save more money for a rainy day."[61] Such a diagnosis ignored the facts of disfranchisement and discrimination, stressing instead the efficacy of individual effort. Not surprisingly, white Progressives agreed. "From my point of view the education that is most needed by everyone, is that personal training which will give a sense of self-respect," wrote white suffrage-leader May Wright Sewall in an endorsement of the agency's work. "This involves a desire to make for oneself a good living, together with the knowledge of how to do it . . . In so far as the Flanner Guild serves this end it deserves well of the public."[62]

By 1912, Flanner Guild faced a crisis. Among the causes were the death in that year of its chief sponsor, white businessman Frank Flanner; the success of a rival organization, the Senate Avenue YMCA; and a financial crisis in which charitable donations and annual grants from the county were no longer sufficient for the programs needed to serve a black population that numbered over 22,000. This last limitation was the most serious. Few settlements solved the problem of funds; very few were as fortunate as Hull House, which received over $1 million from the wealthy philanthropist Louise de Koven Bowen.[63] For settlements that served blacks, one alternative to bankruptcy was to be "adopted" by a white church or religious body. Like other black agencies that first tried to maintain some independence from white control, Flanner Guild allowed itself to be taken over by a white missionary body, the Christian Women's Board of Missions, in 1913. A missionary arm of the Protestant Disciples of Christ denomination whose headquarters were in Indianapolis, the CWBM trained missionaries for evangelical work at home and abroad at its Missionary Training School in the Indiana capital.[64]

The move probably saved Flanner Guild from financial collapse. When Richard Wright refused a similar offer by a white Chicago church to take over his Trinity Mission and Cultural Center in Chicago's Black Belt, he sealed its fate for the settlement closed down in 1911.[65] CWBM support enabled Flanner House to survive and expand: by 1918 it was operating on a budget of almost $4,000 a year. And the Missionary Training School provided students to staff the agency's programs and faculty volunteers to direct them. Because professional social workers, especially blacks, were few, trained workers like these white urban missionaries were valuable in the settlement's educational work. Yet the absence of Flanner House "graduates" as social workers was a sign that the new management intended to keep control of the settlement firmly in the hands of whites.[66]

By 1918, the CWBM provided 74 percent of the settlement's funding and exercised a dominant role in the black agency. The settlement's governing board of eight members included three members of the CWBM executive committee and two faculty members of the College of Missions, "thus giving the practical control into the hands of our Board," it was noted in the CWBM executive committee minutes.[67] The relationship between

Flanner Guild and the CWBM lasted until 1923, when the settlement entered the Community Fund.[68]

The change to white leadership was marked by the arrival of a new superintendent in 1917. Charles Otis Lee was a graduate of the University of Chicago in religion and sociology. His "New Aspects of the Negro in the Industrial World," a summary of the problems of black Americans in 1918, shows that he brought a sympathetic understanding and a keen mind to his work.[69]

Lee's analysis began not with moral failings, but with economic realities. Discrimination was keeping even educated members of the race from the advancement they deserved, Lee pointed out. A black doctor could not practice at any hospital in Indianapolis except an inferior, segregated one, and black girls with high-school diplomas were reduced to seeking domestic work. "Opportunities that are almost forced upon white children must oftentimes be gained by the colored boy or girl only after paying a tremendous price of toil and hardships."[70] As for conditions among those newly arrived from the South, the wartime influx had worsened problems of health and housing, making the work of the settlement house ever more difficult. "The upward pull of the schools, the churches, and such institutions as Flanner House are every day nullified because of these conditions existing in the improper housing of the great bulk of the Negro citizens."

The settlement director demanded more opportunities for African-Americans in industry and the professions and called on city government to improve the health and housing conditions of its black residents.[71] This was more than a summary of conditions, it was a demand for redress, reflecting a confidence that wartime labor shortages would result in permanently improved prospects for black employment. The war had already produced a dramatic improvement in black industrial employment: a survey of five major Indianapolis companies found that since 1916 employment of blacks had almost doubled, from 1,230 to 2,100 in 1918.[72] The response of the white community was not quite the square deal that Charles Lee demanded, however.

Instead, it is clear from a report issued in 1918 that the city's white leaders saw Flanner House as an ally to control and contain the problems created by the Great Migration. The report named the conditions existing among the black population, now numbering 35,000, as the city's greatest challenge: "The distinctive problems called up by race prejudice, the inability of the large number of colored people recently arrived from the South to adjust themselves to the life and housing conditions of a large city, created dangers both of a moral and health character."[73] The authors of the report enthusiastically endorsed settlement houses like Flanner House which could organize "the efficient members of the race to assist others and to teach

Figure 3. Flanner House Baby Clinic, about 1918. The old Flanner House Building on Colton Street was soon abandoned for better quarters. Courtesy of the Indiana State Library, Indianapolis.

the newly arrived how to maintain sanitary living quarters, how to find the best employment and . . . proper recreation."[74] They noted that Flanner House--"a mission" with a "staff of white people cooperating with and working among the colored people"—had the ideal arrangement. The biracial board of directors ensured white control and would "secure more stability in the work than would be the case if the money were turned over to a staff consisting exclusively of colored workers." Whites should remain firmly in control of such efforts, the authors implied.[75]

The 1920s saw important changes in both the internal and external history of the settlement house. Superficially, these were changes for the better. The CWBM purchased new buildings for the settlement and spent about $10,000 to modernize them. They were a great improvement over the settlement's previous facilities, described in the 1918 Survey of Social Agencies as "dilapidated . . . primitive and inadequate"—in sad contrast to the "commendable" spirit of the settlement workers.[76] By 1922, Community Chest contributions amounted to $15,020 out of the settlement's annual budget of $17,712. In 1923, the formal connection of Flanner House with the CWBM ended altogether, and the agency entered under the umbrella of the Community Chest, gaining financial stability as part of a citywide network of public and private social service agencies. Community Chest control ensured the viability of the agency but also guaranteed that its activities would not stray outside the parameters of conservative "adjustment" programs.[77] In a decade when the NAACP was mounting a vigorous legal challenge to segregation locally and nationally and when a new sense of racial consciousness was finding expression in numerous "new Negro" organizations, the settlement played a different role. Like the Urban League, Flanner House helped ease migrants' adjustment to industrial society, provided information about jobs, housing, and health, and worked for better race relations. Offering blacks a range of helping services, the agency at the same time implicitly promised whites that it was "keeping things under control."[78]

Better funded and with new buildings, Flanner House now provided many essential services to the black community. The day nursery cared for the children of working mothers; the Friendly Visitor called on neighborhood people with helpful advice. Weekly clinics—dental and baby clinics and the tuberculosis clinic—made Flanner House a source of desperately needed health care. The educational work of the settlement included a Red Cross home-nursing course and a Mothers' Council that taught about health and nutrition. Settlement clubs for boys and girls offered recreation as well as instruction in sewing and music. The settlement also continued to encourage residents to spruce up the neighborhood by sponsoring Yard and Home contests.[79]

In addition, the settlement sponsored and carried out several ambitious surveys of economic and social conditions in the black community. These culminated in the very comprehensive *Indianapolis Study* of 1939 which summarized the needs of blacks and assessed how well the settlement house was meeting them. Not surprisingly, the study found insufficient income to be the basic cause of all the problems that blacks faced.[80]

The Great Migration both coincided with and contributed to a marked deterioration in race relations. The 1920s saw the resurgence of the Klan, the increased segregation of schools and housing, and continued erosion of black civil rights. Whites organized "civic leagues" to contain black housing areas, and in 1926 the city council passed a zoning ordinance that permitted segregated housing, a decision that the Indianapolis NAACP successfully challenged.[81] In contrast, Flanner House was not associated with an open challenge to racism. White support, which allowed the settlement to maintain and expand its programs, also helped shape the agency's agenda. Its programs reflected compromises between white interests and black demands.

Blacks continued to have a say in running and staffing the settlement: they helped to shape the two major programs of the settlement in the 1920s, the campaign against tuberculosis and the organization of female

Figure 4. The Employment Office, Flanner House. Waiting for a call for domestic work, 1922. Courtesy of the Indiana State Library, Indianapolis.

domestic workers. Both these initiatives were object lessons in progress through accommodation, both were viewed favorably by whites; at the same time, the black middle class tried to shape the settlement's programs for the betterment of the black community.

As early as 1905, Flanner House sponsors were calling for action to meet the crisis of tuberculosis in the black community. With poor housing and living conditions, blacks accounted for about one-half of all the city's TB deaths although they were only one-eighth of the population. Yet they were excluded from the city's only treatment facility, the City Hospital.[82] Between 1905 and 1918 a coalition of black female community activists, physicians, and reform organizations led by the WIC energetically organized to provide for blacks as a charity the health services that public authorities were providing for whites as a right. Flanner House lent its effort to this campaign, holding clinics for the diagnosis and treatment of tuberculosis, staffed by volunteer black and white physicians. Cooperation between the settlement and the WIC culminated when the women's reform organization funded a resident visiting nurse at Flanner House in 1918.[83]

However, public funding was not made available for the settlement's TB work until 1919, and then in a changed context which favored strengthening black institutions, rejected integration of treatment facilities, and advocated home care over institutionalization. Public support of a citywide

Figure 5. Flanner House Tuberculosis Clinic, 1919. Nurse Lilian Kazaka and Dr. Henry L. Hummons. Courtesy of the Indiana Historical Society Library (neg. no. C2221).

tuberculosis tax levy to fund a network of segregated clinics might have been partly a response to the grave public-health situation produced by the wartime migration of thousands of poor blacks from the South.[84] The Flanner House superintendent played on white fears of the spread of disease from the black community as he pointed out how closely blacks and whites lived and worked together in Indianapolis—especially as mistresses and servants.

> They ride in the same cars with us, they work in the same factories; they handle the same money and they buy at the same shops—trying on, in many cases, the very garments we wear. What is more important, they cook much of our food, wash our clothes and dishes, handle our linens, clean our houses and make our beds.[85]

Government must take responsibility for checking the spread of contagious disease from the black community, he declared. In February 1919, Lee wrote to the Marion County Tuberculosis Society, again demanding that some provision be made for the approximately 13,000 cases of tuberculosis among blacks in the city.[86]

Whether city government was responding to such invidious arguments, to the campaigns of the WIC, or simply to the pressures to "do something" about the needy population in their midst, the result was a "reform" that meant more not less segregation, one in which the black settlement house played a major role. First, admission of black patients at the City Hospital was ruled out: the 1918 report by the "expert" National Bureau of Municipal Research explained why the need for segregation outweighed the claims of equal treatment:

> Practical experience shows that it is not advisable to care for colored and white people in the same ward or in fact to care under the same roof for patients whose habits and social status differs widely . . . In planning for hospital treatment . . . one cannot give the first consideration to ideals of social equality and equal justice . . . Experience shows that in order to make the hospital treatment of tuberculosis effective, separate institutions or at least separate units must be provided for groups who are differentiated by prejudice of color and social habits.

Medical experts obligingly affirmed the superiority of home over institutional treatment.[87]

But the report's main recommendation—a separate publicly funded hospital for blacks—was ignored. Subsequently, both the WIC and Flanner House responded defensively, the WIC by establishing a private hospital for blacks, Flanner House by developing programs within the black community for education about and diagnosis of tuberculosis. When the Board of Health established the first unit of a planned citywide network of tuberculosis clinics at Flanner House in February 1919 it was as an alternative to the integration of public facilities.[88] In the 1920s Flanner House health services consisting of programs for the education, diagnosis, and treatment of tuberculosis became pivotal to health care in the black community. The WIC employed Daisy Brabham, wife of a Presbyterian minister, as a visiting nurse based at the settlement. She became a familiar presence in the neighborhood, calling at peoples' homes to encourage "a general sanitary uplift that would render it more difficult for this disease to get hold of its victims."[89] The black community could take pride in the community-based health center that employed black physicians and nurses, even though all these services took shape in a context of increasing racial segregation. But it was significant that, at a time when public authorities refused to take action, the settlement, led by the Progressive Lee, had become the means by which a coalition of black reformers had attacked the health crisis in the black community. It was not until 1938 that black sufferers from TB were admitted to the city hospital, however.[90]

Widespread denial of rights, barriers in employment, and the increased segregation of schools and housing amounted to a worsening situation for blacks in the 1920s. But the appearance of separation—of two races living in the same city but apart—was an illusion. For thousands of black women were becoming domestics in white homes, replacing the immigrant girls, the typical domestic worker of earlier times. The percentage of servants and waitresses in Indianapolis who were black rose from 34 percent in 1910 to 61 percent in 1920, reflecting a national trend.[91]

At the same time, changes in the organization of domestic work were making this area one of particular concern to settlements. Before the war, most domestics had lived with their employers, but in the 1920s day work was rapidly replacing live-in work as the norm. This shift accompanied the change from white to black "help." As domestic work became increasingly done by black women, they, too, sought to shape the terms on which they entered employment. Many welcomed the change from live-in to day work since it enabled them to combine paid employment with care for their own families.[92] However, this reorganization of domestic work also had the effect of casualizing domestic labor. It was a change that released workers from the potentially exploitive situation of live-in help but threw them into a precarious labor market where many did not know where the next day's wage was coming from.

The Flanner House initiative arose from its concern about blacks' economic survival and quality of life. At the national level, settlement leaders like Jane Addams were at best ambivalent about paid employment for mothers, yet they recognized that poverty and high rates of male unemployment forced thousands of black women to seek work as domestics, laundresses, or maids.[93] The settlements were among dozens of reform groups, from the National Urban League to the YWCA, concerned about reforming domestic work. Some reformers sought to protect domestic workers from exploitation, others to ensure that middle-class housewives had a reliable source of domestic workers, and others to improve the quality of domestic "help." The Flanner House employment agency did all three.[94]

Compared to the efforts of other reform groups nationally to reorganize and rationalize domestic work, the Flanner House domestic employment agency enjoyed remarkable success. The agency, first developed in 1904 to find places for unmarried mothers, by 1918 was supplying maids and servants to over 2,000 homes.[95] With wages and hours regulated and a graded pay scale based on experience, the agency represented an attempt to standardize conditions and protect domestic workers. It offered them what amounted to a contract guaranteeing a certain rate of pay for an eight-hour day, more for overtime. It required employers of day workers to provide a good lunch and considerate treatment. A growing number of black women chose to participate in this program—(although widespread poverty among African-Americans in the 1920s makes the notion of "choice" somewhat illusory). By 1921 the agency had 2,000 workers on its files, and by 1923 the settlement was supplying work to 3,500 of the 4,000 to 5,000 black women estimated by the settlement to be engaged in domestic work in Indianapolis. Up to seventy women were placed in day work by the settlement house each day, two-thirds of them laundresses.[96]

The settlement house presented its employment department differently to different constituencies. To the public, it was advertised as a progressive program to regularize domestic work, to make it more efficient and more like industrial work. Employers were encouraged to use the agency because the settlement guaranteed the quality of its workers, grading them "A" or "B" according to skill and experience (wage rates differed accordingly).[97] Borrowing from the language of skilled labor, Flanner House claimed that settlement training programs were a six-week apprenticeship whereby maids, servants, and laundresses improved their skills and acquired knowledge of the latest electrical appliances. Hearty approval of the domestic-employment agency by a white middle class always in need of "good help" dictated that the settlement would continue to be identified with its employment agency in the 1920s. (The same was true of other settlements in this study, such as Neighborhood House.)[98]

Behind the confident-sounding endorsements of the settlement's work in newspapers and annual reports lay another reality. The settlement's effort to reform domestic work was in fact a gamble, a race against the changes taking place in household technology which offered middle-class housewives the possibility of doing without servants altogether. Owners of electric washers, wringers, irons, and ranges had no use for untrained, ignorant women from the rural South who were unfamiliar even with a faucet.[99] To meet this problem, the settlement planned to establish several training schools that would feed into the employment department. Flanner House "graduates" would then be expert in the use of the latest household equipment, and white housewives would be able to use servants along with their modern machinery, instead of using machinery to replace them.[100]

The first of these Flanner House training schools, a school for laundry workers, was established in 1924 with a $3,000 grant from the CWBM and the Community Chest. An account in the white missionary press stressed the expertise of the Flanner House staff, the fact that the apprentices received pay, and the up-to-date equipment. The new laundry school, superintendent Charles Lee wrote in an enthusiastic description in the missionary magazine, *World Call*, was a place "Where Washing Is a Science." More practically, he pointed out that the training black women received at Flanner House would increase their earning power and "aid them in the battle for adequate support."[101]

A similar school for maids was started at Flanner House a few years later. Instructors were white students of home economics from the Teachers'

Training College. Maids were instructed in cooking, "proper table setting and service at the table"; they were also taught appropriate dress and manners that would help them retain a job once they found one.[102]

But Flanner House also promoted its programs for domestic workers in very different terms from this language of efficiency and "science." The settlement was trying not only to upgrade domestic workers but also to dignify the lowly but essential work it offered black women, and for this it used the language of racial advancement. Settlement literature tried to elevate the enterprise by portraying domestic work as a vocation, equating household service with an almost-religious call to service that dignified the worker and the work.[103]

We cannot assume that the success of the settlement's employment department meant the acquiescence of black women in work that was, after all, menial drudgery. This, at least, is suggested by Flanner House literature describing the domestic agency: settlement reports read like one side of an argument, the other side of which has been lost. The writers "protest too much," portraying domestic work not as an unfortunate necessity, but as a happy opportunity for poor women to come into contact with better standards of living and a higher culture. Passing over in silence the menial and in fact servile aspects of domestic work, they stress instead its role in racial uplift. "While disappointed again and again, our hearts are constantly gladdened by the higher standards of life that come to these women through this contact," Lee declared in one report.[104] Was such hyperbole a response to black women's resistance to domestic work with its menial associations? We can only speculate.

This issue highlights the irony of settlement-sponsored reform. All settlement houses taught domestic subjects, but this teaching signified different things according to whether the settlement's clients were black or white, struggling or independent. Settlements with clients that were white Americans or European immigrants taught working-class women skills that would make them better managers in their own homes. Settlements working with black women were teaching them to be better homemakers, but also better domestics. By educating black women in housework, laundry, and service at table, settlements like Flanner House were training them to fill positions as paid workers in the homes of whites, should that become necessary. As one historian of domestic work has written about Nannie Burroughs' Training School in Washington, D.C., a contemporary and similar enterprise, the domestic-training program was based on the assumption "that black women would move back and forth between doing their own and others' housework, as the vicissitudes of racial oppression required."[105] Household training, though it may have led to exploitation, was also an insurance policy.

These programs to train domestic and service workers enabled thousands of black women to earn a wage and served to lift the sense of helplessness from families struggling with poverty and discrimination. They were a realistic response to the actual conditions of the time. But Flanner House programs also served to institutionalize the black female as a domestic worker and thus to remove her as a competitor with white and immigrant women for more lucrative and higher-status jobs. These programs clearly served the self-interest of whites and allowed the settlement to make a bid for the support and goodwill of the white community. By becoming identified with an agency for "colored help," Flanner House was conceding that for blacks, progress might mean less than equality.

Such conservative programs contrast strongly with the lofty goals enunciated in the settlement's public statements. One such statement, a declaration on the cover of a Flanner House report of 1923, eloquently declared the settlement's purpose:

> The chains of chattel slavery have been for ever broken from the wrists of the American Negro, but the shadow of an insistent race caste has continually darkened his pathway of emancipation and hindered his progress at every turn.
>
> To work for the clearing away of this shadow; to stand for a square deal relative to the Negro in education, in industry, in justice, in recreation and in housing; to labor for a kindlier sympathy between the races; for the spirit of Jesus to be the controlling principle in all our dealings—this is our aim. [106]

Measured against such a bold declaration, the settlement's policies seem conservative, its programs practical and undramatic. But what was the alternative? In a decade when hooded Klansmen marched through the heart of the downtown business section, when the lines of segregation were tightening, when news of bloody race riots in East St. Louis, Chicago, and Springfield warned blacks of the consequences of demanding rights that were theirs by law but were violated every day, the possibilities of action for the black settlement house were limited.

Flanner House operated in a context that limited its ability to confront the serious problems blacks faced as workers and citizens, but more than context limited the settlement. Because it was controlled by conservative whites and their black allies its goal remained adjustment rather than empowerment. Analysis of the role Flanner House played in its first three decades suggests that such dualisms as social control or social reform, oppression or empowerment, are inadequate for what was really a more complex picture. If contemporaries saw no contradiction between social control and social reform, neither should we. [107] The two purposes, reform and control, coexisted in the agency from the beginning: in the black settlement house the goals of white philanthropy merged with the black elite's goal of racial uplift to carry out progressive reforms without disturbing the basic relations of class and race.

White direction did not mean that blacks derived no benefit from the agency, however. Flanner House brought improvements in health care, recreation, and education that deserve the name "reform." Blacks used the settlement, despite the conservative intentions of its founders, benefiting from programs that improved neighborhoods, cured disease, sustained family income, and cared for children. But, paradoxically, at the same time, the settlement was also helping to reinforce policies of segregation and inequality that barred black progress.

PART II

Gary: The Political Economy of an Indiana Steel Town

The Twelfth General Meeting of the American Iron and Steel Institute at the Waldorf Astoria in New York City on May 25, 1917, had the largest attendance ever. Over 800 heads of the industry listened as Elbert Gary, president of the institute and chairman of the United States Steel Corporation, warned them that America was at war against a "barbarous despotism." But, he reassured them, "the great majority, if not the total, of our inhabitants appreciate what our Republic, with its protective institutions and manifold opportunities, means to every citizen; and . . . they will . . . rally round and follow the stars and stripes, their emblem of honor, of liberty and of justice."[1]

Gary was addressing his own doubts as well as those of his listeners. The tremendous expansion of the American steel industry since the late nineteenth century had been made possible by the unskilled, heavy labor of thousands upon thousands of foreign immigrants. In 1908, nearly a quarter of all steelworkers spoke no English, many were illiterate, and most were peasants with no experience of industrial life. Working twelve- or even fourteen-hours shifts, they saved for a return to their homelands and took little part in American life. Forty-nine out of every hundred immigrants who arrived between 1908 and 1910 returned to their native lands. For the rest, their assimilation to either American material standards or ideology seemed at best problematical. "A good job, save money, work all the time, go home, sleep, no spend," was how one steelworker described his life in America.[2] In Gary, Indiana, the city built by U.S. Steel which bore the chairman's own name, the foreign-born made up a staggering 54 percent of the population in 1910, compared with a United States percentage of 34. The Gary police records for 1916 showed arrests of people of forty-two different nationalities and the city directory for 1914 listed a manufacturer of "flags of all nations."[3]

In 1905, the United States Steel Corporation bought 1,500 acres of sand barrens in Calumet Township, Lake County, for a new steel works. The new steel town would form one of a semicircle of satellite cities around Chicago. The location in northwest Indiana provided cheap water transportation for ore boats, nearness to markets and to labor supply, favorable taxes, an excellent railroad system—the site seemed ideal. The construction of the Gary works began in April 1906. In July 1906 the city was incorporated and named for Elbert Gary, chairman of the board. Gary had been created a "city by fiat," and on the sand dunes where, a few years before, parties of wealthy Chicagoans came for the duck shooting, a new steel works rose. Within a few years, seven U.S. Steel subsidiaries had offices and plants there. The steel corporation created two subsidiaries to manage the new enterprise: the Gary Land Company, charged with laying out the town, and the Indiana Steel Company, which was to build the steel mills.[4]

Gary's population growth was astonishing. From an estimated 16,000 in 1910 it increased to 55,000 in 1920 and to over 100,000 in 1930. Gary was an industrial city. Of the male work force of 21,559 in 1920, 67 percent were employed in manufacturing and mechanical industries.[5] But although U.S. Steel had created the town and dominated it, Gary was not, in the strictest sense, a company town. The Pullman experience with paternalism was a disaster fresh in the minds of Gary's managers and planners. They determined that U.S. Steel would be neither landlord to its workers nor supplier of utilities, as Pullman had been.[6]

This was in fact what happened. The section of Gary actually developed by the Gary Land Company was a small percentage of the whole. North of the Grand Calumet River rose the great mills, the Illinois Steel Company, the Coke Ovens, the American Sheet and Tin Plate Mill, and the American Bridge Company (see Map 5). Industrial plants lined eight miles of Lake Michigan's shoreline. Immediately south of the river was the First Subdivision, laid out by the Gary Land Company. By 1916, 506 houses had been put up and sold at prices between $2,000 and $5,000. The American Sheet and Tin Plate company erected 110 cement houses and rented them to its skilled workers, mostly Americans and English. Similarly, the American Bridge Company established its subdivision, Ambridge, with about 300 houses for workers. These housing districts were characterized by straight streets, well laid-out housing, and well-planned utilities—Gary was "a city

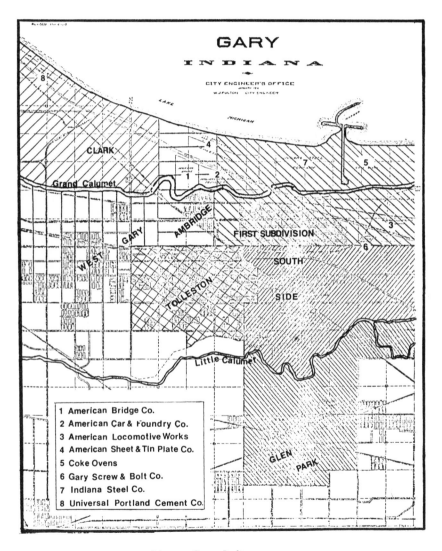

Map 5. Gary, Indiana, 1914

complete from the start." Rich black soil was even brought in from Illinois to start lawns and gardens.[7]

Thus far, the corporation, through its created subsidiaries, had directed the building of both mill and town. But the rest of Gary developed outside the control of the corporation, on 800 acres of land that had never belonged to U.S. Steel and lay in an unexpected direction—namely, to the south. Speculators bought up land on each side of Broadway, the main north-south street (land that the corporation's planners had not thought to purchase), and built an instant slum as they responded to the urgent demand for dwellings. The "South Side," or "the Patch," as this part of Gary was called, escaped all the standards and regulations as to buildings, utilities, and sanitation that prevailed in the First Subdivision.[8]

Gary's immigrants settled in the Patch; renamed the Central District, it would be home to the immigrants of the twenties, the blacks and Mexicans. There were actually two Garys, a contemporary noted:

> the North Side characterized by regulation, order in planning and in building, good housing conditions, and only two places where intoxicating liquors are sold; and the South Side, where are most of the saloons, crowded conditions, houses of prostitution, unsanitary conditions and poor living conditions. In the North Side live, in general, the better-to-do: skilled workmen, professional men, business men—principally the higher social and economic classes of native-born Americans and the Old Immigration. In the South Side, in general, live the unskilled common laborers and Colored, but with the lower social and economic classes of Americans and the Old Immigrants.[9]

Thus well-marked geographical divisions in Gary paralleled social and economic divisions. A survey of wages in 1918 revealed the gulf that separated white American workers from immigrants, and both groups from blacks. Among the native-born white families surveyed, annual earnings of the chief breadwinner were in the range of $1,450 to $1,859, whereas the median among immigrants was $1,050. For blacks the range was $850 to $1,049. Fourteen percent of native-born whites surveyed earned less than $1,050, but 36 percent of immigrants did so, and 50 percent of blacks; and while 15 percent of native-born whites earned over $2,250, only 4 percent of the foreign-born did so (see Table 4). Poor living conditions on the South Side were reflected in statistics of health. Among American cities that registered births in 1917, the rate of infant mortality was 100 per thousand live births. In Gary, it was 125 per thousand, and higher for immigrants. These inequalities in income and quality of life were not an unfortunate and unforeseen by-product of industrialization but a reflection of U.S. Steel Corporation's labor policies which aimed to attach skilled workers

Table 4
Annual Earnings of the Chief Breadwinner, by Color and
Nativity of the Mother, Gary, 1917

Annual Earnings of Chief Breadwinner in 1917	Total		Native White		Foreign-Born		Black	
	No.	%	No.	%	No.	%	No.	%
Under $850	851	14.1	122	6.6	673	17.1	56	24.1
$850–1,049	923	15.3	135	7.3	729	18.5	59	25.4
$1,050–1,249	1,065	17.7	239	13.0	775	19.7	51	22.0
$1,250–1,449	843	14.0	255	13.8	570	14.5	18	7.8
$1,450–1,849	1,049	17.3	474	25.7	548	13.9	18	7.8
$1,850–2,249	378	6.3	201	10.9	174	4.4	1	0.4
$2,250-and over	441	7.3	280	15.2	156	4.0	3	1.3
No chief breadwinner and no earnings	129	2.1	31	1.7	92	2.3	6	2.6
Not reported	344	5.7	106	5.8	217	5.5	20	8.6
Total	6,015	100.0	1,843	100.0	3,934	100.0	232	100.0

Source: U.S. Department of Labor, Children's Bureau, Children of Preschool Age in Gary, Ind., Bureau Publication no. 122, p. 151.

to the company by means of good wages, pension schemes, homeownership plans, and bonuses, but neglected the unskilled.[10]

In contrast to the frankly repressive policies of his predecessors, Elbert Gary, who became chairman of the U.S. Steel Corporation in 1910, announced a new era of benevolent paternalism in labor-management relations. Noblesse oblige and the Golden Rule would now guide management's dealings with labor in the steel industry, he promised. A corporation lawyer who seemed, one admirer wrote, "A statesman rather than a man of affairs," Gary carefully cultivated public opinion and confounded critics of the corporation by sanctimonious statements about his regard for the workers and his willingness to cooperate with reformers in improving conditions in steelmaking. Some of this was obviously bluff, such as his statement that the chairman of U.S. Steel was perfectly open to complaints: any worker with a grievance could march into Gary's Fifth Avenue, New York, office at any time.[11] The main features of U.S. Steel's welfare policy emerged two years later in 1911 when the steel corporation established a Bureau of Safety, Sanitation, and Welfare and began a well-publicized and expensive "welfare" program (see Table 5). Improvements in the workplace, company restaurants, hospitals, safety programs, and bonuses were among the compensations for the workers' supposed renunciation of unions. Some of this expenditure—the supply of pure water to workers, for example, or basic sanitation in company towns—was not welfare, but ordinary "housekeeping." Moreover, Gary's benevolence had a price. In exchange for such welfare programs, workers were required to be loyal to the company, an attitude of mind inconsistent with union activity. In 1909, U.S. Steel announced a definite nonunion policy in most of its subsidiaries. There is, Judge Gary announced, "no necessity for labor unions." Autocratic control rather than benevolence thus characterized the steel industry in the nonunion era; it was, one critic said, a policy of "detectives and toilets."[12]

The welfare policy of the U.S. Steel Corporation could be seen in its full flowering in mill towns such as those run by the Tennessee Coal, Iron and Railroad Company in the South; in towns near large urban centers like Gary, paternalism was less evident. There, the corporation trod softly. Corporation officials complained that intervention, even benevolent intervention, into the community was attacked as paternalism—while failure to intervene was condemned as neglect. Since the choice had to be made, in Gary the corporation erred on the side of neglect. It was not the main builder of housing for sale or rent. Gary would not be another Pullman.[13]

Although not avowedly paternalistic the corporation nevertheless dominated the city of Gary in several important ways. Historian David Brody has identified three "sources of stability" which helped the corporation maintain power in the steel towns in the nonunion era. These sources of

Table 5
Welfare Work of the U.S. Steel Corporation, 1918

Description	No.
Number of Dwellings and Boarding Houses Constructed and Leased to Employees at Low Rental Rates*	25,965
Churches	23
Schools	43
Clubs	17
Restaurants and Lunch Rooms	53
Rest and Waiting Rooms	171
Playgrounds	181
Swimming Pools	11
Athletic Fields	86
Tennis Courts	88
Bandstands	16
Practical Housekeeping Centers	16
Piped Systems for Drinking Water	355
Sanitary Drinking Fountains	2,835
Comfort Stations	1,390
Water Closet Bowls	6,837
Urinals	2,329
Washing Faucets or Basins	16,479
Showers	2,446
Clothes Lockers	110,759
Base Hospitals	25
Emergency Stations	279
Training Stations (First Aid and Rescue)	64
Company Surgeons, Physicians and Interns	156
Nurses	154
Visiting Nurses	62
Teachers and Instructors	209
Safety Inspectors	25
Employees Now Serving on Safety Committees	22,000
Employees Who Have Been Trained in First Aid and Rescue Work	16,637

* Over 15,000 of these houses are for workers outside the steel areas.

Source: This summary of the company's welfare work was provided for the Senate Committee on the Steel Company, 1918, by Elbert Gary, and is reproduced from Interchurch Commission of Inquiry, *Public Opinion and the Steel Strike* (New York: Harcourt, Brace, 1921), pp. 244–45.

stability and control can be identified in Gary also. First and most obviously, U.S. Steel was the major industrial employer. Gary prospered or declined

according to the fortunes of steel. And however often independent businessmen met at the Gary Chamber of Commerce to complain about the over-
dependence on a single industry, they were unable to prevail over the more
powerful Gary Commercial Club headed by Captain Norton and representing the U.S. Steel interests. The fortunes of the town continued to be
bound up entirely with those of the steel industry.[14]

A second source of the corporation's control was its influence over city
government. Before 1913, the Democratic party led by the flamboyant and
popular Thomas Knotts challenged the power of the mill, but the defeat of
Knotts in the race for mayor in 1913 ended this independent challenge.
From then until 1935, a close political alliance prevailed in Gary between
the Republican party and the steel corporation. The real mayor, it was com-
monly said, was not William F. Hodges, but Horace S. Norton ("Captain"
Norton) of the Gary Land Company. Norton's bodyguard, Pontius Heinz,
was chief of police, and Ralph Rowley, chief engineer at the Gary Works of
U.S Steel, became president of the city council and continued on the council until the 1930s, a position from which he effectively controlled the city's
budget. Norton and William Gleason, superintendent of the Gary Works of
U.S. Steel went each week to consult top management in Chicago. They
spoke for the corporation in Gary and, as the following chapters will show,
had a decisive influence on the town's affairs.[15]

A third source of stability in Gary was the corporation's alliance with
the small shopkeepers, engineers, foremen, and professionals who constituted Gary's middle class. In this Gary resembled other steel towns. Mill
officials also enjoyed amicable relations with the city's clergy. In 1913, a
useful alliance was cemented when the corporation assumed a number of
church mortgages, thus allowing several congregations to begin the expensive task of building and maintaining new churches and church schools. In
the mayoral race of that year the clergy, financially dependent on the corporation, helped the triumph of the Mill party over the Democrats, already
mentioned.[16] During the steel strike of 1919 the clergy were mainly silent,
a silence generally interpreted as sympathy with the corporation. They were
accused of helping to recruit strikebreakers and of supporting the Loyal
American League, a law-and-order committee of one hundred businessmen
who organized escorts to the mills to protect strikebreakers and mounted a
campaign of propaganda in Gary's press designed to demoralize the workers
and defeat the strike.[17]

The corporation's power also reached down into the private and voluntary sector of the community. David Brody alluded to this in his 1965 study,
and more recently David Montgomery in *The Fall of the House of Labor*
suggested that "corporate muscle began to be put behind older welfare
causes" and "corporate executives assumed control of local Americanization
efforts, displacing the American grocers, clergymen, and organized nativists

who had sponsored earlier campaigns to change immigrants' beliefs and behavior."[18]

Already before the World War, reformers and churchmen had been directing their attention to Gary's immigrants with a mixture of sympathy and alarm. They struggled with the social problems created by the rapid growth of the city and its teeming immigrant population, a population which, by one estimate, turned over every three months in Gary's first few years as construction workers and railroad gangs came and went.[19] Reformers were appalled by the living conditions of these foreigners and distrusted their politics. Something should be done for them, but what? The Gary *Daily Tribune* described the problem as one of order: "They are for the most part a religious, kind-hearted well-meaning people; but they were born and reared in oppression, and the freedom they enjoy here has undisciplined them, until they sometimes run riot like so many wayward children who have escaped from the control of wiser and older heads."[20]

Like the reformers, the steel-plant managers also expressed concern about the volatility of their mainly foreign-born work force, which by 1916 numbered 20,000. Company policies designed to encourage homeownership were of little use so long as many immigrants were single men, without the stabilizing and civilizing factor of families; among the foreign-born, men outnumbered women by three to one in 1910.[21]

Among the welfare agencies working with Gary's immigrants were two settlement houses, Neighborhood House, founded in 1909 and Campbell House, founded in 1914, supported by the Methodist and Presbyterian churches, respectively. Their goals included Americanization, religious evangelizing, and the improvement of the immigrants' health, housing, and morals. What made their work, and that of other Americanization agencies, of interest to U.S. Steel was the explosive situation produced by World War I and the Red Scare that followed it.

A halting start at Americanization had been made when the war challenged the precarious unity of Gary and brought to the fore questions of assimilation and the right of steelworkers to belong to a union. A tidal wave of patriotism swept over Gary during the World War as it did over every American city. In September 1918, patriots unfurled a huge banner, eighteen feet high by thirty feet wide, across Broadway between Sixth and Seventh Avenues. At the center was a painting of Uncle Sam, fourteen feet tall, and above, the inscriptions, "Are You Worthy of Being Fought and Died For?" and "Buy Liberty Bonds." Vividly illuminated at night by powerful electric lights, the banner remained there until the end of the war, causing a thrill of warning to those who passed beneath.[22]

America was at war for Democracy, but on the home front over half of Gary's population was foreign-born. Were they, too, worth fighting and dying for? Foreignness, disloyalty, and radicalism were interchangeable terms

Figure 6. Men leaving the mill at noon, Gary, 1913. This landscape of "anomie" was the context for the settlements' attempt to re-create the human values of an earlier era based on home and neighborhood. Courtesy of the U.S. Steel Collection, Calumet Regional Archives, Indiana University Northwest.

to the champions of "100 percent Americanism." The call for victory abroad became one for unity at home. Declaring April 28, 1918, "Patriotic Day," Mayor William F. Hodges announced that the day would demonstrate to Gary's fighting men "that the cause for which they are called is one of a united people," and the organizer of a bond drive that raised a quarter of a million dollars declared that "in spite of the more than fifty-seven varieties of peoples that compose the population of the fourteen year old city its Americanism ranks high."[23]

It was dangerous to criticize American institutions. When one Frank Petroni shot a man who shouted, "To Hell with the United States!" a patriotic jury in neighboring Hammond took only two minutes to acquit the murderer. In the atmosphere of national emergency, patriotic organizations flourished. A group calling itself Gary War Mothers declared war on "anything that has a semblance of treason, disloyalty or rebellion to the constitution of our Country." It defined its goals as "Fostering such a Democracy

Figure 7. Patriotic meeting at the machine shop of U. S. Steel, April 1918. The call for victory abroad became one for unity at home. Courtesy of the U.S. Steel Collection, Calumet Regional Archives, Indiana University Northwest.

as our sons, brothers, fathers and husbands found in the trenches, and assisting in the Americanization of foreigners and the recognition of our flag."[24]

The Calumet Township Council of Defense, founded in June 1918, worked for "universal patriotism," and pledged itself to stamp out "disloyalty, sedition or treason." It investigated and made reports on the number of pupils studying German or attending churches where the German language was used; it followed up Gary's candidates for naturalization, sending to the chief of the Naturalization Service in Washington, D.C., reports including details of the applicants' "morals, character, patriotism, sentiments, families, relations, etc." It put pressure on Gary's theater managers to prevent the showing of plays that "in the opinion of the council might tend to discourage patriotism." Finally, it encouraged Gary's industries to submit to the council names of men "who did not work steadily or regularly." These miscreants were required to appear before the Patriotic Committee and "show cause for their idleness."[25]

In Gary's steel mills, as in the community, propaganda was used to silence dissent, and the same steelworkers who trudged to and from the mills under the great patriotic banner might pick up a copy of the Illinois Steel Company magazine, *Gary Works Circle*, any time in 1918 and read articles in which slacking off or airing grievances at work was made the equivalent of treason to the United States. "Your daily work is your contribution to America's victory," an article in the September-October issue declared. "Are you making as much success of your job Over Here as the American soldier is making of his work Over There?" "Beware of the grumbler," another article warned. ". . . If he complains of the conditions under which he works, say, 'Have you a friend or relation in the trenches in France?' That ought to wake him up."[26] While the war lasted, the campaign for loyalty was successful. G. M. McGinnis of the Gary Tin Mill reported of his company during the war, "Our force included no slackers and the subscription of our employees, not only to the loans, but to the Red Cross . . . was practically 100 percent in all departments." Workers in Gary's industries gave $222,852 in one Patriotic Fund Drive alone, an amazing $240 per worker.[27] A significant shift had occurred among Gary's immigrant steelworkers during the war. They had made a great financial and emotional commitment to help their adopted country win. Now that victory was won, they would expect their sacrifices to be recognized and their just claims to be met by management.

This was not to be, however. At the end of the war there was no sign that U.S. Steel was prepared to modify its labor system which continued to be based on the exclusion of labor unions and on welfare policies for skilled and native-born white American workers, accompanied by expressions of paternalism toward employees. But such benevolence was no longer sufficient to stem the tide of unrest among the steelworkers. Many still worked a twelve-hour day and seven-day week amid the hottest, most dangerous conditions in American industry.[28] Moreover, wages for common labor were insufficient to maintain a minimum standard of living: after a careful study of prices and wages in steelmaking, economist Charles Gulick concluded that "for the first seventeen or eighteen years of its operation the Corporation did not pay to the average common laborer in its employ sufficient wages to enable him to support a normal size family in health and decency."[29] Company restaurants, flower beds, and tennis courts were insignificant compared to these basic grievances over hours and wages.

The war had irrevocably changed relations between labor and capital. The National War Labor Board's recommendation that the steel industry abandon its open-shop practices encouraged steelworkers to demand the right to form unions, and in August 1918 the AFL began an organizing drive in the steel towns. But with the ending of the war, U.S.

Steel acted swiftly to forestall the unionization campaign. Freedom of speech and rights of assembly were for all practical purposes suspended in the steel towns, the press was manipulated, and men who joined the union were fired and blacklisted. Blatant intimidation was used to prevent immigrants from joining the unions. For example, in October 1918, the Illinois Steel Company appealed to immigrant workers to sign a "Pledge of Patriotism," promising "loyalty to our country and to the company for which I work."[30]

Propaganda themes were not abandoned but only subtly altered with the ending of the war. Judge Gary of U.S. Steel continued to speak as if he believed that industrial relations could return to the "normalcy" of prewar paternalism and welfare work. But the demand of the steelworkers for union recognition and the eight-hour day could not be ignored. For the steelworkers, everything seemed altered. Rapid inflation cut real wages, unemployment threatened, and the democratic right of collective bargaining was denied by the autocratic Gary. For steelworkers, the cause of union representation seemed a matter of simple patriotism: they had fought a war for democracy in France and now they were going to fight for industrial democracy at home.[31]

The history of the Great Steel Strike, which began in September 1919, has been told at length elsewhere—how the company defeated the strike by use of labor spies, troops, control of the press, and repression of liberties; how it exploited the divisions of Gary (and other steel towns) between the skilled and unskilled, Americans and immigrants, black and white; how the strike finally collapsed when Judge Gary stubbornly refused to talk to the strike leaders—all these have been documented and analyzed.[32]

What I am concerned with here is the impact of the upheaval of 1919 on the nexus of relationships in Gary in the 1920s. Inside the plants and mills corporate managers exercised absolute control. An article in *Gary Works Circle* one month after the steel strike had collapsed warned workers about the need to be "dependable." The Dependable Worker, it said, "has no time to indulge in fault finding . . . knowing that well directed zeal and faithful work will lead him to success. He leaves his fault finding comrades far in the rear; they only too soon slacken their pace and finally drop out of the race. Be a dependable worker."[33] The corporation could be sure of control in the plants, but not in the community: people could become hostile to the interests of the corporation—1919 had shown that. Now in the 1920s the practitioners of welfare work were joined by the exponents of a newer expertise—personnel management. "Scientific" hiring of the right men, careful public relations, and alliances with church and community leaders were sought. As the head of Illinois Steel's department of labor and safety put it,

The superintendent . . . must not only be aware of the location of all the groups of foreign settlements in the community, but he must become personally acquainted with the individual boarding bosses, steamship agents, clergymen, and other influential agents with whom the immigrant maintains a close contact. These are his supply depots, and only by perpetual, personal reconnoitring can he remain familiar with the quality and quantity of available applicants.[34]

The following chapters will show how the steel company used the institutions of the community, including its social-welfare institutions, to build a consensus favorable to the corporation. Some of the reasons for the company's continuing hegemony in Gary in the 1920s lay with factors quite independent of relations in the community, of course. Worker discontent abated as real wages rose after 1922; the twelve-hour day was abolished in 1922 (although only after an irresistible public campaign, culminating in a plea by President Harding himself); and the virtual ending of European immigration in 1924 helped allay some of the nativists' anxieties. A buyer's market for labor strengthened the corporation's hand; meanwhile, the Steel Company benefited from the competition for common labor jobs between blacks and whites and among different ethnic groups.[35]

The defeat of the strike and the resulting bitterness were followed in Gary by a wave of boosterism created by the press and steel-company allies that visitors found overbearing. "No American city, lest it be Los Angeles or Miami, is so completely cursed by boosterism," wrote one ascerbic commentator.[36] Boosterism also entailed a continuing crusade of Americanization—had not foreign radicals been behind the strike? Wasn't an IWW identical to a radical, a socialist, and an AFL agitator?[37]

Along with boosterism came a return to paternalism. On January 21, 1919, Elbert Gary gave the presidents of U.S. Steel subsidiaries his recipe for good labor relations. He made no mention of unions. "Make the Steel Corporation a good place for them to work and live. Don't let the families go hungry or cold; give them playgrounds and parks and schools and churches, pure water to drink, every opportunity to keep clean, places of enjoyment, rest, and recreation."[38]

All four of Gary's settlement houses were affected by these developments. First, Campbell House and Neighborhood House, which before the war had been quietly engaged in Americanization of the foreigners, suddenly found their crusade was the steel company's also. Both agencies received financial support in the 1920s for their work with the immigrants.

Second, two new groups had entered Gary since 1919. Catholic immigrants, especially Mexicans, and blacks from the southern states had been recruited to Gary to help break the strike in the steel mills in 1919 and

Table 6
Population Shifts in Gary, Indiana, 1920–30

	1920		1930	
	No.	%	No.	%
Total	55,378	100.0	100,426	100.0
Native White	33,584	60.6	59,647	59.4
Foreign-born White*	16,294	29.4	19,345	19.3
Blacks	5,299	9.6	17,922	17.8
Mexicans	166	0.3	3,486	3.5

*Excluding Mexicans
Source: U.S. Department of Commerce, Bureau of the Census, *Fourteenth Census of the United States, 1920: Population* 2:63, 760–61; *Fifteenth Census of the United States, 1930: Population* 3: 715, 720.

1920; both groups became a permanent factor in the city's population (see Table 6). By 1930, the Gary work force was 14.6 percent black, and the European immigrants who had crowded into the South Side in the early years began to move out.[39] U.S. Steel cooperated with community and church leaders to establish settlement houses for both groups. Gary-Alerding Settlement, established for Catholics in 1923, will be described in Chapter 6, and Stewart House, set up for blacks in 1920, in Chapter 7.

One measure of U.S. Steel's involvement with the community-welfare agencies was its growing financial commitment. By 1923, it was estimated that U.S. Steel and Judge Gary personally had given a total of $5 million to Gary's churches, welfare agencies, and other benevolent projects. A notable example (though one that predated the strike) was the splendid YMCA built with $250,000 of steel company money in 1912.[40] Exact amounts of steel-company donations to Gary agencies cannot be determined for the 1920s, but one piece of evidence suggests its dominance: in 1926, according to a Chamber of Commerce report on charitable giving, almost 10,000 donors responded to various charitable appeals, but while the median donation was between $1 and $3, two donors together gave a total of $72,319![41]

On the face of it Gary was a success. Steel sheets and bars rolled from its mills; profits soared. Gary was praised as a thoroughly modern city. But poverty continued to exist alongside prosperity. Down on the South Side, European and Mexican immigrants crowded into slum housing, blacks and Mexicans faced racial discrimination in housing and in the mills.

How effectively did the settlement houses deal with these problems? What role did they play in the steel town, torn by issues of economic justice and political power, of racial and ethnic rivalry? Could settlement houses help reform the conditions of working-class families when these agencies were financially sustained by the very corporation whose abuses they sought to correct? The following chapters detailing the relationships among the churches, the racial and ethnic groups, and the steel mill will provide some answers.

CHAPTER FOUR

"To Christianize and Americanize These People": Campbell Friendship House—The Settlement as Mission

America presents to-day the most economic, the most kaleidoscopic, the most engaging, the most inspiring, the most important field of missionary operations upon the Globe.

—*The American Home Missionary*
40 (1909), 21

"The name, 'Settlement' as well as the idea on which the movement is founded have been and are increasingly abused," protested Caroline Williamson Montgomery in her Introduction to the Fourth Edition of the *Bibliography of College, Social, University, and Church Settlements.*[1] It had become fashionable for all kinds of institutions—missions, schools, parish houses, and others—to label themselves "settlements," she complained. Montgomery found especially disturbing the rapid proliferation of religious settlements. A settlement's task was to teach, reform, and uplift, but did this extend to teaching the gospel? Should settlement workers deal with the spiritual emptiness of city dwellers, as well as their everyday, down-to-earth problems? As they battled for clean streets, safe playgrounds, and honest government, should they also worry about the absence of churches, the flourishing of vice and materialism? Did saving a neighborhood involve bringing its inhabitants to church?

Caroline Montgomery and other settlement leaders did not think so, but the question caused dissension in the 1890s and continued to nag at the movement for decades. Some declared vehemently that settlements were not missions in modern dress, while their critics pointed out correctly that many settlement houses were just that, agencies where social work functioned as an adjunct to the work of conversion. Ignorance, crime, vice, exploitation—these were the problems that settlements should address, Jane Addams wrote. To add a religious purpose to the settlement's work was to violate the basic pragmatism of the movement: a social agency that works to pass on a received truth is not a settlement, she wrote, but a mission. A settlement, on the contrary, "shares the perplexities of its time and is never too dogmatic concerning the final truth."[2]

If historians have not readily acknowledged the religious affiliations of the settlement movement, it is perhaps because contemporary settlement leaders themselves so vehemently denied the connection between their movement and organized religion. The new social-work professionals, especially, were scathing in their denunciation of settlements that tried to combine missionary work and reform. National social-work leader Mary Richmond disliked the amateurishness of many settlements. In her opinion, enthusiasm, especially religious enthusiasm, was a poor substitute for expertise. "Under the name of settlement," she wrote, "the old-fashioned mission, distributing a cheap and sprinkly sort of charity, can do more harm than under the right name." Richmond and others like her saw that many social settlements, those strange new institutions where educated, middle-class people lived and worked in the slums, were missions in disguise, collections of religious enthusiasts who pretended to be engaged in a program of social work, but whose real purpose was proselytizing.[3]

By the end of the nineteenth century, some Protestants were still attempting to reverse the church's retreat from industrial populations, establishing missions and institutional churches that were a practical response to poverty and need. Historian Aaron I. Abell has summed up the achievements of this Social Gospel movement between 1865 and 1900 as follows: "In attempting to satisfy the demands of the urban poor, Protestants had measurably Christianized their social and economic attitudes, formulated and developed a far-flung system of social service and sacrificed sectarian concerns to basic religious needs."[4] The urban mission that combined relief and preaching was an important feature of Social Gospel Christianity. "Til the cravings of hunger are satisfied, we cannot develop the moral nature," a spokesman for the mission movement explained in 1872. Missions established a presence for many denominations in working-class and ethnic areas that their congregations had fled. Institutional churches were larger and more ambitious than missions; they combined social service work and recreational programs with religious observance. Enormously successful, they were another sign that the churches were seeking to regain lost ground among America's urban masses.[5]

At first glance, there seemed little difference between the missions and institutional churches on the one hand, and the settlements on the other. Like missions, settlements saw themselves as beacons in the twilight world of tenements and slums. And like institutional churches, they frequently combined social work with religious work. In 1900, 29 percent of one group of settlements surveyed admitted that their programs included sectarian religious instruction; by 1910, the percentage had risen to 46 percent. Many settlements were headed by a minister, and a majority of settlement workers surveyed were members of some church.[6] Moreover, a number of settlement workers had gone into settlement work as an alternative to foreign-mission work.[7]

Yet despite evident similarities between settlements and missions, the first generation of settlement leaders denied the link between their institutions and organized religion, promoting the settlement house as a secular reform agency. The logic of their situation compelled them to do this, they claimed: since 90 percent of settlements were located in areas heavily populated by immigrants, settlement workers must be completely impartial in religion. If settlements pursued Protestant mission goals they would find it harder to secure the trust and cooperation of neighbors who were Catholic, Orthodox, or Jewish. Then not only their religious mission, but also their practical reform work would be jeopardized. While religious teaching might be "part of the general task of uplift," Robert Woods conceded, a settlement's task would be harder if it advertised a religious affiliation. Woods had changed the name of his Andover College Settlement to South End House for this reason.[8]

A settlement could not and should not be a mission, Julia Lathrop of Hull House explained to a meeting of the National Conference on Charities and Corrections (NCCC) in 1894. Hull House offered no religious instruction, she stated, "and I think very few settlements do. . . . It would be impossible to harmonize in clubs of men or women or in societies of boys and girls, as we constantly do, various religious faiths and nationalities, if we undertook any sort of religious propaganda." In fact, "undertaking to do the one, it would be impossible to do the other."[9]

Settlement leader John Gavit argued that a fundamental difference of approach distinguished settlements from missions. A mission "comes from *outside* to a neighborhood or community which it regards as 'degraded'," Gavit wrote. "The settlement bases its existence, its hope, its endeavor on the firm foundation of Democracy—on the thesis that the people must and can and will *save themselves*."[10]

A survey of forty-four settlement houses conducted by the NCCC in 1896 revealed that many houses in the movement's first decade excluded religious activities. Of the twenty-seven agencies responding, nineteen said that they had no religious observance. Typical was the response of Philadelphia College Settlement. "Each resident attends her own church and we encourage our neighbors to do the same," head-resident Katherine Davis wrote. "Our influence is distinctly *for religion*, but not for any denomination or creed." Princeton House in the same city, a settlement used for training Princeton theological students, was unusual among the houses surveyed. Its work was mostly religious, the reply claimed, "undenominational, but

Evangelical." More typical was the response of Lillian Wald's New York Nurses' Settlement which returned the cryptic if ungrammatical answer, "As a settlement, nothing is said of religious teaching."[11]

Because of this refusal of the major settlements to be identified with the missions and institutional churches of the Social Gospel, it was not long before settlements were even being accused of being irreligious. Settlement workers combated this accusation in several ways. At the 1896 NCCC meeting, Dean George Hodges admitted that "some good people are troubled by what they take to be a lack of religion in the settlement." But this was a misunderstanding. "The settlement is not a church," he insisted. "The church has its work in the community and the settlement has its work, and there is as much difference between them as there is between the errand of the parson and the errand of the doctor." What, anyway, was "the real meaning of religion" but doing good? he asked.[12]

The settlements took an important ideological step in the 1890s: all their work was religious because it was ultimately redemptive, they claimed. The settlement mission was to revive, or redeem, each city neighborhood and thus to create, in the words of Walter Rauschenbusch, "a Christian social order which will serve as the spiritual environment of the individual." When a visitor to College Settlement, New York, protested, "But where is your religious work?," the settlement worker replied, "We think all our work is religious."[13]

The effort of settlement leaders to cut their movement free from association with organized religion was not just a feature of the 1890s. It amounted to a long, drawn-out campaign. This was partly because they were aware that the church as an institution, although speaking the language of brotherhood and reconciliation among social classes, was continuing to lose ground among the working classes. Dozens of mainstream Protestant churches had left the inner cities and established themselves in the comfortable complacency of the suburbs. It was the failure of the church as an institution, in fact, that by the 1880s had impelled a search for alternative institutions such as the settlements.[14]

But there was also an ideological reason for the efforts of settlement leaders to distance themselves from the churches. By carving out a territory within the field of late-nineteenth-century reform, they sought to distinguish settlements from other agencies and to cut the movement off from its English antecedents, which from Toynbee Hall on had been predominantly religious. Hence the definition of an ideal settlement that emerged by 1900 was of a distinctly American reform institution that was both pluralistic and secular. When Jane Addams tried to explain to the warden of Oxford House, an Anglican-affiliated settlement, why even interdenominational services had been discontinued at Hull House, she stated that the residents of Hull House "come together on the basis of the deed and our common aim," not on the basis of a shared faith. "This diversity of creed was part of the situation in American settlements, as it was our task to live in a neighborhood of many nationalities and faiths."[5]

Yet while Jane Addams and other settlement leaders laid down what might be called an orthodox settlement policy of separation between churches and settlements, events took their own course. All over urban America in the first decade of the twentieth century, earnest reformers inspired by evangelical fervor came together and launched settlements. Soon there were hundreds of such institutions. Attempts of the leaders to discipline them were unsuccessful. When Robert A. Woods and Albert J. Kennedy compiled an official *Handbook of Settlements* in 1911, they were forced to acknowledge the existence of large numbers of religious settlements that combined missionary and social work. The ideal settlement, "under American conditions," was one that provided "neutral territory traversing all the lines of racial and religious cleavage," they declared. "Nevertheless it is clear that there is a considerable number of houses having a high degree of the settlement spirit while including some of the functions of a church. . . . Where such specific religious effort is conducted without willing or conscious invasion of other religious loyalties," the authors reluctantly included such settlements in their account.[16]

In New York, an attempt to discipline the proliferating settlement movement resulted in the formation of a federation of settlements, the United Neighborhood Houses, in 1920. The federation excluded from membership all settlements that represented a single denomination. In its view, these could not come up to the desired standards of impartiality. With all the denominational houses barred from the federation, it is not surprising that historian John Herrick, writing of the UNH, found an admirable standard of open-mindedness among the settlements that *were* members. "Most American settlements," Herrick concluded rashly, "unlike their English counterparts, were non-denominational in their work, and in fact prided themselves on their openness and ability to respond spontaneously to the problems of their neighbors."[17]

In the 1920s, when social work was becoming professionalized and secular, settlement leaders were still trying to discipline the smaller settlements that were conducting themselves like missions. Mary Simkhovitch, in *The Settlement Primer: A Handbook for Neighborhood Workers*, first published in 1926 and reprinted in 1936, found it necessary to restate the orthodox settlement position on religion. The fact that the discussion of religion was pushed to the end of the book, fifty-second out of fifty-three subjects covered, suggests a reluctance to treat a topic that had long been a bone of contention within the settlement movement. Simkhovitch declared, "As in the nation we are committed to the separation of Church and State so in the Neighborhood House should there be a similar delimitation. If the House undertakes religious services or instruction it changes its character and is really, no matter what it may call itself, a mission."[18]

The continuing complaints of contemporary settlement leaders reveal that the mission approach persisted. Many settlement workers, like the two young women who founded Christamore, believed that the neighborhood needed "not only the outward friendliness and cheer of our work, but the inward change of heart and purpose." Such language points to the persistence of evangelical goals in the settlement movement.[19]

Evidently, there were divisions within the settlement movement that historians have not adequately described. Officially, the movement was committed to helping and understanding immigrants of many faiths, but many settlement workers were equally dedicated to evangelizing them and drawing them into an "American" church. Few settlement leaders genuinely valued immigrant traditions or defined goals for the movement that came close to what a later generation calls "cultural pluralism." Most settlement workers only became aware of their clients' separate culture as they worked for its extinction. No wonder historians have had difficulty in finding generalizations that covered the whole movement, and while most accounts stress the secular nature of the settlement movement, they leave out religious settlements and thus deny the religious roots of most of them.[20]

One such religious settlement, an agency of conversion and Americanization, was Campbell House in Gary, Indiana. Part of the Home Missions movement of the Methodist Episcopal church, Campbell House was a spearhead of that denomination's attempt to win converts among the immigrant peoples of northwest Indiana. Campbell House, or Friendship House as it was sometimes called, was founded by Methodist churchwomen in 1912.[21] Between 1912 and 1919, it carried on a program that combined social and religious work among Gary's foreign population in the South End. In the 1920s it became part of the Americanization drive in Gary. The history of Campbell House calls into question the account of the settlement movement that has stressed its commitment to secular goals; it reveals that settlement houses often drew strength from the Protestant missionary impulse, that churchwomen's organizations founded and sustained them, and that after 1916 their original purpose was subtly changed by the Americanization campaign.[22]

Campbell Settlement was the idea of Mrs. Myron Campbell, a native of South Bend, Indiana. Mrs. Campbell had long been active in the Methodist church and had founded the Northwest Indiana Branch of the Women's Home Missionary Society in 1883. Her daughter, Vera Campbell, described in homely terms the beginnings of the Gary settlement.

It took place in the kitchen of my mother . . . while we were washing dishes. She had been Treasurer of Northwest Indiana Conference Woman's Home Missionary Society from the time of its organization, and her mind naturally ran along missionary lines. As we talked of the interesting new city being built in our neighborhood she said, "There will be a wonderful opportunity for Christian Americanization in this new city and The Woman's Home Missionary Society ought to get in and begin work with these foreigners at once." With her, thought always led to action, so it was not long before the women of that Conference had petitioned the national Society for permission to begin a conference work in Gary, and when permission was granted work began.[23]

In 1913, Mrs. Campbell appealed successfully to the steel corporation for support. Its subsidiary, the Gary Land Company, donated land valued at $2,000 for the settlement house. Donations for the building were raised from various Methodist churches, including $1,000 from Mrs. Campbell's South Bend church. The site, at 2244 Washington Street in the heart of the foreign section, was ideal for the work contemplated by the "home missionaries." The settlement house, a three-story, red-brick structure costing $6,000, was dedicated on September 27, 1914.[24] Although the steel company had donated the settlement's site, it refused further help; a request by the First Methodist Church for $5,000 was turned down by the U.S. Steel chairman in October 1911. Ten years later, however, steel-company officials would prove more receptive to appeals from the self-appointed guardians of morality, religion, and "Americanism" in Gary.[25]

The Methodist churchwomen were more successful in getting support from the national office of their denomination. A visit by Mrs. Kendrick, president of the WHMS, and Mrs. Wilson to Washington, D.C., in October 1913 resulted in assurances of support from the national body. They also obtained the backing of the North Indiana Conference, which would subsequently sponsor the settlement jointly with the Northwest Conference until November 1919, when it would pass directly under the control of the National Conference of the Methodist Episcopal Church.[26]

The Home Missions movement of which Campbell House was a part was dedicated to a combined propaganda of Protestantism and Americanism. The Protestant churches had earlier been able to congratulate themselves that "immigration was part of God's providential plan for building the most Christian nation on earth." But it had become more and more difficult for Protestants to sustain this view of immigration as they faced the fact that the "new immigration" was mainly Catholic, Orthodox, and Jewish and that mass conversions to Protestantism were unlikely. Instead, the Home Missions movement promoted evangelization and Americanization as two sides of the same process. If America was to be the "Redeemer Nation," its first duty was to the foreign enclaves in its cities. To its advocates, the Home Missions movement was the domestic equivalent of imperialism abroad, and Protestant religion the cement of civil society. "Let a foreigner become a citizen of the Kingdom of Christ, and he . . . will love this country and its institutions more than any other, because [they are] more Christian than any other."[27]

"The United States is not a preserve for little Germanys, or little Italys, or little colonies of any nation," wrote Joseph Clark, secretary of the Congregational Home Missionary Society in 1903. "The least that Americans can ask of those who come to the United States for its benefits is that they shall become Americans; and to this end, however distant, home missionary effort is steadily aiming."[28]

Despite such confident rhetoric at the national level, Americanization did not begin in earnest at the local level until the war and the Red Scare created an atmosphere in which foreign beliefs and culture became intolerable. In Gary the male-dominated board of the First Methodist Church at first kept its distance from Campbell Settlement, which they patronizingly referred to as a project of "the Ladies." To its residents, and perhaps its clients as well, Campbell House appeared a women's institution: women had founded the settlement, as they had thousands of other religious and reform institutions. Faith, optimism, and pride in their achievement were all evident in the corresponding secretary's excited comments on the occasion of the Campbell House dedication in September 1914. "We feel sure it is the result of God's direction and guidance. The House is our beacon light, our saving station, our Friendship House—it is ours, Ours, OURS!"[29]

Vera Campbell recalled her conviction that God was calling women to assert their special influence for good in Gary.

> Possibly in no city of the United States was there greater need for what we call "settlement work" than in this strange, new city in the years of its infancy. No homes, no schools, no churches—everything must be built! And so few women to give their spiritual guidance and help! Men, men, everywhere![30]

She expressed the spirit of the settlement house in a poem that celebrated the settlement as a Woman's Work for the Church.

> Here in the midst of Gary sands,
> Where people have gathered from many lands,
> Has risen a "House not made with Hands."
>
> It was planned by women of vision keen,
> Who Gary's needs have clearly seen,
> To the Heavenly Vision they true have been.

So this house is founded on FAITH, firm and strong,
For they prayed together and labored long—
Their's, Faith that triumphed over wrong.

This building brings HOPE to the neighborhood,
An easier way for the child to stay good,
And help for overworked motherhood.

Thru all a spirit of LOVE shall shine,
As radiance from Thy light divine—
O, God of Love, all Love shows us Thine.

Service and sacrifice here have wrought
In the Friendship House the Master's thought,
When little children to Him were brought.

So, instead of a "mansion over there,"
We have this House of Friendship, where
The needy HERE may breathe Heaven's air,

And learn in this friendly atmosphere
That the Kingdom of Heaven can come near,
Thru Faith, Hope and Love—made real here.[31]

Campbell House's first task was to establish contact with the foreign families of the neighborhood. Trained personnel were employed to lead the social work. Miss Alma Schultz, a deaconess and graduate of a Washington, D.C., training school, established a day nursery at the Froebel School building even before the settlement had its own building. Helping Miss Schultz was Miss Jean Stone, a trained nurse who was a graduate of the Baptist Hospital in Chicago. The two women supplemented their work with the children by visits to the homes of immigrant families, where they gave advice on health, work, and domestic problems. There was such a good response to the settlement's clubs and classes that the agency soon found its facilities under severe strain. By 1919, remodeling was necessary and the building was enlarged; additional living rooms for staff were now added, and a building was erected on an adjoining site that served as a gymnasium for the whole neighborhood.[32]

The Methodists viewed the influx of immigrants into Gary as an exhilarating challenge but also a fearful threat to the forces of religion and order. Gary's Methodist churchwomen had been the first to react to this challenge by founding their "mission house," as the settlement was called. But by 1916, the male leaders of the church also began to organize a response. The settlement passed under male direction when a Dr. Stecker from Findlay, Ohio, became superintendent; under his leadership, according to one account, "great strides were made in the work at the Settlement."[33]

By 1920, the Methodists had drawn up a plan for their work in Gary that involved Campbell House, Stewart House, and a grandiose new "Downtown Church." There was a strong precedent for their actions in the urban-mission movement. "Organize or perish" had been the substance of Josiah Strong's famous warnings to organized religion at the end of the nineteenth century:

> If the churches do not soon organize for the prosecution of social reforms they will lose their opportunity of leadership and with it their great opportunity to regain their lost hold on the masses and to shape the civilization of the future.[34]

The General Conference had accepted a similar position at their 1896 meeting, declaring,

> Methodism in our cities should be slow to abandon what are called downtown populations because of changes from native to foreign and rich to poor. The greater the challenge, the more need of our remaining. Combine the plants if need be; adapt them and the services to the new surroundings but remain and save the people.[35]

Remain and save the people they did. The year 1916 marked a new religious offensive in Gary, the sinful city where, Rev. William Grant Seaman wrote, "The name of God is taken in Vain in forty-three different languages and His praises are sung in only sixteen languages."[36] Gary became, in the words of the historian of the Northwest Conference, "the great missionary and reform field for the church."[37] Bishop Thomas Nicholson's first step was to select Reverend Seaman as minister of Gary's First Methodist Episcopal Church. Seaman, a graduate of Boston University School of Theology, had been head of the Philosophy Department at DePauw University, Indiana, and subsequently president of Dakota Wesleyan University. He left a promising academic career to plunge into Gary's swirling currents. Blessed with a bright, optimistic outlook that had earned him the nickname "Sunny Jim" at DePauw, Seaman was an easygoing man who was soon meeting on friendly terms with the powerful Horace Norton—another DePauw alumnus—and other Gary civic leaders, at weekly meetings of the Gary Rotary Club.[38]

Shortly after his appointment, Seaman wrote to Rev. D. D. Forsythe in Philadelphia about the needs of the Gary region. Quoting figures to show that Gary's foreign population was enormous—the "Big Plant" alone enrolled 10,307 men, only 26 percent of whom were American citizens—and that Gary was "the fastest growing city in the world," Seaman went on, "The fact that our city is for the most part yet to be built makes it an ideal opportunity for laying out a scientifically constructed program for dealing with home missionary problems of the sort found here."[39] The time was right for some experimentation, Seaman wrote, for the innovative Gary School system had made people more willing to try large schemes. Now a bold program of religious social work should be planned. The other denominations had a head start, he warned; the Baptists and Presbyterians, with their Home Missionary societies, already had "complete plants." Begging his superior to visit Gary and see for himself, the harried Seaman ended, "Come over into Macedonia and help us!"[40]

Seaman's statement of the Gary situation was revealing. He clearly viewed the presence of a large foreign-born population in Gary as a challenge to the church. Campbell Settlement could play a much greater role in meeting this challenge, he explained in a memorandum written for internal circulation among Methodist church leaders. The South End was the area most in need of this kind of institution: there was "no preaching in English and no Protestant preaching in any language for white people south of 21st Avenue and the Pennsylvania tracks." "There are several thousand white people with a sprinkling of Protestants among them. . . . It is a distinctively Mission field and probably will remain that way for many years."[41]

Both a settlement and a church would be needed to "christianize this population," for the task was one of practical as well as moral reform. Seaman feared the rootlessness of immigrants who were incapable of choosing a new loyalty even more than the possibility that many would adhere to the Catholic church: social control and religious conversion went together. Gary had a large volatile population of single men; among the immigrants, males outnumbered females by three to one. The recreational infrastructures that Seaman proposed—the clubs, classes, and entertainments—would be an attempt to restructure the leisure time of these new urban dwellers. Everything hinged on the building of a modern institutional church to serve mainly "individuals who are outside any social group. It must tie them into such groups and provide group socials and pastimes for them."[42]

The Americanizers believed that immigration was a disorganizing experience for immigrants which loosened older ties of religion and custom; a religious settlement such as Campbell House offered the immigrants both standards of behavior—how to dress correctly, how to set a table, practical skills such as how to write a letter of application in English—and the religious beliefs that were a corollary to American behavior, namely Evangelical Protestantism.[43] Reverend Seaman was optimistic about the possibility of converting the immigrants: if the Catholic church found itself under impossible strains because of the centrifugal forces of immigrant nationalism, might not this be turned to the advantage of the Protestants, the churchman mused. "Many of the young foreigners will tend to slip away from their foreign speaking churches and a strong Protestant work should be carried on among them. A settlement house will tend to create a constituency for Protestant Evangelism. The denomination that supports the Settlement House would be the one that could more easily reach the people."[44]

Even Protestant immigrants needed the moral control and stabilizing influence of the settlement house, Seaman wrote, for immigration could erode a person's beliefs and moral standards. "If a Protestant, he often becomes indifferent. . . . Moral ties are loosened with the religious. The intervening process which occurs here between his abandoning the old state of things and fitting himself to the new, is not favorable to morals and character."[45]

It was true that immigrants had to choose between competing patterns of behavior in the new land. The dominant culture, pragmatic and secular, promised the American dream of material success, but was it right? Secularism and materialism threatened both traditional Protestantism and the authority of the Catholic hierarchy. Immigrants faced a bewildering array of codes of behavior exemplified by a variety of ethnic and religious groups. Seaman and other church leaders hoped that when immigrants chose among these competing cultures they might opt for the "American," that is, Protestant, church that was a counterpart to other new patterns of behavior and that promised material success along with the best adaptation to American conditions.[46]

The entry of the United States into the World War put Americanization on the national agenda. Some settlement workers had previously looked with indulgence on foreign cultures, but now no aspect of foreignness was above suspicion. Methodist churchwomen were urged to rededicate themselves to the settlement house effort and its great task: "to Christianize and Americanize these people," just as foreign missionaries were doing abroad.[47] The startled delegates to the 1917 meeting of the Northwest Conference were given a dramatic account of the situation in the Gary region. "Capital and men are pouring into the region in overwhelming tides, new enterprises are springing up overnight, great factories doubling and trebling their facilities, the figures of to-day must be thrown upon the scrap-heap of tomorrow, and one is bewildered by the rush and roar of this amazing development." Most alarming were the political ramifications of immigration. "Practically all the nations of the earth meet here and unless they are fused with our national life and ideals will prove a menace to our free institutions," the speaker warned.[48]

Other Protestant denominations also saw the Calumet area as a missionary field. When it attempted to carry out a survey of the population, the Baptist Home Mission Society discovered an amazing variety of nationalities and a rate of mobility that made planning impossible. The authors added in exasperation, "While we were making a survey of the Calumet

District in March 1917, one new community of six hundred souls moved into one section of Gary in a week."[49]

But Methodist work was moving ahead in Gary. The Methodist Board of Home Missions and Church Extension announced a national "Centenary" Campaign to raise money for the extension of Methodism in Indiana. Dr. H. R. DeBra, president of Epworth Seminary, Iowa, was appointed superintendent of a new Calumet Missionary Society, his goal: to raise $250,000 "to plant Methodism in this region and give it a commanding position."[50]

Reverend DeBra outlined his strategy of religious social work at the 1919 Conference. It was obvious that the old-fashioned methods of the church had failed, he began. In order to reach the foreigners, the church must study them—their history, their antecedents, "what there is in their past worthy of our appreciation." But admiration must give way to action: the separateness of the immigrant population from American influences was deeply disturbing: "We still face the grave problem of actual contact. We walk among these people, we live in the same communities with them, . . . and yet we live apart—we have nothing in common with them."

What was needed was a strategy that combined social work and religious teaching, "the social approach." This would bring back face-to-face relations.

> The process of building parish houses, settlements, or missions, the bringing in of trained workers to live among the people, the kindly ministry in the institution and in the homes, by which to win the confidence of the people, the holding of night classes, the teaching of English, the patient work with the children—all this and much of it, perchance before there is the slightest opportunity for preaching what we would ordinarily call a "gospel sermon."[51]

But when the Calumet Missionary Society presented its report to the conference the following year, the result was calculated to produce alarm rather than self-congratulation. Merely for the immediate needs of the region, the report stated, $250,000 would be required for mission work, while for settlement houses and churches $1 million would be needed in the next five years. "We absolutely must have an adequate church and working plant in Gary," DeBra appealed to the conference. But how could this money be raised? It was unrealistic to expect support from the immigrants themselves. Nothing could be expected of the thousands of "birds of passage," migratory workers who stayed in America only until they had saved enough to return to their homelands; their donations to any church were small.[52] Other immigrant groups harbored attitudes hostile to the church as an institution; the Italians were notorious for not supporting their priests, expecting not to give, but to receive charity from the church. Mexicans, too, shared a strong tradition of anticlericalism. The Methodist Conference confronted the uncomfortable fact that the Catholic hierarchy was also facing: settlements and missions would all have to rely on outside funding—they would be institutions founded *for* immigrants, but not supported *by* immigrants.[53]

It was far from the million-dollar expenditure projected by the conference to the small amount actually available to Campbell Settlement after the war. As part of the reorganization of the postwar years, the settlement passed under the direction of the National Conference of the M. E. Church in 1919. Between 1919 and 1943, the National Society financed the entire salary budget and two-thirds of its operating costs. The other third came from donations, including those from the steel corporation.[54] But in the postwar years money was tight. The WHMS reported to the 1921 Conference that they had spent $3,000 on the settlement. "The Calumet Missionary Society is urging us on to greater achievements," they noted, yet the WHMS was unable to meet the needs of the people as it wanted.

In 1921, however, Methodist Centenary funds to the amount of $3,960 were made available to Campbell House; the settlement now added a Community Hall and a welfare department.[55] Behind the expansion of the settlement's work in Gary lay important changes produced by the World War and the steel strike of 1919. The end of the war brought the return of thousands of men to Gary, resulting in dislocation and unemployment. A "Red Scare" swept across the nation and the presence of large numbers of foreign-born in the Calumet Region increased the pressures for Americanization: the goal was no less than cultural and political homogeneity. A stream of propaganda in the press routinely equated foreignness, radicalism, and immorality.[56]

The church could not escape these pressures; it might even turn them to its advantage. On the eve of the 1919 strike, a new publication, the *Calumet Federation Messenger*, appeared under a strident headline, "The Calumet Region: A Field for Christian Americanization." The problems of the region resolved themselves into the single problem of an excess of aliens, the writer claimed. The remedy consisted of an immediate campaign to convert foreigners into Protestants and Americans.[57]

To facilitate its contacts with the foreigners, Campbell House had begun to use social workers of immigrant background. For example, in 1918, the settlement had employed a trained Serbian social worker. A convert to Protestantism, Mr. Mijarovitch formed Boys' Clubs and preached at the settlement both in English and in Serbian. With the coming of the Red Scare, however, Campbell House and other settlements became defensive about their work among foreigners. They had taken a step toward their neighbors by employing nationality social workers but now they risked being labeled agencies of foreignness.[58] Reflecting this pressure, the settlement's published statements took on an additional edge of patriotism. Christian American-ization was designed to counteract socialism and to interpret America to the foreigners, a settlement appeal for funds dated 1922 declared. "Ideals of Lib-erty, Equality and Equal chances in life become dangerous ideals unless there is also given the fundamentals of Christianity," it added darkly.[59]

Historians find little or no evidence that socialism inspired the 1919 steel strike, as was alleged in the reactionary press. If immigrant workers were discontented, it was not because of "bolshevik plots," but because the intolerable pre-1919 conditions in steelmaking persisted after the war. With the collapse of the strike in January, the steel company restored the twelve-hour day in the mills and its whole prewar labor policy. For the next few years, it sponsored several benevolent and paternalistic projects in the city of Gary designed to take the edge off discontent and improve its tarnished image in the nation. In the months following the strike, the corporation increased its contributions to Gary agencies until, as the historian of the Calumet Region writes, there was "scarcely a church, hospital, fraternal, or civic organization in Gary that has not received a contribution from the United States Steel Corporation." Campbell House also began to receive annual subsidies from the corporation.[60]

In June 1922, a new period of consensus and (for the steel industry) prosperity was celebrated when Elbert Gary came to the city on what was virtually a "state visit." He declared to a crowd at the Commercial Club that U.S. Steel would help build Gary "on a foundation that will stand. Good schools and churches, law and order."[61] Elbert Gary praised Reverend Seaman, who accompanied him during his visit, and Reverend de Ville, the leader of Catholic Americanization, as gentlemen "whose work is our work."[62]

At the national level, however, some church leaders were attacking the steel corporation for maintaining the twelve-hour day. Such hours of work were a barrier to Americanization, for they left no time for family life, wholesome leisure activities, or self-improvement, critics claimed. "The church and every other American institution has a duty to perform to the immigrant workers and . . . this duty cannot be performed until the twelve hour day is abolished," the Interchurch Report declared.[63] But once the corporation phased out the twelve-hour day in 1923, such criticism abated. No challenge arose to the ascendancy of the corporation in Gary during the 1920s.

Gary's Methodists approached the postwar reconstruction with ambitious plans. There were to be church schools and a Methodist hospital; two set-tlement houses, Campbell House and Stewart House (the black settlement founded in 1921), were to be strengthened and expanded. In a confidential planning paper entitled "Askings," Reverend Seaman laid out the projected needs of Gary Methodism. One hundred thousand dollars would be required to improve Campbell House, he estimated. He hoped to secure half this amount from the steel company and the remainder from the WHMS and the Centenary Fund. Seaman did not approach Elbert Gary directly, however, but wrote to Captain Norton, head of the Gary Land Company. Norton and William Gleason, superintendent of the Gary Works, traveled each week to consult with top management in Chicago and were the recognized spokesmen of steel company policy in Gary.[64]

Early in 1920, Seaman addressed a letter to Captain Norton describing at length his plans for Gary Methodism and asking the steel company for support. He might have taken comfort from the fact that Elbert Gary was a lifelong Methodist who liked to remind people that he had been both a lay preacher and a Sunday-school teacher.[65] Yet he began by insisting, "The growth of Methodism is not our impelling motive"; these institutions were planned as "instruments of community service not of Methodist propaganda." Norton's reply was sympathetic. Agreeing with Seaman that "the Christian church cannot continue its retreat and remain a dominant factor in civilization," Norton promised his support for the projected downtown church.[66] In late June or early July 1920, Seaman, Dr. Diffendorfer, secretary to the Methodist Centenary Committee, and Dr. Burns held a meeting at Norton's Gary home. There were areas of common concern to them all, Seaman wrote to Norton some days later. The question was "to determine just what would most advance the fundamental interests both you and we have at stake."[67]

Meanwhile Seaman had scored a notable success. Judge Gary had agreed to cooperate in the downtown church project. Beatrice Lewis described how it happened:

> At a banquet in New York City, Judge Elbert Gary . . . was sitting next to Dr. Ralph Diffendorfer who was secretary to the Centenary Movement of the Methodist Church. . . . In casual conversation, Dr. Diffendorfer said to Judge Gary, "Judge, we have a Methodist Church in a midwestern city to be named after you and I think it would be a wonderful thing if you would aid in the developing of the new center there." Judge Gary thought for a moment, then asked, "What do you think I should do?" "Well," Dr. Diffendorfer said, "you might go on a 50-50 basis with us for a new, model church building." Judge Gary always carried a pencil in his pocket but no writing paper. True to his custom, he rolled back his coat sleeve and on his old-fashioned starched cuff, made a note to consider the matter. Later Dr. Seaman received word that the United States Steel Corporation would be willing to help on a 50–50 basis.[68]

The promise was confirmed at a meeting held between Diffendorfer, Buffington, and Gary in the latter's New York office on June 30, 1920. Seaman's dreams for Gary were coming true. But the part to be played by the settlement house was no longer so clear. Gary was unwilling to give more money to Campbell Settlement because of the fluid situation on the South Side. He demanded "a further study of the Negro situation" as a first step before he would consider helping the settlement.[69]

Campbell Settlement, founded to serve the immigrant population, was now presented with what Reverend Seaman euphemistically referred to as "the challenge of our brothers in black, coming from the Southland in a continuous stream." Gary's small African-American population of a few hundred increased rapidly as thousands came north to seize the opportunity of a job during the steel strike. Now black families were moving into the area already crowded with foreigners where Campbell Settlement was located.[70] The impression of instability was overwhelming. Yet Reverend DeBra insisted that the Methodists should not give up the Americanization work at the settlement. One possibility was to move Campbell House, "if one could tell where to put it in order that it might be central to a population of white foreigners."[71] DeBra expected the steel corporation to continue the policy (begun in 1919) of building racially segregated housing areas (see Chapter 7). When the residential segregation of blacks was complete, he wrote, it would be easier for the church to target immigrant populations. As a makeshift solution, he suggested, "We should erect temporary buildings at strategic locations and in them carry out a strong program until such time as the Steel Company shall have developed their colored section and it shall appear what the population is to be in this region."[72]

"Friendship House is poorly located for its work as a settlement," another report admitted frankly. Several developments had made its work with the foreign-born difficult. The movement of black families into the neighborhood had encouraged some foreigners to move out, especially since the public school that had previously been close to the settlement at 24th and Adams had now been relocated. In addition, many foreign families lived on the other side of the Pennsylvania railroad tracks. Running along the north side of the settlement neighborhood, these were like a "Chinese Wall," deterring people from coming to the settlement. The house should be relocated, this report concluded, where the foreign-born population was the densest. This would "guarantee a sufficiently large white population to justify the proposed investment in plant and workers."[73]

Meanwhile a major investment in Gary's religious life had been made by the steel company: Seaman had secured $425,000 for his downtown church. This was not only a church but also, in the social engineering language of the time, an "entire plant" with clubs, recreation rooms, classrooms, and an auditorium. The building of this church absorbed the energies of the enthusiastic Seaman and the major donation of Judge Gary (who, however, modestly declined the complement of having the church named after him).[74]

Despite uncertainties about its future, Campbell Settlement in the 1920s played an important part in the life of the Central District, as the South Side was now called. The settlement's varied social-service work made it indispensable to needy people who had few alternatives. By 1923, the settlement employed five social workers, and the extensive health programs included dental clinics, weekly eye and ear clinics, and an infant health station. In addition, there were clubs and classes offering recreation and instruction to children and adults. During one year, a settlement report noted, the agency had performed 42,911 services.[75]

At the same time, Campbell House continued the Americanization work among the district's diverse immigrants. English classes, an Italian mothers' club, and a Croatian mothers' club drew small numbers of foreigners. Efforts with the children were the most successful, however. Settlement-house movies (provided by the Indiana University Extension Service) drew in crowds of Gary children. And while the young audience was still spellbound, settlement workers stepped up to explain the programs and opportunities of the settlement house and lead the children in the singing of "popular, patriotic, and religious songs." "These weekly gatherings furnish the House a splendid opportunity of bringing the whole program before their attention as well as to give them an evening of wholesome entertainment," the settlement's 1922 report noted with satisfaction.[76]

Settlement clubs were designed not just to amuse but to instruct. The Campbell House "Blue Birds" club taught homemaking skills to little immigrant girls. They used dolls and doll furniture to practice making beds in the American manner, "with sheets, quilts, pillows, pillow-cases and spreads." Americanization meant giving up the featherbeds of the old country, which were impossible from a sanitary point of view. This, a settlement report noted with enthusiasm, was "a bit of practical Americanization."[77]

Such teaching was important for a way of life that was fitted for the hamlets and sunlit valleys of Europe was ill-adapted to the smokey, crowded living conditions of an American steel town.[78] The settlement's stand on the issue of prohibition was a quite different matter, however. The Methodists' insistence that the use of alcohol was sinful put a gulf between them and the immigrants. Prohibition was so widely violated in Gary that in one roundup of lawbreakers in 1920, Gary Mayor Roswell O. Johnson was among those indicted for violating the Eighteenth Amendment. A poll taken in 1926 showed that seven out of eight persons interviewed were against the dry law. There is no doubt that this issue strained relations between the settlement and those it sought to help.[79]

By the 1920s, the missionary activities of the social agency had become a source of tension between the settlement and its immigrant neighbors. The social-service activities of Campbell House in the 1920s remained secondary to its religious goals. The settlement retained a full program of religious services and instructions. Sunday school, women's Bible classes, vesper services, sermons, and religious programs were among the regular offerings. Although the settlement's literature emphasized the practical good that the settlement had achieved and downplayed its mission aspect, Campbell House was, in fact, engaged in an effort to detach Gary's immigrants from their churches. The Catholic churches viewed the settlement's efforts as a threat and moved to oppose them. "That will shut many doors to the work of the Friendship House," Reverend Seaman noted sadly in 1920. Gary's Catholic priests warned their parishioners that Protestant social settlements were agencies of propaganda in disguise. In 1923, the Catholics established their own settlement house, the Gary-Alerding Settlement. (Its work is described in Chapter 6.)[80]

The founding of the Gary-Alerding Settlement was part of a drive by the Catholic church to win back Italians, Mexicans, and other immigrants to the church. Several contemporaries spoke of the tensions caused by this rivalry between competing religious settlement houses in the 1920s. More religious tolerance was "urgently needed" in Gary, Father de Ville declared in an article in the Gary *Post Tribune* in 1926. There was "a considerable degree of mistrust, misunderstanding and even downright animosity in matters connected with religion," he noted.[81]

Sociologist Paul Taylor in his lively study of Mexicans in the Calumet Region also found evidence of the role played by social agencies in the keen rivalry between Protestants and Catholics in Gary. "Some charitable aid has been extended by Protestant mission churches," Taylor wrote.

> This greatly incenses Catholics, who also give some charity through their churches, for they regarded it as religious proselytizing with charity as the bait. . . . There was the typical (and doubtless true) story of the recipient of aid who attended the Protestant mission, but upon the approach of death called the priest. In 1924 the version was that the particular Mexican also attended mass in the morning before attending the mission.[82]

In another case, a Protestant social worker related to the investigator,

> We had permission from the railroad to hold meetings from three o'clock to four in a box car, and the priest had the place at four. Promptly at four he would pound on the door and demand the car, and as the children came out he would say, "You know better than to come here; don't you know you are going to hell?"[83]

Although the hold of the Catholic church over some immigrants was loose, this did not mean they were ready to flock to the Protestant camp, as this example showed:

> Miss X tried to mix social work with religion. They did not like it. They are Roman Catholics by name only; but the priests teach them that the Protestants are heretics. Some of the Mexicans say, "they are not trying to teach me English, but to make me a Protestant."[84]

Even when the settlements concentrated their efforts on the children, they met resistance. A Campbell House worker was surprised to be told, during a class discussion of what made a Christian father, "Why, he can't be a Christian, he's a Protestant."[85]

Inevitably, some immigrants attended the settlement only in order to take advantage of its services and remained untouched by its propaganda. American social workers noticed the opportunism of Mexicans who told the helping agencies they were Protestant, but who became "Catholic in emergencies."[86]

Despite all the efforts of agencies like Campbell Settlement, only small numbers of Catholics joined Protestant churches nationally. The investment of millions of dollars in the effort to convert the immigrants was largely unrewarded. From the Catholic side, worries about what was known as "leakage" of Catholics to Protestant agencies such as Campbell House were often expressed. But Gerald Shaughnessy, later bishop of Seattle, was able to answer the question "Has the Immigrant Kept the Faith?" in the affirmative. Catholic immigrants had, by and large, resisted the proselytizing efforts of Protestant agencies, he found.[87] The national parishes established in immigrant communities by Poles, Germans, Slovaks, and others attested to the vitality of immigrant religion (or perhaps to the persistence of immigrant nationalism in religious form). As for the Italians and Mexicans, they seemed immune to the propaganda of both Protestants and Catholics.[88] Of the Italians, historian Rudolph Vecoli writes,

> After half a century of missionary labors by *both* Catholics and Protestants, the majority of the Italian immigrants remained either nominal Roman Catholics or without church ties of any kind. . . . While the free-thinkers and socialists remained aggressively anticlerical, for the majority, religion continued to be what it had been in their *paesi*: a belief in the efficacy of magic and devotions to their saints and madonnas coupled with a basic indifference to and distrust of the institutional church.[89]

The changing racial composition of urban neighborhoods in northern cities during the 1920s produced a crisis in the settlement movement during the 1920s. When blacks first began to move into Gary during the World War, Campbell House excluded them, fearing that the settlement would not be able to serve these newcomers while continuing its programs with immigrants. Ethnic barriers were already evident in the steel city, according to an Urban League study; different groups did not join the same organizations, churches, or social groupings.[90] Paul Taylor found that members of antagonistic groups would not use the same agency, no matter how much they stood in need of its services and that, when Mexicans used an agency, it deterred other users. Although Gary's housing patterns were racially mixed in the early years, racial barriers and antipathies began to rise in the 1920s.[91]

When blacks moved in large numbers into the Christamore district of Indianapolis, the settlement managers relocated the house in an immigrant section. But Campbell House did not take this step. It remained at 2244 Washington Street and eventually extended its services to blacks who needed its services as much as immigrants, and perhaps more so. By 1929, the settlement had integrated its programs, hired a black social worker, and was looking for a second one. To its credit, the settlement defined its goal as serving people of all races and backgrounds. The 1931 report declared, "It has been a joy to see the increasing friendliness and cooperation between the white and colored children." Sometimes the ethnic variety of the settlement neighborhood complicated the settlement's task beyond reason: in 1931, Campbell House had five separate Boy Scout troops—Polish, Russian, Croatian, Greek, and Negro.[92]

Unlike many of the foreign immigrants who had come to the Calumet Region as single men, black migration consisted mainly of families. The female wage-earner was an important sustainer of these families. Campbell House, like Flanner House, aided the entry of blacks into the work force in Gary by offering the services of an employment agency to women seeking domestic work. Through the employment bureau, the settlement house was able to reach out to the black population. While the women waited at the settlement for calls for daywork, settlement workers conducted sewing classes, taught the women to mend and alter garments, and also held informal discussions on matters such as "personal appearance, sanitary habits, thoroughness of work, dependability, helping them to become better fitted to get and keep positions."[93] A new chapter had opened in the history of Campbell House: the settlement that had started as a mission and had become an agency of Americanization was now a social-service agency serving blacks, Mexicans, and a diminishing number of European immigrants.

Surveying the settlement movement in 1922, Woods and Kennedy noted sadly that settlement workers were not achieving the desired standard of impartiality in matters of religion. The settlement should be "a miniature world of culture and resource," and settlement workers should be of every background, religion, and nationality, they stated.[94] But despite the official stance against the use of settlements for proselytizing, settlement houses like Campbell House resembled missions in many ways. The fact was that the pool of those available for settlement work contained far more people motivated by faith than driven on by altruism or by generalized (and nondenominational) feelings of goodwill. Those who were prepared to leave comfortable lives and live as brothers and sisters to the poor often did so out of religious motives. They regarded rural Americans adrift in the city, city dwellers seduced by materialism and secularism, and even members of immigrant churches as lost sheep who might, with effort and God's grace, be gathered out of the confusion of city life into the fold of Protestantism.

Historians of the settlement movement need to restore the religious and missionary motives of many settlement workers to a central position. Only then can we understand those committed activists who struggled in the nation's worst slums. Many settlements, like Campbell House, were born of an effort to achieve the goals of the Social Gospel. Although they were later swept up in the intolerant crusade for cultural and political uniformity known as Americanization the strength of the settlement workers' commitment resulted from the fact that they believed themselves engaged in a battle not only against poverty, ignorance, and vice, but also against sin.

CHAPTER FIVE

"Give Them Home Life": Neighborhood House, the Steel Company, and the Domestic Ideal

The comforting thing to a lover of human kind is that men in all grades of employment are securing for themselves homes of their own.

—*Bulletin of the American Iron and Steel Institute*, 1917

The settlement house is really an addition to every little tenement home. Its books and pictures, the nursery and play spaces, the lobby and living room, the music and flowers, the cheery fireplaces and lamps, the auditorium for assemblies or social occasions and dancing, are an extension of the all too scant home equipment of most of the neighbors.

—Graham Taylor, *Chicago Commons through Thirty Years* (1936)

It seems clear that the new industrialism wants monogamy.

—Antonio Gramsci, *Selections from the Prison Notebooks*[1]

The immigrant steelworker in Gary on the eve of World War I lived in two different worlds. At work, he was under pressure to use English, adopt American habits of work, and shed his foreign peculiarities. Several years of improvements in the physical conditions of the workplace had resulted in the provision of such amenities as showers, toilets, lockers, and company restaurants.[2] However, when the steelworker returned to a family housed in a shack on Gary's South Side, without running water or toilet, where no one but the children spoke English, it was of no concern to his employer. For the U.S. Steel Corporation had specifically rejected the idea that it should play a directly paternalistic role in Gary. As Eugene Buffington, president of the Illinois Steel Company and personally charged with directing the construction of the steel town, declared in an article for *Harper's Weekly* in 1909:

> The most successful attempts at industrial social betterment in our country are those farthest removed from the suspicion of domination or control by the employer. Fresh in the minds of all of us is the failure of the Pullman Company to maintain its authority over the village affairs of Pullman, Illinois. . . . American ideas and atmospheres are inherently antagonistic to such plans of community life.[3]

The steel corporation was "not in the real estate business," another official stated; it had no intention of being a landlord to its workers, another Pullman. Thus, the corporation made little or no provision for housing the thousands of construction workers who flocked to Gary to build its industrial plants and railroads, to work in its steel mills and blast furnaces, and to settle in the "South End."[4]

Gary was a town "divided at the Wabash tracks." North of this line in the First Division and Ambridge the U.S. Steel subsidiary, the Gary Land Company, developed an area of about 800 acres for housing skilled workers and managers, mostly American-born and white. This part of Gary was "a city in harmony with modern ideas of sanitation and progress." As the *Iron Age* put it:

> The miles of streets paved with concrete are kept clean and bright, the lighting system is exceptional. . . . The sewage disposal system conforms to the best practice of sanitary engineers, and the sanitary code . . . is looked upon as a model. The water supply drawn from a point far out in the lake leaves nothing to be desired. Lots are sold under restrictions as to buildings . . . [and] the city is kept free from dives and slums.[5]

However, most of Gary's residential development took place toward the south, on land that had never belonged to the corporation or its subsidiaries and in a direction where U.S. Steel had never planned the city to grow. If Gary seemed free of "dives and slums," it was because they had all been swept to the South End. Here, where the majority of the unskilled workers lived, private, speculative building had produced a jerry-built, unsanitary slum. Hundreds of workers lived in the long, single-story boarding houses, arranged in parallel rows with a three-foot passage in between, one faucet and one toilet to twelve families. Others lived in the small detached houses of tarpaper, boards, or sods, stuck here and there in the sand.[6] In the official Gary, the company permitted only two bars (and these were to be run, on Judge Gary's instructions, by "fine outstanding Christian gentlemen").[7] But in "the Patch" there were an estimated 238 saloons in 1911. In contrast to the First Subdivision homes, supplied with water at no cost by the Gary

Heat, Light, and Water Company so that the homeowners could coax pleasant lawns out of the sandy soil, 22 percent of homes on the South Side had no inside water supply, and one in three depended on an outhouse for sanitation.[8]

In 1911, the U.S. Steel Corporation launched an ambitious and elaborate program of "welfare" work in all of its plants. Embarrassed by the Stanley Committee hearings and by bad publicity created by the Pittsburgh Survey, the corporation set up a Bureau of Safety, Sanitation and Welfare which spent $750,000 annually for the next few years on improvements in all aspects of working and living conditions (see Table 5). In some towns where the corporation was the sole or chief employer it played a paternalistic role, attempting to reform living conditions and employing visiting nurses and company social workers to investigate and help immigrant families. Sometimes ill-conceived and always invasive, such welfare activities nevertheless, in the judgment of historian David Brody, "added the measure of betterment needed to win the steelworker's consent to the terms of his employment."[9]

Despite its original intentions not to make Gary "another Pullman," the steel company began as early as 1911 to sponsor improvements in the community serving to stabilize the industrial situation. In this year, the corporation's Finance Committee voted $1.5 million for the construction of new housing for higher-paid workers, in order to encourage homeowning.[10] Employees who participated in the homeownership plans benefited from a favorable mortgage scheme that allowed them to buy existing houses or construct new ones. The modern housing built in the First Subdivision and in Ambridge was for sale, not for rent, and the majority of purchasers were skilled workers or managers, mainly native-born Americans. Unskilled workers could not afford to participate. As the company frankly admitted, "The housing provided by the Corporation is perhaps better suited to the needs of the skilled workmen than to the wages of the unskilled laborers [who are] . . . largely foreigners without families . . . These men earn low wages, out of which they seek to save the utmost amount possible."[11]

Company-built housing was expected to decrease labor turnover, a problem that United States corporations were viewing as a near-crisis.[12] But the policy had a political use also: ownership of a company-built house was both a sign of loyalty to the company and a reward for loyalty. As a "Home-Owning" issue of the *Bulletin of the American Iron and Steel Institute* remarked in 1917, many homes had been bought out of the proceeds of stock in the corporation "acquired under its thrift inspiring policy of encouraging men of all grades to become partners in the Corporation." Since "the owning of a home is calculated to increase a man's proper pride in himself and his business," the extension of homeowning among employees was a matter for congratulations. By cementing skilled labor to the company, it ensured the stability of the labor system in the steel town and forestalled efforts to organize unions.[13]

So far these welfare policies had not affected the foreign-born steelworkers who formed the great majority of the Gary work force. As the steel town's population continued to increase from an estimated 16,802 in 1910 to 55,378 in 1920, steelworkers and their families experienced the discomforts and hazards of crowded, unsanitary dwellings. A Gary probation officer estimated in 1916 that fewer than half the men working in Gary could find housing there. The rest spilled over into "the Patch," which became synonymous with crime, vice, drunkenness, and disorder.[14]

Already by 1912, the company had begun to connect the unruly lifestyles of the immigrants to unsatisfactory practices in the workplace. The result was that efforts to streamline production in the plants became an ambition to remake the working-class community itself.

In part, this took the form of a company-sponsored educational campaign aimed at improving the immigrants' living conditions and Americanizing their values. The Illinois Steel Company's publication, the *Gary Works Circle*, targeted immigrant workers with feature stories about immigrants whose perseverance and good character had won them success in the end. Domesticity was an important ingredient in the American dream portrayed in this journal. Company propaganda encouraged immigrant workers to adopt habits of hard work, discipline, and regularity in the workplace; but it also promoted an ideal of the individual, family-owned home, with the wife and mother constantly presiding over all its activities. From such homes would go forth well-fed, satisfied men and healthy children. The rewards for the worker, according to this propaganda of domesticity, were the complementary ones of upward mobility at work and the domestic ideal at home.

A movie made in 1912 for showing to steel-company employees entitled *An American in the Making* conveys the flavor of this domestic ideology. It portrayed Americanization as a transformation of character as well as customs. It was the story of "an ignorant Hungarian peasant, who, if he had remained in his native land would never have risen above the dull worthless level of his surroundings," but who came to join his brother at the steel plant in Gary. Here he became aware that "there were chances of advancement if he cared to take advantage of them," night schools where he could learn English, technical schools to help him get ahead, "innocent amusements in plenty at the clubhouse or the YMCA which saved him from wasting his pay and ruining himself physically in the saloons." At work, a thoughtful management had placed doctors and nurses to care for him and had worked out provisions for his safety. "He took advantage of his oppor-

Figure 8. Children at Gary Neighborhood House, 1919. The settlement, or mission, represented the reforming presence of women and the gospel in an agency of Americanization. Courtesy of the Neighborhood House Collection, Calumet Regional Archives, Indiana University Northwest.

tunities, and today he is an intelligent and industrious workman, a happy husband and father, and although he does not expect ever to become a millionaire he has money in the bank and no apprehensions regarding his future."[5] A photograph accompanying the text showed the hero at the family dining table with his wife and child, lace curtains framing the picture of contented, working-class domesticity.

Such company propaganda implied that only lack of character or perhaps information prevented immigrant workers from achieving a higher standard of living; however, studies of wage levels in steel-making tell a different story. Economist Charles Gulick found that, until the 1920s, the steel corporation did not pay the average common laborer "sufficient wages to enable him to support a normal size family in health and decency."[6]

By 1916, U.S. Steel policies in the city of Gary had already undergone several changes: the early vision of the model city had been rejected as too paternalistic and replaced with "welfare" policies that gave benefits to skilled workers but not to the unskilled. World War I now caused the company to modify its labor policies once more, intensifying its campaign for Americanization and reaching out more ambitiously into the community to change ideology as well as habits of life.

But well before the steel company became interested in Americanization, nativists of various persuasions were engaged in a crusade to Americanize Gary's immigrant homes. Such homes were the nurseries of new Americans—but would they produce good workers, steady and loyal, or radical misfits? Could immigrant homes become the breeding ground of all that was un-American? Employers were not immune to such nativist nonsense. The company could go some way toward controlling immigrants at work, but the home environment was the principal source of ideology and culture. The experiment carried out at Ford, where between 1914 and 1921 the Sociological Department employed one hundred social investigators to record minutely the physical and moral conditions of workers' domestic lives, was only an extreme example of the new gospel of management: that a worker's efficiency in the mill was inextricably bound up with his home conditions.[17] By 1920, advocates of Americanization had persuaded management that a worker could not be efficient and loyal if his home was dirty, diseased, foreign, or, as a writer in the American Iron and Steel Institute *Bulletin* put it, "abnormal."[18]

In Gary, steel-company-sponsored Americanization took several forms. The corporation began English classes at night for employees (though many were too tired to attend); the Goodfellows Club offered health services to families of steelworkers; a visiting nurse was employed to visit the homes, making inquiries about morals as well as physical well-being.[19] The company also increased its campaign to persuade immigrants to become naturalized. An article published in the *Gary Works Circle* in 1918 entitled "What Americanization Is" showed that intolerance of foreignness had escalated to include matters previously considered private or trivial. Among ten points listed as criteria for Americanization were the use of American foods, American methods of cooking, and American attitudes toward child care.[20] And in 1920 the same magazine carried an article entitled "A Message for Mothers," which began, "This is a letter to you, little mother. No doubt it will find you at home and perhaps a bit lonesome." The writer appealed to the immigrant woman not to be left out while her whole family became Americanized.

> Do your best to learn English, go to the Mother's Club at the Settlement House if there is one near you. Maintain your place in the home and keep the respect of your husband and children by learning as much as you can about what is going on in the new country . . . By so doing you will not only retain the place of honor you should have as wife and mother but you will be adding to the sum of your happiness and usefulness.

Fail to heed this advice, the writer warned, and the immigrant woman would become "a stranger in a strange land."[21]

Figure 9. English class at Neighborhood House. The spruced-up appearance of these young men suggests that such settlement classes appealed to the upwardly mobile and easily Americanized. Courtesy of the Neighborhood House Collection, Calumet Regional Archives, Indiana University Northwest.

When the steel corporation developed its programs for foreign employees to plant American standards in their homes and loyalties in their hearts, several private agencies, including two settlement houses, had already begun an intense effort to reach Gary's immigrant women. Reformers and civic leaders laid the blame for the vice, crime, and dirt of the South Side squarely on the immigrants and especially on immigrant homes. Wherever they looked, whether at infant-mortality statistics, at illiteracy, at filth and disease, or at political radicalism, they always came back to the foreigners and the foreign homes that kept them immured and separate from American influences. With their foreign churches and clubs, their newspapers in strange languages, expressing heaven-only-knew-what alien ideas, their homes redolent of foreign food, their odd clothing, the foreigners, who made up over half the population in 1910, were an alarming alien presence. Several Children's Bureau investigations were also under way; they would provide the detailed statistical data to add weight to the campaign for the Americanization of immigrant homes.[22]

The most vigorous Americanization campaign in Gary was that directed through the Gary schools at immigrant children. In addition, the Gary school board ran night-school classes to Americanize adults. This program, which claimed enrollment of 10,000 by 1922, has been characterized as reflecting "a harsh and unyielding demand that immigrants abandon old-country ways and quickly conform to those of the new land."[23] Was the settlement-house Americanization campaign equally "harsh and unyielding"? In extending the process of Americanization to the families of immigrants and to immigrant women in particular, how did the settlements interpret their goal to "give them home life"? Did the female-staffed and dominated agencies intervene in ways supportive of the immigrant woman, as wife, mother, and worker? How did the social-service workers, backed by Gary's powerful elite, translate Americanization into a system of power and gender relations in the immigrant community?

Neighborhood House, founded by Presbyterian churchwomen in 1909, combined religious activities and social work. Like Campbell House, it was known both as a settlement and a mission. The settlement began when two wealthy sisters, Kate and Jane Williams, from Howe, Indiana, conceived the idea of establishing a kindergarten for the children of Gary's immigrant steelworkers. Gary already had the reputation of frontier roughness, if not violence. "Ladies, ladies," a Chicago businessman protested when he heard of their plans, "you should not venture into this Gary of which we hear so much in the papers."[24] Undaunted, the Williams sisters traveled to Gary where they sought out Rev. Fred Walton, minister of the First Presbyterian Church. At their insistence, Reverend Walton and Dr. George Knox of the Home Missions Committee, who was visiting him at the time, toured the mission field, Gary's South Side or "the Patch," as it was known, in the only transportation available, a shiny, black funeral car.[25]

What they saw on the South Side convinced them that it was not only a mission field but also an area where the services of a settlement house were desperately needed. Everything that had been planned carefully for the steel-company subdivisions was lacking here. Inadequate, even shocking, living conditions were only part of the problem, they agreed. More serious, from the reformers' viewpoint, was the abnormal situation in Gary caused by the predominance of men. Gary was a boomtown, vibrant and exciting, but to the reformers it seemed full of rootless, brawling men, without a stake in the town or in America. To the settlement workers and their religious allies the immigrants seemed like men who had thrown off the restraints of the old country but had not acknowledged the responsibilities of the new. They determined to provide what Gary lacked—the influence of religion and women, stable influences to turn wild young men into family men, drifters into regular, disciplined workers, foreign women into American wives and mothers.[26]

Neighborhood House began modestly. Soon after their first memorable visit to Gary, Jane and Kate Williams founded two kindergartens for immigrant children, one on 14th Avenue in May 1909 and one on 25th Avenue in the fall of that year. They also started a sewing school and a Sunday school. In these efforts they had the support of the First Presbyterian Church of Gary.[27]

In January 1910 when Rev. B. M. Baligrodski and his sister arrived as directors, the kindergartens had already been drawn into the Gary public-school system, and a settlement house or mission (it is not clear which) was in operation at 1533 Washington Street. This was the "South Side Mission," housed in a shack with the words "Bibles for Sale" boldly over the door. When the Gary *Daily Tribune* described the settlement as "Gary's Hull House," it aroused expectations of reform and neighborhood improvement. It was to be a model home, with Miss Baligrodski as both social worker and housekeeper, visiting immigrant homes and "doing such turns for the children of the neighborhood as only a mother can do." The settlement represented both the reforming presence of women and the spiritual refreshment of the Gospel. It offered educational and cultural opportunities for immigrant women and girls—a library and a reading room, a night school, sewing classes for girls and women, and classes in domestic science. Its religious work included both worship services and Sunday school.[28]

The settlement had no link with the steel company, but it was immediately applauded by Gary's civic and religious leaders. On February 14, 1910, under the title "Americanizing the Foreign Born," the Gary *Daily Tribune* heralded Neighborhood House, "a new settlement devoted to the uplifting of the foreign born." The settlement's goal of improving the homes of the foreigners in order to create an environment that would nurture American values drew its hearty support. "If these people are to have the ballot, as the constitution provides, they must be prepared to exercise it wisely and well," the editorial declared. "They must be made over into real Americans as the forefathers of us all were made over. . . . The work must be done in the homes and largely with the children." Under the title "Give Them Home Life," the same newspaper described the settlement's purpose. However, the writer's tone of condescension made it doubtful whether the foreign "wards" would be encouraged to retain any of their customs or culture.

The general plan under which Mr. Baligrodski will work is to *invite his wards into the home that is the settlement*, bringing with them their own songs and customs of the fatherland. From a practical standpoint the colonists of the south side are to be taught the English language, sanitation, hygiene, homemaking—in fact everything that pertains to the uplifting of the man, and the purifying of his home.[29][emphasis added]

Reverend Baligrodski related a revealing encounter with some of Gary's immigrant men. The missionary had gone to visit one of the South Side boarding houses.

> Upstairs there was one big room, with two rows of beds with an aisle between them. The room was full of tobacco smoke and not one window was open. I offered the Bible to some of the men. [One young man could read.] . . . The men gathered about us while he read selections here and there. After a while he turned to the book of Psalms and he and a few other men began to sing them. Many of the other men became interested and bought Bibles. . . . One of them, noticing that I had a newspaper, asked me to read and tell them what was going on in the rest of the world. I was glad to answer their questions and talk with them.[30]

Although the encounter ended when Reverend Baligrodski had to leave "on account of the closeness of the room and the foul air," his experience nevertheless convinced him that many immigrants wanted what the settlement had to offer—its spiritual message and its promise of literacy. The missionary recognized, however, that the physical living conditions of Gary's immigrant men posed a grave problem. "It seemed incredible that human beings could exist in such a place," he mused.[31]

If the settlement's contacts with Gary's immigrant men were tentative, its main work was with immigrant women and children. We do not know enough about the personnel who lived at Neighborhood House in this early stage, but evidence suggests the predominance of female settlement residents and of activities centered on immigrant women and children. Sarah Burton, a trained nurse who carried on a busy schedule of home visiting and social work, earned the affection of the neighborhood along with the name "Dobra Pani," the "Good Lady."[32] Such home visiting was an effective method of Americanization, "serving as a connecting link between these homes and the outside world of opportunity," one social worker wrote. "The tactful, considerate and sympathetic visitor who is concerned with the hygienic aspect of the home she enters, can win the confidence of the foreign-born women and so teach them many household needs and household methods that make for real Americanization."[33]

By October 1911, the settlement's director was Reverend Backora, a Hungarian educated in the United States.[34] With demand for the settlement's services growing, there were plans to expand its buildings. The Presbyterian Board of Home Missions, acting with the synod, purchased lots at 17th and Adams. Fifteen thousand dollars had already been donated by the Presbyterian Synod of Indiana, and in November 1912 the first unit was dedicated. The new buildings included a dormitory for young men, a nursery for the children of working mothers, a public-library branch, and public baths. Soon the meeting rooms were being used for Slovak and Russian religious services and for educational lectures. The settlement, earlier referred to as "the Gary Settlement," now acquired the name "the Neighborhood House."[35]

The population of the South Side continued to grow and so did demand for the settlement's services. In 1914, it was necessary to rent two outside buildings. Significantly, one was for use as a nursery, presumably for the children of working mothers or for children being temporarily cared for; one was a residence for women settlement workers.[36] In 1914 also, Grace Mary Warmington arrived to direct the social work of the settlement. Warmington became the settlement's Lillian Wald, a social worker and visiting nurse who traveled on bicycle—or on foot where the sand made the going too difficult—on an exhausting round of visits to South Side homes.[37]

Instability of leadership had been a problem during the settlement's first years. But in 1916 the settlement acquired a new director, Rev. Ralph Cummins. Trained in Yugoslavia, Cummins had a background that would help him in his contacts with the immigrants. In the words of a settlement history, his arrival "completed our organization, gave us a fine permanent leadership, and terminated our preliminary transitional period." He also married Grace Warmington. (We should not rule out the possibility that those who wrote the history of the institution equated male leadership with permanent, professional leadership—this, despite the fact that the settlement was a female-staffed agency that focused on immigrant women and children.)[38]

A significant change in the governing board took place in 1914 when that body, which had previously included only denominational representatives, was enlarged by a number of Gary citizens, men and women. The settlement was no longer just a home-mission effort of the Presbyterian church, but was becoming part of a community-wide crusade in which religious, moral, sanitary, and social-control motives flowed together. And in an important move designed to tie the Americanization work of the steel company to that of the settlement house, the U.S. Steel Safety Department in 1916 sent an employee, Bernard Coggan, to be resident at Neighborhood House. Coggan was put in charge of English-language teaching and citizenship classes at the settlement. The steel company now had a direct link with the social agency and its Americanization work.[39]

The settlement expanded again in 1916 when a second part of the main building was opened. New quarters included nursery rooms for boys' and girls' activities, living quarters for staff members, and an office. Since it was only four blocks from Froebel, the school attended by most of Gary's foreign-born children, Neighborhood House was in a good location for the combined missionary and Americanization effort known as the "Gary Plan of Church Schools." Under this scheme, children were released from the public schools to attend the religious schools of their choice. Neighborhood House was one center for this activity. The settlement carried on a strong program of evangelism among the foreign-born children.[40]

The settlement's location also made it a natural choice as a base for Gary's first public-health nurse. Now officially designated as a "city welfare station," the settlement brought substantial improvement to the neighborhood health situation by holding clinics and classes, teaching about hygiene, and giving pre- and postnatal care. A school physician estimated that the health work of the social settlement was responsible for a 25 percent drop in infant mortality during 1916. Many immigrants were not reached, however: a 1923 survey revealed that fewer than one-third of foreign-born women received prenatal care from a physician. One-half of live births were still attended by a midwife.[41]

In 1916, Neighborhood House could claim with some justification that it had become a vital part of the South Side community. It sponsored a playground and an employment department, nationality and language schools, classes in handwork, scouting, and a Vacation Bible School. Protestant worship services were held there. In 1918, average attendance at Slovak worship was twenty-one; at Italian, fourteen; and at services in English, fifty.[42] Eager to make contacts in the foreign community, the settlement offered its facilities for meetings of many ethnic, cultural, and mutual-benefit societies, including the Sicilian Union, the First Italian Society, the Italian Band, the Spanish-American Club, the Lithuanian Educational Society, the Lithuanian Alliance of America and the Lithuanian Benefit Society, the Czecho-Slovak Alliance, the Royal Neighbors (Slavic), the Zivena Beneficial Society (Slavic), and the Albanian Union. In addition, labor organizations such as the Ukrainian Progressive Workers' Association met there, as did religious organizations such as the Slavonian Calvinist Presbyterian Union. This indicated "the place the House holds as a Community Center," a settlement report noted with satisfaction.[43]

Sometimes the close contacts between the reformers and their potential converts were disappointing. When the settlement board made efforts to draw nearer to its immigrant neighbors by hiring part-time workers who were themselves immigrants, older national and racial rivalries sometimes surfaced. An Italian pastor attached to Neighborhood House in 1918 complained to the board of his difficulty in reaching the Italians with his gospel message, but blamed the fact that "most of [them] . . . are Sicilians, ignorant and prejudiced." Generally speaking, however, the settlement workers were glad to make contact with ethnic organizations even if this amounted only to sharing facilities.[44] After 1917, work at the settlement continued amid increasing hostility to foreigners in the wider community, hostility that was raised to the boiling point by the 1919 steel strike and the subsequent "Red Scare." Anxious to legitimize its work among aliens, Neighborhood House was careful to point out in its published literature that it was not a foreign agency, but rather an agency for Americanization. If the year's total of attendance at clubs, classes, visits, lectures, and so on amounted to anything at all, the 1920 report declared, it was "the Making of Americans."[45] Citizenship training now became an urgent task for the settlement; 290 sessions were held at the House during 1920, with an average attendance of twelve. The expanding activity of the settlement in these years was also reflected in the increase of its operating budget from $5,426 in 1914 to $12,650 in April 1919.[46]

A change in the composition of the settlement's governing board became important in the twenties. Before the war, the board had been reconstituted to include not only denominational and synodal leaders but also members of the civic and business elite. By the 1920s, the board included some of Gary's most prominent citizens: the mayor of Gary, W. F. Hodges, H. B. Snyder, owner of the Gary *Post Tribune*, real-estate men and lawyers, and the wives of prominent mill officials.[47] Steel-company support also increased. The social upheaval glimpsed during the 1919 strike made the corporation more interested in supporting civic and social-welfare efforts. In November 1920, the settlement received a promise of $2,000 from the Illinois Steel Company. Thereafter, sizable contributions came each year. By 1924 the steel company was meeting one-third of the running expenses of the settlement house.[48] This was in addition to an in-house "settlement" for steel-company workers and their families, the Gleason Center, which offered cooking classes, health clinics, day care, and other services designed to serve the needs and reform the habits of immigrant families.[49]

Before turning to analyze the settlement's work with immigrant women, it is necessary to summarize the changes that were occurring in the 1920s. A transformation in the population of the Central District, which began in 1920, posed a new challenge to the settlement house. Neighborhood House had been founded to Americanize the immigrants who still made up about 30 percent of Gary's population in 1920. But by 1930, their percentage had fallen to 19 percent (see Table 6). No fewer than ten churches of six different denominations had begun by meeting at Neighborhood House; now all had buildings of their own. An International Institute Report of 1929 described the situation in Gary's Central District:

> Each group has had its turn at this section of town. What was once Italian and Polish, then Polish and colored has become almost entirely colored. The Italians have scattered to all parts of the city, most of them having bought their own homes. The Polish people . . . are selling . . . [their] homes as rapidly as possible and are renting . . . to colored people.[50]

Like Christamore and Campbell House, Neighborhood House faced the choice of remaining and opening its doors to blacks or following its immigrant families to the greener pastures of suburbs like Glen Park. The agency had originally been launched as an institution to make foreigners Protestant—but blacks needed neither Americanization nor evangelizing. The "Minutes" of the Neighborhood House staff meetings reveal the confusion that these changes produced. At first the settlement staff tried to take care of blacks in segregated classes, while they discussed opening an annex for them at a cottage west of the settlement.[51] But, since ever larger numbers of blacks needed the settlement's services while ever fewer immigrants did so, these arrangements seemed unreasonable. In April 1924, the board referred the matter to the executive committee of the Synod on National Mission and to the executive committee of the house.[52]

Uncertainty was resolved in April 1925 with the decision to admit blacks to the main settlement building. The settlement would remain in the Central District, serving blacks and Gary's newest arrivals, the Mexicans. By 1925, the settlement was claiming that black children were cared for in the kindergarten and admitted to classes, clubs, employment, and aid "in every way that the white children are being benefited."[53] The house soon had a black minister to assist at religious services, and by 1929 a black social worker as well. Neighborhood House, like Campbell House, thus entered the thirties as an agency serving both races. Neighborhood House pioneered with children's recreation in 1929; when it took twenty children to summer camp this was the first time such a camp experience had been available to Gary's black children. However, not until the early 1940s, when attendance at the settlement was two-thirds black, was a black person invited to sit on the settlement's board of trustees.[54]

Neighborhood House was also coming into contact with Gary's newest immigrants, the Mexicans. Like previous immigrants, these were rural people trying to adapt to industrial life. Not only did they suffer from unhealthy living and working conditions, but in addition, like the blacks who were arriving in the Calumet region at the same time, they faced racial discrimination in employment, housing, and public accommodations. Neighborhood House workers recognized the Mexicans' need of the settlement's services—but also saw them as a group that might be attracted to Protestantism. On November 17, 1925, the settlement's governing board decided to open the social agency to Mexicans (an admission, incidentally, that they had previously been excluded).[55] In an attempt to interest the Mexicans in its religious message, the settlement tried open-air preaching in Spanish and hired a Spanish-speaking Mexican national. Neighborhood House also tried to foster the Mexicans' national culture: Mexican Independence Day was celebrated each year at Neighborhood House with great

Figure 10. Gary Neighborhood House Chorale. Settlement entertainments showed the settlement in the dual role of Americanizer and preserver of immigrant culture. Courtesy of the Neighborhood House Collection, Calumet Regional Archives, Indiana University Northwest.

fanfare. The Protestant settlement had arrived at a more sophisticated understanding of how to reach immigrants when it appealed to their pride in their heritage, rather than marching toward them with outstretched arms over the ruins of their culture.[56]

By the 1920s, Gary Neighborhood House had developed into a full-fledged social agency, part of a broad Americanization drive that enjoyed the support of the steel company, the Protestant churches, and civic leaders. Choosing racial toleration over exclusion, it was attempting to serve all ethnic and racial groups in Gary's Central District. In the remainder of this chapter, I will describe and analyze the settlement's work with immigrant women and families. The settlement had defined its task as Americanizing Gary's immigrant homes—but what was an "American Home"? What assumptions about the family and about women's roles underlay the social workers' attempts to Americanize immigrant women, and how did these differ from the beliefs of immigrants themselves?

We can get some idea of the agenda of settlement Americanization programs from the statement drawn up by Woods and Kennedy and appended to their 1922 book *The Settlement Horizon*, under the title "An Experimental Definition of the American Standard of Living." The statement lists the various aspects of Americanization, from language (English); to food; "room"; cleanliness; clothing ("inconspicuous"); association; child nurture; and "moral idioms" ("a general attitude of hope and opportunity toward communal activities").[57]

Before turning to the content of the settlements' Americanization activities, however, it is important to note the context in which these took place. In Chicago, Philadelphia, New York, Buffalo, and other large cities, immigrant women toiled in mills, factories, canneries, and sweatshops. In these cities, settlements worked for the reform of industrial conditions, started working-girls' clubs, and sometimes encouraged labor organizations such as the Women's Trade Union League. But mill towns like Gary presented settlements with a different configuration of needs and possibilities. Few women in Gary were employed in manufacturing. According to the United States Census, female labor-force participation was only 13 percent in 1920 and 20 percent in 1930; of those recorded as wage-earners in 1920, only 11 percent were employed in manufacturing.[58] Even during World War I, when the departure of about one-fourth of the immigrant steel workers to their home countries caused a serious labor shortage, the steel mills did not seek female labor but instead recruited male black and Mexican workers. Steel-mill officials and social workers seemed to agree that the benefits to social stability of having women in the home outweighed their value as wage-earners.[59]

Why, then, did the settlement workers complain constantly about "overworked motherhood" among their immigrant neighbors? The answer can be found in a Children's Bureau Report for 1917 which reveals a strikingly different picture of immigrant women's employment in Gary from that in the census. The report found that, even in families with children aged two to seven, mothers' employment rates were high. In those families with preschool children the mother was employed in 31 percent of white families, 41 percent of foreign-born families, and 52 percent of black families. Among immigrants, ethnicity was associated with differing labor-force participation rates: 59 percent of Lithuanian mothers in Gary worked for wages, but only 34 percent of Hungarians. Perhaps because of the war, perhaps because of need, many working-class mothers were employed for wages, a practice that the social workers felt bound to condemn.[60]

For their part, too, most immigrants opposed women's wage-work outside the home. Cultural norms were breached when young women engaged in work that caused them to associate with others not of the same family or ethnic group, or that exposed them to sexual encounters. Moreover, factory work was an unattractive prospect for working-class women: it brought neither good wages, improved status, nor even psychological benefits—the domestic role offered more.[61] Children's Bureau figures showing that work-force participation was associated with low income confirm that it was economic necessity that forced these women out into jobs: in families where the chief breadwinner earned under $1,050, 41 percent of mothers were employed. Where the earnings were more substantial, $1,850 or over, only 30 percent of mothers worked. But in families reporting "no chief bread-winner or no earnings," 79 percent of mothers of preschool children were employed for wages.[62]

Poverty, then, seems associated with high rates of female labor-force participation. For example, blacks, with lower income than either immigrants or white Americans, had higher work-force-participation rates: in 1918, when the cost of living for a family of five was calculated to be $1,375, data from the Children's Bureau survey showed that in 41 percent of native-born white families, 70 percent of immigrant families, and 79 percent of black families, the breadwinner earned less than $1,449. As noted in other chapters, settlements suspended their disapproval of mothers working outside the home when black women were involved. At Flanner House, at Campbell House, and at other agencies, the social workers actually facilitated the entry of black and other poor women into the paid work force by operating employment agencies that sent them out, mainly as domestic workers. This curious "double vision" of Progressivism on the issue of paid work for mothers not only contradicted the general stance of the settlements on women's wage-work, but also created tensions within a movement whose major social-policy triumphs were protective legislation for women and the mothers' pension movement, both of which accelerated the withdrawal of most married women and widows from the paid work-force.[63]

Meanwhile, poverty forced immigrant women to seek paying work as it did black women. With the breadwinner's wage insufficient to sustain the family, income from other family members was essential. The solution was keeping boarders and lodgers: the Children's Bureau report found the practice in 86 percent of homes where mothers declared themselves gainfully employed. According to the report, 18 percent of children of native-born whites lived in homes with lodgers, compared to 25 percent of blacks and 30 percent of children of immigrants. An impressionistic but sympathetic International Institute Survey of Gary in 1919 described keeping boarders as "the chief industry of all the foreign homes."[64]

Boarding and lodging provided shelter for the thousands of single men who made up the majority of Gary's early population. They aided chain migration, immigrants often coming from the same regions of the European homeland or being acquaintances or even kin of those they boarded with. And for working-class women, taking in boarders and lodgers meant getting around prohibitions against wage-work while fulfilling both home and family duties and making a major contribution to family income.[65]

The settlement workers' attempts to discourage the keeping of boarders were doomed to failure; the practice was a temporary one that reflected necessity, not choice. Income and boarding figures from the 1923 Children's Bureau survey showed that families resorted to taking boarders at certain stages in the family life-cycle, and only when it was economically necessary. When they needed the extra income, immigrant families were willing to put up with crowded housing as a temporary inconvenience. The second generation of immigrants reaped the benefits for which the first had sacrificed. The author of an International Institute survey of 1929 grasped this fact. "Many times, while the children are small, a family will rent out most of the rooms and endure discomfort in order to get enough money that they may live in comfort later in life," the writer noted.[66]

Settlement workers, social workers, Children's Bureau experts, and also, presumably, the steel-company welfare workers all disapproved of mothers leaving the home to work; they also disapproved of boarding. The Progressive ideal of the American home stressed privacy and the single-family dwelling, with the mother as full-time housekeeper. Settlement workers like Grace Warmington were less inclined to regard the boardinghouses as a sign of immigrant resourcefulness than as an unsatisfactory practice arising from cultural or ethnic traits that produced a tangle of social problems: crowding led to bad health, lack of privacy to vice, and the task of caring for as many as a dozen men put impossible strains on immigrant women who had to fetch water, cook, wash, and clean for their large households. The settlement was particularly critical of boarding because of the strain it placed upon the city's inadequate housing supply. The Neighborhood House social worker found as many as fifteen boarders in some homes in beds occupied both day and night because the men worked in shifts. One house on the South Side inspected by the Children's Bureau investigator in 1918 was described as follows: "Six of the rooms were occupied by a Spanish family of six and their six lodgers, and its basement, containing three rooms, housed a Polish family and lodgers, eight persons in all. These twenty individuals were dependent on a single toilet under the outside steps."[67]

Immigrants would never enjoy an American home life unless these housing conditions could be improved, Grace Warmington wrote. Instead, the "great army of foreign men" would continue to come off their shift at the mill and head for the "solid block of saloons" on Broadway, instead of going directly home. "Are you surprised that they should want to stop in the saloons rather than return to their room?" the social worker asked her audience of middle-class American women, after describing to them the shocking housing conditions in Gary. Was it any wonder that immigrant husbands and boarders took refuge in the saloons when their wives remained so ignorant of domestic skills?[68]

Since they could do nothing to stop the practice of boarding, however, the settlement workers tried to help immigrant women become better housekeepers, more able to cope with their heavy burden of housework. At times when they despaired of Americanizing the isolated and conservative immigrant women, they turned to the more receptive immigrant daughters. Settlement girls' clubs did not concern themselves with civics, history, or subjects leading to a fuller citizenship or to occupational mobility, as boys' clubs did, but concentrated on fitting girls for lives as homemakers and consumers. Settlements should aim to teach "the real dignity of toil," a national settlement leader declared. For boys this could be achieved in the settlement's manual-training class. However, "[Girls] . . . whose future may be as wives of plain workmen, learn that to cook, to sweep rooms, and to make beds, is not undignified, nor menial, only to do these things fretfully and after a slovenly fashion." The social workers polled in *Young Working Girls* recommended that girls be required to do housework in the evening—even if they had been employed in the factory all day. Such remarks point to a tension between immigrant girls enjoying the freedom symbolized by a paycheck and the delights of commercial entertainment, and social workers counseling sexual restraint, self-control, and the dignity of toil. Meanwhile, if women were doing their housework "fretfully," might it not be because working-class districts of cities such as Gary lacked municipal services that middle-class suburban dwellers were taking for granted, or because, on steelworkers' wages, families could not afford the labor-saving machines that, by the twenties, were becoming necessities in middle-class homes?[69]

Settlement classes for girls provided not only socialization and instruction in homemaking, but also moral guidance and shelter. As one social worker put it, "The young working girl's search for recreation is fraught with moral danger at many points." Settlements provided an alternative to the "cheap amusements" of commercial entertainment such as movies and dance halls.[70] But the results were often disappointing: it was difficult to persuade immigrant girls who had worked all day at the Gary Screw and Bolt Company, or in the offices and shops along Broadway, to attend a settlement cooking class rather than to see a movie. And at times immigrant girls took the settlement's offerings, only to subvert them to their own ends: immigrant resourcefulness triumphed over the agenda of the Americanizers when a young Spanish woman took the housekeeping classes at Neighborhood House, then got married and used her training to manage a household of twenty-four boarders.[71]

Central to the settlement's vision of American domesticity were standards relating to diet and to the cooking and serving of food. The Woods-Kennedy definition of the American standard of living stated it as a principle that the family should meet together at meals "at least once a day." Settlement workers also were concerned about the healthfulness and purity of food consumed and whether working-class women knew how to buy food that was nutritious but inexpensive. Public-health reformers and employers wanted workers to be well-fed and contented. They also wanted them sober: as we have seen, U.S. Steel strictly limited the number of saloons that could be built in the "official" Gary.

The settlement workers, public-health reformers, and government experts who wrote about working-class diet expressed grave concern about a decline in domestic skills, especially cooking, for which they unfairly blamed the immigrants. Citing the fact that so many young women worked for wages before marriage, just at the age (it was argued) when they should be learning the domestic arts from their mothers—these reformers seem to have feared that a whole generation of urban dwellers had lost touch with the art and science of homemaking—it was as if the work of Catharine Beecher had to be done all over again. In fact, women of all income levels were spending less time cooking in the 1920s than their mothers had done. Urbanization had brought an increase in commercial food preparation so that more women were purchasing bakery-produced bread and cakes and using canned foods.[72] Settlement workers might have welcomed these changes that lightened women's work. Baking bread, for example, was an impossible chore in the cramped kitchens of most of Gary's working-class houses. Instead, the settlements and other Americanizers regarded these changes as an aberration from a fixed standard of domesticity to which they hoped American homemakers would soon return. As for the numerous single men, they further contributed to this deficit of "proper homes": Gary had restaurants and hotels in place of homes, one social worker noted.[73]

Settlement cooking classes were an attempt to stem this tide of ignorance and indifference, to Americanize the immigrant diet, and to tackle other social problems. Take divorce, for example. Good cooking was the basis of a happy marriage, social workers agreed; bad cooking filled the saloons with restless men, causing desertion and divorce. Even so sensible an observer as Jane Addams recounted the story of a young woman, a factory worker who married without adequate preparation, and whose husband became "so desperate after two years of her unskilled cooking that he had threatened to desert her and go where he could get 'decent food.' " Luckily, she took the Hull House course in cooking, and "at the end of six months reported a united and happy home."[74]

Cooking skills were not taught in isolation. At Neighborhood House in 1923 it was reported, "Besides learning to cook, the girls serve and eat what they cook, learning nice customs and enjoying the social intercourse." Three thousand were enrolled in these classes in Gary—a crash course in middle-class manners for aspiring immigrant girls.[75]

Immigrant girls could be useful allies in Americanization if they carried American practices and values back from the settlement house into their own homes. Neighborhood House invited mothers and daughters to attend cooking classes together so that the girls could interpret the mothers' questions about American foods. "The girls had learned so many new and tasty dishes in the cooking class and wanted them for home so that the mothers had come to learn too."[76]

Settlement houses also offered cooking courses because they believed that immigrant women's ignorance of nutrition was to blame for the poor health of their children. A Children's Bureau report published in 1923 exposed the bad dietary habits of Gary's immigrants and contrasted the actual diets of the children with an ideal children's diet, defined as "mild, bland foods simply cooked, . . . no tea, coffee, rich pastries, or other unsuitable articles. The meals . . . at moderately regular hours . . . no promiscuous eating between meals, and the dinner or "heaviest" meal . . . at noon."[77]

In practice, the basic rules of good nutrition, so obvious to the investigators, were everywhere violated. Despite the "rule," "a quart of milk a day for every child," only one-fifth of the children received even as much as a pint a day. Cultural preference was very important: three-quarters of Italian children and 70 percent of Hungarian and Slovak children, Gary's largest foreign group, received no milk at all. Worse yet, "not only did more than 90 percent of the children drink coffee, but practically three fourths of them drank it two or more times a day."[78]

The children's diets were lacking in many essentials, about half of the total receiving no vegetables and 60 percent no fruit. Gary's preschoolers, it turned out, were living on meat and potatoes, but "meat alone cannot save a diet from inadequacy," warned the report. "With an income of under $850 a family would unquestionably be better nourished if meat were foregone entirely and the money put into more essential foods."[79]

Not surprisingly, the investigators found a correlation between poor diet and poverty—"the proportion of adequate diets increases gradually from the lowest income level to the highest." Despite this, they blamed low income less than ignorance and "racial dietary prejudices." The Italians had the poorest record of all. Three-fourths of the children did not receive milk, "approximately 85.3 percent drank coffee, had no cereal, and ate between meals; about two-thirds were without eggs, and the same proportion lacked four or more of the specified items." Of 2,890 children on the South Side only 2.7 percent were found to have adequate diets, as defined by the study.[80]

Not only was the content of immigrant diets defective, but the whole attitude toward the child's needs also seemed un-American. Immigrant families did not regard children as having special dietary needs. "The meals were prepared for the father and . . . all the family from the two year old up ate the same meal." American family experts knew better: settlement workers trained in nutrition and child health tried to teach immigrant mothers that their young children needed special food, specially prepared.[81] The Americanization of the immigrant family involved both democratization and specialization: the different needs of the generations should be considered and, what is more, given equal weight, the Americanizers insisted.

In some cases the intervention of settlement workers was helpful: when the Neighborhood House nurse advised a family to obtain milk for a sick child, she told them which dairy was hygienic. In other cases, the intervention was unwise or unwelcome: the decision of foreign families to exclude milk from their diet was not always a "racial dietary prejudice." It may have been a sensible precaution in view of the fact that dairies in Gary were not uniformly safe.[82]

Cleanliness, named by Woods and Kennedy "an indispensable factor in the American standard," was also the hardest for Gary's working class to attain.[83] Clean clothes and bodies both promoted physical health and symbolized moral purity. The physical and the moral—Cleanliness and Godliness—were often linked. For example, a "Clean Kid" Club at Katherine House in neighboring East Chicago required members to be "clean in word and deed and to have a minimum of two baths a week." A clean shirt or blouse might help an immigrant secure employment. But poor conditions made clean clothes and regular baths an almost impossible standard for Gary's working-class housewives. In 1918, almost one-third of the homes of foreign-born children were without water, and three-fourths of the children of immigrants lived in a home without a bathtub (compared to 30 percent of children of American-born mothers). Children's Bureau investigators found that, even in summer, only one-fourth of children of immigrants took the "minimum" of one bath per week, far fewer than their American counterparts.[84]

Unlike the settlement workers at Hull House or the University of Chicago Settlement who agitated for the extension of city services to the slums, Neighborhood House took the less activist approach of providing, in the settlement house itself, the conveniences that its neighbors' houses lacked—showers, baths, and laundry facilities.[85]

For immigrant women whose homes lacked running water and who had the clothes of their family and of perhaps ten boarders to wash, the settlement laundry was a useful resource. On a typical morning at Neighborhood House in 1920, women entered with large baskets of clothes, paying twenty cents at the office and leaving their names before going to the basement to wash for their families and boarders.[86] Many contacts between immigrant women and the settlement began in the settlement-house laundry. A social worker must be there in the morning to greet the women when they arrived to do their laundry, the director of Katherine House in neighboring East Chicago advised her staff. She should collect the tickets and "make friendly contacts with the women." The social worker at Neighborhood House noted the names of those who used the laundry and later invited them to attend settlement classes and other functions.[87]

The settlement baths were less popular than the laundry. In 1915, for example, twelve people on average took a bath each day at Neighborhood House. Most people wanted a bathroom in their own home; only those with no alternatives used the settlement baths. As living standards rose and more Gary houses had indoor water, the settlement's facilities became less necessary. Like the settlement library and health clinic, the settlement baths and laundries eventually fell into disuse.[88]

In the early days of the settlement movement, feminists had believed in the potential of the neighborhood house with its public kitchens, laundry, and day-care facility to socialize housework and revolutionize women's household labor. But by the 1920s the ideology of material feminism was largely forgotten; the demonstration kitchens at Hull House and elsewhere were abandoned. In 1922, the conservative Woods and Kennedy expressly repudiated the settlement as a cooperative institution. "Under American conditions," they wrote, "public baths and laundries are felt even by immigrants to be visible acknowledgements of financial and sanitary insufficiency, . . . serving chiefly . . . to meet the needs of newcomers until they acquire American habits of living."[89] Facilities like this were an interim measure, not consistent with the American standard of living that settlements stood for, they implied. Settlement laundries and demonstration kitchens could have become the precursors of cooperative laundries and restaurants, freeing women from the unspecialized labor of the household. Instead they were regarded—by the social workers, and perhaps by immigrant women themselves—as stopgap arrangements, far less desirable than the individual, private facilities that gradually replaced them. The settlements' potential for revolutionizing household labor thus gave way in the 1920s to an emphasis on consumerism and the private household.[90]

No aspect of Americanization so much symbolized immigrants' surrender of European ways as their adoption of American dress. In many parts of Europe, clothing marked a person's place of origin, but American clothing disguised origins and even class: an Americanized immigrant woman was indistinguishable from others. No wonder that among some immigrant women, purchasing a new set of clothes was the first step toward adaptation to a new land.[91]

But ten years after Gary's beginnings, an observer could still distinguish the immigrant women by their dress. Social worker Edna Hatfield Edmondson described the immigrant section of Gary where "cows, horses, dogs, geese, pigs, chickens, and beautiful children in droll looking clothes tumble over each other in the sand."

> In the evening the women come in along the path from the prairies, wearing their shawls and kerchiefs over their heads, and their short, full skirts, and bending under bundles of sticks tied on their backs. As they gather in groups laughing and chatting, . . . the red of the setting sun behind them throws this picture of peasant life into bold relief that quite blots out another picture only two squares away, a picture of the hustle and bustle of an American business day drawing to a close.[92]

Settlement workers believed that it was to the immigrants' advantage to shed their traditional dress, whether it was picturesque or whether it was the heavy, black, woolen kind. Odd-looking clothing singled immigrants out, making them the butt of jokes, the victims of confidence tricksters. The settlement-house solution was to offer sewing classes where the immigrant woman could learn to make simple, American-style clothes for herself and her children.[93]

The settlement was not interested in sewing as a traditional art, even though embroidery was part of the heritage of many European immigrants.[94] Instead, the settlement sewing class was a bit of practical Americanization, an economical way for women to make clothes for themselves and their children while gathering with other women under settlement auspices. The immigrant woman "made herself over" as she constructed modern American clothing.

Sewing classes at Neighborhood House were so popular with immigrant women that they overflowed. Eighty were enrolled in 1916. Immigrant women realized that, in encouraging them to modify traditional dress, the settlement was helping them to remove at least the visible marks of a second-class citizenship. Settlement workers, for their part, could congratulate themselves that, in gathering together immigrant women in the settlement house, they were hastening the Americanization and the homogeneity of the ethnically mixed community.[95]

The sewing class was also an occasion for other kinds of teaching. Immigrant women sewing were, in a sense, a captive audience. Thus the first class at Neighborhood House in 1909 was a sewing class where, as they worked, girls of every nationality and religion were taught Christian Bible stories and Protestant hymns. A Jewish girl who returned from the settlement singing Protestant hymns was at first forbidden by her father to attend the sewing class again, but he relented and allowed her to go: she could learn to sew—so long as she paid no attention to the songs, he said. And

Figure 11. Sewing class at Neighborhood House. Immigrant girls learned a new domesticity in America; they heard lessons on health, the Bible, and English as they sewed. Courtesy of the Neighborhood House Collection, Calumet Regional Archives, Indiana University Northwest.

Grace Warmington, herself a nurse by training, found the settlement sewing class the most receptive audience for her instruction on matters of health, hygiene, and child care. The first classes held at the settlement house for black women, in 1916, were also sewing classes.[96]

Americanization also involved a new attitude toward children. The hallmarks of an American standard of child care, according to Woods and Kennedy, were "devoted care for health, cleanliness, and dietary; constant oversight of play . . . watchfulness for the appearance of talent . . . "[97] This close attention to the needs and rights of children implied that professionals had a duty to intervene in order to correct the mother's well-meaning, if instinctual, care for her child. On the national scene by the 1920s there was an array of experts giving advice to mothers about child care, nutrition, play, and emotional health. Settlement workers lent their voices to this call for expert intervention in families—and by the 1920s, settlements like Neighborhood House (even if still headed by a minister) were staffed by experts, men and women with training in nursing, social work, casework, or child development. It was this specialized training that justified their intervention into working-class homes, not (as had been true in the early years of the settlement movement) simply altruism or a good-hearted desire to help.[98]

Sometimes this intrusive intervention caused resentment in immigrant and working-class families. A Protestant pastor who worked among Italian families told about social workers who

> burst into their homes and upset the usual routines of their lives, opening windows, undressing children, giving orders not to eat this and that, not to wrap babies in swaddling clothes . . . The mother of five or six children may, with some reason, be inclined to think that she knows a little more about how to bring up children than the young-looking damsel who insists on trying to teach her how to do it.[99]

Sympathy for overworked single mothers, a desire to help those who had to go out to work, a determination to influence foreign children toward American ways, and a sense of religious mission—all these motives, in addition to the interest of professionals in their clients, came together in the settlement day-care center.

A nursery was begun at Neighborhood House in 1914 and moved into the new addition in 1916. Soon it was reported that fifteen to twenty babies were being cared for every day, enabling their mothers to earn, "collectively," $3,000 a year. From 1924 to 1925, 2,158 children were looked after while their mothers worked, a ten-cents-per-day charge covering the two meals the children received. In 1920, the nursery was given a state license to handle up to forty children per day.[100]

The discussion of the day nursery in the Neighborhood House literature reveals settlement workers deeply divided on the issue of wage-work for married women. The elaborate justifications with which the settlement literature surrounded the provision of day care betray the anxiety that settlement personnel felt lest they be accused of aiding women to escape domestic responsibilities. Work outside the home was an undesirable thing for mothers, settlement workers agreed, but often there was no alternative. Descriptions of this program referred to mothers in heroic terms—the phrase "mothers who have to go out to work" was almost formulaic. "Widowed or deserted mothers or mothers whose husbands are incapacitated for work can bring their little ones while they themselves bravely go forth to provide a living for their little flock."[101]

Official settlement descriptions justified the day nursery as a beneficial influence on mothers and children. Cruel necessity was transformed into a positive good when mothers and children were brought into contact with the settlement house and its programs. The children cared for received training in useful skills and good citizenship. "The Nursery children always assist the matron in the necessary activities of the nursery such as sweeping, dusting, cleaning, setting and cleaning the table and washing and wiping the dishes. In this way many are learning habits of industry and thrift at a very impressionable age."[102]

According to these self-serving and defensive descriptions of its programs, the settlement house embodied both scientific expertise and rules for right living that could have wonderful effects when applied in working-class homes. "The nursery is one of the finest branches of the work," wrote its superintendent, Rev. Henry David Jones, in *Twenty Years of Neighborliness*.

> The children learn courtesy, unselfishness, cleanliness and many things as they live together during their long day away from home. They have proper food and rest and plenty of fresh air which often brings the question from mothers, "why do my children sleep all night after they have spent the day in the nursery. At other times they are so restless." The home then improves as the mother learns helpful things for home and babies.[103]

It would be a mistake to read the settlements' efforts to organize child care for working mothers as an attempt to usurp the mother's place as primary child-rearer. Settlement-house nurseries were neither a contradiction to the settlements' support of a primarily nurturing role for women nor an attempt to socialize child care or to "liberate" working-class women from family responsibilities. Instead, settlement literature justified the provision of day care in terms that reinforced the primacy of motherhood as the goal of all women.[104]

Rather than a threat to a happy home life, then, the settlement-house day nursery could be the means to achieve it. The following, very typical, anecdote illustrates how settlement workers projected the nursery as the salvation—the word is not too strong—of a working-class home.

> Not long ago four little children whose mother was a widow were found in a home where filth was almost unbelievable and were brought to the Neighborhood House nursery and given a few months' care. A subsequent visit revealed not only a cleaner and much better kept house, but where before one saucepan and a few spoons had sufficed to serve the family meals, five tin cups, five granite plates and five spoons were now carefully set out on the table three times a day, and under the supervision of the ten year old girl the meals were begun with grace and served with all the courtesies of the nursery table.[105]

The impact of the settlement day nursery should not be exaggerated. The Children's Bureau study shows that Gary's immigrant mothers left the home to work only as a last resort or because of economic necessity—such women were in many cases the main breadwinner. In 1917, only 8 percent of those with young children left them in order to work, and most of these mothers used relatives or friends: such informal arrangements were far more popular than formal, institutional arrangements such as the settlement-house nursery.[106]

While settlements promoted Progressive Motherhood as an ideal for all women, they left a loophole for women who had to find paid employment. In Gary, poor women, mostly blacks and immigrants, were encouraged by the Neighborhood House employment agency to take day work as domestics, cooks, maids, and laundresses. Again, the settlement's explanation of this program illustrates the contradictions that beset women's wage-work and the settlement's endorsement of it. In caring for the children of these working mothers, it claimed, the settlement enabled them to hold their homes together. "Can you imagine a more noble task?" a settlement pamphlet of 1916 asked. But black and immigrant women might have asked who was served when they were "permitted" to leave their own children in the settlement day nursery in order to clean the houses of other women.[107]

By 1920, the settlement's domestic-help agency had become one of the most useful parts of its work. Neighborhood House was best known in Gary as a domestic agency, the superintendent admitted frankly, and people were "constantly" telephoning to ask for domestic workers. Reverend Jones explained the benefits of the program less in terms of the wages (which at $1.58 a day hardly guaranteed economic independence) than in terms of the uplift that domestic work provided to unlettered rural women. Just as the nursery could effect the reform of working-class homes, the settlement claimed, so the experience of domestic work helped to raise the standards of black women and to Americanize immigrant women, who "get a glimpse into American homes and are able to learn from them as well as receive pay for their services."[108]

As for the immigrants, by 1929 the alchemy of Americanization was working. A survey of the foreign-born conducted by Gary's International Institute in 1929 contained questions directed specifically to immigrant women. "Are the homes here better or not so good? Are the women happier in their homes than in their home country or not? Why?" were among the questions asked of a number of leaders from the various ethnic groups.[109]

In responding, many immigrant women spoke of improved material conditions in America. The homes had "more luxuries and comforts," a Polish lawyer told one investigator, and a spokeswoman for the Greek community described their living conditions as "much better, more conveniences and necessities."[110] Other women mentioned experiencing improved status in America. Polish women were happier in America than they had been in Poland, another investigator was told, "because they do not feel so dependent on their husband and would be taken care of if something happened to their husband." Twenty-five Greek women who had taken out citizenship boldly named their goals as "to better themselves and become more independent."[111]

These were changes that social settlements and other Americanizing agencies encouraged. When the settlement house invited women to clubs and classes, advised them on marital troubles, and offered shelter in cases of domestic violence, it was intervening within the traditional, patriarchal family. Immigrant husbands sometimes actively opposed their wives' participation in settlement activities. The director of a Gary night school told how "the husband of one [immigrant woman] . . . happened to come one evening and, discovering that his wife was there using the facilities of the gymnasium and the swimming pool, ordered her to go home. But he himself immediately went into the gymnasium."[112]

Incidents like this are more than amusing anecdotes. They show Americanization going beyond changes in clothing, language, and table manners to involve shifts in the balance of power in the family. Among the Mexicans, for example, conflict resulted when the wife sought new opportunities and status. Neighborhood House workers in the thirties noted, "The husband brings Old World ideas of the place of his wife in the home, while the new environment of the American city is conductive [sic] to the desire for more freedom for the wife."

Neighborhood House worked with the public schools, the Public Welfare Department, and other agencies to effect "satisfactory adjustments" in these cases. Often these adjustments must have meant the lessening of men's power over women and children.[113] Settlement-house activities for different members of the family already acted to erode immigrants' traditional culture. In the song *El Enganchado* (The Contract Laborer), a Mexican husband expressed his disgust at the change America had wrought in his wife and family:

> Even my old woman has changed on me—
> She wears a bob-tailed dress of silk,
> Goes about painted like a piñata
> And goes at night to the dancing hall.

> My kids speak perfect English
> And have no use for our Spanish.
> They call me "fader" and don't work,
> And are crazy about the Charleston.[114]

The settlements may have been advocates for immigrant women's rights, but immigrant women did not flock to them for leisure or recreation. Few abandoned their traditional leisure activities—visiting with neighbors, friends, and relatives, sewing, talking—in order to attend Americanization classes. In fact, for immigrant women and their daughters escaping patriarchal power at home, commercial leisure, movies, and dance halls had more to offer than the awkward, half-understood exchanges with well-meaning Americanizers at the settlement house. And immigrant women who did come to use what the settlement offered had to balance the opportunities for Americanization against the controls that it implied—controls that the commercial culture was urging them to discard.[115]

Sewing classes, day care, mothers' clubs, and cooking classes have brought us far from the concerns of the steel company. And yet, in a way, the settlements, by contributing to the Americanization of the immigrant woman, were part of that larger process of homogenization and the obtaining of consent that marked the 1920s as a crucial transition to the unchallenged hegemony of corporate capitalism.

The view that the settlements were doing the work of the steel company—that they were "the servants of power"—must be qualified by two important reservations. First, immigrant women were more than just the objects of the social controllers: their needs, tastes, and preferences helped to shape the programs of the social agencies. Immigrant women were opportunistic about the settlement's programs, and settlement workers, for their part, learned to compromise. Second, running as a counterpoint in the discourse about social control and Americanization was a theme that bound social workers as women with their clients who were also women. Settlements like Neighborhood House were not feminist institutions, if by that term we mean that the settlements worked to individualize working-class women, making them equal to men. They *were* feminist if we take that term to mean that the settlements recognized women as a separate class of persons with common experiences and needs and sought to improve their conditions *as women.*[116]

Ties of gender bound controllers and controlled, even when class and color separated them. If American settlement workers often had unrealistic expectations of immigrant women—misunderstandings over boarding and lodging, diet, or the use of liquor—at the same time individual settlement workers came to admire immigrant women for their strength and resourcefulness. Living amid the dirt and poverty of the South Side, the settlement workers knew firsthand about the struggles of working-class housewives. At a period when many men worked a twelve-hour day in the mills, working-class women also bore a heavy burden at home. As a result, along with the tone of irritation at immigrants' bad habits and ignorance, a note of undisguised admiration comes through in the writings of the social workers. "These women do so many things for themselves that American women have long ago given up," Edna Hatfield Edmondson wrote. "They bake their own bread, half-sole their children's shoes, make their own sauerkraut in the fall. . . . Many of them make beautiful crocheted lace, executing the most intricate patterns."[117] And Grace Warmington wrote the following appreciation of immigrant mothers:

> There are no other groups of people that I have ever known that can compare with some of these foreign mothers. Admitting their ignorance, their pitiful weakness, the dirt in which they often live, the drinking in so many cases, . . . You see these women standing up under the blows of fate, holding up their children, holding up their families, working themselves to death in the space of a few years for those children.[118]

As for the slogan "Give Them Home Life," there was no need for the settlements or the steel company to preach about the joys of an "American home" to immigrants who, more than native-born Americans, black or white, were purchasing homes in ever-increasing numbers and beginning to catch just a glimpse of the American dream.[119] What *was* still to be decided was the structure of this Americanized family in its privatized dream house, and particularly the woman's place within it. Some scholars have suggested that the settlements, and other welfare agencies, public and private, by chipping away at the patriarchal relations within immigrant and other working-class families, were helping to level the working-class family, laying it open and defenseless before the greater patriarchy of the corporate state. Although the dimensions of this important change lie outside the scope of this study, it is important to note that the legal changes rescuing women as individuals from their husbands' authority would result in women exchanging the authority of domestic patriarchy for that of "the State as Parent."[120]

CHAPTER SIX

"A Splendid Investment": Gary-Alerding Settlement House and Catholic Americanization

I might speak to you of Father de Ville, and over here Dr. Seaman, and many other gentlemen whose work is our work.
—Elbert Gary, chairman, United
States Steel Corporation, public
address, Gary, Indiana, June
1922

By 1920, there were two settlement houses in Gary, Indiana, actively engaged in Americanization and in religious social work among the city's foreign-born population—Campbell House and Neighborhood House. From 1920 on, the percentage of foreigners in Gary began to decline, falling from about 30 percent of the total in 1920 to about 20 percent in 1930 (see Table 6).[1] During this decade, the Gary schools were having an important Americanizing impact, rendering the children of immigrants and of American-born parents practically indistinguishable from each other. The school system was "training 6,000 children daily to salute the flag and revere the great leaders of America," an observer noted in 1923. It had been "immensely effective in producing Americanism."[2]

Despite the ending of European immigration the pace and urgency of Americanization in Gary increased after 1920. Gary's Americanization campaign, previously identified with Protestant denominations, was led in the 1920s by a Catholic priest, Rev. John B. de Ville, who played the part of intermediary between the Catholic hierarchy and the steel corporation. His efforts led to the building in 1923 of the largest and most elaborate of the city's settlement houses, Gary-Alerding Settlement House, an agency named jointly for Elbert Gary, head of the steel corporation, and Herman Alerding, bishop of the Fort Wayne Diocese.

In order to understand these developments it is necessary to go back to 1913, when the city was only seven years old. In this year, the steel-corporation managers in Gary began to extend financial support to the clergy, assuming the mortgages of a number of churches. This alliance soon bore fruit, for the clergy's support in the election of that year helped the mill party defeat its opponents in the Democratic party, led by the Knotts brothers.[3] Subsequently, cooperation between the churches and mill officials would be an accepted feature of the city's political life.

It was especially important for mill managers to establish a working relationship with Gary's Catholic leaders in view of the strength of Catholicism in Gary. Although the polyglot population included numbers of Orthodox believers, Jews, and a variety of Protestants, Roman Catholics were a majority. In Lake County, where Gary was located, 64 percent of church members described themselves as Catholic in 1916.[4]

From the point of view of the steel corporation it made more sense to support a Catholic agency of Americanization than the two existing Protestant settlement houses, Campbell House and Neighborhood House, since the Protestant agencies tended to tie Americanization to the remote, even quixotic, goal of converting Gary's Catholic and Orthodox population to Protestantism before, or in the process of, Americanizing them. This fact seriously limited their effectiveness as Americanizing agencies.

A much more effective campaign for Americanization could be conducted in Gary if only the city's Catholics could be kept, or reconfirmed, in their traditional faith and if only the company could secure the cooperation of Catholic priests and bishops.

United States Steel officials also sought control in Gary, but they did not want direct political involvement—some critics called it power without responsibility.[5] The essential thing for the corporation was to have a situation of stability that would ensure the uninterrupted operation of the mills and the continuing profitability of steelmaking. With 20,000 men on its payroll in Gary in 1916, U.S. Steel and its subsidiaries were prepared to make an investment in Gary's churches for the sake of stability.[6] William P. Gleason, superintendent of the Gary Works of U.S. Steel, must have had this kind of consideration in mind when he approached the bishop of Fort Wayne, Herman J. Alerding, in 1913, and asked him to organize a social-work agency for Gary's Catholics.[7]

The Catholic hierarchy also sought some control over the situation in the steel town. Immigrant Catholics had been quick to begin schools and establish congregations where they worshiped in their own languages. These democratic, lay efforts served the immigrants as a defense of cultural values, while aiding their adjustment to life in an American industrial environment.[8] The first Croatian parish in Gary, for example, began with the decision of thirty Croatian lay people. They secured the services of a pastor from another city and began to celebrate mass, using an empty storeroom as a church. Soon they had established a parish organization, and only after these initial steps did they inform Bishop Alerding, in Fort Wayne, requesting that he send them a permanent pastor. Similarly, Poles had their parish, St. Hedwig's, with a church and a parochial school that enrolled as many as 1,000 children during the 1920s. These institutions enabled Polish immigrants to keep the culture, language, and history of their homeland alive.[9]

Such lay efforts, although they proved the vitality of immigrant Catholicism, raised questions of authority and control which worried the hierarchy of the church. Bishop Alerding privately expressed his fears about the position of the Catholic church in Gary. The growth of the Gary population was rapid and alarming, and 60 percent of the newcomers were Catholics, he estimated.[10] The immigration of these thousands of nominal Catholics (Slavonian, Croatian, Polish, Lithuanian, and Hungarian) presented the hierarchy with the urgent but delicate task of finding priests who would be acceptable to both the church and the people and raising funds for church and school buildings. The immigrants themselves did not have the resources to support parochial establishments or buildings. "You may readily appreciate," he complained later in a letter to Cardinal Gasparri in Rome, "what a task devolved on me, as bishop, to take proper care of this multitude."[11]

Bishop Alerding was receptive when William Gleason, superintendent of the Gary Works of U.S. Steel, approached him suggesting that the steel company and the church cooperate in providing much-needed social-service and religious work in Gary. Despite poor health and advancing age, Bishop Alerding traveled to New York in March 1913; he and de Ville then met with Elbert Gary at the corporation's headquarters and discussed the situation in the steel town.[12] Returning to Fort Wayne on March 10, Alerding wrote to the head of U.S. steel, summarizing the reasons why the corporation should support the work of the church in Gary. The letter stated the terms of this cooperation and struck themes that would be repeated in their correspondence over the next decade.

After complimenting the steel-corporation chairman on building "a delightful modern city . . . ," which he called, "the wonder of the twentieth century," Bishop Alerding went on to express fears of the political consequences that might result from the tremendous and rapid growth of Gary's foreign population.

> Coming from countries that denied them the liberty American citizens enjoy, it is but natural that these foreigners should interpret liberty to be synonymous with freedom from every restraint, going from one extreme to the other. They become an easy prey to the revolutionary doctrines of economic theorists, such as the socialists . . . What wonder that under these conditions Capital and Labor, instead of being friends working hand in hand, become inimical and destructive of each others' interests.

Since a majority of the foreigners were nominally Catholic, the best method of combatting socialism was for the U.S. Steel Corporation to support the Catholic church in Gary, the bishop argued. "The organization of parishes for these foreigners would ensure peace and contentment for the city and the steel works," Alerding assured Elbert Gary.

Four national parishes should be set up to serve Gary's Catholics.

> We must organize these foreigners into parishes or congregations: a parish for each nationality, . . . supply each nationality with buildings, . . . and place over each of them a priest or pastor of the nationality of the parish. In this way we have hopes of holding them together, shielding them against evil and revolutionary influences and making of them peaceful, law-abiding citizens.

The problem was that these people were "poor laborers"—indeed, "poverty induced them to come to this country." Thus the church must "rely upon assistance from those who appreciate the importance of this work," Alerding concluded, in a thinly veiled reference to the steel corporation.[13]

The bishop's bid for the financial support of U.S. Steel was desperate. In May 1913, the church had made a similar appeal to the directors of the Inland Steel Company but had been refused. "We can look for nothing from any other source and . . . [Elbert] Gary was and is the only one," Alerding confided to de Ville.[14]

Fortunately for the bishop, important steel-company officials in Gary itself, notably Eugene Buffington, president of Illinois Steel Company, reacted favorably to the churchman's appeal.[15] Soon after the New York meeting among Elbert Gary, de Ville, and Alerding, the U.S. Steel chairman agreed to contribute $50,000 to the church in the steel city. The money was to be divided into $10,000 for each of the five national parishes: Holy Trinity for the Croatians; Sacred Heart parish for the Poles; St. Casimir for the Lithuanians; Holy Trinity for the Slovaks, and St. Emeric for the Hungarians. Historians have usually viewed the creation of the immigrant national parish as a sign of lay, democratic initiative and cultural defense. But in Gary, the steel corporation played an important part in funding national churches (as it would do in establishing the Catholic settlement house). These immigrant religious institutions were indeed a sign of "cultural defense," but they were also capable of being used by employers and the church hierarchy to increase control over the situation in the steel town.[16]

Acknowledging the donation, Bishop Alerding expressed his "heartfelt gratitude." "It is my honest conviction that your Corporation will be benefited by assisting the good work in hand in having peaceful and interested laborers in your Steel Mills," he wrote. A month later he reported to Gary, after a visit to see the progress of the foreign churches at first hand, "I have every reason to believe that the establishment of these parishes will exercise a beneficent influence on these foreigners in every respect."[17]

From the point of view of the Catholic hierarchy, however, these "national parishes" represented a compromise. By acknowledging the nationalism of the different ethnic groups—their "clannishness," as Alerding called it—the Catholic hierarchy hoped to keep them within the fold until a more complete assimilation could occur. "We must deal with them as we find them," he wrote, "Catholic in religion and foreign in their various nationalities."[18] The immigrant churches were necessary for social peace, but they were hardly vehicles of Americanization—in fact, they helped to keep foreign language and culture alive in Gary.[19] In 1917, when Americanization became urgent, the bishop would begin a new initiative, aiming at a more efficient Americanization of the foreign-born in Gary.

At the same time as the Catholic church was struggling with the problems caused by the rapid expansion of the immigrant population, the steel corporation in Gary was working to Americanize its labor force. Some foreign-born workers came to Gary's steel mills from the industries and mills of Chicago or the Pennsylvania region.[20] But the majority were peasants who faced problems of adapting to urban living and industrial work in America. For example, 70 percent of 2,602 Polish iron and steel workers interviewed listed their previous occupation as agriculture.[21] Through Americanization classes in the plants and Americanization programs such as those offered by settlement houses in the community, the steel corporation was trying to increase the efficiency of workers already employed, to attract and hold "steady" workers, and to combat unions. Americanization and in-plant "welfare" policies were thus part of the same policy: settlement work with workers' families and similar community efforts served to amplify the in-plant Americanization programs.[22]

Like other large manufacturing organizations of the time, U.S. Steel Company in Gary had in-plant English classes for its employees. Iron-and-steel manufacturers gave strong verbal support to programs of Americanization. Some manufacturers even called for legislation to make night-school attendance for employees compulsory.[23] Illiterate or foreign-speaking workers meant as much as a 10 percent reduction in a plant's efficiency, according to one expert in industrial relations. "Think of a large factory with nearly nine tenths of the employees foreigners and not an interpreter in the place. Consider another case with no foreign-speaking foreman and no English-speaking workmen, both just blundering through their jobs." As it was, many foremen could only communicate with workers by shouting, cursing, and gesticulating.[24]

Increased efficiency and more plant safety would follow if only workers could speak English, promoters of Americanization argued. Between 1912 and 1919, U.S. Steel spent between $500,000 and $1 million annually on accident prevention, part of which went toward classes in the mills. The results were a dramatic decrease in accidents: nationally, the numbers of serious and fatal accidents were about half in 1919 of what they had been in 1906, "We have saved 25,853 men from serious or fatal injury," Charles Close, manager of the Bureau of Safety, Sanitation and Welfare, declared in 1919.[25]

U.S. Steel also expected political benefits from its Americanization programs. Americanizers argued that English-speaking employees were more open to the appeals of their employers, whereas foreign-speaking ones were vulnerable to the arguments of those who sought to spread "radical" ideas and to cause labor troubles. Education in the English language and American ideals would enable aliens "to meet the arguments of agitators who prey upon ignorance of the English tongue and American conditions," an editorial in the *Iron Age* said in 1913.[26] Employers hoped that eventually the public schools would provide Americanization classes; meanwhile, they shouldered the burden themselves, for until their workers could speak English there could not occur what one writer called that "assimilation to American ideals and the shaping of the foreigners' conceptions of human relations and rights to what they are generally recognized to be here."[27]

The war added a sense of urgency to the problem of Americanizing employees. "Now is the time to enlist every agency for the spread of our language and all the ideals that follow in its trail," declared a writer in the *Iron Age* in December 1918.

> For language is the primary contact of the foreigner with our institutions. Without the language he is . . . a source of danger to himself and to all others in our industrial plants. Production halts because of his ignorance. Accidents thrive by reason of his deafness to words of instruction. He is not of us unless he knows. Until that time arrives, he cannot be for us and for what is meant by our flag.[28]

Americanization was also promoted as an answer to the wartime problem of labor turnover. Americanization was a "stabilizer of labor," industrial-relations experts agreed. "To minimize turnover is to increase the number of employees who will become more permanently connected with an individual concern . . . This means decreased restiveness and increased loyalty."[29] The estimated cost of replacing every worker with a new one was as high as $300, said industrial-relations expert Magnus Alexander; in order to employ 6,697 men in a factory labor force, Alexander estimated, it had been necessary to hire 42,570.[30]

By 1917, Americanization had become so urgent that Bishop Alerding began a new initiative among Gary's Catholic immigrants. The bishop and

steel officials now supported the idea of a settlement house, an agency outside the parish structure, and one that would combine a propaganda of religion and patriotism with useful services to Catholic parishioners.

By 1917, both the Catholic church and the steel-corporation officials
had, for their own reasons, come to accept the need for programs of Americanization. Between 1917 and the 1920s, Americanization became a joint
preoccupation as the bishop attempted to absorb the city's foreign churches,
and as the company pursued the last labor "radical" out of Gary in the wake
of the failed steel strike of 1919.

The new initiative began with the visit to Bishop Alerding in Fort
Wayne of a delegation headed by steel-company superintendent William
Gleason and Reverend Jansen, pastor of the Polish Holy Angels Parish, a
beneficiary since 1913 of steel-company generosity. They made an urgent
representation to Bishop Alerding, citing the rapid growth of the city and
the increasing number of nominally Catholic foreigners in Gary. Eighty percent of all the Polish people in Indiana now lived in Lake County, the
delegation pointed out. The situation was such as "to challenge the attention and earnest consideration of the Catholic Church."

> These people are nearly all Catholic, but, being unfamiliar with Ameri-
> can ways and customs, are not as closely allied with the Church and her
> teachings as they should be. They are easily influenced to regard their
> religion lightly because the Catholic Church has not interested herself in
> their social and spiritual welfare, sufficiently, to make of them faithful
> Catholics and useful citizens.[31]

When the committee asked Bishop Alerding for his support in establishing
several Catholic settlement houses, the bishop agreed. The situation in
Gary was one that the church must address, he wrote in a memorandum
probably intended for Gary's priests. Protestant denominations had become
aggressive in their activities among the foreigners, "establishing community
centers in the form of settlement houses where children and their parents
are, by degrees, led to disregard the teachings of their faith, and, under the
guise of kindness and helpfulness, are gradually believing that Catholicity is
un-American."[32] Thousands of Gary's Catholic children, he went on, were
attending public schools—there were 1,800 Catholics in one public school
alone. These children received no instruction in Catholic doctrine, and
after school large numbers of them went to the Protestant settlement house
near the school to take baths and showers and to enjoy games and club
activities.

The situation was urgent, and the solution lay at hand. "We must take
care of our people," Alerding declared. A Catholic settlement house would
be a place for "instructive and innocent amusement" in the immigrant's

own neighborhood. It should contain "all the facilities lacking in the homes of the people for whose benefit the work is undertaken."[33]

It would be five years before the Gary-Alerding Settlement House, the realization of this dream, was built. And the intervening years were hard on Gary's immigrants. The atmosphere of perfervid nationalism revitalized the Protestant settlement houses, Neighborhood House and Campbell House. They had been quietly working on Americanization, but now their work seemed to take on a new importance. Neighborhood House was not just helping poor people: its task was "the Making of Americans," the settlement's literature proclaimed, while Campbell House described its work as innoculating new Americans against the germs of radicalism and welcoming them into "an American Church" as well as into American citizenship.[34]

Bishop Alerding viewed the activities of the Protestant agencies with concern. Gary was "a hotbed of proselytism," he wrote to Rev. J. S. Burke, chairman of the Catholic Welfare Council, "and something should be done to counteract its venomous influence."[35] That "something" was the appointment of Rev. John B. de Ville in 1919 to lead a Catholic Americanization drive, which through meetings, classes, and the showing of patriotic films would reassert the leadership of the church in Gary and reaffirm its commitment to "Americanism."

The success of de Ville's campaign owed much to types of organization that had emerged during the wartime drives for loyalty and patriotism in Gary. In the frenzied activity of 1918, organizations such as the Red Cross and the Calumet Township Council of Defense had risen to the challenge of winning the war "At Home." They had reached out into the whole community with fund drives and propaganda, raising enormous amounts of money for the war effort. In the atmosphere of emergency, Gary's civic, industrial, and ethnic leaders formed associations that would in many cases carry on into the postwar period. The Red Cross committee after the war, for example, was composed of the triumvirate—H. B. Norton, Ralph Snyder, and A. B. Dickson—representing, respectively, the steel corporation, the press, and the YMCA. And when a General Relief Committee was formed during the 1920–21 depression, it was composed of social workers employed both in the mills and in the city. This later became a permanent City Welfare Association. The cooperation of steel-mill officials with community and church leaders was becoming a permanent feature of Gary life.[36]

During the various bond drives of 1918, Gary's ethnic groups had been organized under "captains." Thus, when the Americanization campaign under Reverend de Ville began in November 1919, it found a civic leadership already self-conscious and experienced. Catholic Americanization in Gary between 1919 and 1923 used the same techniques as the wartime bond drives and worked with businessmen who had been active during the loyalty campaigns. The Rotary Club was a major backer of the Catholic Americanization drive and raised much of the money for the settlement house. But whereas wartime propaganda had been directed against the "Hun," now the targets were Bolsheviks and Socialists, enemies doubly dangerous to Catholics since they were both radical and atheistic.[37]

The steel strike that began on September 22, 1919, pursued the moderate goals of better wages, an end to the twelve-hour day in steelmaking, and the right to collective bargaining.[38] However, Gary's mill managers portrayed it as a radical insurgency that proved beyond the shadow of a doubt the dangers of a town full of unassimilated aliens. Foreign radicals were blamed for instigating the strike, and there were alarming rumors of Bolshevik plots hatched on the South Side by wild-eyed anarchists. Though these rumors were unsubstantiated, they provoked a defensive response from the self-proclaimed forces of law and order. In September 1919, the nativist Loyal American League was formed. This vigilante group of businessmen and war veterans was a revived form of the anti-German American Protective League of 1918. In October the mayor of Gary, frightened by a series of parades and strike meetings, called in the state militia, and when fighting broke out between strikers and strikebreakers on October 7, he requested federal troops. Although the strike was not formally called off until January 8, 1920, by the end of November 1919 the mills were estimated to be working at 90 percent capacity. Gary resembled an armed camp, and an uneasy peace reigned.[39]

This was the situation in November 1919 when Rev. John de Ville arrived in Gary to lead the Americanization campaign among the city's foreign Catholics and to found the settlement house. He was well equipped by experience and background for the task. Born in the Austrian Tyrol in 1873, de Ville spoke Italian, French, and German as well as English. He had received an education in classics at Trento and in theology in Rome before emigrating to the United States at the age of nineteen. He studied for the priesthood at St. Bonaventure's College, Albany, New York, and spent the next twelve years organizing and starting parishes among immigrant coal miners in Western Pennsylvania. After working in Chicago, de Ville was an assistant at Holy Angels Church in Gary during 1909 before going to Huntington, Indiana, to be assistant editor of the new and enormously successful Catholic paper, *Our Sunday Visitor.* Founded by Rev. John F. Noll in 1912, this paper was intended as the church's answer to the rampant socialism and secularism that were the twentieth century's challenge to religion.[40]

The outbreak of war in Europe drew de Ville into a different field. Between 1914 and 1917 he was active in occupied Belgium, arranging the transport of over 1,500 Belgian refugees to the United States, but with the entry of the United States into the war, these activities became too dangerous. De Ville spent 1917 and 1918 traveling across the United States, speaking on behalf of Belgian refugees and appealing for Liberty Bonds. When he arrived in Gary in the fall of 1919 to take on his new task, de Ville was already a celebrity, with a reputation for courage and a cosmopolitan aura. He was a scholar, a priest, a social worker, a propagandist, and a fighter for the Faith.[41]

Installed in an office at 664 Broadway, de Ville began the Americanization work that he called "the Gary Americanization and Social Settlement Endeavors." He directed a Catholic Instruction League where 2,400 children who did not attend parochial schools received religious instruction. Meetings, classes, and films created a strong propaganda for Americanization among the immigrants. The league's work increased until it occupied six centers, "situated conveniently near the new public schools," and included 4,000 children. The league also did some relief work, especially during the postwar depression, and helped Gary families with immigrant problems such as the detention of relatives at Ellis Island.[42]

But it was understood that the benefits of de Ville's work were political as much as spiritual or social. The Catholic Instruction League and the Americanization program were not agencies of conversion, a church publication claimed. Rather, they were "of the utmost value in counteracting the socialistic and bolshevistic tendencies of certain elements among the foreigners who constitute the majority of the inhabitants of Gary."[43] And although the Gary *Daily Tribune* quoted de Ville as saying that Americanization was "a purely educational affair," the newspaper's detached tone was belied by the strident headline that proclaimed, "Great Move for Loyalty Under Way."[44]

Like wartime campaigns for patriotism, the postwar Americanization campaign superficially recognized ethnic separatism but in fact aimed at conformity. Since Gary's ethnic groups grounded their identity in their affiliation with ethnic churches, foreign-language and parochial schools, and ethnic associations, the strategy of the Americanization program was to approach them through these organizations. The flocks were to be rounded up separately, only to be shepherded, in the end, into the fold of Americanism. De Ville explained this in an interview published by Illinois Steel Company's *Gary Works Circle* in 1920. "We are getting each race together in groups," he stated. The "officers" of each group composed a "cabinet," or federation of groups, watched over by a committee of prominent citizens. By this arrangement national leaders were kept in touch with "Americanism." At the same time, "Through the leaders, who are selected from the brightest minds of each nationality, a community can keep in touch with its foreign population." Gary's ethnic churches and associations were providing their members with educational, charitable, and religious services. To be successful, the Catholic settlement house must duplicate these services or better them. The Catholic settlement movement represented a move to co-opt the social and service functions of the existing Catholic organizations in Gary and to extend these services to Catholic immigrants, such as the Mexicans, who had previously been excluded from them.[45]

While de Ville's Americanization plan offered a broad tolerance of cultural differences, it demanded absolute political conformity. As an immigrant, de Ville understood the affection that immigrants held for their native country and language.

> The trouble with many Americanizers is that they begin by telling the foreigner to stop speaking in his native tongue and cease reading foreign newspapers. The foreigner who comes here at a mature age is naturally attached to the language of his native country . . . Our Americans living abroad love to get together to speak English and read American newspapers and magazines.[46]

It was not necessary for foreigners to forget their mother tongue in order to become Americanized, de Ville insisted.

> In fact, one who could so easily forget his affection for the country where he was born and raised would make a very poor citizen . . . One does not need to sacrifice love and adoration for his mother to become a good husband or father.

What was essential was "the absolute necessity of renouncing allegiance to foreign powers," de Ville wrote, and this was to be the basis for the Americanization program in Gary.[47] To be American was to accept and love America's ideals and institutions. Despite de Ville's tolerance of cultural diversity, there was no room for political dissent in his view.

The Catholic settlement house was to be the keystone of the Americanization program for Gary's Catholics and a symbol of political and religious orthodoxy. De Ville turned to Bishop Alerding, requesting help with financing the settlement, and on March 6, the bishop assured de Ville of his support. "The Gary Americanization and Social Settlement Endeavors, under Catholic auspices . . . has my cordial approval and best wishes," he wrote. "You can rely on me for whatever it may be in my power to do for the noble purposes of this praiseworthy undertaking."[48] Alerding was as good as his word. A week later he addressed a letter to "The Honorable Elbert Gary, New York," "commending most highly the establishment of a recreational and educational center for our foreigners of Gary, which de Ville . . . and his associates have been trying to establish." Not only would the settlement house do much for the "mental improvement" of the foreigners, Alerding pointed out, but "under Father de Ville's wise guidance, it will also result in more and more amicable relations between employer and employee."[49]

The timing was good for an appeal to the corporation. Two months after the end of the long and bitter steel strike the corporation still had not made any concessions to labor. It had neither ended the twelve-hour day nor recognized the unions. During the strike, the churches had been either friendly to the corporation or neutral, but now America's religious leaders were calling for capital to make some concessions to the just demands of labor. In an editorial entitled "The Bolshevik, the Socialist and the Remedy," the *Indiana Catholic and Record* warned, "It is not enough to rave and scream in denunciation of Socialism and Bolsheviki spirit. Something must be done to remove the causes of discontent and to give the working masses hope. It is of no use to raise wages 50 per cent if the cost of living has been raised 100 per cent."[50]

In response to the public outcry about conditions in steelmaking, and in order to mollify its critics and improve its image, the corporation now began what one historian has called a "flurry of welfare efforts." It is in this context that the corporation agreed to Bishop Alerding's suggestion that it support the building up of the Catholic churches in Gary as part of the social "reconstruction" in that city.[51]

But financial times were bad for steel, and with steel prices falling disastrously low, Alerding's first appeal went unanswered.[52] In October 1920, he again asked help from Elbert Gary, this time for the five parishes that had received U.S. Steel money in 1913. The steel corporation should consider the benefits of ensuring the financial stability of these foreign churches, the bishop wrote, since "together the five parishes comprise a large percentage of the population of Gary." The corporation would only be acting in its own interests. "They are all quiet, law-abiding citizens. Citizens of that class are an important asset for business," Alerding pointed out. And if the city of Gary had returned to tranquility after the strike, "the establishment of these parishes has been largely instrumental in bringing about the desired result." Let there be no doubt: the U.S. Steel Corporation's gift of $50,000 in 1913 had been "a profitable investment." Gary's Catholics could not be expected to support their own parishes. Not only were they too poor, but also they came, in many cases, from countries where the church was state-supported. "May these parishes have still further reasons to thank God and implore His blessing on the future of the United States Steel Corporation," the prelate concluded.[53]

Staunch Methodist though he was, Elbert Gary was moved. In February 1921, Alerding wrote jubilantly to de Ville, "I have received the long-expected check for $100,000 from Mr. Gary." Thirty thousand dollars of the donation was for de Ville's own use. It was earmarked for a church for the Mexican, Italian, and Spanish people in Gary, the planned first phase of the settlement house.[54]

Yet the donation fell short of what he had hoped for, and de Ville led an aggressive fund-raising campaign during 1922 to supplement it. Again he could count on influential allies in the community. From headquarters in the Gary Hotel, and helped by a committee that included representatives of over forty businesses as well as prominent professional people, de Ville raised $30,000 by October 1922.[55] The Gary *Post Tribune* commented, "The appeal of the settlement house is one of the strongest ever presented to the citizens of this city and one of the most powerful campaign organizations ever seen here is being assembled to carry on the work of solicitation."[56]

The settlement house would not duplicate existing institutions such as the Red Cross, the YMCA, or the recently established International Institute, its supporters promised. Instead, it would be a "dispensing point" for Americanization and social services. Its name would signal the cooperation of company and church that had brought it about.[57]

Meanwhile de Ville's relations with Gary's business leaders continued to be close; his work in Gary was understood to have the support of the corporation. When Judge Gary visited the steel town in 1922, he referred in a speech to Reverend de Ville and Dr. Seaman as "gentlemen whose work is our work." De Ville returned Judge Gary's confidence. He became an outspoken defender of the corporation; when a *Chicago Tribune* writer attacked Elbert Gary because of his refusal to end the twelve-hour day in steel, de Ville wrote an open letter defending the U.S. Steel chairman in his indefensible stand against shorter hours.[58]

In March 1923, de Ville announced plans for the settlement-house building at 17th Street and Van Buren Avenue, near the Froebel School. The cost was estimated at $75,000.[59] Plans for the building grew more elaborate as de Ville's hopes of securing more money from the corporation grew brighter. Privately during 1923, de Ville and Alerding were still angling for more steel-corporation money.[60]

By 1923, a sharply improved economic situation prevailed in steel. The city of Gary was riding on a crest of prosperity because the abolition of the "Pittsburgh plus" pricing system made its products more competitive.[61] Postwar labor problems had been especially acute with the ending of unrestricted European immigration. But now the corporation turned to southern blacks and Mexican immigrants to fill its demand for unskilled labor. Mexicans in Gary numbered only 166 in 1920, but by 1930 there were 3,486. By 1928, they comprised 6.4 percent of the Illinois Steel work force in Gary and 8.6 percent of the work force at Gary's Tin Mill.[62]

The Mexicans, although at first largely comprised of single men, *solos*, constituted a new ethnic community in Gary and a new Catholic group.

Excluded from other Catholic churches in the region, Mexicans were a people in search of a parish. They also badly needed the helpful social services of a settlement house, yet they were faced with discrimination everywhere. The press increased hostility toward the Mexicans by publishing lurid articles linking them with vice and crime (while ignoring positive features of Mexican community life); moreover, stories about poor health and living conditions put the Mexicans' suitability for assimilation in further doubt. De Ville deplored the presence of communists among them.[63] The steel-corporation chairman must have been convinced of the desirability of building the settlement house to serve this problematic new immigrant people, for some time during 1923, de Ville received from Gary a check for an additional $100,000.[64]

These important donations allowed the Catholic hierarchy to finalize its plans for the settlement house. The building when completed was an elaborate one, containing forty rooms; on the ground floor there were classrooms and a bowling alley, pool and billiard tables, and showers for boys and girls. There was a large auditorium, which doubled as a gym and was placed at the disposal of all Gary's parishes for concerts, meetings, and dances. The second floor housed a clinic staffed by doctors and nurses from Mercy Hospital, and upstairs also were living quarters for the Sisters Catechists and other paid settlement workers. Father de Ville had "an attractive residence" attached. The settlement house was also the heart of a new parish, Our Lady of Guadalupe, the first Mexican parish in the Midwest. St. Anthony's Chapel, attached to the settlement house, welcomed Mexican, Spanish, and Italian worshipers who had previously had no church in Gary.[65]

Gary-Alerding settlement incorporated many of the features of what could be called a "classic" settlement house: its Italianate porches, where, de Ville hoped, children from nearby tenements would shelter and play, could serve to tempt children inside and into the influence of the house. Inside, de Ville, an aesthete and avid collector, arranged many beautiful objects, old books, prints, and paintings, many of which were the gifts of grateful Belgian friends. He also placed on display an educational exhibit of war relics that he had shipped from Belgium in 1923. "You know how I loved to be surrounded by beautiful things," the priest later wrote to a Gary friend when he was ill in Italy. "When I built the Judge Gary-Bishop Alerding Settlement at Gary, I filled it with such objects . . . I convinced myself that those refining influences would have a good effect upon the boys and girls of the working classes that would frequent it and that I could develop latent artistic tendencies in some of them."[66] De Ville need not have been apologetic, for he followed in a settlement tradition by then thirty years old. In 1889, Jane Addams had taken pleasure in arranging in Hull House some good pieces of "family mahogany," furnishing the settlement house so as to awaken the interest of its working-class visitors in art and a higher culture.[67] To de Ville, however, the elaborate fittings of the settlement recalled the fact that the building later became an expensive liability.

The settlement house opened in December 1923 in an atmosphere of wild celebration and well-engineered hoopla. It resembled a political-campaign celebration more than anything. To mark the occasion, a circus came to town. All Gary residents, "regardless of religious or other affiliations," were invited to take part in a week of celebration. Thirty dollars in gold was given away every night in prizes and, to top it all, a Rickenbacker automobile. Great crowds came to the circus to enjoy the animal and pony performances and "high class musical acts" on the stage of the Gary-Alerding House assembly room.[68]

But a thoughtful observer would have found more significant the settlement's dedication ceremony five months later in May 1924, a day when religious and political symbols combined and merged in one great celebration of faith in God and America. Fortunately, Gary's most famous journalist, Tom Cannon, left a vivid account of the day's proceedings.

First there was the parade. Nothing like it had been seen since the great parades of wartime. "Led by a platoon of Police, and the Salvation Army band . . . the men's organizations of the Polish, Hungarian, Slavish, Lithuanian, Italian, Spanish and Croatian churches with their bands and banners, were followed by the Knights of Columbus and the Catholic Order of Foresters."[69]

This great procession, representing the diversity within unity of Gary Catholicism, was watched by the visiting clergy from the balconies of the Commercial Club. For the moment, the representatives of Gary Catholicism enjoyed their position as the guests and allies of Gary's business leaders, scores of whom attended the proceedings. William Gleason, representing U.S. Steel, was present, and many mill superintendents marched in the procession or went in automobiles to the dedication. The alliance of business and church was referred to many times in the speeches of that day.

When the procession at last reached the settlement house at 16th Street and Van Buren, it became obvious that the crowds were too large for the auditorium. The speakers therefore improvised, going up to a roof garden and addressing the crowd, estimated at 25,000 from there. Tom Cannon caught the spirit of the moment:

> A sea of upturned faces; scores of American flags fluttering in the breeze; the tramp of thousands of marchers; the music of a quartet of bands; the chanting of the impressive litanies of the church by full-gowned priests and white-robed choristers; the fervency and enthusiasm of the dedication ceremony—all these marked the consecration of what is planned to be a melting pot wherein all nationalities are to be fused into an indissoluble bulwark of American patriotism.

A speech from Elbert Gary, read in his absence by Captain Norton, emphasized the theme of Catholic Americanization.

> If the foreign-born people who have come to our shore can be kept in the faith of their forefathers in the lands from which they came, this country will remain safe from enemies within as well as from enemies without. That is the purpose of this institution—to keep these people to their ancient faith, to make Christians as well as Americans out of them. In doing that, this building will be a splendid investment, and it will be repaid an hundred fold.[70]

And in the formal dedication address, a speech marked by hyperbole and complete with references to Motherhood and Abraham Lincoln, Father Seidenberg, a prominent Catholic liberal, emphasized again the alliance of church and industry. "The names of the two men who built the settlement are sufficient guarantee of its high purpose," he declared. "One is the head of one of the greatest industrial corporations in the world. The other is the head of this Catholic diocese. One is working for the betterment of world conditions and the other is working for the betterment of spiritual conditions. Both are engaged in a holy cause" (see Figure 12). Bishop Alerding struck the same theme in his speech. The settlement house was one of the "greatest monuments of the Church," he said, "because it represents the unity of industrial and spiritual activities in a common cause."[71]

But in reality the alliance between the churches and the steel corporation, produced by the extraordinary events of the war, the strike, and the Red Scare, could not be sustained. By the late twenties, Americanization no longer carried the sense of urgency that it had in 1920. Mass European immigration stopped in 1924. In Gary as elsewhere, many immigrants achieved promotion into the ranks of skilled labor, bought homes and businesses, and became pillars of the community.[72]

At the same time, American employers were turning away from paternalistic types of welfare capitalism including involvement in community work. While the level of financial involvement of corporations in social work was maintained or even increased after the World War, the style of involvement began to change; Community Chests replaced the variety of ad hoc committees that had administered "welfare" for businesses in America's cities. Gary's industries continued to support, and direct, social agencies in the city. In fact in 1929, 14 percent of the contributors to the city's social agencies provided nearly 74 percent of their funding.[73] But intervention was cautious. Tempers were high because of the 1919 strike, and opposition to anything smacking of paternalism in Gary was so great that even the company's announcement of a generous and elaborate park plan for Gary was viewed with suspicion and hostility.[74] Welfare work in the mills, too, was downplayed. In 1922, an editorial in the *Iron Age* was referring to a general

Figure 12. The dedication tablet for Gary-Alerding Settlement House symbolized the partnership of the steel corporation and the Catholic church in Gary in the 1920s. Courtesy of the Gary Public Library.

"liquidation of welfare work in industrial establishments" in the wake of the depression. At a conference on industrial relations in 1920, the president of the Chicago Link Belt Company declared that welfare work had been "overdone." "The proper relationship between employer and employee was a business relationship," he said.[75] Workers did not want a bathtub put into a company clubhouse for their use, agreed a labor-union leader at the same meeting. They wanted sufficient wages to put a bathtub into their own homes.[76]

Having given a major donation of $100,000 to the Gary-Alerding Settlement, U.S. Steel officials were not willing to give more. When, sometime after 1924, Reverend de Ville appealed for a further $30,000 to complete the chapel, U.S. Steel officials attached to the donation the written rider that this appeal to the corporation would be the last. And when de Ville again approached the steel corporation asking for financial support, a steel-company executive merely opened the files and drew out the previous agreement. Direct steel-company involvement with the agency was at an end.[77]

Moreover, death soon removed all those who had been the promoters of the settlement house. Elbert Gary, a distant but benevolent patron, died in 1927. Bishop Alerding was killed in an automobile accident in November 1924, and his successor, Bishop John Noll, was much less enthusiastic about the Gary project. The settlement house, a handsome and elaborate building, expensively equipped, became a thorn in his side that he described in his *History of the Diocese* as "an immense burden on the diocese." Indeed the agency was a serious financial liability, carrying a debt at the time of Alerding's death of over $200,000.[78]

De Ville, now a Gary celebrity, continued to direct the settlement's activities until illness forced his retirement in 1930. Mexicans made up the majority of those who used the settlement house and attended religious observances in St. Anthony's Chapel. Their children took part in the recreational and club programs. Mexican women attended nursing and sewing classes.[79] De Ville not only directed the agency but also entertained and entranced Gary audiences with speeches on a variety of subjects. Increasingly, though, he dwelt on the declining morals of the age, parental neglect of children, the dangers of socialism.[80]

The settlement remained closely identified with the corporation, as its name suggested. And that close identification doubtless prevented Mexican laborers and steelworkers from feeling that the settlement truly expressed their own political or cultural aspirations. Not only had lay initiative been notably lacking in the establishment of the Mexican church and community house, but de Ville also continued to be an apologist for the corporation and to defend the steel corporation against its critics. "I think that loyalty to those who are responsible for the creation of Gary should be the first requisite," he said on one occasion. "There is a disposition in many quarters to find fault, to suspect selfish motives . . . in everything the Corporation and its officials do concerning their interest in Gary's civic, social and business activities. Any fairminded individual ought to realize that without such help and leadership, Gary would not be what it is today. Such cooperation we should welcome and not criticize."[81]

De Ville's enthusiasm for the steel corporation was not matched by enthusiasm for his Mexican parishioners, however. Apparently, they were not

people after his own heart. Differences in language and culture partly accounted for his failure with the Mexicans. De Ville was an intellectual and
aesthete who was cool toward the uncouth Mexican peasants: "We have
shut out European immigrants and have accepted the uncivilized Mexican
in his place," he declared in a surprisingly frank speech to the Gary Rotary
Club in 1927. In the same speech he sounded a common theme of American Catholics in the 1920s, that of anticommunism. Perhaps trying to
counter the popular prejudice that "alien" often meant "radical," de Ville
conceded that many Mexicans were indeed guilty of disloyalty: there were
five hundred "organized Communists" in Gary, and they were nearly all
Russians or Mexicans, he declared. His concluding comment, "You can
Americanize the man from southeastern and southern Europe, but you can't
Americanize a Mexican," seemed a confession of the failure of the church's
religious and political mission toward the Mexicans. Rather than defending
Gary's Mexicans against discrimination, de Ville echoed the strident racism
of the time that labeled Mexicans too different and too undesirable to be
assimilated.[82]

De Ville sounded like a disillusioned man. In 1930, he became seriously
ill. He returned to the mountain valleys of Moena to die amid his beloved
Alpine scenery.[83]

Under Father Costello, who replaced de Ville, the settlement house, recently launched with such bright hopes, foundered during the Depression.
The agency became a relief station for the hungry and homeless. A soup
kitchen fed hundreds daily, and the main concerns of the settlement's staff
were not recreation, but job placement, the distribution of clothing, and
emergency help. By 1935, the settlement began to resume its earlier programs, but lack of funds was a problem until the agency joined the Community Chest in 1941. Through the chest, Gary's businesses again affirmed
a responsibility for and interest in the city's social agencies, and under Rev.
James Cis, the settlement house restored the level of activity it had
achieved before 1930.[84]

CHAPTER SEVEN

Between Church and Mill:
Stewart House—The Making of a
Black Settlement House

Elbert Gary—"You have a colored church I suppose?"

George Crawford (president, Tennessee Coal, Iron, and Railroad Company)—"Well, we have the appropriation, but we have not had the labor to do it . . ."

Elbert Gary—"It is a great thing to keep in touch with the priests and the clergy."

Eugene Buffington (president, Illinois Steel Company)—"Especially the colored clergy."

Elbert Gary—"Well, in all nationalities. The pastors are in contact with the families and the working men themselves . . ."

—Addresses and Statements of
Elbert H. Gary.[1]

In November 1926, as the swirling migrations of the war years hardened into the now-familiar patterns of racial segregation in America's cities, black minister Frank S. Delaney of Trinity Methodist Church sat in the comfortable surroundings of the Gary Commercial Club with some of the city's most powerful white men to read aloud the sixth annual report of Stewart House, a settlement of which he was director and which had been established in 1920 by steel-company officials and black and white church and civic leaders to serve the city's black community.[2]

The Commercial Club was an apt setting for the ceremony that symbolized the relationship between the U.S. Steel Corporation and Gary's black community. Housed in an imposing three-story building on Broadway, the Commercial Club was shortly to move into quarters described by one contemporary as so opulent they "would satisfy the Grand Turk."[3] The Commercial Club symbolized both the power and wealth of the corporation in Gary. It was a meeting place for the U.S. Steel officials and civic leaders who formed Gary's elite, sitting on the boards of its institutions, promoting or opposing civic efforts, funding or starving its institutions. By supporting the black settlement house, the white establishment was setting its seal on an alliance with Gary's black community, represented that day by Reverend Delaney and attorney William C. Hueston. The two black leaders, for their part, saw the settlement house as a way to advance the interests of their race in the steel town. Whether or not they were correct readers will be able to judge.

The directors of the settlement house present at the ceremony included many of Gary's most prominent white citizens. There was Mayor Floyd E. Williams, the Ku Klux Klan candidate in the mayoral race of 1925, a staunch Republican and steel-company friend; C. Oliver Holmes, state senator, bank president, businessman, and prominent Methodist layman; and the Rev. William Grant Seaman of the First Methodist Church, a civic and religious leader who was himself the beneficiary of steel-company largesse, his $500,000 City Church having been recently completed (see Chapter 4).[4] Also present were the township trustee, Mary Newlin, an official who knew at firsthand the poverty of Gary's black migrants, and H. B. Snyder, millionaire founder-owner of the Gary *Post Tribune*. Representing the steel corporation was "Captain" Norton—the "real mayor" of Gary, some called him, who as manager of the Gary Land Company, U.S. Steel's real-estate subsidiary, had made the major planning decisions for the city since 1906.[5] Reverend Delaney and attorney W. C. Hueston represented the black community. Hueston had earlier earned a reputation as a spokesman for black civil rights and opponent of segregation, but in the 1920s he exchanged the politics of confrontation for those of patronage, becoming a political boss reputedly able to deliver Gary's black vote to the Republican party. Now Hueston was acknowledging on behalf of Gary's blacks some of the fruits of his cooperation with the white elite: Stewart House, named after John Stewart, a black missionary to the Wyandote Indians in the early nineteenth century, delivered relief and social services to poor and needy blacks. The settlement house was an interracial venture typical of the politics of cooperation of the 1920s.[6]

Unlike Campbell House and Neighborhood House, settlements originally founded to serve foreign immigrants, Stewart House was for blacks only. Like Flanner House in Indianapolis it was a segregated agency, operating under a biracial board of directors. Serious divisions had occurred among black leaders in the period since the World War. Some, disillusioned by the betrayals of the war years, when African-Americans had been brought North to break the strike, then fired in the thousands with the return of "normalcy," pursued goals of legal equality and integration. Their voices were heard through the Gary branch of the NAACP, founded in 1916. Others joined the United Negro Improvement Association (UNIA) and embraced the liberating rhetoric of Garveyism, with its emphasis on racial pride and economic advancement and its rejection of integration. Reverend Delaney sympathized with the UNIA, but Stewart House represented a less confrontational approach than black nationalism, an attempt to advance the race materially and educationally through interracial cooperation.[7]

Black and white Progressives of the 1890s had not envisioned settlements like Stewart House, which mediated among business, white philanthropists, and the black community, but had thought of settlements as institutions capable of transforming social relations along democratic and communitarian lines. One of the black Progressives who had shared in this dream was the young W. E. B. Du Bois, who had lived from 1896 to 1898 in a room over Philadelphia's Spring Street Settlement, "in the midst of an atmosphere of dirt, drunkenness, poverty, and crime," gathering data for his pathbreaking book, *The Philadelphia Negro*.[8] To Du Bois and other intellectuals at the turn of the century, the settlement house seemed less important as an agency of social work than as a base for scientific observation of the slum. Settlement residents would quantify poverty, vice, and crime, mapping out the city wards and their inhabitants. "I determined to put science into sociology, through a study of the conditions and problems of my own group," Du Bois wrote. "I was going to study the facts, any and all facts, concerning the American negro and his plight, and by measurement and comparison and research, work up any valid generalization which I could."[9]

To Du Bois and others of his generation, the settlement house was both a symbol and a tool of social "scientific" reform; sociologists resident in the settlement would generate the facts on which reforms could be grounded, reforms that they themselves would help to draft. The result would be a sociology harnessed to the ends of race advancement.

The surveys were completed, the data on poverty, ill-health, and bad housing conditions were collected, but the reform promise of the settlement movement was not realized; in the end it was easier for the settlements to collect data than to transform society.[10] Soon, as previous chapters have shown, settlements were busy Americanizing immigrants, making religious converts, or serving as domestic-employment agencies. White-run settlements that served blacks, like Flanner House, instead of promoting racial reform, displayed a cautious reformism that bowed to racism and oppression.

The failure of reform was not everywhere the same process, but occurred within specific social and political contexts. Stewart House, an agency developed "between church and mill," reveals the settlement as playing a conservative role in Gary in the 1920s, although still contributing to betterment for the black community.

The focus of this chapter is not on the internal history of Stewart House. Detailed analysis of the settlement's programs has been omitted, since

Chapter 3 contains an extended discussion of that topic. Instead, "Between Church and Mill: The Making of a Black Settlement" places the agency in the context of power and race relations in Gary and examines the formal and informal alliances—between the white elite of steel-mill officials and civic and religious leaders, black and white—that sustained the settlement between the steel strike and the Great Depression. The chapter then considers how effective the settlement was in advancing the interests of blacks in Gary in this period.

"The negro entered the iron and steel industry either as a strike breaker or at the time of great labor shortage," sociologists Horace Cayton and George Mitchell wrote in their 1939 study, *Black Workers and the New Unions.* In 1907, only 1.5 percent of steel workers in the East and a tiny 0.1 percent of the steel workers in the Midwest were black.[11] The great change came after 1915. The war created an unprecedented demand for steel at a time when immigrant steel workers were leaving the mills in thousands to return to their countries of origin and when European immigration had practically ceased. Escaping disastrous conditions in southern cotton agriculture, blacks came North to fill the demand for unskilled workers in the mills. In Gary, where the majority of steel workers were immigrants, one in four had left their jobs to serve in the armed forces. Desperate for labor, steel companies sent agents to the rural South to recruit workers. The numbers of blacks employed at the Gary Works of U.S. Steel jumped from 189 in 1915, only 1.4 percent of the work force, to 407 or 2.9 percent in 1916, and then in 1919 to 1,325, 8.8 percent of the work force (see Table 7).[12] Black workers came to Gary, as to other northern industrial centers, to escape southern violence and an iniquitous system of justice. They sought an education for their children and full citizenship rights for themselves. Entering the mills and furnaces at the level of unskilled workers, blacks were hired for the hottest, heaviest, and most dangerous work in steelmaking.[13] Hours were long: a twelve-hour day and a six-day week still prevailed in steel, a schedule that produced broken men—"Old Age at Forty," economist John Fitch called it. Yet even with these hours, investigators found that the corporation paid wages inadequate to support a family.[14]

Gary had no black ghetto to begin with. Blacks found housing on the crowded South Side along with European immigrants. As a later history of Stewart House pointed out, "From the beginning, Gary was a carefully planned community, with attention given to homes, streets, schools and facilities to serve the large work force . . . at the Gary works. However the growing Black population was not included in these plans."[15]

Just as this wartime migration was settling down, the steel strike brought another wave of migrants. Between 20,000 and 30,000 blacks came to northern steel towns in 1919, William Z. Foster estimated. Exactly how many of them came to Gary will never be known, but one observer recalled seeing as many as a hundred a day getting off trains in Gary.[16] Blacks were hired by U.S. Steel to help break the AFL strike; as a result, the number of blacks employed in the Gary steel mills surged to 2,060 in 1920, 13.7 percent of the work force, though dropping again to 1,686 in the depression of 1921 (see Table 7).

In the 1920s, blacks formed a permanent and growing part of Gary's working class, making up just over 9 percent of the population in 1920, and nearly 18 percent in 1930 (see Table 6).[18] The goals of the white elite were mutually contradictory. On the one hand, they desired social control and, to achieve this, they wanted blacks integrated into the society. On the other hand, they supported policies of increasing segregation. Jane Addams articulated this conflicting position in 1930 when she remarked that complete racial segregation was always undesirable because it resulted in placing blacks "outside the immediate action of that indispensable but powerful social control which influences the rest of the population."[19] The problem (as the white elite saw it) was to devise a form of social control that would place the black masses under reliable black leadership with institutions that, although separate, shared the values of self-help and individualism. Conversely for blacks, as Vincent Franklin has argued, the need was to tie their cultural values such as religious faith and belief in education to a progressive economic program while at the same time providing desperately needed social services.[20] In Gary, as historians Elizabeth Balanoff, Raymond Mohl, Neil Betten, and Ronald Cohen have carefully documented, between the time of the war and the Great Depression, white leaders pursued the goal of racial segregation in every area of the city's life while at the same time seeking to encourage in the black community itself the churches, welfare agencies, and schools that would be agencies of uplift and of discipline. White ministers began casting around for black allies to lead these institutions.

Public opinion was alerted to the need for new white-directed institutions in the black community by a series of newspaper articles. In July 1916, the Gary *Daily Tribune* called its readers' attention to the great migration that was taking place. "By tens of thousands the negroes have left the farms of the South and have gone north to take the place of European laborers called home or kept home by the great war."[21] Now was the time for Gary's white citizens to "take up in earnest the uplift of the colored population," the paper declared. Another editorial writer significantly described the task of uplift in the language of imperialism: "The white man's burden lies at our doors and not thousands of leagues away across continents and seas," he wrote.[22] Special, separate institutions were needed, the editorial insisted; it commended the efforts of white Presbyterian pastor Fred E. Walton to set up a neighborhood house for "colored" and endorsed the idea

Table 7
Employment of Blacks at the Gary Works of U.S. Steel, 1909–34

Year	No. of Blacks Employed	% Total Employees
1909	66	0.5
1910	105	0.9
1911	151	1.3
1912	287	2.3
1913	316	2.4
1914	220	1.7
1915	189	1.4
1916	407	2.9
1917	1,072	7.4
1918	1,295	8.6
1919	1,325	8.8
1920	2,060	13.7
1921	1,686	11.6
1922	2,826	18.8
1923	3,181	20.5
1924	2,402	16.0
1925	2,700	17.4
1926	2,680	17.3
1927	2,368	15.3
1928	2,683	16.8
1929	2,560	15.6
1930	2,271	14.7
1931	1,853	15.0
1932	1,682	14.8
1933	1,963	14.9
1934	2,216	15.3

Source: John Foster Potts, "A History of the Growth of the Negro Population of Gary, Indiana" (M.A. thesis, Cornell University, 1937), p. 7.

of a separate branch of the YMCA. "If Gary is to become a clean, well-governed city we must look after our colored people," Reverend Walton wrote in 1916. "It is unfair to criticize them and to exploit their weakness and faults if we do nothing for their moral and social uplift."[23]

At first these appeals fell on deaf ears. Only $250 was raised, and a few months later a modest donation of another $250 from Judge Gary of the steel corporation to an A. M. E. Zion church only showed that the corporation did not seek any special relationship with the black community at that time. A black minister who asked the corporation for $5,000 to build a Presbyterian church received only $500.[24]

But U.S. Steel's policy toward blacks changed in 1917 with the announcement by Captain Norton of the Gary Land Company and the Gary Realty Board that the company would build low-cost homes for blacks in an area east of Virginia Street and south of the Michigan Central tracks.[25] Previously, the steel company had developed housing only in the First Subdivision and only for skilled workers and managers who were mostly white, native-born Americans. Almost certainly, this scheme for a planned black neighborhood with company-built housing was designed to increase stability. Employers wanted to reduce labor turnover, real-estate interests sought to prevent blacks from buying property outside the South Side, and at least one Protestant denomination saw an opportunity for religious and moral reform work in the black neighborhood.[26]

Informally seeking support in the black community for the proposed subdivision, the steel corporation came up against unexpected resistance. A black preacher, interviewed in 1934, recalled: "In 1919 the company tried to get a Negro subdivision, and they wanted me to put my church there." Because he refused, he noted, "they have never helped me at all." This preacher was not the only black leader to speak out against the plan. Several prominent blacks denounced the scheme to introduce segregated housing; they ignored Norton's lame assurance that the company's only motive was to relieve the shortage of housing on the South Side and to give blacks "special opportunities."[27]

White industrial and civic leaders, on the other hand, expressed support for the new policy. "Colored people everywhere prefer to live together and this new subdivision . . . is going to permit them to live in the same neighborhood decently and well," an editorial in the Gary *Evening Post* commented approvingly. The Calumet Church Federation, composed of the area's white Protestant ministers, passed a resolution thanking the Gary Land Company for their action in providing the separate housing for blacks and asking the company "to continue to develop that subdivision which they have set apart for these people."[28]

For Gary's white leaders, the segregated subdivision was a necessary first step in reforming conditions among blacks on the South Side. A survey conducted by Rev. John Lee of the Board of Missions for Freedmen of the Presbyterian church confirmed their worst fears about the moral dangers of the South Side district, where immorality, vice, and crime were rampant. Asked where a "colored man" could find wholesome recreation in Gary, one interviewee replied, "Nowhere."[29]

The Great Migration northward had led to blacks founding their own educational, religious, and cultural institutions—churches, lodges, clubs, and societies—but white church leaders considered many of these unsatisfactory. They claimed that fewer than half of Gary's blacks belonged to a church and implied that moral disintegration was at hand. The Calumet Church Federation went so far as to recommend "that financial and moral support be withheld from colored religious and welfare organizations until they have secured recommendations from the Calumet Church Federation."[30]

White church and civic leaders looked to the steel company for money and support in dealing with the problems presented by the black migration into the Calumet Region. In a frank and revealing letter to Captain Norton written early in July 1920, Rev. William Grant Seaman of Gary's First M. E. Church reviewed the interests that the steel corporation, as Gary's major employer, and the white churches had in common with regard to the city's black population. Seaman expressed his denomination's support for the corporation's proposed segregated subdivision, and appealed to Norton for the steel company to join the M. E. church in establishing and supporting a black settlement house and church there.[31]

Whether Seaman believed the series of half-truths and slanders contained in his letter, or whether he sought to appeal to the bigoted Norton, we cannot know. Whichever was the case, Seaman's argument was based on a view of the Negro as both morally and intellectually inferior. "The colored people are very ignorant, and morally undeveloped," Seaman began. Although the church was "the outstanding social institution of colored people, the one to which they give their hearts most fully and to which they respond most readily," their pastors were in most cases unsuitable men, "the blind leading the blind." There must be white control over Gary's black institutions, the churchman concluded, and his own denomination was the best equipped to exercise it. What was needed was an institution of uplift involving religious, educational, and social-service functions. The solution was a "two unit plant," a settlement and a church. The settlement would then act as a check on the black church by including white leaders on its board of directors. "The settlement having a separate board, with white leaders as members, would be the means of bringing the colored preacher and his abilities and character before a tribunal capable of testing same, and which could easily bring about a change if he did not measure up in any essential particular."[32]

The settlement was needed for the uplift of blacks, who were "not far from the jungle," Seaman argued, "not so much viciously immoral as they are unmoral"; their "looseness" and disregard for property rights were notorious. White leadership was as essential in matters of morals as it was in religion, he implied. But political considerations should also persuade the steel corporation to support the settlement plan, the minister continued. Black congregations that were independent of white leadership tended to be independent in politics, he warned. In some cases they were "cultivating in their people the sense of being wronged . . . [and] . . . building up in America a distinct group of people apart from the rest of Americans, and in a very real sense a foreign body in our land." How dangerous this could be had been shown in the recent strike, Seaman went on, when a black attorney (he meant Caldwell) was "quite noisy in behalf of the strikers." The building of the steel corporation's black subdivision was exactly the right kind of policy, for it created an arena for the operation of steel-corporation interest and white benevolence. The controversy over the black subdivision had clearly illustrated the value for the corporation of having allies in the black community. "When this project was announced and the colored people objected to it on the grounds for segregation a very little effort lined up our colored people for the project."[33] They should all be encouraged by the fact that most of Gary's black professionals had been trained at Methodist colleges such as Meharry and shared the values of the "better class" of whites. Getting down to business, Seaman spelled out his proposal to Captain Norton. The cost of the church and settlement house was projected to be $100,000, of which $60,000 would come from the Methodist Conference and $10,000 from local donations. The steel company was asked to donate the site, plus $50,000. The plan promised a good return for a total investment of about $150,000.[34]

"Hearty enthusiasm" among officials of the corporation greeted the proposal for a black settlement house,[35] but this enthusiasm can only be explained by factors far removed from the concerns of the Methodist churchman. To understand these concerns, it is necessary to see the role played by blacks in the corporation's labor force after 1919.

By 1920, U.S. Steel was facing severe labor shortages because of the impending restriction on the entry of European immigrants who had performed the unskilled heavy labor in steel-making since the corporation was formed. Worse still, pressures were increasing on the corporation to shorten the workday for common labor from twelve to eight hours. Should U.S. Steel be forced to run three shifts a day instead of two it would have to hire an estimated 60,000 more men, just at a time when its traditional and preferred labor source was drying up.[36] The role that blacks had played as strikebreakers in the events of 1919 suggested to mill management that there would be definite advantages in making them a permanent part of the steel work force. Thus, although employment managers continued to regard blacks as the least desirable workers, they also continued to send labor agents to the South to recruit them.[37] Figures supplied by William S. McNabb, superintendent of industrial relations at the Gary Works, on March 12, 1937 show that in the twenties, blacks varied as a percentage of the Gary Works from 20 percent in 1923 to about 14 percent in 1930 (see Table 7).

By the time of Reverend Seaman's letter to Captain Norton, U.S. Steel had already taken two steps toward more direct control over its black workers. The first, the separate housing area, has been mentioned. The second, not coincidentally, also occurred in 1919, when the corporation created the position of "welfare worker" at Illinois Steel and gave it to a black man named John Russell. Welfare workers like Russell were employed in many U.S. companies in the period between 1918 and the Depression to keep workers informed about company goals and policies and also to keep managers, especially employment managers, informed about their employees. They aided with hiring, providing employers with reliable workers and screening out troublemakers. Welfare work was intended to improve the quality of employees, reduce labor turnover, and combat unionism. It was also expected to produce dividends in employee goodwill and to improve the public image of the corporation.[38]

The needs of the steel corporation for a stable force of black laborers coincided with concerns of white church and community leaders about stability and social control in the black community. As welfare work was useful in the workplace, so the settlement house would be useful in the community. White church leaders sought to bring black churches under white sponsorship and thus to create more allies for the corporation. "It is a great thing to keep in touch with the priests and the clergy," Elbert Gary told the heads of U.S. Steel subsidiaries in 1919, for they are "in contact with the families and the working men themselves."[39]

Although it was fear of "a dangerous separatism" that prompted U.S. Steel's sponsorship of Stewart House, separatism was to be the basis of black-white relations in Gary in the 1920s. It was a matter of devising the right kind of separation, one not based on opposition or challenge to Gary's power structure, but one that facilitated communication without challenging inequality of power and fostered racial pride under an umbrella of shared values. Black welfare organizations could serve this purpose (while performing useful work as well), just as patronage politics had integrated blacks into politics without giving them power. The founding of Stewart House should be seen in this context.

Since about 1916, Trinity Methodist Episcopal Church had existed as a small congregation of black worshipers meeting in each others' homes and in a series of temporary quarters, with a succession of ministers that included an elderly, retired minister who continued his trade as a shoemaker and a ministerial student. However, in 1920, leaders of the white First Methodist Episcopal Church, as part of their "Centenary" program, announced their intention to put Trinity M. E. Church on a firmer foundation, to move it into a permanent building, and to add a settlement house that would serve the black community as an agency of community uplift and social control. Since Reverend Seaman and other white church leaders believed that none of Gary's black ministers was suitable for this position, they took steps to import one. Accordingly, two Methodist laymen,

Dr. H. R. DeBra and black physician Dr. W. A. Hardy, visited the session of the Methodist Episcopal church in Springfield, Ohio, early in 1920. Hardy, a founding member of the black church, was doubtless able to explain to his religious superiors the problems that the little congregation had with temporary quarters (they met in a tent, which occasionally blew down during the service) and with a succession of ministers. Bishop Anderson's answer was the appointment of Rev. Frank S. Delaney, who was working at the time in Chicago. Delaney, a native of Ohio and a graduate of Gammon Theological College, Atlanta, became the minister of Trinity M.E. Church and superintendent of the planned settlement house.[40]

The steel company supported this initiative. It provided a new site for the church and settlement at 1527 Massachusetts Avenue. The Methodist Episcopal church was to provide Delaney's salary while the steel company was to meet the expenses of the building. In 1921, the name Stewart House was adopted and a board of directors organized that included prominent citizens of both races. The settlement adopted the motto "Christian ideals and racial goodwill."[41]

The social-work agency arose not from a reform challenge to the hegemony of the steel corporation, but from the shared concerns of mill officials and the black and white elite. As sociologist Horace Cayton commented on the community relations in the towns he observed, "the 'good' colored people and the 'good' white people have seldom failed to get together upon questions of policy." The presence of black professionals and business leaders on the Stewart House board of directors shows that many middle-class blacks supported the idea of the social-work agency. These included attorney W. C. Hueston, as president, and architect William W. Cooke, as secretary, as well as Dr. Hardy. Gary's black women's federated clubs also supplied three members of the board. These black professionals pursued the accommodationist strategy of furthering race advancement through an alliance with powerful whites. White directors were banker and businessman C. O. Holmes, Methodist lay leader Dr. H. R. DeBra, and Reverend Seaman. In 1926, they would be joined on the board by a wide array of other prominent citizens, including Norton (who was on the executive board) and W. P. Gleason.[42]

If the circumstances of the founding of Stewart House boded ill for the transformation of race relations in Gary, the benefits that the settlement house would secure for blacks through its relationship with the steel company soon became apparent. To a greater extent than was the case with white settlements, Stewart House was a relief-giving agency. The depression of 1921 resulted in layoffs in the steel industry; discharged soldiers and new arrivals from the South swelled the ranks of unemployed blacks. In the first year of the settlement's operation, "hundreds of returned soldiers walked our

streets, homeless and hungry," Reverend Delaney recalled. Two Gary
women who headed women's auxiliaries of veterans' organizations, Mrs.
J. H. Eppler and Mrs. H. V. Snyder, worked with Delaney to enlarge the
services of the settlement-house building to cope with the needs of the unemployed. The settlement-house building served as a church on Sunday, but
during the week it was used to provide lodging for the homeless, serve
meals to the unemployed, and distribute repaired shoes and used clothing.

Although the depression lifted in the spring of 1922 the settlement continued to be an important provider of social services to Gary's African-
Americans. Delaney described Stewart House as "an entry point into the
community and as a stabilizing factor." And one former user of the house
recalled that "Getting Folks Settled" was its main work. Hundreds of needy
people came for advice about employment, medical, or legal problems. Mrs.
Leila Delaney, the minister's wife, was the secretary and ran the baby clinic
and mothers' club, and his sister ran the day nursery. There was a free
medical clinic and dispensary, meeting places for clubs, and supervised
recreation for children. Heavy use of the agency required the rental of additional buildings, and soon plans were being drawn up for a new Stewart
House building.[43]

The new Stewart House which opened in November 1925 was a com-
manding structure. To many blacks, the institution, designed by black architect W. W. Cooke and built by a black contractor from Chicago,
symbolized black pride and aspirations: Delaney's own congregation pledged
$10,000 for the new building. A later history described the settlement
house as a "a monument . . . to the constructive ability of the Negro race
in Gary."[44] Many churches and other institutions of blacks in the city were
burdened with debt, but the steel corporation paid off the debt on Stewart
House within two years of its opening. "This donation to Gary's black community proves that a giant of steel has a heart responsive to the call of
humanity," Clarence Walker, a youth worker at Stewart House, declared at
a ceremony marking the occasion.[45] However, some critics suggested that by
letting the steel corporation pay the $60,000 indebtedness on the new
building, Reverend Delaney had incurred debts that he might come to re-
gret. In an article entitled "Our Mendicant Priests," published in the black
newspaper the Gary *Colored American* in 1929, a writer complained that
black churches were always asking money from whites. Politicians did not
give without expecting some return, he warned. "Nor do the masses of Negroes gain anything. The preachers sell the race's respect for the few dollars
they beg. Let us build and conduct our churches to suit our means. If we
cannot support huge institutions and edifices, let us not build them on such
a scale of grandeur."[46]

But such open expressions of criticism were rare. The kindly, self-sacrificing work of the Delaneys won the hearts of even those who might have been critical of the settlement's accommodationist stance and its ties to the steel corporation. Certainly, the disasters of war and the strike had not been followed by race riots in Gary as they had in neighboring Chicago, and black anger at the corporation, momentarily glimpsed in 1919, seemed to have vanished. Black attorney L. I. H. Caldwell who had declared in 1919, "I will be one man whose mouth will not be shut by that damnable steel corporation bunch," afterward seems to have regretted his intemperate words, for he apologized to Reverend Seaman in writing.[47] By the mid-1920s this erstwhile critic of the steel company had taken his place on the board of Stewart House along with attorney Hueston. Other prominent members of the black community associated with Stewart House in the 1920s were physicians Dr. Royal Grubbs and Hardy; school principals H. Theo Tatum and Blanche Liggett; social worker and later journalist Thyra Edwards; architect William Cooke; and councilman A. B. Whitlock.[48]

Located "between church and mill," the settlement house was a pivotal institution, expressing the "goodwill" of the corporation toward its workers by distributing services to them and their families. Even after the death of its most sanctimonious exponent, Elbert H. Gary, in 1927, paternalism continued to characterize the relations between the corporation and black workers at least until the great unionizing drives of SWOC in the 1930s. Between the 1919 strike and the rise of industrial unionism, corporation spokesmen generally referred to industrial relations in terms of personal relationships and mutual obligations. Sometimes steel spokesmen in Gary even tried to draw on the fund of goodwill among blacks in terms that evoked the personal labor relations on southern farms and plantations.[49] It was Judge Gary himself who should be thanked for Stewart House, Captain Norton told an audience gathered at the dedication ceremony of the settlement in November 1925. The steel chairman was their great benefactor, for by hiring blacks as steelworkers he made it possible for them to buy homes, secure education for their children, and realize their aspirations for advancement.[50]

Norton was right about the aspirations of his black listeners but wrong about their progress toward these goals. An Urban League study of conditions among blacks in 1928 belied his claims about racial advancement. As for industrial goodwill, the essence of steel-company paternalism was not benevolence, as Norton alleged, but unequal power between ununionized, marginalized black workers and an all-powerful employer.[51]

Stewart House was an institutional expression of this quasi-feudal relationship between blacks and the steel company. The material relief that was channeled through the agency to needy families and the unemployed created a constituency for the steel company, validating the view of the employer as benefactor. Thus steelworkers interviewed during the Depression realized that Delaney was distributing material help for the steel company, that it was behind him, so to speak. Many saw Delaney as a spokeman for the corporation, occupying the same morally ambiguous ground as the black political bosses who urged Gary's blacks to vote Republican. "Vote for your friends, those who employ you," W. C. Hueston, first president of Stewart House and black political boss, urged.[52]

To its white supporters, Stewart House was important as a symbol of racial cooperation (though they usually did not discuss the terms of this cooperation). To blacks, it was *their* settlement house, one where dozens of social, cultural, and benevolent organization met each week. Adult organizations meeting there included the Gary Noonday Business Club, the City Federation of Colored Women's Clubs, Welfare Clubs, Neighborhood Clubs, nine lodges, and benevolent and industrial organizations.[53]

Especially strong links existed between the black settlement house and the campaign for black business—a very significant movement in Gary in the 1920s as elsewhere. Advocates of black economic development formed the pro-UNIA black businessman's club, the Gary Noonday Business Club, which met at Stewart House. Among its organizers were the Stewart House directors, Cooke, Grubbs, and Tatum. In the fall of 1927, the club sponsored an exhibition about black business at Stewart House with William Cooke as chairman.[54]

The Gary *Sun*, published between 1916 and 1929, supported the goals of the UNIA and was also an advocate of black business. The newspaper's admiration of entrepreneurship even produced a flattering portrait of Elbert Gary as a model of entrepreneurship whose "Horatio Alger" career was a lesson to all. "The late Judge Gary's rise from humble circumstances to that of a captain of industry ought to furnish inspiration to the struggling businessmen of the Negro race," it said. "His career is full of many good examples of business insight, business aggressiveness, and business system."

> There are lessons in business for the Negro businessman in Judge Gary's career, which shows clearly how the Negro lawyer may increase his usefulness and become a big business leader among his group . . . The moral to be pointed out is as applicable in the lives of the Negro doctor, minister, teacher and merchant as it is in that of the lawyer.[55]

But such praise of the corporation by black leaders was more an acknowledgment of their dependence on the steel company than a blueprint for success. The opportunity structure that had allowed the rise of "captains of industry" in the late nineteenth century was notably absent in the twentieth-century steel town. For African-Americans, in fact, opportunity was narrowing as segregation increased. There was nothing inevitable or "natural" about this process, as historians Raymond Mohl and Neil Betten have shown:

> The segregation of Gary's population did not develop accidentally out of housing patterns. Rather, discrimination and segregation in education, housing, employment, public services and recreation was established and carried out by the city's white elite—businessmen, bankers, realtors, educators, steel company officials, and local government leaders.[56]

Although detailed analysis of the process of segregation lies outside the scope of this chapter, a grasp of its dynamics is essential to understanding the range of possibilities facing the Stewart House leadership in the 1920s. What strategies were available to Delaney and other black leaders? One strategy—outspoken opposition to segregation and uncompromising demands for political, social, and economic equality—was out of the question for the black minister, given the fact that U.S. Steel and the conservative Methodist Episcopal church had sponsored Stewart House, donated its land and buildings, and paid the minister's salary. It is doubtful whether a confrontational stance could have been successful in the Gary of the 1920s. For example, although the Gary branch of NAACP regularly protested segregation, it was generally ineffective, received little support in the black community, and rarely moved to action beyond formal protests.[57] Although Delaney himself was at one time on the executive committee of the NAACP, he avoided taking a public stand against segregation. During the park protests led by the NAACP in the 1930s, Delaney would take the side of the mill managers against the demands of blacks for access to the whites-only park.

But if he avoided confrontation, Delaney was not simply an accommodationist: the very existence of Stewart House was witness to the unmet needs of the black citizens for food, shelter, and jobs; to their demand for equal access to education and health care. On the other hand, the settlement was also an institutional expression of blacks' continuing hopes for betterment. It was a meliorist institution, and thus one very much in line with middle-class values in the black community itself, namely, the belief in education, self-improvement, and religious faith.[58]

Between accommodation on the one hand and confrontation on the other, a new movement arose. The year when Stewart House began—1920—was also the beginning of an enormously influential UNIA movement in Gary that was to involve nearly all its black community, if not as actual members then as supporters—and, one might add, believers. Tremendously important in instilling racial pride, Garveyism did not view segregation as necessarily inimical to black progress, for separate, black-only institutions could be the basis for economic progress as well as racial pride. At their most extreme (and, some said, misguided) black nationalists viewed the development of segregation as creating conditions favorable for racial progress: housing segregation meant an opportunity for neighborhood-based black business, separate schools promised jobs for black teachers and a curriculum that included black history; it was even said that white racial exclusiveness made possible black racial purity. Segregation proceeded more rapidly in the 1920s than it would have done because of a convergence between the racist views of Gary's white leaders and the separatist views of some black leaders. As a blacks-only institution, Stewart House was part of this movement: the separate social agency employed black social workers, black schoolchildren were taught African-American history (which they did not learn in school); and the segregated institution, even though born of white racism, became a source of racial pride.[59]

But pragmatic considerations rather than philosophical adherence to Garveyism in the abstract inclined blacks to support Stewart House and to accept Delaney's cautious approach. Black councilman and businessman A. B. Whitlock endorsed the work of Stewart House in his newspaper, the Gary *Colored American*. When the settlement house received its deed from the steel company in 1927, the *Colored American* commented that the occasion "showed graphically the racial good-will and amity existing between the better classes of the two races." However, in the thirties the paper took a more outspoken and less accommodationist stance; it led campaigns for better housing and for more municipal jobs for Gary's black citizens and supported the "buy black" and "hire black" campaigns that succeeded eventually in opening up white-collar employment to black women in downtown stores and banks.[60]

White support for Stewart House was expressed in the influential Gary *Post Tribune*, owned by H. B. Snyder. A member of the first executive committee of Stewart House in 1921, Snyder and the Snyder family were important financial supporters of the agency; the newspaper's coverage of racial affairs articulates the reasons for this support. Whether reporting the opening of a new black church, Judge Gary's gift to an A. M. E. church in 1916, or the news that Mayor William F. Hodges had successfully blocked the showing of the racially inflammatory film *Birth of a Nation*, Snyder's newspaper condemned race hatred and supported "interracial" institutions. By this, whites meant segregated institutions that served the black community only but that were tied into the existing white power structure.[61]

Coverage of Stewart House in the white-owned press gave it visibility and made it respectable to white readers. For example, in 1928 the *Post Tribune* featured a short history of the settlement house that mentioned its "humble beginnings" and then described how in the years under Delaney,

the settlement had "obtained the endorsement of such citizens as Captain
H. S. Norton, Dr. William G. Seaman, State Senator C. O. Holmes, Mrs.
J. R. Eppler, Dr. H. R. DeBra, Mr. W. P. Gleason, etc." The citizens of
Gary should not hesitate to support an institution that had such prominent
white sponsors, the writer implied. It portrayed Delaney as an interracial
goodwill ambassador, "capable of understanding and interpreting the traits
and the aspirations of both the white and the colored people."[62]

Delaney's approach to race relations can be sampled in a series of pieces
that he wrote in the late 1920s for the *Colored American*. Here the minister
laid out his moderate and eclectic philosophy. Sometimes he articulated a
Garveyite racial pride under a title such as "Fate of Race in Its Own
Hands." At other times he preached moderation, as in "Negro Cannot Win
Promoting External Opposition." Sometimes there was uncertainty about
the roots of African-American culture as in "Negro Should Absorb White
Culture." Unconcerned about ideological inconsistency, Delaney always
stressed the practical. A typical column preached to black readers on the
work ethic and the subject of avoiding debt. "Beware the lure of credit," the
minister warned. "Pay your bills promptly. Get along with what you have.
Save money. Buy homes. Contribute to the good of the race and community." Another column entitled, "Prejudice," contained the advice, "Be just
and fair to all men, even at the cost of disadvantage to yourself." Unfortunately, Delaney's column often had to share a page with one by W. E. B.
Du Bois. The comparison was not flattering to Delaney. Where Du Bois was
outspoken, pithy, and direct, Delaney was circumspect, pious, and vague.
His caution often looked oddly inappropriate next to some news item which
trumpeted the injustices blacks suffered such as the following: "Dying
Woman Is Turned Away from D.C. Hospital. 'We do not take colored patients,' Says Doctor to Mother Dying of Gunshot Wounds."[63]

A bitter opponent of the settlement house and of clientage politics
claimed that "mendicant priests" like Delaney, dependent on whites, only
"sold the race's respect"—that the masses of Negroes gained nothing. It is
important to examine whether blacks gained anything from Stewart House
other than racial peace and the approval of whites. In order to answer these
questions we turn to examine the progress that Gary's blacks made in the
1920s in four areas: housing, health, recreation, and jobs. How effective
was Delaney in bringing improvements to the black community? Did his
position "between church and mill" enable him to secure gains for blacks?

High rents and substandard, unhealthy dwellings characterized housing
conditions for blacks in Gary's early days, but at least in "the Patch" they
shared these conditions with other groups.[64] However, the segregation of
housing proceeded rapidly after the steel company opened its "colored subdivision" in 1919. As Gary's ethnics moved out to West Gary and

Tolleston or south to Glen Park, real-estate interests began to refuse to sell to blacks in these areas and conspired to contain Gary's blacks in the Central District (formerly the South Side). A National Urban League survey showed the trend toward the development of a ghetto: by 1928, 89 percent of white residents were concentrated in white areas, and Negro areas were up to 90 percent black. The Fifth Ward, which had been 27 percent black in 1920, was 72 percent black in 1930; its foreign-born population dropped by half in the same decade, from 34 percent of the total to 15 percent in 1930.[65] Shortage of housing meant that rentals for blacks were higher than for whites: in 1928, blacks had to pay $22.57 per dwelling, compared to $16.00 for whites. Rents in Gary were comparable to those in Harlem; only Philadelphia and Baltimore rents were higher. And because many families kept lodgers in order to help pay the rent, crowding resulted. One-fourth of black homeowners had lodgers, while one-third of black tenant families did so. Ten persons on average occupied white-owned homes in Gary, but for blacks the figure was twenty.[66]

Figures for homeownership in Gary show that blacks were far less successful in buying their own homes than other groups. In 1920, 35 percent of all homes in Gary were owner-occupied, but only about 9 percent of black homes. Figures collected by the U.S. Census Bureau in 1940 permit a comparison among different groups: while almost 39 percent of white homes were owner-occupied, only 19 percent of black homes were.[67] Twenty-six years later, an Urban League Study revealed continuing problems with housing. In 1944, 80 percent of nonwhite families in Gary were still tenants rather than owners, and two-thirds of the units that they rented needed major repairs or were without indoor toilet or bath.[68]

Although there were numerous black protests against racial barriers in housing such as restrictive covenants, Stewart House did not take part in any overt efforts to change prevailing patterns of racism. However, the settlement and its allies did make some attempts to help blacks buy homes. Beginning in 1919, the Calumet Church Federation led a movement to improve the quality of housing available to blacks. The federation appointed a committee to approach building-and-loan associations, requesting them to formulate building restrictions so as to "secure the erection of sanitary and suitable houses in those parts of the city occupied by the colored race."[69] But despite the federation's instruction to its chairman to take up the matter with the city council nothing seems to have come of this initiative. In the mid-twenties, Reverend Delaney was among the organizers of the Gary Building and Loan Association which was set up in order to provide better credit and lower mortgage-interest rates to blacks to help them buy homes. Unfortunately, it too soon ended in failure.[70]

But if the settlement could do nothing about the housing discrimination, it did try to combat the poverty and ignorance that compounded these problems. Like other settlement houses, Stewart House tried to encourage cleanliness and self-respect; it led campaigns for cleaner neighborhoods in line with the teachings of Garveyism which stressed racial pride. Such efforts brought some improvements that were practical but undramatic. For neighbors whose homes lacked even water, the settlement house had public shower baths and a community laundry.

In the second area, that of health, bad conditions also resulted directly from poverty and racial discrimination. Blacks in Gary as in all American cities had higher disease and mortality rates than whites; the death rate for black children under one year in 1931 was 86 per thousand, as compared with 59 for white children. The incidence of tuberculosis was especially shocking—nearly 150 per 100,000 for blacks, but only slightly over 22 for whites.[71]

These health problems were compounded by discrimination in health-delivery services. Blacks were not admitted to either of Gary's two major hospitals, Methodist and Mercy. In 1923, Reverends Delaney and Seaman tried unsuccessfully to challenge this situation. Significantly, they did not attack discrimination head-on but by subterfuge. When the light-skinned wife of U.S. Steel welfare-worker John Russell needed hospital treatment, the two ministers conspired to smuggle her in as white, in order to establish the principle that blacks could receive treatment there. However, the plan misfired when Mrs. Russell resisted this undercover tactic, phoning the hospital to ask outright whether black patients were admitted. When she was refused, the game was up. The test case showed the hopelessness of integrationist hopes in the 1920s—and the limitations of the kind of interpersonal "interracial politics" that Delaney represented. John Russell was a light-skinned, well-to-do black man. The only black member of the Gary Realty Board, which was dominated by Captain Norton, he seemed to enjoy the confidence of both black and white elites. This case revealed to the black community that Gary's much-vaunted interracial cooperation could not be used as a lever to gain blacks access to white facilities. Delaney did not lead a public protest against discrimination in health services—such an action would have brought confrontation with his sponsors—but he and Seaman worked behind the scenes to reverse the hospital's decision, without success. Perhaps as a result of this case, in the mid-1920s, Mercy Hospital established a segregated ward for blacks though only white doctors were permitted to practice there. But Methodist Hospital did not take a similar step until the 1930s. In the 1920s blacks were driven back into reliance on their own health institutions, mainly two small private hospitals, run and staffed by black doctors. According to one source, it was this failed challenge to the mill and the white elite that caused Reverend Seaman to leave Gary a few years later in 1928.[72]

Unable to challenge segregation in health care, the settlement concentrated on providing alternative services. For example, there were several health clinics where black doctors could practice; there was a visiting nurse and an infant clinic recognized by the Infant Hygiene Department of the State Board of Health. Mrs. Leila Delaney presided over the mothers' clinic. Despite shortages of money the settlement's health services were a significant resource to the black community. Stewart House also did important health-education work. It promoted National Negro Health Week, held health and hygiene classes, and offered a Better Baby Club to promote maternal health and child nutrition.[73]

Like immigrants, blacks saw access to educational opportunity as vital to their advancement and that of their children: hope of securing better schools had been an important factor in moving to the North, and, once in Gary, black children had higher school-attendance rates than foreign-born children in every decennial year from 1910 to 1940. But Superintendent of Schools William Wirt planned from the very beginning to segregate black children, and in this he had the approval of Gary's mill officials and white elite. Between 1907 and 1938, Wirt developed a system of schools for Gary's black children that was both segregated and second-rate, reproducing the faults of the system blacks had left in the South.[74]

Serious disagreements among black leaders arose over what strategies to adopt in the face of the relentless pressure from U.S. Steel and civic leaders to segregate the schools. Some, like UNIA advocate, black school-principal F. C. McFarlane, thought that blacks should not fight the process that was pushing them into separate schools but should try to view the separation as a precondition for racial progress, where black teachers could find employment and black culture and history could find a place. Blacks "no longer whine about segregation," he said in 1930. When the plan for a separate high school for blacks was first announced in 1927, the UNIA in Gary spoke in favor of it, saying that integration would "destroy class and race consciousness."[75] But not everyone agreed with the UNIA and with McFarland. In 1924, W. C. Hueston had written to Wirt protesting the segregation in the schools.[76] And Delaney's friend and associate H. Theo Tatum believed in integration and was an outspoken critic of the emerging segregated system. As Gary moved toward the segregation of its schools, the *Colored American* published a stinging attack on separate schooling and on those blacks who supported it: "Black people have been fighting to get this segregated, stigmatized institution for seven years, and now, not with chagrin, but with foolish pride and pitiable pomp, they glow and gloat over the evil that they have wrought."[77] The NAACP also launched bitter protests, but was generally ineffective. The 1927 Emerson School strike and the subsequent controversy over Roosevelt School, Gary's new black high school which opened in 1931, threw into relief the difficulties of Delaney's position.

To oppose segregation was to oppose the steel company, which had thrown its influence behind segregation ever since it built Gary's first black neighborhood with its segregated Virginia Street School, and Delaney could not oppose the steel company. A. R. McArthur, the mill representative on the Gary school board, was also on the executive board of Stewart House. At a meeting held to discuss Roosevelt School in 1930, Delaney was booed when he tried to rebut an attack on some black ministers who were absent. Black preachers who spoke out in favor of separate institutions were accused of "importing segregation from the accursed Southland."[78] The role of a moderate was unpopular in a crisis where many blacks believed that what they needed was not an arbitrator, but an advocate. Thus, it was easier for Delaney to accept the new $1 million school as a symbol of progress than to challenge the policies of the men who sat on the governing board of his settlement house as well as on the school board. As time went on, the black community became proud of Roosevelt School; former integrationist Tatum accepted the post of principal and did not protest that the school was for blacks only.[79]

Stewart House was itself an educational institution, of course. Its classes for children in black history, the weekday church school, the young peoples' clubs, the Scouts and Camp Fire Girls, were all educational. Music lessons were given at the settlement, and musical organizations met there, including an orchestra, a band, and a chorus. Adults, too, benefited from a range of classes. The subjects taught included not only practical skills like lampshade making but also academic subjects. In 1935, the settlement employed four paid teachers who taught civics, homemaking, Negro history, and Spanish. Education, broadly defined, made Stewart House a valuable resource to the black community.[80]

The pattern of action and inaction was replicated in the area of organized recreation. One of the reasons for founding the settlement house had been to provide clean, safe recreation for blacks, who were excluded from white facilities. The new settlement building, completed in 1925, contained rooms for games and clubs; hundreds of children came after school to play and learn at the settlement house. Young people could participate in the dramatics club, or in sports such as basketball, volleyball, and tennis. However, Stewart House had no gymnasium, and Stewart House children were given only occasional and grudging access to the Friendship House gym. Plans for a second building containing a gym were sabotaged by the Depression.

In 1944, the Urban League study found the recreation facilities of Stewart House inadequate and described it as badly designed for its purpose. It still had no gym at this late date.[81]

Another serious problem concerned access to parks and beaches. Despite Gary's position on Lake Michigan, blacks were not allowed access to the lake for recreation or swimming until the 1960s. Protests by prominent blacks like the respected Tatum failed to have any effect. The two original parks laid out by the Gary Land Company were in the First Subdivision and inaccessible to South Side inhabitants. When the Gary Parks Board, headed by the ubiquitous W. P. Gleason, set out to give Gary the parks that its growing population needed, it followed a policy of racial separation: blacks were excluded from parks used by whites and given inferior ones for their own use. Thus two parks were built in Gary in the 1920s—South Gleason Park, a 310-acre park for whites, and Riverside or North Gleason Park for blacks, a 48-acre park with inferior facilities which the Gary *American* sarcastically referred to as "a few sunswept acres." Why should blacks go to the small Jim Crow park named after "their chief crucifier," the writer asked.[82]

A test case involving the segregated Washington Park in the 1930s involved Delaney in an embarrassing and hopeless challenge to his steel-company backers. Gary NAACP president Mrs. Hallie Hayes and others began to try to integrate the park by taking their own children to play there. Unable to keep blacks out, park officials retaliated by letting all the water out of the pool and taking down the swings, but Mrs. Hayes persisted. The steel company used intimidation to deter black users of the park; an official from the mill—occasionally even Gleason himself—came to the park every day, and if he recognized a black steel worker there threatened to fire him. Several people testified that the employment manager at Illinois Steel Company stood at the mill gates during this park crisis, warning blacks to stay away from the park.[83]

Delaney refused to lead this movement to integrate public facilities. When he was approached and asked to lead a protest march to the park, the minister claimed that the crisis was "irritating" race relations in Gary and that there were "hot-heads on both sides." Instead, after a visit to corporation headquarters, Delaney came back to the protestors with the warning that if they or their children were seen in the whites-only park they would lose their jobs. Delaney's role in this crisis must have damaged his effectiveness in the black community, for when blacks challenged segregation they came up against the power of the steel corporation, and Delaney had thrown in his lot with the corporation. A steelworker interviewed in 1934 called the minister a "stoolpigeon" for the corporation.[84]

In the fourth area, employment, Stewart House alleviated suffering, but was unable to change the underlying causes of high unemployment for blacks. Years before the Great Depression, blacks suffered more from unemployment than other groups because of racial discrimination. Since the settlement's first winter, when hundreds of unemployed ex-servicemen came to Stewart House for help with lodging, food, and information about work, the settlement was often called on to provide such services. In view of the close relations between Delaney and Norton, it is probable that Stewart House played a role in supplying black workers for the steel corporation, and from Delaney's general accommodationist stance there is little doubt that as an employment agency the settlement house was a source of nonunion workers that the corporation could depend on.

But the role of the settlement was not simply supplying workers to the steel mills and other employers. Blacks were a new element in the labor markets of the North, and as historian Herbert Gutman has shown, rural people did not adjust immediately or easily to industrial life. A function of social work sponsored by corporations was to aid the adjustment of rural folk entering new conditions of work and life. Similar adjustment work was done for blacks by the National Urban League—what historian Nancy Weiss calls "integrating capitalism." Like the Urban League, settlements also helped new migrants adopt industrial discipline, the habits and values that would make them acceptable as workers.[85]

Little statistical evidence about the employment work of Stewart House remains; the settlement had an employment bureau, headed by the hardworking Mrs. Delaney. A few reports list the numbers that were helped with locating work: for example, in 1926 the report claimed that Stewart House placed over four hundred men and women in employment. Black women were probably placed mainly as domestic workers, maids, and laundresses. But Stewart House was less involved in functioning as a domestic-work agency than Flanner House, Campbell House, or Friendship House. Perhaps Gary's black community was not content to have its social-service and cultural institutions become the source of cheap domestic labor for white middle-class homes.[86]

The Delaneys worked hard to relieve the immediate needs of the unemployed before and especially during the Great Depression. The settlement collected and redistributed used clothing and shoes, and operated a woodyard to provide people with fuel. On the problem of employment, however, the settlement could do little. Apart from employment in laboring or domestic positions, there were few alternatives to the steel company as employer. In 1932, the NAACP led the campaign to open sales jobs in the Central District to black women with the slogan "Don't buy where you can't work." There is no evidence that Delaney played a part in this campaign.[87]

Black males were dependent for employment on the steel corporation; UNIA adherents argued that this dependency would continue until the black community established strong economic institutions, including black-owned businesses and banks. Meanwhile, the homely and often-heard remark was "Don't bite the hand that feeds you."

Yet even employment in the steel mills, though highly sought after, did not guarantee blacks steady work, good wages, or the possibility of promotion. Excluded almost completely by the older AFL unions, blacks had been vulnerable to offers of employment during the steel strike of 1919. Consequently, the role they had played as strikebreakers in that crisis increased racial animosity in the steel town and reinforced the tendency for Gary's European immigrants to adopt racist attitudes as part of their Americanization.[88] Racial divisions within the steel work force became a fact of life, one that only strengthened the hand of the corporation. At a time when conditions for the average steel-maker were improving, with better pay and shorter hours, and when many immigrant workers were being promoted into the ranks of skilled labor, blacks still remained trapped in the worst-paid and most dangerous jobs. The hiring policies and employment practices of the steel corporation blocked upward mobility for blacks and kept them as a marginal source of labor, confined to unskilled work and vulnerable to high unemployment. The evidence for this is partly anecdotal, partly statistical. For example, a common practice of the corporation in the twenties was the setting of quotas on the employment of blacks.[89] At a large steel-products works, the superintendent told one interviewer,

> When we got [up to 10 percent] colored employees, I said [to the employment manager] "No more colored without discussion." I got the colored pastors to send colored men whom they could guarantee would not organize and were not bolsheviks, and when a Negro brought another Negro to the plant I told him if the new man wasn't as good as he was, I would let both of them go.[90]

This superintendent also explained how Mexicans were used to balance blacks at the Gary Works in the twenties.

> It isn't good to have all of one nationality: they will gang up on you . . . We have Negroes and Mexicans in a sort of competition with each other. It's a dirty trick, but we don't have the kind of work that will break a man down.[91]

"The Mexicans were first employed here to dilute colored labor," another superintendent told Paul Taylor, this time at a foundry in the region. The black newspaper, the Gary *Sun*, called in an editorial for the restriction of the Mexican immigration: as long as Mexicans and blacks competed for the unskilled jobs, unemployment and powerlessness would be the result for both groups.[92]

The labor policies of the corporation belied the promise that hard work would be rewarded with success. It was an open secret that Superintendent

Gleason and other mill officials were prejudiced against blacks; and the only references to Horace Norton in the typed history of the NAACP call him a "bigot" and "a forceful intolerant person."[93] During the twenties, blacks remained in the lowest-paying jobs in steel, while many of the foreign-born workers were advancing into semiskilled positions. Whereas 30 percent of blacks held skilled or semiskilled jobs in steel at the Gary Works in 1918, by 1928 they had slipped back until only 21 percent of them did so. In 1928, 98 percent of skilled jobs at the South Works were held by whites, only 1.6 percent by blacks. Almost one-half of white workers were classified skilled, but only 5 percent of the black workers. "The attitude of management seems to be that some jobs are for white only," one black U.S. Steel employee remarked in 1944. Even when blacks and whites held the same jobs, there was at least a 10¢ hourly difference in pay between the average black and the average white worker.[94]

The philosophy of Stewart House was based on the belief in upward mobility. That a poor man could pull himself up to self-sufficiency was the basis of the American dream, but it was also rooted in African-American culture with its steadfast belief in self-improvement. Yet this belief was sadly inappropriate in a society characterized by wide inequalities of power and wealth, where race and class, not virtue or effort, determined upward mobility.[95]

In view of how little Stewart House was able to challenge the racist policies of Gary's steel mill and civic elite in housing, education, recreation, or employment, it is a credit to Delaney (or a reflection of the hopelessness of the times) that he received the thanks and affection of the black community. The paunchy, balding minister and his wife were friends and advisers to hundreds who dropped into the settlement every day with heartbreaking stories of need. On Delaney's death, the community renamed Trinity Church "Delaney Church," and when Gary's first black housing project was completed in 1940 it was named "Delaney Project."

Delaney was a versatile race leader, a religious leader who moved easily between the black working class, black leadership, and what contemporaries always called the "better class" of whites. He was often invited to speak as a "representative Negro" at fund-raising luncheons of prominent whites. But when necessary Delaney could play the populist, preaching in overalls to a large and appreciative audience.[96]

But it was hard to disguise the fact that Delaney maintained his position at the pleasure of the powerful white establishment. This would have mattered less so long as the black minister could have used his access to steel management to secure improvements for blacks in jobs, health, or employment. But the history of Stewart House in the 1920s shows that this was not the case. The settlement's welfare efforts ameliorated conditions, but could not remove the main causes of black poverty in Gary: the Jim Crow practices of schools, employers, and realtors, and the racist labor policies of the corporation—unofficial quotas, differential wages, and job ceilings—which kept blacks in the lowest-paying jobs and blocked their advancement. The black settlement was powerless to check the development of segregation in all areas of the city's life—indeed, it was itself a product of segregation.

Like black political bosses of the 1920s who attached themselves to white-dominated political parties in the patronage system and became detached from the masses they claimed to represent, the black minister was seen by more militant blacks as a creature of the corporation. Delaney was said to be the only black man who could go into the steel-company management office at any time. This access, while it gave him influence with the white establishment, undermined his credibility with blacks.[97] To give one example, during the 1920s, Stewart House, like many other settlement houses, held a Sunday-evening forum where prominent speakers of both races were featured and lively debates often ensued. But at least one black steelworker believed that Delaney "would keep the company posted." Although the forums were popular, we may assume that discussion was guarded.[98]

Interviewed in August 1934, a few years before his death, Reverend Delaney thoughtfully summed up the relationship between the settlement house and the mill.

> Yes, the steel companies have been willing to help us. They have aided most of the churches in a material way. The establishment of this agency [a social center] was brought about through the joint enterprise of the company and the church. The company was not satisfied with the progress of the churches. So . . . they bought this property and said they would share dollars in the erection of this building. They have cooperated in the activities. I don't want you to think that I am a tool for the company, but there are circumstances that . . . [99]

Another black minister, one who had not benefited from the company's support, interviewed in 1934, spoke of the close relations between black churches and the steel company in much more critical tones.

> Because the company controls this city, there are few of us who are not afraid to go against the wishes of Mr. _____ , who runs this town. To work here you must work for some part of the mill directly or indirectly . . . There is no way the colored have to say anything against this . . .

The churches had become "subsidiaries of the steel corporation," he concluded, "and the ministers dare not get up and say anything against the company."[100]

Reverend Delaney tried to put the best face on the situation. Stewart House, he declared in 1938, summing up the settlement's seventeen-year history, "has not concerned itself so much about formulating programs which it desires people to conform to, but finding people in their own strata with their own needs and helping them get up on their feet and walk."[101] Delaney's distaste for "formulating programs" was the reluctance of one who maintained a moderate or conciliatory stance during all the controversies of the preceding years, in some cases acting as mediator between opposing factions, in other cases working closely with the white establishment. It was the hesitancy of an opportunist to be pinned down.

Even in 1936, when the Steel Workers Organizing Committee under John L. Lewis was conducting a drive to organize Gary's steelworkers, including blacks, a drive where they expected and in fact assumed the opposition of black ministers, Delaney tried to hold things together. "As you go along with us, I want to assure you that we will do our best to go along with you to make our community . . . a better one in which to live," he told the predominantly white audience at a Stewart House fund-raising lunch. This mild statement might have struck some of his listeners as astonishing in view of the labor situation: while the steel-company officials were approaching black workers individually, asking if the company could "depend on them" as it had in 1919, Delaney was publicly assuring the white elite that it could count on the support of the black middle class.[102]

The history of the rise of the New Unions need not concern us here. U.S. Steel suddenly agreed to recognize the CIO, and the struggle was over almost before it began. Shortly after this, in 1939, Delaney died. In a piece in the Gary *American*, February 17, 1939, entitled "The Job at Stewart House," the writer summed up the black minister's contribution to race improvement in Gary: "The late lamented leader served, sacrificed, and made contributions to the uplift of the community that will not be expected of his successor. He made friends of the institution and the race that we hope will be retained."[103] A replacement minister for Trinity Church would be easy enough to find, the writer conceded. But Delaney's achievement had been to "tie in" to the institution such people as Norton, Snyder, and others, people who "represent Gary's best." The task for the Stewart House board and the trustees of the church was now to find someone "whose cogs would mesh with the present set-up."[104]

But was the "present set-up" worth keeping? Those who tried to prevent the segregation of Gary's schools, who sought equal access to Gary's parks, and who tried to organize black steel workers against the opposition of the black clergy, did not think so. One CIO spokesman in Gary complained, "All we have met from the Negro preacher . . . is discouragement. They don't seem to care anything about the low wages and bad working conditions their people suffer, nor the feudal condition which exists in the plants here."[105]

Of course, this was vastly unfair. Delaney and other black ministers cared deeply about the poverty and oppression that they witnessed every day. And although the settlement house was founded in part by elite groups who sought to control blacks, it nevertheless brought the black community tangible benefits. Delaney had judged his position carefully: he believed that he could do more as an intermediary between the races than as an adversary, and the quasi-feudal power of the corporation and the sorry failures of the NAACP to challenge it in this period may show that he was correct. It was just that in accepting white money and steel-company sponsorship, Delaney and Stewart House were unable to correct the fundamental injustices from which blacks suffered.

Conclusion

Seven settlement portraits are not the same as a portrait of the whole settlement movement. Nevertheless, these Indiana settlements can tell us much about the national scene, especially about the second-tier settlements that numbered in the hundreds in America's cities in the early twentieth century. Differing from each other and from the Hull House "model" in their origins, alliances, and client populations, these settlement houses serve as a reminder of the variety that existed within the settlement movement, a variety that has not always received sufficient attention in general accounts. Much less well endowed than the famous settlements like Hull House, these "second tier" settlements made little impact on the national scene. Yet, at the local level, they were "spearheads for reform," promoting improvements to their neighborhoods in public health, education, and recreation, sponsoring day nurseries, kindergartens, libraries, and night schools. Settlements were ahead of their time, pioneering services, such as the neighborhood health clinics, that would be repudiated in the conservative twenties as too "socialistic."[1] In an age when business and government looked to the private sector for solutions, the settlements were voluntary, idiosyncratic agencies that tackled some of urban America's worst social problems. In so doing, they helped put in place many of the programs that would become the charge of government in the New Deal and after.

Yet if the settlements of this study had done no more than replicate the famous models—if they had only confirmed what we already knew about Hull House and the larger settlements—their story would be hardly worth telling. In fact, the Indiana settlements differed significantly from the Hull House model in several ways. They provide evidence about the settlement movement that was not available from the major settlements alone; they reflect tensions within the wider movement and within Progressivism itself.

First, religion played a much greater role in the settlement movement than many historians have recognized. Hull House had no affiliation with a church, and its residents held to a secular "religion of humanity." As neighbors to immigrants of all faiths, they believed that a nonsectarian and undogmatic approach was best. And although Jane Addams and the women of Hull House used a language of reform that was embedded in Protestant

Evangelicalism, Addams insisted that religious observance had no place in the settlement's programs.

But this secular stance denied the two great parent movements of the settlements: the Social Gospel of Toynbee Hall with its Anglican affiliation, and the missions to freedmen in the post–Civil War South where, it has been suggested, American settlements also had their origins.[2] These Indiana case studies show that religious faith was an important motive for many settlement workers. And the church, as an institution, was an important sponsor of settlements in the Progressive period. Many settlements were headed by ministers; some even used their social-service programs to function (in the frank expression of Gary's Rev. William Grant Seaman) as "feeders to the church." Despite the fact that the National Federation of Settlements excluded from membership those that acted like missions, settlements like Campbell House and Neighborhood House continued to glory in their evangelical purpose and to receive funding from their respective denominations—Campbell House and Stewart House from the Methodist Episcopal church, and Neighborhood House from the Presbyterian church.

Gary-Alerding, the Catholic settlement house, was different again. Created as a result of an initiative by the Catholic hierarchy, and therefore more identified with the purposes of the church leadership than the settlements of what I have called the "heroic account," Gary-Alerding may nevertheless have been typical of the hundreds (by one count, thousands) of Catholic settlements across the country which have generally been left out of the history of the settlement movement.[3] The church used Gary-Alerding settlement to wage war on several fronts at once: to combat anticlericalism and indifference among Catholic immigrants on the one hand, to neutralize the proselytizing efforts of the Protestant agencies on the other, and all the while to fight off socialism as well. Clearly, such settlements were different from the secular, pragmatic cosmopolitanism associated with the Hull House model.

While some settlements, like Christamore, became more secular with time, others went the other way. Flanner House and Immigrants' Aid Society's Foreign House (later American Settlement) had their origins in secular Progressive reform movements—municipal reform on the one hand and charity organization on the other. Yet both these originally secular settlement houses were driven by financial need into the arms of a church: both eventually accepted the support of the Disciples of Christ denomination and subsequently tacked religious teaching, Sunday school, and worship services onto their other programs. Christamore, on the other hand, which had initially been identified with this same denomination, abandoned its religious affiliation and programming after it joined the National Federation of Settlements in 1911.

Previous accounts of the Progressive-era settlements emphasized the importance of the "social science" settlements which like Hull House were conceived as laboratories of the new social science, centers for pioneering techniques of sociological inquiry and measurement, as well as centers for reform.[4] But the residents of these Indiana settlements, so far as we can tell, owed more to the Social Gospel than to sociology. They counted poverty, dirt, and ignorance as sin and witnessed to their faith by caring for sick babies, visiting the poor, and teaching immigrant mothers to sew. They were less interested in social science than in saving souls.

A second important difference between these seven settlements and the "heroic account" concerns their relations with immigrants. As Americanizers, these settlements were not agencies of cultural pluralism, as many historians have assumed. The five settlements of this study that worked with immigrants together present a great deal of evidence about the goals of settlement Americanization programs, and it is evidence that contradicts the Liberal Progressives' account at several points. It thus reinforces the movement already under way toward the reinterpretation of Hull House as an Americanizing agency.[5]

The settlement workers of this study were not cultural pluralists, but missionaries for the American Way. While they spoke of accepting immigrant "contributions" to American life, they did not conceive of American society as malleable or in progress toward a new synthesis. We will look in vain in the settlement literature for the idea that immigrant culture had anything of permanent value to contribute to American society; instead, the settlement workers saw American culture as something already fixed, to which immigrants would soon conform. The goal was "adjusting their life to ours." While close contact with foreign immigrants and their culture often inspired the admiration of settlement workers, it did not deflect them from working to hasten the assimilation of the immigrants to American standards and culture. Grace Warmington's appreciation of the struggles of Gary's immigrant mothers, or Mary Rigg's sympathetic and intelligent word-portraits of Indianapolis immigrants show that individual settlement workers were kindly observers of the immigrant community. But sympathy and admiration are not at issue. What is important is how settlement workers viewed immigrant culture and how they interpreted their task of Americanization.

The settlements' relationship with the immigrants, whether in Indianapolis's Foreign District or on Gary's South Side, was characterized by impatience with immigrant cultural practices and a determination to end ethnic separateness. Indianapolis's Foreign House was established by civic reformers out of near-panic at the presence of separate ethnic communities within the Hoosier capital, "ignorant of our language, methods of government, and national ideas."[6] The settlement's sponsors saw the immigrant colonies as not only a menace to health and order but also a barrier to the success of the wider Progressive campaign against dirt, disease, and political corruption; their intervention into the immigrant community had characteristics both of protection and coercion. Learning was to be a one-way process, as settlements brought immigrants up to American standards. True, settlements sometimes seemed to play the dual role of Americanizer and preserver of immigrant culture. But when settlement programs encouraged expressions of ethnicity—whether singing or dancing, cooking special dishes, or observing immigrants' national holidays—it was generally within the context of attracting immigrants to the settlements' wider purpose of Americanization. And when settlement workers interpreted Americanization to include drawing immigrants into an American Protestant church—what the sponsors of Campbell House unabashedly called "Christian Americanization"—they not only threw up new barriers between themselves and the immigrants, but also stepped over the line from social work to cultural imperialism.

This is not to say that the settlements did not hold out some attraction to the upwardly mobile or unusual immigrant. As some of the case studies in Chapter 2 show, many immigrants benefited from the settlements. English classes helped them write a letter of application for work; instruction in manners and conventions helped them hold a job, make money, and improve their status. Playgrounds, sports programs, and gyms were popular with the children of immigrants even if their parents kept aloof. On the other hand, as historian Rivka Lissak has suggested, the immigrants most attracted to the settlements might often have been those most marginal in the immigrant community—Romanian Baptists, for example, or Italian intellectuals without any ties to the peasant-based Italian ethnic associations. Most important, settlements never succeeded in diverting the immigrant communities from building their own institutions of worship, mutual benefit, and cultural defense.[7]

Most previous studies of the settlement movement did not so much misstate questions of race as omit them. For example, in his important monograph *Spearheads for Reform: The Social Settlements and the Progressive Movement, 1890–1914,* historian Allen F. Davis described the role played by settlement workers Mary White Ovington, William English Walling, Jane Addams, and Lillian Wald in founding the NAACP in 1909; he noted the contribution of settlement residents such as John Daniels to the social investigation of conditions among urban blacks. However, he did not fully discuss the relations of settlements with blacks or inquire into the origins or role of the black settlements. Since that work appeared, historians have begun to fill in these gaps: they have analyzed the programs of white-led settlements for blacks and traced the process by which the white-only settlements became racially integrated since 1945. They have also begun to retrieve the history of the settlements founded in the North and South by blacks themselves.[8]

This book has continued the process. It has shown the impact on the Indiana settlements of black migration into the cities and traced the efforts of "white" settlements such as Christamore to flee black populations, efforts that were ultimately unsuccessful. It has shown how white philanthropists and reformers established two settlements, Flanner House and Stewart House, to serve the rapidly growing population of needy blacks in their respective Indiana cities. An important finding has been the extent to which the black settlements, though controlled by conservative black and white elites, nevertheless became effective reform institutions. For example, in Gary in the 1920s, Stewart House, a segregated settlement, worked in the space "between church and mill" to help blacks improve their lives. Both these settlements were created by exclusion, yet both became a source of improvements in their respective black communities. Flanner House functioned as a center for voluntary service providers in the black community. Though not resident in the settlement, middle-class black women made Flanner House a catalyst for neighborhood improvement at a time when most male race leaders stood aloof: soon, a "community of women reformers" gathered around the settlement. Despite the denial of rights that made the "Progressive era" a time of repression for African-Americans, blacks used the settlements to achieve some gains in their living standards and opportunities.

To incorporate race as a category of analysis in the settlement movement broadens our understanding. A portrait that focused only on the well-known white settlements gave the false impression that the movement was confined to cities of the North and Northeast, served mainly immigrants, and was disassociated from missions on the one hand and charity organization on the other. It also suggested that a program combining social service with recreational, educational, and health activities at the neighborhood level was unique to the settlements. But such a generalization ignores the evidence of important self-help organizations among blacks. In excluding "mission" settlements, the National Federation of Settlements also excluded most black social-service organizations, however complete a "settlement program" of education, recreation, and health care they might have had. In addition, treating the black settlements as a unique form of social-service activity has obscured the fact that settlements run by whites for blacks were part of an older tradition of white philanthropy among African-Americans.[9] This study has shown the need to "reintegrate" the history of the settlements by including in it the black social-service agencies whose histories are being written by such historians as Sharon Harley, Cynthia

Neverdon-Morton, Jacqueline Rouse, Rosalyn Terborg-Penn, Evelyn Brooks Higginbotham, and others. Many voluntary agencies, religious and secular, worked to uplift and adjust poor people, including blacks and immigrants, but only a minority of these agencies joined the settlement movement.[10]

The Progressive-era settlement movement has come to occupy an important place in the history of American feminism. Indeed, some who have based their generalizations on Hull House as typical have claimed all the settlements as feminist institutions. Female Progressives, so the argument goes, made the settlements into a "woman's space," where collective living produced a supportive sisterhood of reform. Settlements were "parallel institutions" to the public ones of male political power. They were private, homelike institutions whose female residents could move, however timidly, into the public sphere. Moreover, it has been argued, the collective-living arrangements of settlement residents demonstrated a pioneering "material feminism" that presented an alternative to the patriarchal, individualist family. Settlements sponsored cooperative housekeeping arrangements for their neighbors—experimental public kitchens, working-girls' cooperative boarding houses, communal laundries, showers and baths—that challenged the emerging norms of twentieth-century middle-class domesticity.[11]

The Indiana settlements have provided an opportunity to test such generalizations about the Progressive-era settlements as feminist institutions. Certainly, settlement living appealed to single, professional women who wanted to live independently of family in the city. The settlement house was an alternative to the "Y" and to the dreary single rooms of "working-girls."[12] For example, between 1905 and 1908, a continual succession of young women came to live at Christamore. How many Sister Carries were saved from seduction because they lived in a settlement, we shall never know. A fine series of settlement biographies has shown how living in a settlement helped some women sustain careers.[13] But in Indiana, most settlement residents seem to have stayed for only a short time: marriage probably ended the careers of most of them. Thus, the long settlement residences of Jane Addams, Alice Hamilton, and Lillian Wald—careers that precluded marriage—were not typical of most settlement workers. The Indianapolis settlements do show us two very long-lasting careers, however: Olive Edwards stayed as director at Christamore for thirty-two years, and Mary Rigg as director of American Settlement for thirty-eight years. For Edwards, a widow, and Rigg, who never married, the settlement provided a solution to vocation and family that recalls Jane Addams's long tenure at Hull House.

An important finding of this study is that the settlement as a "community of women reformers" existed as a stage in the development of several settlement houses. At Christamore it was strongly evident before 1911. And in Gary, the churchwomen who started Neighborhood House did so against the advice of male ministers and initially without the support of church leaders. Similarly, the Methodist churchwomen who founded Campbell House claimed it as a women's institution: "It is ours, Ours, OURS!"[14] However, within a few years, all these settlements had come under male domination: Christamore was drawn into a citywide federation of professional social work, the two religious settlements into the male-led urban mission organizations of their respective denominations. Flanner House, a focus for female-led reform, as noted above, was nevertheless almost continually under male leadership.

The records of the Indiana settlements hold few examples of the ferment of feminist reform associated with Hull House. Only Christamore among these settlements resembled the Hull House model. There, Anna Stover and Edith Surbey, loving friends and fellow reformers, shared an intense evangelical faith that sustained them through setbacks and exhaustion as they sought to bring the Kingdom of Heaven to their slum neighborhood. A Hull House, yet with a strongly religious flavor, Christamore was probably a much more typical settlement than its more famous model two hundred miles away in Chicago.

Some features of "material feminism" were present in the settlements of this study: communal laundries, day nurseries, and baths served the settlements' neighbors. However, there is no evidence that settlement residents saw these arrangements as anything but temporary expedients, stopgap measures for the neediest working-class families. In fact, this account has shown how the settlements provided services for working mothers in terms that tended to reinforce the ambiguities about women's roles along with traditional notions of motherhood. For example, although they provided day care for the children of working mothers, the Indiana settlements never conceded that motherhood was other than women's supreme duty and role. They released mothers for day work—but they understood the day nurseries to be a way to enhance the motherhood of their clients, not to supersede it. In this, the Indiana settlements confirm what is emerging as a new picture of how class, race, and gender established conflicting and sometimes contradictory meanings for terms such as "Progressive" and "reform." If the settlement workers were single women and professionals, the message they conveyed to working-class clients was nevertheless one of femininity, not feminism, a vision of reform that rested on a greatly enhanced role for motherhood, rather than on equality or individualism, on mothers' duties, not women's rights.[15]

But if the identity of the Indiana settlements as feminist institutions seems problematical, this study has shown that, whether their neighbors were poor whites, like those in Christamore's first neighborhood, blacks like those at Flanner House, or immigrants on Gary's South Side, the settlements were continuously concerned with the health and welfare of working-class women and their children.[16] Clubs, classes, health clinics, and socials targeted neighborhood mothers, and after-school activities targeted their daughters. Alongside the national campaigns of settlement leaders like Jane Addams and Mary McDowell for the vote, that symbol of women's equality as citizens of the Republic, ran a current of reform that stressed the need to protect the nation's mothers. Most settlements were far more committed to the goals of special treatment for women than to the principle of equality. The papers of the Indiana settlements contain little about suffrage; instead, they exploit gender differences in order to call for special protection for women.

More than any other issue, that of wage-work for mothers reveals the settlements' divided mind. Settlements generally opposed it because it interfered with women's supreme task, child-rearing. Yet, when their clients were black, the settlements of this study suspended their disapproval and encouraged black women to seek paid work, even if they had young children. Because of poverty in the black community and because discrimination made it hard for their husbands to find work, black mothers were often driven to seek paid work as domestics, maids, and laundresses. Unlike the Hull House social feminists such as Julia Lathrop and Florence Kelley who discouraged working-class mothers from seeking paid work, these Indiana settlements (Flanner House, Campbell House, and Neighborhood House) facilitated the entry of black women into the labor market, providing day care and operating employment agencies for them. Justifying these activities in the same terms in which it justified its prohibition on work by other women, settlement literature spoke of the experience of domestic work as one that enhanced the black woman as mother to her own children and domestic worker in her own home. If a working mother could be the ruin of a white family, apparently she could be the salvation of a black one.[17]

The settlements' policies on working women were inconsistent because they reflected contradictory intentions: settlement workers wanted to protect Motherhood, but they were also concerned about the work ethic; they believed in improving the care of children in the home—but they also knew that the settlement nursery provided better influences than many poor homes; mothers should not "have to" work, but if they had to, then the settlements should facilitate work for them; mothers were always potential workers, but never the most desirable workers. These private agencies display the same conflicts as were being debated in public policy. Progressive-era public-policy successes, such as mothers' pensions, which acted to withdraw many women from the labor force, had their counterpoint in other Progressive policies that pushed other classes of women out into the work force. As historian Alice Kessler-Harris writes, "Clearly, some women had to be socialized into staying home while others were encouraged to work."[18]

That the settlement-run domestic-employment agency at Flanner House achieved genuine protection for black domestic workers was important. These programs at Flanner House, Campbell House, and Neighborhood House helped the survival of black families struggling with poverty. And they enhanced the role of the black woman as breadwinner, contradicting the thrust of mainstream Progressives (including labor unions and social feminists) toward the goal of the family wage. That they also channeled black women into domestic work reveals the undertow of repression in the Progressive tide that pulled black Americans in another direction from that of white Americans and immigrants.

Another theme of this study has been how the settlements functioned within the social relations of capitalism. In their programs to get poor people into the industrial work force (or, in the case of women, into the paid, unskilled work force), they were at once more conservative and more practical than the more famous settlements. Their attitude toward industrial work contrasts with that of early theorists of the movement. Frederick Denison Maurice and Charles Kingsley, nineteenth-century forerunners of the English settlements, had believed in a cooperative commonwealth that would turn aside from the ugly materialism of industrial society with its deep class divisions, where wealth would be produced by labor without exploitation. Through Toynbee and Ruskin, such ideas about work and community influenced the American settlement movement, especially Hull House, and led to two of that settlement's best-known experiments. In 1900, Jane Addams and Ellen Gates Starr founded the Hull House Labor Museum in order to make a statement about the fact that work in industrial society had become mechanical and soulless. The museum displayed traditional work processes such as spinning and weaving so that the children of immigrants could come to appreciate the skills of their parents. And immigrants, though employed all day in industries or sweatshops, could learn handicrafts and restore a wholeness to work and life. Ellen Starr's Hull House bookbindery was based on similar principles. Both presented a critique of standardization, the decline of crafts, and the separation between work and the management of work processes.[19]

The Hull House experiments made an important statement about the passing of the older craftsmanship, but it was just that—more epitaph than alternative. Most settlements organized a more practical response to the problem of work in capitalist society. (Hull House, too, soon turned to more practical programs.) Whereas the Hull House Labor Museum celebrated the role of the skilled craftsperson, the settlements of this study helped workers compete more effectively for whatever jobs existed: they sought to adapt people to industrial society, not to change the way the political economy was organized. Thus, as rural folk, black and white, and foreign immigrants continued to arrive in the cities, the settlements organized classes for vocational and manual training, night schools, employment bureaus, and domestic-service agencies, all with the goal of assisting people to find work, of whatever kind. Indeed, although settlement programs encouraged individualism and upward mobility (values often at odds with the immigrants' own beliefs), their long-term goal was to speed the proletarianization of the newcomers into an undifferentiated working class. Only in rare cases, such as at Flanner House in the 1920s, did the settlements manage to control the terms of this work, set wages and hours, or secure conditions favorable to the workers.

From this it follows that the settlements' activities posed no threat to business. Again, the Hull House example presents a misleading model, for Hull House was, at least in its first two decades, often critical of business. Hull House residents picketed, supported striking meatpackers and garment workers, and cheerfully got themselves arrested for their pro-labor activities. Jane Addams opened Hull House to labor-union meetings and invited anarchists to dinner. "At Hull House one got into the labor movement as a matter of course, without realizing how or when," settlement resident Alice Hamilton wrote.[20] Other prominent settlements, too, worked with labor allies and were sometimes criticized for their stand on labor issues. Of the major activist settlements, Allen Davis wrote, "As a group they offered important and genuine support to organized labor at a time when labor had few friends."[21]

This book has analyzed in some detail the relations among the seven Indiana settlements and business. It has found no link between organized labor and the settlements in Indiana, instead it has revealed increasing involvement by business in funding and controlling these voluntary agencies. In Indianapolis, progressive businessmen were influential in setting up the Foreign House (Immigrants' Aid Society) in 1911; however, most support for the settlements came not from business but from religious groups. Business involvement with the settlements increased with World War I, however, and was formalized by the establishment of the Community Chest in 1923. In Gary, where the whole infrastructure had to be built from scratch and where the agencies of social control, such as churches, were just starting up, the steel corporation played a much larger role in establishing and supporting voluntary agencies, including the settlements. After 1919, when labor unrest and even militancy seemed to threaten corporation hegemony, U.S. Steel infused money into the settlement movement, supporting the two Protestant settlements and establishing the two additional settlements,

Stewart House and Gary-Alerding Settlement, in cooperation with the Methodist Episcopal church and the Catholic church, respectively, as described in Chapters 6 and 7.

What was the basis of business support for the settlements, an alliance so seemingly incongruous when measured against the Hull House model of what a Progressive-era settlement was? Did business corporations support the settlements because, as contemporary sociologist Thornstein Veblen suggested, they "enhanced the industrial efficiency of the poor"? Plenty of evidence exists to document the sense of crisis felt by early-twentieth-century corporate employers about labor costs and efficiency. Absenteeism, unions, high turnover, foreign workers who could not understand English and were a danger to themselves and others—such "labor problems" prompted corporations such as U.S. Steel to embark on systematic programs of Americanization and welfare work. This book has traced the development of such programs in Gary. It has noted the pragmatic alliances formed between the corporation and the social workers as both sought to Americanize workers—with social workers concerned for living standards and morality, employers for any conditions in the homes or in the community that would foster unions, increase instability, or challenge the company's power.

Such evidence puts the settlement movement back into the historiographical mainstream of early-twentieth-century reform. Earlier interpretations of progressivism as a movement that enlarged American democracy by curbing the power of corporations are now widely discredited; Robert Wiebe, James Weinstein, Gabriel Kolko, Judith Sealander, and others have shown how business values and business interests in fact shaped many aspects of Progressive-era reform.[22] Emerging social-work institutions, too, were shaped by business: settlements and other voluntary social-work agencies were private, but their work had public consequences. Viewed in this context, settlements were part of Progressive-era reform aiming to discipline and modernize the urban masses—and American business was vitally interested in the outcome. Labor historians have dubbed the early-twentieth-century workplace a "contested terrain"; this study shows that the community, too, was a contested terrain. Social workers, dependent on corporate dollars yet sympathetic to the poor, had to choose sides, and how they did so has formed one of the themes of this book.[23]

Veblen's aphorism that settlements served to enhance the industrial efficiency of the poor accurately identified the weakness of a reform impulse issuing from within the industrial order itself. The history of these second-tier settlements confirms the correctness of his insight into the limits of settlement-led reform. But it does more: such a criticism can also help to explain the decline of the settlements after 1914, including the eclipse of the more radical Hull House–type institutions.

In her book *Settlement Houses and the Great Depression* (1975), historian Judith Trolander described how the rise of the Community Chest in most American cities coincided with the decline of activism in all but a small handful of settlements. Trolander's second book, *Professionalism and Social Change: From the Settlement House Movement to Neighborhood Centers* (1987), continued to explore the reasons for what she saw as the decline of activism in the settlement movement since the Progressive era. She cited the changing racial composition of settlement neighborhoods from immigrant to black, a change which settlements were slow to reflect and which alienated them from their working-class constituents. She also blamed professionalization, which meant that settlement workers (increasingly males, not females) became mobile and career-oriented—no longer resident "friendly neighbors," and no longer identified closely with their neighborhoods.[24]

Although Trolander convincingly documented these changes in the settlements in the 1930s and after, she made the assumption that the settlements of the Progressive era set a standard of activism from which their successors declined. But to read the history of the settlements as a history of "declension" is to overlook the essential conservatism of the settlements even in the Progressive era. Even the burst of activism at Hull House was a glorious but untypical phenomenon and Hull House reformers were meeting serious defeats by the 1920s.

Rather than seeking the cause of the decline of settlement activism in the 1930s and after we should recognize how limited settlement activism was, even in the Progressive era. If the settlements failed to transform society, it was because this was never their goal. For example, although the residents of Hull House and some university settlements engaged in collecting social statistics as a prelude to reform, these "social-science settlements" were few. Most settlement workers busied themselves with a succession of urgent needs; they rarely had time for legislative or national solutions or for theorizing. Moreover, settlement workers' efforts to encourage self-help and to build character resembled the charity-organization solution—individualistic and moralistic—more than the settlement leadership ever acknowledged. And in the 1920s, many settlement workers and social workers would slide over into the conservative school of social diagnosis that focused on the psychological maladjustment of individuals rather than on systemic problems of capitalist society.

Meanwhile, settlement workers who believed in nothing less than the fundamental reform of society found the settlements inadequate. Florence Kelley was often critical of the settlements, though she was a resident both of Hull House and Henry Street Settlement; Mary Simkhovitch eventually rejected the settlement as a reform institution; Raymond Robins and Robert

Hunter became socialists. Radical feminist Charlotte Perkins Gilman began by admiring the settlements but ended up critical of their views on women and family; Emma Goldman lampooned them as institutions "where the poor learn to eat with forks."[25]

Conservatism was not a disorder that overtook the settlements late in their careers. In the Indiana settlements, at least, it was present in the configuration of possibilities from the beginning. Settlement workers hoped for the transformation of neighborhoods, but often had to be content to change some individuals. Each settlement resident could tell success stories of the individual, once the grubby, bright-eyed star of the settlement boys' club, who had become a successful businessman or civic leader. From such examples, they drew the lesson that "the American dream" was real: after all, if one or two could rise, then success lay within the grasp of anyone with character.

But there were limits to what such reform could achieve. Gertrude Barnum, a prominent Women's Trade Union League activist, explained why she had "graduated" from the settlement movement to the labor movement.

> As I became more familiar with the conditions around me, I began to feel that while the settlement was undoubtedly doing a great deal to make the lives of working people less grim and hard, the work was not fundamental. It introduced into their lives books and flowers and music, and it gave them a place to meet and see their friends or leave their babies when they went out to work, but it did not raise their wages, or shorten their hours. It began to dawn on me, therefore, that it would be more practical to turn our energies toward raising wages and shortening hours.[26]

Barnum was right. Not only were the settlements unable to make fundamental changes in the conditions around them, but during World War I, they also enthusiastically joined the crusade for Americanization and for an efficient, well-adapted work force. Obituaries for the Progressive movement can be wearisome, but Robert Wiebe's still deserves attention. In a chapter called "The Illusion of Fulfillment," Wiebe suggested that Progressive-era reformers had mistaken the approach to reform for reform itself. "[They] had built no more than a loose framework, one malleable enough to serve many purposes," he wrote.[27] The settlement house as an institution was such a framework. Established not to empower but to uplift the poor, the settlements that remained after the Progressive tide receded merged with professional social work to become part of a new partnership with business and with local elites. Settlement leaders Rev. William Grant Seaman, Father de Ville, and Rev. Frank Delaney worked tirelessly for the people of Gary, but despite their efforts they were seen as tools of the corporation. Elbert Gary, the fatherly chairman of U.S. Steel, had the last word after all when, on his famous visit to Gary in 1923, he praised the settlement leaders as "Gentlemen whose work is our work."[28]

If chance had removed, by fire or flood, all the attendance records of these seven settlement houses but left intact all the evidence documenting the intentions of their founders, there would be good reason to revive a "social control" interpretation of the settlement movement. Such an interpretation might lay stress on how poor people were manipulated by agencies offering social services but in fact intending to control and co-opt them. I have shown how those who established the settlements of this study did so in order to promote more distant goals—Americanization, the suppression of political dissent, the triumph of Protestantism (or Catholicism). They founded settlements to speed up the assimilation of immigrants, to guarantee the triumph of WASP values, or to assure a work force that was clean, sober, and content. The settlements were part of the Progressive "Search for Order," a broad restructuring of American society.

But the attendance records are there. Thousands of people, young and old, black and white, Americans and immigrants, came to settlement classes, clubs, and socials, used settlement facilities, and attended settlement events. Were they duped and manipulated? Did they abandon ethnic traditions and class-based values in exchange for a modicum of health care, some English lessons, and a chance to use the settlement gym once a week? Such an interpretation is hardly convincing. People came to the settlement because they needed what it had to offer. For people who had no alternative, the weekly health clinic was an important resource. For children of the city, the settlement playground, with its grass and seesaws, was better than the streets. The settlement dance, though inconveniently chaperoned, had a middle-class aura that appealed to the upwardly mobile. For immigrants, the night schools, cultural programs, and English classes of the settlements could make the difference between a low-paying job like Gabriel Potcova found, "cutting up cows," and a chance at clean, higher-status work. If Gary steelworkers attended night schools at the settlement or the plant after a twelve-hour day, it was because they saw that workers with a command of English got ahead, while the unassimilated "Hunkies" continued to work amid the searing heat and danger of the blast furnaces and rolling mills. "The crucial fact," David Brody wrote, "is that in the steel mills immigrants did rise."[29]

A generation of historians has noted the existence of contradictory tendencies within Progressive reform. To Christopher Lasch, the Progressives were "torn between their wish to liberate the unused energies of the submerged portions of society and their enthusiasm for social planning, which led in practice to new and subtler forms of repression." To Don Kirschner, progressivism led both toward social justice and social control; it left behind an ambiguous legacy.[30]

Such ambiguity is not news to historians of social welfare; three decades ago, social-work expert Ralph Pumphrey wrote his important essay "Compassion and Protection: Dual Motivations in Social Welfare."[31] In exploring the tensions within the settlement movement this study has discovered the dualisms that Pumphrey spoke of—compassion and protection, reform and coercion. Combining the sympathy of humanitarians, the science of experts, and often, too, the zeal of missionaries, settlement workers entered the slums with brave but contradictory purposes: to help the poor and to control poor people, to assist foreigners and to eradicate foreignness, to deal with the "colored problem," that is, the problems blacks faced—but also with the problems that whites had in accepting them. Segregated black agencies, with interracial boards of control, promised to do both.

By showing how social work created new forms of social order, this study points toward the need for a reinterpretation of the settlement movement as a whole. The settlements, long immune from the historiographical revisionism that has transformed our understanding of most other aspects of Progressivism, were in fact as full of contradictory purposes, of noble dreams, well-meaning interventions, and tragic failures, as the wider Progressive movement of which they were a part.

Notes

Introduction

1. Arthur S. Link and Richard L. McCormick, *Progressivism* (Arlington Heights, Ill.: Harlan Davidson, 1983), p. 72; Michael B. Katz, *Poverty and Policy in American History* (New York: Academic Press, 1983), p. 201, n. 10.

2. The settlement-house leaders were an articulate and self-conscious lot; by one estimate, they produced over forty-five books. See Stephen Kalberg, "Commitment to Career Reform: The Settlement House Leaders," *Social Service Review* 49 (December 1975): 612. Judith Trolander calls Jane Addams "a superb publicist." Judith Ann Trolander, *Professionalism and Social Change: From the Settlement House Movement to Neighborhood Centers, 1886 to the Present* (New York: Columbia University Press, 1987), pp. 15–16. Settlement autobiographies include Jane Addams, *Twenty Years at Hull House* (New York: Macmillan, 1910; repr. ed., Signet, 1960); *Second Twenty Years at Hull House* (New York: Macmillan, 1930); Lillian Wald, *The House on Henry Street* (New York: Henry Holt, 1915), and *Windows on Henry Street* (Boston: Little, Brown, 1943); Alice Hamilton, *Exploring the Dangerous Trades: The Autobiography of Alice Hamilton* (Boston: Little, Brown, 1943); Graham Taylor, *Pioneering on Social Frontiers* (Chicago: University of Chicago Press, 1931); Florence Kelley, *The Autobiography of Florence Kelley: Notes of Sixty Years*, ed. Kathryn Kish Sklar (Chicago: Charles H. Kerr, 1986); Vida Scudder, *On Journey* (New York: E. P. Dutton, 1937). Biographies of settlement workers by friends and colleagues include Robert L. Duffus, *Lillian Wald: Neighbor and Crusader* (New York: Macmillan, 1938); Josephine Goldmark, *Impatient Crusader: Florence Kelley's Life Story* (Urbana: University of Illinois Press, 1953); Jane Addams, *My Friend, Julia Lathrop* (New York: Macmillan, 1935); Eleanor Woods, *Robert A. Woods: Champion of Democracy* (Boston: Houghton Mifflin, 1929); Edith Abbott, "Grace Abbott: A Sister's Memories," *Social Service Review* 13 (September 1939): 351–407, and "Grace Abbott and Hull House, 1908–21," *Social Service Review* 24 (September-December 1950); 374–94, 493–518.

3. Allen F. Davis, *Spearheads for Reform: The Social Settlements and the Progressive Movement, 1890–1914* (New York: Oxford University Press, 1967). Richard C. Wade, in his Foreword to this first edition of *Spearheads for Reform*, called the settlements "the principal instruments of this first war on poverty," p. vii.

4. Jacob Riis, *How the Other Half Lives* (New York: Scribner's, 1890). Surveys of the Progressive-era social-justice movement begin with Harold U. Faulkner, *The Crusade for Social Justice* (New York: Macmillan, 1931), and include Robert A. Bremner, *From the Depths: The Discovery of Poverty in America* (New York: New York University Press, 1956); and Paul Boyer, *Urban Masses and Moral Order in America, 1820–1920* (Cambridge: Harvard University Press, 1978). See also David Ward, *Poverty, Ethnicity, and the American City, 1840–1925* (New York: Cambridge University Press, 1989), pp. 46–93. Intellectual underpinnings are dealt with in Robert M. Crunden, *Ministers of Reform: The Progressives' Achievement in American Civilization, 1889–1920* (New York: Basic Books, 1982), and James T. Kloppenberg's *Uncertain Victory: Social Democracy and Progressivism in European and American Thought, 1870–1920* (New York: Oxford University Press, 1986). Numerous studies deal with specific Progressive reforms. Among them are Roy Lubove, *The Progressives and the Slums: Tenement House Reform in New York City, 1890–1917* (Pittsburgh: University of Pittsburgh Press, 1962); Martin J. Schliessl, *The Politics of Efficiency: Municipal Administration and Reform in America, 1880–1920* (Berkeley: University of California Press, 1977); Dominick Cavallo, *Muscles and Morals: Organized Playgrounds and Urban Reform, 1820–1920* (Philadelphia: University of Pennsylvania Press, 1981); James H. Timberlake, *Prohibition and the Progressive Movement, 1900–1920* (Cambridge: Harvard University Press, 1963). The extensive literature on Progressive reform in education, juvenile crime, immigration law, child labor, and other aspects of living and working conditions can be consulted in numerous bibliographies, beginning with the Bibliographical Essay in Link and McCormick, *Progressivism*, pp. 119–40.

5. Davis, *Spearheads for Reform*, pp. 26–39. The "settlement impulse" is best stated by its founders. For the English movement, see Canon Samuel Barnett and Henrietta Barnett, *Practicable Socialism* (London: Longmans, Green, 1915); John Knapp, ed., *The Universities and the Social Problem* (London: Rivington, Percival, 1895). For the American movement, see Addams, *Twenty Years at Hull House*; Charles Henderson, *Social Settlements* (New York: Lentilhon, 1895); Mina Carson, *Settlement Folk: Social Thought and the American Settlement Movement, 1885–1930* (Chicago: University of Chicago Press, 1990).

6. Allen F. Davis, *American Heroine: The Life and Legend of Jane Addams* (New York: Oxford University Press, 1973); Allen F. Davis and Mary Lynn McCree, eds., *Eighty Years at Hull House* (Chicago: Quadrangle Books, 1969); Doris Groschen Daniels, *Always a Sister: The Feminism of Lillian D. Wald* (New York: Feminist Press, 1989); Kelley, *Autobiography of Florence Kelley*; Wade, *Graham Taylor*; Barbara Sicherman, *Alice Hamilton: A Life in Letters* (Cambridge: Harvard University Press, 1984); Lela B. Costin, *Two Sisters for Social Justice: A Biography of Grace and Edith Abbott* (Urban: University of Illinois Press, 1983).

7. Addams, *My Friend, Julia Lathrop*; Molly Ladd-Taylor, *Raising a Baby the Government Way: Mothers' Letters to the Children's Bureau, 1915–1932* (New Brunswick, N.J.: Rutgers University Press, 1986), pp. 1–46 and passim.

8. Nancy Schrom Dye, *As Equals and as Sisters: Feminism, Unionism, and the Women's Trade Union League of New York* (Columbia: University of Missouri

Press, 1980); Elizabeth Anne Payne, *Reform, Labor, and Feminism: Margaret Dreier Robins and the Women's Trade Union League* (Urbana: University of Illinois Press, 1988); Allen F. Davis, "The Women's Trade Union League: Origins and Organization," *Labor History* 5 (Winter 1964): 3–17.

9. John F. McClymer, "The Pittsburgh Survey: Forging an Ideology in the Steel District," *Pennsylvania History* 41 (April 1974): 169–86; Paul U. Kellogg, *The Pittsburgh Survey*, 6 vols. (New York: Charities Publication Committee, 1909–14); William Steuck, "Progressivism and the Negro: White Liberals and the Early NAACP," *The Historian* 38 (November 1975): 58–78.

10. Eric F. Goldman, *Rendezvous with Destiny* (New York: Knopf, 1953); Clarke A. Chambers, *Seedtime of Reform: American Social Service and Social Action, 1918–1933* (Ann Arbor: University of Michigan Press, 1967 [1963]).

11. Boyer, *Urban Masses and Moral Order.*

12. Influenced by the French Annales school, the new social history began in the United States with the work of Stephan Thernstrom and others on "anonymous Americans"; historians produced revolutionary studies in the fields of immigrant, black, and working-class history. Stephan Thernstrom, *Poverty and Progress: Social Mobility in a Nineteenth Century City* (Cambridge: Harvard University Press, 1964); Tamara Hareven, ed., *Anonymous Americans: Explorations in Nineteenth Century Social History* (Englewood Cliffs, N.J.: Prentice Hall, 1971); James Borchert, *Alley Life in Washington: Family, Community, Religion, and Folklife in the City, 1850–1970* (Urbana: University of Illinois Press, 1980); Josef J. Barton, *Peasants and Strangers: Italians, Romanians, and Slovaks in an American City, 1890–1950* (Cambridge: Harvard University Press, 1975); John Bodnar, Roger Simon, and Michael P. Weber, *Lives of Their Own: Blacks, Italians, and Poles in Pittsburgh, 1900–1960* (Urbana: University of Illinois Press, 1982); Herbert G. Gutman, *The Black Family in Slavery and Freedom, 1750–1925* (New York: Pantheon, 1978). Surveys of the new social history are in *Journal of Social History* 10 (Winter 1976); James A. Henretta, "Social History as Lived and Written," *American Historical Review* 84 (December 1979): 1293–1333; Peter N. Stearns, "Toward a Wider Vision: Trends in Social History," in Michael Kammen, ed., *The Past before Us: Contemporary Historical Writing in the United States* (Ithaca, N.Y.: Cornell University Press, 1980), pp. 205–30. Clarke A. Chambers, "Toward a Definition of Welfare History," *Journal of American History* 73 (September 1986): 407–33, judiciously summarizes the impact of social history on the writing of social welfare history.

13. Examples are Virginia McLaughlin, *Family and Community: Italian Immigrants in Buffalo, 1880–1930* (Ithaca N.Y.: Cornell University Press, 1977); Raymond Mohl and Neil Betten, "Paternalism and Pluralism: Immigrants and Social Welfare in Gary, Indiana, 1906–1940," *American Studies* 15 (Spring 1974): 5–30; Thomas Lee Philpott, *The Slum and the Ghetto: Middle Class Reform and Neighborhood Deterioration, Chicago, 1880–1930* (New York: Oxford University Press, 1978); Paul McBride, *Culture Clash: Immigrants and Reformers, 1880–1920* (San Francisco: R & E Research Associates, 1975); Ronald J. Butera, "A Settlement House and the Urban Challenge: Kingsley House in Pittsburgh, Pennsylvania, 1893–1920," *Western Pennsylvania Historical Magazine*

66 (January 1983): 25–47; Jeffrey A. Hess, "Black Settlement House, East Greenwich, 1902–1914," *Rhode Island History* 29 (1970): 113–27.

14. Frances Fox Piven and Richard A. Cloward, *Regulating the Poor: The Functions of Public Welfare* (New York: Pantheon, 1971), was enormously influential, despite the fact that as historical explanation it contained serious limitations. See Walter I. Trattner, ed., *Social Welfare or Social Control? Some Historical Reflections on "Regulating the Poor"* (Knoxville: University of Tennessee Press, 1983). Social-welfare histories influenced by the Social Control thesis included John A. Alexander, *Render Them Submissive: Responses to Poverty in Philadelphia, 1760–1800* (Amherst: University of Massachusetts Press, 1980); Raymond Mohl, *Poverty in New York, 1783–1825* (New York: New York University Press, 1971), and Anthony Platt, *The Child Savers: The Invention of Delinquency* (Chicago: University of Chicago Press, 1969). See also Marvin E. Gettleman, "Charity and Social Classes in the United States, 1874–1900, I," *American Journal of Economics and Sociology* 22 (April 1963), and II, 22 (July 1963): 417–26; William A. Musaskin, "The Social Control Theory in American History: A Critique," *Journal of Social History* 9 (Summer 1976): 559–69; David Rochefort, "Progressive and Social Control Perspectives on Social Welfare," *Social Service Review* 55 (December 1961): 568–91.

15. Howard Jacob Karger, *The Sentinels of Order: A Study of Social Control and the Minneapolis Settlement House Movement, 1915–1950* (Lanham, Md.: University Press of America, 1987); David Whisnant, *All That Is Native and Fine: The Politics of Culture in an American Region* (Chapel Hill: University of North Carolina Press, 1984); Rivka Lissak, "Myth and Reality: The Pattern of Relationship between the Hull House Circle and the 'New Immigrants' on Chicago's West Side, 1890–1919," *Journal of American Ethnic History* (Spring 1983): 21–50.

16. Blanche Wiesen Cook, "Female Support Networks and Political Activism: Lillian Wald, Crystal Eastman, Emma Goldman," in Nancy F. Cott and Elizabeth H. Pleck, eds., *A Heritage of Her Own: Toward a New Social History of American Women* (New York: Simon and Schuster, 1979), pp. 412–44; Kathryn Kish Sklar, "Hull House in the 1890s: A Community of Women Reformers," *Signs* 10 (1985): 658–77; Ellen DuBois, Mari Jo Buhle, Temma Kaplan, Gerda Lerner, and Carroll Smith-Rosenberg, "Politics and Culture in Women's History: A Symposium," *Feminist Studies* 6 (Spring 1980): 26–58; Estelle Freedman, "Separatism as Strategy: Female Institution Building, 1870–1930," *Feminist Studies* 5 (Fall 1979): 512–29; Ellen Fitzpatrick, *Endless Crusade: Women Social Scientists and Progressive Reform* (New York: Oxford University Press, 1990); Robyn Muncy, *Creating a Female Dominion in American Reform, 1890–1935* (New York: Oxford University Press, 1991).

17. Trolander, *Professionalism and Social Change*, p. 5; Karger, *Sentinels of Order*. Differing interpretations of the settlements doubtless reflect historians' awareness of ambiguities and conflicts within the wider Progressive movement. See Don S. Kirschner, "The Ambiguous Legacy: Social Justice and Social Control in the Progressive Era," *Historical Reflections* 2 (Summer 1975): 69–88 and Daniel T. Rodgers, "In Search of Progressivism," *Reviews in American History* 10 (December 1982): 113–32.

18. Roy Lubove, *The Professional Altruist: The Emergence of Social Work as a Career* (Pittsburgh: University of Pittsburgh Press, 1965); Don S. Kirschner, *The Paradox of Professionalism: Reform and Public Service in Urban America, 1900–1940* (New York: Greenwood Press, 1986).

19. Barry D. Karl and Stanley N. Katz, "The American Private Philanthropic Foundation and the Public Sphere, 1890–1930," *Minerva* 19 (Summer 1981): 236–70; Robert A. Arnove, *Philanthropy and Cultural Imperialism: The Foundations at Home and Abroad* (Bloomington: Indiana University Press, 1980).

20. This point is made in John F. McClymer, *War and Welfare: Social Engineering in America, 1890–1925* (Westport, Conn.: Greenwood Press, 1980).

21. Ibid, p. 41; Robert Wiebe, *The Search for Order, 1879–1920* (New York: Hill and Wang, 1967).

22. Boyer, *Urban Masses and Moral Order*, p. 367, n. 2 and passim; Jean B. Quandt, *From the Small Town to the Great Society: The Social Thought of Progressive Intellectuals* (New Brunswick, N.J.: Rutgers University Press, 1970); Patricia Mooney Melvin, *The Organic City: Urban Definition and Neighborhood Organization, 1880–1920* (Lexington: University Press of Kentucky, 1987).

23. "Clients have used institutions and organizations for their own purposes, shaping them sometimes in ways quite at variance with the intentions of their sponsors. In actual practice . . . the roles of social institutions have been complex, not easily deduced from the statements of sponsors or administrators." Michael B. Katz, *Poverty and Policy in American History* (New York: Academic Press, 1983), p. 59.

24. Rochefort, "Progressive and Social Control Perspectives on Social Welfare," p. 584.

Part 1: Indianapolis

1. Booth Tarkingon, *The Turmoil* (New York: Harper and Brothers, 1915).

2. U.S. Dept. of Commerce, Bureau of the Census, *Fifteenth Census of the United States, 1930*; vol. 1, *Population*, p. 330; Robert Barrows, "A Demographic Analysis of Indianapolis, 1870–1930" (Ph.D. dissertation, Indiana University, 1977). For comparative data on geographical mobility and "persistence" in American cities, see Stephan Thernstrom, *The Other Bostonians: Poverty and Progress in the American Metropolis, 1880–1970* (Cambridge: Harvard University Press, 1973), pp. 222–23.

3. Clifton J. Phillips, *Indiana in Transition* (Indianapolis: Indiana Historical Bureau, 1968), p. 367; Frederick Doyle Kershner, Jr., "A Social and Cultural History of Indianapolis" (Ph.D. dissertation, University of Wisconsin, 1950), pp. 94, 115–20.

4. Kershner, "History of Indianapolis," pp. 106 ff.

5. *Fifteenth Census of the United States, 1930*: vol. 2, *Population*, 210.

6. U.S. Dept. of Commerce, Bureau of the Census, *Fourteenth Census of the United States, 1920*: vol. 3, *Population*, p. 308; Theodore G. Probst, "The Germans in Indianapolis, 1850–1915" (M.A. thesis, Indiana University, 1951).

7. Mary Ann Armborst, "Immigrant Groups in Indianapolis" (Honors thesis, Marian College, Indianapolis, 1963); Elavina S. Stammel and Charles R. Parks, "The Slavic Peoples in Indianapolis" (M.S. thesis, Indiana University, 1930). See Chapter 2.

8. U.S. Dept. of Commerce, Bureau of the Census, *Negroes in the United States, 1920–1932* (Washington, D.C.: Government Printing Office, 1935), p. 55.

9. *Fourteenth Census of the United States, 1920:* vol. 5, *Agriculture,* p. 18; vol. 9, *Manufactures,* p. 375; Phillips, *Indiana in Transition,* p. 277. In order to avoid revealing statistics of Lake County industrial operations that might have formed a basis for antitrust actions against U.S. Steel the Census did not give statistics of individual firms in 1920. Powell A. Moore, *The Calumet Region* (Indianapolis: Indiana Historical Bureau, 1959), pp. 193–99, 230–41, 327–31; Isaac J. Quillen, "Industrial City: A History of Gary, Indiana" (Ph.D. dissertation, Yale University, 1942).

10. U.S. Dept. of Commerce, Bureau of the Census, *Twelfth Census of the United States, 1900: Manufactures,* pt. 2, pp. 218–21; Twelfth Census, 1900: *Occupations at the Twelfth Census,* pp. 574–76; *Thirteenth Census of the United States, 1910:* vol. 9, *Manufactures,* p. 325; *Fifteenth Census of the United States, 1930: Population,* vol. 4, *Occupations by States,* p. 501.

11. *Census of Manufactures,* 1914, 1:395–96; Kershner, "History of Indianapolis," pp. 89–90; Phillips, *Indiana in Transition,* pp. 311–13.

12. U.S. Dept. of Commerce, Bureau of the Census, *Census of Manufactures,* 1914 1:395; Kershner, "History of Indianapolis," pp. 86–87; George W. Starr, *Industrial Development of Indiana,* Indiana University Studies in Business, no. 14 (Bloomington: Indiana University School of Business, 1937), pp. 32–38; George D. King, "The Industrialization of Indiana" (Ph.D. dissertation, Indiana University, 1963).

13. Kershner, "History of Indianapolis," p. 142.

14. Ibid., pp. 145 ff.; Phillips, *Indiana in Transition,* p. 382. Colonel Eli Lilly was the club's first president.

15. Indianapolis *Daily Journal,* November 3, 1973, p. 7; W. R. Holloway, *Indianapolis: A Historical and Statistical Sketch of the Railway City* (Indianapolis: Indianapolis Journal Printing Co., 1870), pp. 37–81; Emma Lou Thornbrough, *Indiana in the Civil War Era, 1850–1880* (Indiana Historical Bureau and Indiana Historical Society, 1965), pp. 274–78, 419; Indianapolis Commercial Club, *Relief for the Unemployed in Indianapolis, A Report of the Commercial Club Relief Committee, . . . 1893–1894* (Indianapolis, 1894); Leah Hannah Feder, *Unemployment Relief in Periods of Depression. A Study of Measures Adopted in Certain American Cities, 1857 through 1922* (New York: Russell Sage Foundation, 1935).

16. Robert Bremner, *From the Depths: The Discovery of Poverty in the United States* (Columbus: Ohio University Press, 1965); Paul Boyer, *Urban Masses and Moral Order in America, 1820–1920* (Cambridge: Harvard University Press, 1978), pp. 191ff.

17. Ruth Hutchinson Crocker, "Making Charity Modern: Business and the Reform of Charities in Indianapolis, 1879–1930," *Business and Economic History,*

2d ser., 12 (1984): 158–70; Genevieve Weeks, *Oscar Carleton McCulloch, 1843–1891: Preacher and Practitioner of Applied Christianity* (Indianapolis: Indiana Historical Society, 1976), pp. 184–89; John R. Seeley et al., *Community Chest: A Case Study in Philanthropy* (Toronto: University of Toronto Press, 1957), p. 82. For the Charity Organization Society see Amos G. Warner, *American Charities: A Study in Philanthropy and Economics* (New York: Thomas Y. Crowell, 1894); Edward T. Devine, *The Practice of Charity* (New York: Lentilhon, 1901); Frank Watson, *The Charity Organization Movement in the United States* (New York: Macmillan, 1922); Boyer, *Urban Masses and Moral Order*, pp. 143–61.

18. National Bureau of Municipal Research, "Survey of Social Agencies in Indianapolis, 1918," typescript, mimeographed. IUPUI; Seeley, *Community Chest*, pp. 88–91.

19. Roy Lubove, *The Professional Altruist: The Emergence of Social Work as a Career* (Pittsburgh: University of Pittsburgh Press, 1965, pp. 22 ff.; Walter I. Trattner, *From Poor Law to Welfare State: A History of Social Welfare in America*, 2nd ed. (New York: Free Press, 1979), pp.

20. Myra Auerbach, "A Study of the Jewish Settlement in Indianapolis, 1850–1915" (Master's thesis, Indiana University, 1937).

21. Weeks, *Oscar Carleton McCulloch*. For the institutional church movement, see Henry F. May, *Protestant Churches and Industrial America* (New York: Harper and Brothers, 1949), pp. 170–71, 184; Josiah Strong, *Religious Movements for Social Betterment* (New York: Baker and Taylor, 1900).

22. Stanton A. Coit, "The Neighborhood Guild Defined," in Lorene M. Pacey, ed., *Readings in the Development of Settlement Work* (New York: Association Press, 1950), pp. 21–28; Jean Quandt, *From the Small Town to the Great Community: The Social Thought of Progressive Intellectuals* (New Brunswick, N.J.: Rutgers University Press, 1970). For an example of a later application of Coit's ideas see, for example, Patricia Mooney Melvin, *Urban Definition and Neighborhood Organization, 1880–1920* (Lexington: University Press of Kentucky, 1987), pp. 11–26.

23. Oscar C. McCulloch, "The Opportunity of the Commercial Club," Address to the Board of Directors of the Commercial Club, July 8, 1890. ISL.

24. Ibid.

25. For "friendly visiting" see Lubove, *Professional Altruist*, pp. 22 ff.; Mary E. Richmond, *Friendly Visiting among the Poor: A Handbook for Charity Visitors* (Montclair, N.J.: Paterson Smith, 1969 [1899]).

Chapter 1: Christamore

1. The first U.S. settlement house was the Neighborhood Guild (later the University Settlement), founded in 1886. Hull House opened in Chicago in September 1889; the College Settlement, New York also in 1889; Northwestern University Settlement in 1891; College Settlement, Philadelphia in 1899. Robert A. Woods and Albert J. Kennedy, *Handbook of Settlements* (New York:

Charities Publication Committee, 1911). On Hull House, see Jane Addams, *Twenty Years at Hull House* (New York: Macmillan, 1910; Signet, 1960); Allen F. Davis, *American Heroine: The Life and Legend of Jane Addams* (New York: Oxford University Press, 1973); Jill Conway, "Jane Addams: An American Heroine," in Robert J. Lifton, ed., *The Woman in America* (Boston: Beacon Press, 1967); Kathryn Kish Sklar, "Hull House in the 1890s: A Community of Women Reformers," *Signs*, 10 (Summer 1985): 658–77.

2. Addams, *Twenty Years at Hull House*, p. 93; "The Subjective Necessity for Social Settlements," in Addams et al., *Philanthropy and Social Progress* (New York: Thomas A. Crowell, 1893), pp. 1–26; Jane Addams, "The College Woman and the Family Claim," *Commons* 3 (September 5, 1898): 3–5; Staughton Lynd, "Jane Addams and the Radical Impulse," *Commentary* 32 (July 1961), 54–59; Daniel Levine, *Jane Addams and the Liberal Tradition* (Madison: University of Wisconsin Press, 1971).

3. Addams, *Twenty Years at Hull House*, p. 92; Addams, "The College Woman and the Family Claim," pp. 3–5; Joyce Antler, " 'After College, What?' New Graduates and the Family Claim," *American Quarterly* 32 (Fall 1980): 409–34.

4. Martha Vicinus, *Independent Women: Work and Community for Single Women, 1850–1920* (London: Virago Press, 1985), is an excellent treatment of this theme, though it is focused on the English experience. Vicinus argues that a "passion for meaningful work" was the "sacred center of nineteenth-century single women's lives and communities. It was the means out of the garden, out of idleness, out of ignorance, and into wisdom, service, and adventure" (p. 1). See also Sheila M. Rothman, "The Protestant Nun," in *Woman's Proper Place: A History of Changing Ideals and Practices, 1870 to the Present* (New York: Basic Books, 1978), pp. 63–93.

5. Davis, *American Heroine*, pp. 24–37. Alice Hamilton's life provides another example. Hamilton's letters reveal "a struggle to find satisfying work that lasted a decade." Barbara Sicherman, *Alice Hamilton: A Life in Letters* (Cambridge: Harvard University Press, 1984), pp. 135–36.

6. "An Appeal for a New Work," February 12, 1889, n.p., in College Settlements Association, *Annual Reports*, vols. 1–7. *The Woman's Journal*, announcing the founding of Hull House, commented:

> One of its chief aims will be to make it also a retreat for other young women, who need rest and change or who desire a safe refuge from the inordinate demands of society, in whom it is believed that a glimpse of the reverse side of life, of the poverty and struggle of half the people, will beget a broader philanthropy and a tenderer sympathy, and will leave less time and inclination for retrospection, for selfish ambition, or for real or fancied invalidism.

Quoted in Davis, *American Heroine*, p. 63. The organization was initially named the College Settlement Association.

7. "An Appeal for a New Work." See also Herman F. Hegner, "The Scientific Value of the Social Settlement," *American Journal of Sociology* 3 (September

1897): 171–82; Roberta Franklin, *Collegiate Women. Domesticity and Career in Turn-of-the-Century America* (New York: New York University Press, 1977), pp. 85–103.

8. "An Appeal for a New Work."

9. Vida Scudder, "The Relation of College Women to Social Need," paper presented to the Association of Collegiate Alumnae, October 24, 1890, pp. 3–5. ACA papers, Sophia Smith Collection.

10. "An Appeal for a New Work"; Helen Hiscock Backus, "The Need and the Opportunity for College-Trained Women in Philanthropic Work," paper presented to the New York Association of College Alumnae, March 19, 1887, ACA Papers. The issue of gender in the making of modern social work is more fully explored in the author's "From Social Mother to Social Worker: Settlements, Social Work, and the Public-Private Dichotomy," paper presented at the Seventh Berkshire Conference of Women Historians, Wellesley, Mass., June 1987, and in the thoughtful written comments by Elisabeth Israels Perry, Vanderbilt University in the author's possession.

11. John P. Rousmanière, "Cultural Hybrid in the Slums: The College Woman and the Settlement House, 1889–1894," *American Quarterly,* 22 (Spring 1970): 62; Jill Conway, "Women Reformers and American Culture, 1870–1930," *Journal of Social History,* 5 (Winter 1971–72): 164–77. Teaching was the career choice of 86 percent of Bryn Mawr graduates who were in paid occupations. The profession was overcrowded, with low pay, uncertain tenure, and demoralization. Kate Holladay Claghorn, "The Problem of Occupation for College Women," *Educational Review* (March 1898): 217–30.

12. Rousmanière, "Cultural Hybrid." See also Robert A. Woods, "The University Settlement Idea" in Addams et al., *Philanthropy and Social Progress,* pp. 57–97; Vicinus, *Independent Women,* pp. 229–31.

13. T. J. Jackson Lears, *No Place of Grace: Anti-Modernism and the Transformation of American Culture, 1880–1920* (New York: Pantheon Books, 1981). Jane Addams described herself after graduation as "clinging only to the desire to live in a really living world and refusing to be content with a shadowy intellectual or aesthetic reflection of it." *Twenty Years at Hull House,* p. 59. Jean Quandt, *From the Small Town to the Great Community: The Social Thought of Progressive Intellectuals* (New Brunswick, N.J.: Rutgers University Press, 1970), has pointed out that the college settlement combined the Progressive drive for reform with progressivism's insistence on useful, applied knowledge, pp. 13–20. See also James T. Kloppenberg, *Uncertain Victory: Social Democracy and Progressivism in European and American Thought, 1870–1920* (New York: Oxford University Press, 1986).

14. "Creative Solution" is historian Allen F. Davis's phrase in *American Heroine,* pp. 38–52. Martha Vicinus emphasizes that although some single women, like Jane Addams, played the role of "mothers," settlement workers were "not mothers living in surrogate families," Vicinus insists, "They were hardworking, ambitious, and visionary women setting forth with great courage upon untrodden paths. But they were also intensely conflicted, deeply emotional women, seeking to fulfill themselves in ways society would approve while still moving

beyond its limitations" (*Independent Women*, p. 44). Elisabeth Israels Perry disagrees. She disputes the notion that settlement workers successfully "bridged the gap" between the domestic and public spheres, pointing out that very few women who became public figures married and that women in public life continued to appeal to the rhetoric of motherhood and domesticity. See her *Belle Moscowitz: Feminine Politics and the Exercise of Power in the Age of Alfred E. Smith* (New York: Oxford University Press, 1987), pp. 34–35, 179–80.

15. This account relies on Anna Stover and Edith Surbey, "Remembrances" typescript, n.d., original in possession of Mr. Ray Spencer, director of Christamore from 1955–65.

16. Stover's Obituary is in the *Butler Alumnus*, 34 (October 1, 1944): 13.

17. Stover and Surbey, "Remembrances."

18. C. B. Coleman, "The College Settlement in Indianapolis," *Indiana Bulletin of Charities and Corrections*, 79 (December 1909): 432–33. The Kindergarten Training School was founded by Eliza Blaker in 1884 and was known as "Mrs. Blaker's College" and later as Teachers' College of Indianapolis. It became affiliated with Butler University in 1930. Clifton J. Phillips, *Indiana in Transition: The Emergence of an Industrial Commonwealth, 1880–1920* (Indianapolis: Indiana Historical Bureau and Indiana Historical Society, 1968), p. 422.

19. Stover and Surbey, "Remembrances." In her study of nineteenth-century female relationships, Carroll Smith-Rosenberg concluded that "Paradoxically to twentieth century minds, their love appears to have been both sensual and platonic." "The Female World of Love and Ritual: Relations between Women in Nineteenth Century America," *Signs*, 1 (Autumn 1975): 313. The view that single women who became settlement workers lived like "Protestant nuns," their sexual energy sublimated into municipal government, tenement inspection, and so on, seems less than convincing. We have no evidence concerning whether the relationship between Stover and Surbey was a sexual or a platonic one. But it seems clear that like the relationship between Jane Addams and Mary Rozet Smith, close companions for forty years, the friendship of Stover and Surbey released their energies for work over many years. Blanche Wiesen Cook, "Female Support Networks and Political Activism: Lillian Wald, Crystal Eastman, Emma Goldman," in Nancy F. Cott and Elizabeth Pleck, eds., *A Heritage of Her Own: Toward a New Social History of American Women* (New York: Simon and Schuster, 1971), pp. 412–44. See also Kathryn Kish Sklar, "Hull House in the 1890s: A Community of Women Reformers," *Signs*, 10 (Summer 1985): 658–77; Carol Lasser, "Let Us Be Sisters Forever: The Sororal Model of Nineteenth-Century Female Friendship," *Signs* 14 (Autumn 1988): 158–81; Lillian Faderman, *Surpassing the Love of Men: Romantic Friendship and Love between Women from the Renaissance to the Present* (New York: William Morrow, 1981).

20. Anna Stover, "Reminiscent History of Christamore the College Settlement from 1905 to 1911," 1911, typescript, p. 7 (copy in the possession of the author).

21. Davis, *American Heroine*, pp. 28–32.

22. "Reminiscent History."

23. Indianapolis Free Kindergarten and Childrens' Aid Society, *Superintendent's Report for June 26, 1906 to March 31, 1908*, Indianapolis Free Kinder-

garten and Childrens' Aid Society Records (Indiana Historical Society, Indianapolis). For Eliza Blaker, see Emma Lou Thornbrough, *Eliza A. Blaker: Her Life and Work* (Indianapolis: Eliza Blaker Club and Indiana Historical Society, 1965).

24. For John H. Holliday, see Jacob Piatt Dunn, *Greater Indianapolis: The History, the Institutions, and the People of a City of Homes*, 2 vols. (Chicago: Lewis, 1910), 1:1008; for Eliza Browning, see 2:955; for Evaline Holliday, 1:1008. By one of those ironies best enjoyed by social historians, Charles S. Grout, secretary of the Indianapolis COS from 1893 to 1916, was employed as a timekeeper at the Atlas Engine Works. Dunn, *Greater Indianapolis*, 2:654–55.

25. *Christamore, the College Settlement Association of Indianapolis* (1911), p. 4.

26. The description of the Christamore district comes from Carlos C. Rowlinson, "The Neighborhood House" (address made to the Local Council of Women of Indianapolis, January 2, 1901, p. 4. In Indianapolis Council of Women Records, Indiana State Library, Indianapolis). Rowlinson's Neighborhood House was later turned from a settlement into a church. See Woods and Kennedy, *Handbook of Settlements*, p. 13. Settlement-house districts rarely corresponded to ward or other recognized geographical areas. They were simply chosen as "the field" by the settlement workers themselves. See also Leander M. C. Campbell Adams, *An Investigation of Housing and Living Conditions in Three Districts of Indianapolis*, Indiana University Studies, vol. 8, no. 8 (Bloomington, Ind., 1910), p. 133.

27. Rowlinson, "The Neighborhood House," p. 2.

28. Adams, *Housing and Living Conditions*, pp. 134–35.

29. Rowlinson, "The Neighborhood House," p. 5.

30. Adams, *Housing and Living Conditions*, p. 137.

31. "Reminiscent History," pp. 13–14.

32. Adams, *Housing and Living Conditions*. "All over the [Christamore] district it is a common thing to see negroes and whites living side by side in a very neighborly manner," Adams recorded in 1910. "It is the belief of the managers of Christamore that the color line is not drawn closely enough in the district. Hence, they, as part of their plan of action, have decided to exclude negroes. The settlement is open only to white people" p. 134.

33. "Misses Pearl Green and Charlotte Carson, two very lovely Kindergarten teachers stayed with us during July and August [1905]. These young women helped us in gardening and visiting and were always greatly admired by the neighborhood." "Reminiscent History," p. 3.

34. The Indianapolis Free Kindergarten Association found that the lack of a dormitory for young women attending the Training School was a serious problem. *Superintendent's Report of the Indianapolis Free Kindergarten Association for June 27, 1905, to June 26, 1906*, p. 30. Box 1527, Blaker Collection, IHS. Discussing the summer course to be offered in social work at the Indianapolis Social Service Department in 1917, Director Edna Henry wrote to President Bryan that she feared many young women would be unable to take the course because of the "insurmountable snag" of lack of suitable lodgings. Edna Henry to President William L. Bryan, May 12, 1917, p. 2. Bryan Correspondence,

1916–18, 44 DC1. IUPUI. Regarding single women in the city in this period, Joanne J. Meyerowitz, *Women Adrift: Independent Wage Earners in Chicago, 1880–1930* (Chicago: University of Chicago Press, 1988); Vicinus, *Independent Women*, pp. 36–37.

35. "Reminiscent History," pp. 9–10.

36. *Butler College Settlement Association, Indianapolis, Indiana* (1905) ISL. This pamphlet lists the officers, trustees, and board of directors of this ephemeral organization. See also *Christamore, the College Settlement of Indianapolis,* (1906–7), n.p.

37. *Butler College Settlement Association.*

38. "Reminiscent History," p. 5; "The College Settlement," p. 433. Christamore continued to call itself "Christamore, the College Settlement Association" until 1928, when its name was changed to Christamore House. James O. Clark, "The First Fifty Years at Christamore House, 1905–1955" (M.A. thesis, Division of Social Service, Indiana University, 1955), p. 23.

39. "Our Settlement House," *Butler Collegian,* January 13, 1906.

40. "Training School for Social Workers, Indianapolis, Indiana," 1912, pamphlet, ISL. For the development of social-work education see Lubove, *Professional Altruist*, pp. 137–56.

41. *Butler College Catalogue,* 1904–5, pp. 54–57.

42. Ibid., p. 55; Charity Organization Society of Indianapolis, *Yearbook,* 1905.

43. Indiana University *Bulletin,* (1917–18), p. 133; Anne Piepho, "The History of the Social Service Department of the Indiana University Medical Center, 1911–1932" (M.A. thesis, Indiana University School of Social Service, June 1950).

44. *Christamore, the College Settlement Association of Indianapolis* (1911), p. 7; Adams, *Housing and Living Conditions*; Robert H. Bremner, *From the Depths: The Discovery of Poverty in the United States* (New York: New York University Press, 1972 [1956]), pp. 140–63.

45. Phillips, *Indiana in Transition,* p. 487; Albion Fellows Bacon, "The Awakening of a State, Indiana," *Survey,* 25 (1910–11): 467–73; Roy Lubove, *The Progressives and the Slums: Tenement House Reform in New York City, 1890–1917* (Pittsburgh: University of Pittsburgh Press, 1962); Phillips, *Indiana in Transition,* p. 487.

46. Under the direction of Edna Henry, the department became a leader in the new specialty of medical social work. Its development can be traced in the correspondence of Edna Henry with Ulysses G. Weatherly and with William L. Bryan, Indiana University President, Edna Henry Collection, IUPUI.

47. Settlement houses were not entirely left behind, for they also embraced the goals and language of professionalization. Judith Ann Trolander, *Professionalism and Social Change: From the Settlement House Movement to Neighborhood Centers, 1886 to the Present* (New York: Columbia University Press, 1987), pp. 38–48 and passim.

48. Coleman, "The College Settlement," p. 433.

49. Settlement workers were influenced by the social philosophies of such thinkers as John Dewey and Mary Parker Follett with their belief that face-

to-face communication was the key to restoring the community ideals of an earlier time. Quandt, *From the Small Town to the Great Community*, passim. Cf. settlement leader Albert J. Kennedy's declaration, "Neighborliness, as an emotional experience, is both means and end." *Settlements and Their Outlook: An Account of the First International Conference of Settlements, Toynbee Hall, London, July 1922* (London: P. S. King, 1922), p. 38.

50. "History of the Indianapolis Free Kindergarten Society" (1930–31). Typescript, Box 166, Free Kindergarten Records; Phillips, *Indiana In Transition*, p. 399; "Reminiscent History," p. 3; Davis, *Spearheads for Reform*, pp. 43–45.

51 *Superintendent's Report, Indianapolis Free Kindergarten Association, June 27, 1905 to June 26, 1906.* Free Kindergarten Records.

52. Indianapolis *News*, March 12, 1925; Indianapolis *Star*, March 6, 1925; "History of the Indianapolis Free Kindergarten Society" (1930–31). R. C. Reilly, president of Republic Creosoting Co., Indianapolis, to Christamore board of directors, October 13, 1932, Box 166, Free Kindergarten Records.

53. "Reminiscent History," p. 3; Coleman, "The College Settlement," p. 433.

54. "Reminiscent History," p. 2, "Formula" is Stover's word.

55. "Reminiscent History," p. 6. The progressive approach to adolescent boys is dealt with imaginatively by Dominick Cavallo in *Muscles and Morals: Organized Playgrounds and Urban Reform, 1880–1920* (Philadelphia: University of Pennsylvania Press, 1981), and David I. Mcleod, *Building Character in the American Boy: The Boy Scouts, YMCA, and Their Forerunners, 1870–1930* (Madison: University of Wisconsin Press, 1983).

56. Ibid., p. 9.

57. Ibid. p. 2. David E. Whisnant, *All That Is Native and Fine: The Politics of Culture in an American Region* (Chapel Hill: University of North Carolina Press, 1983), dealing with the Hindman Settlement School in Eastern Kentucky, is an excellent case study of the interaction between settlement workers and their Appalachian clients. Whisnant describes social workers who were well meaning but failed to understand the culture of those they sought to help.

58. Dolores Hayden, *The Grand Domestic Revolution: A History of Feminist Designs for American Homes, Neighborhoods, and Cities* (Cambridge: MIT Press, 1982 [1981]), especially pp. 162–79. "Settlement houses were the great practical success of cooperative housekeeping in the period between 1890 and 1920, the middle-class reformers' proof that collective cooking, cleaning, laundering, and central heating . . . could really work," Hayden writes, "yet this was an achievement that settlement workers rarely spoke about" p. 174. The few community kitchens established by settlements like the Hull House Public Kitchen set up in 1894 were rarely successful. See pp. 165–67.

59. "Reminiscent History," p. 2.

60. Ibid., pp. 5–6. *Christamore, the College Settlement of Indianapolis* (1906–7), n.p.

61. "Our Settlement House."

62. Helen Worthington Rogers, "A Modest Experiment in Foster Motherhood: The Work of the Pure Milk Commission of the Children's Aid Association

of Indianapolis," *Survey* 22 (May 1, 1909): 176–83; "Fighting to Save Indiana Babies," Indianapolis *Sunday Star*, November 17, 1907, p. 1. The production of milk for sale in Indiana rose from 6,723,840 gallons in 1879 to 36,562,105 in 1899, and to 45,167,166 gallons in 1919. Phillips, *Indiana in Transition*, p. 163.

63. Rogers, "A Modest Experiment in Foster Motherhood," p. 176.

64. "Reminiscent History," p. 12; *Christamore, the College Settlement Association* (1911), p. 5.

65. "Reminiscent History," p. 7; *Christamore, the College Settlement in Indianapolis* (1906–7), n.p.; "Our Settlement House," *Butler Collegian*, January 13, 1906; *Christamore, the College Settlement Association of Indianapolis* (1911), p. 5.

66. "Reminiscent History," p. 7.

67. Ibid., p. 11.

68. National Bureau of Municipal Research, "Survey of Social Agencies in Indianapolis," 1918, pp. 33, 36, 230. Typescript, mimeographed, IUPUI. For a discussion of settlement-house design see Guy Szuberla, "Three Chicago Settlement Houses: Their Architectural Form and Social Meaning," *Journal of the Illinois State Historical Society* 14 (1977): 114–29.

69. Stover and Surbey, "Remembrances"; *Christamore, the College Settlement Association* (1912), p. 3; Clark, "First Fifty Years at Christamore House," p. 14. Clark repeats the story that both women resigned because of ill health. The account in "Remembrances" hints that the real reason for their retirement was their difference with the settlement board about the question of "worldly entertainments." Stover's memoir speaks of pressures to make the settlement "more of an educational and recreation center, introducing worldly amusements." For the Disciples of Christ, see Phillips, *Indiana in Transition*, pp. 448–89. The denomination split at this time over the issue of instrumental music in church services. The minority anti-organ faction of the church adopted the name Churches of Christ. See also U.S. Department of Commerce, Bureau of the Census, *Religious Bodies*, 2 vols., 1906, 1: 308–10; 1916, 1:258–59.

70. Clark, "First Fifty Years at Christamore House," p. 14.

71. Robert A. Woods and Albert J. Kennedy, in the "official" statement of what settlements stood for, the 1911 *Handbook of Settlements*, stated, "The typical settlement is one which provides neutral territory traversing all the lines of racial and religious cleavage" p.v. "If the word 'mission' means a finished message passed on to others, then the settlement is not a mission," wrote Mary Simkhovitch. "The settlement, made up as America is made up, of various types of people with varying points of view, cannot fasten upon any one aspect of truth, political or religious." Simkhovitch, "The Settlement and Religion," in Lorene Pacey, ed., *Readings in the Development of Settlement Work* (New York: Association Press, 1950), p. 139. See Chapter 4.

72. National Bureau of Municipal Research, "Survey of Social Agencies in Indianapolis," p. 35.

73. *Butler Alumnus*, 34 (October 1944): 13; "Edith Surbey," Deceased Alumni Files, Butler College Alumni Office.

74. *Christamore, the College Settlement Association of Indianapolis* (1912), p. 7.

75. National Bureau of Municipal Research, "Survey of Social Agencies in Indianapolis," p. 35.

76. Clark, "First Fifty Years at Christamore House," pp. 13–14; Kennedy, *Settlements and Their Outlook*, p. 186.

77. *Christamore, the College Settlement Association* (1911), p. 2.

78. *Christamore, the College Settlement Association of Indianapolis* (1912), p. 7.

79. Adams, "Housing and Living Conditions," p. 134; U.S. Department of Commerce, Bureau of the Census, *Thirteenth Census: 1910, Population 2*: 574; *Fourteenth Census: 1920, Population 3*: 308; *Fifteenth Census: 1930, Population 2*: 206; Emma Lou Thornbrough, *Since Emancipation: A History of Indiana Negroes 1863–1963* (Indianapolis: American Negro Emancipation Centennial Authority, 1963), pp. 70–76; U.S. Department of Commerce, Bureau of the Census, *Negroes in the United States, 1920–1932*, pp. 230–31, 269–71.

80. Clark, "First Fifty Years at Christamore House," pp. 17, 19.

81. In 1914, the Christamore board of directors was considering a possible merger with the Indianapolis Boys Club or with the Christian Women's Board of Missions. Clark, "First Fifty Years at Christamore House," pp. 14–18. Edwards's proposal to the board was that black women be allowed to use Christamore's gymnasium one afternoon a week.

82. Trolander, *Professionalism and Social Change*, documents the changing racial composition of settlement personnel and settlement clients since World War II.

83. John Seeley et al., *Community Chest: A Case Study in Philanthropy* (Toronto: University of Toronto Press, 1957), pp. 90–94.

84. National Bureau of Municipal Research, "Survey of Social Agencies in Indianapolis," pp. 36, 231, 233.

85. Clark, "First Fifty Years at Christamore House," pp. 17–18.

86. Head Resident's Report, October 1921, quoted in Clark, "First Fifty Years at Christamore House," pp. 20–21. A postscript concerns the fate of the settlement-house building, which had been praised as "ideal" by the 1918 survey, only to be abandoned in 1921. The Christamore College Settlement Association sold its property on Columbia Avenue to the Board of Park Commissioners in 1921, with the intention that the building should become a social agency for blacks. This plan was stalled for several years by protests from some white property owners, with the result that the Christamore building was reserved for whites only. It later became the J.T.V Hill Community Center. *Christamore House Report. Over a Period of Twenty-Five Years, 1907–1932*.

87. "Dr. John Elliott Gives Christamore Dedication Speech," clipping, [1924?]. Charities file, Indianapolis Public Library; Clark, "First Fifty Years at Christamore House," p. 23.

88. "A New Type of City Department," *Survey* (July 19, 1919), 605–6. For the professionalization of social work, see Abraham Flexner, "Is Social Work a Profession?" NCCC *Proceedings of the Forty-Second Meeting*, Baltimore, pp. 576–90, 1915; Robert A. Woods, "Social Work: A New Profession," *Charities and the Commons* 15 (January 6, 1906): 469–76; Trolander, *Professionalism and Social Change*; Lubove, *The Professional Altruist*; *Encyclopedia of Social Work*, "Professional Organization," by David W. French (New York: National Association of Social Workers, 1965); Bertha Leming, "Indianapolis Chapter, American Association of Social Workers, 1923–1946," June 1946. Pamphlet, IUPUI.

89. "Questions Propounded at the St. Louis Conference" (1910) in National Federation of Settlements, Conference Reports, 1910–22. Bound together. United Neighborhood Houses of America, Inc. (UNH); Porter R. Lee, "Social Work: Cause and Function," National Conference of Social Work, *Proceedings* (1929), pp. 3–20. For the role of national social-work leaders in articulating the goals of wartime and postwar reconstruction, see Clarke A. Chambers, *Paul U. Kellogg and the Survey: Voices for Social Welfare and Social Justice* (Minneapolis: University of Minnesota Press, 1971); Guy Alchon, *The Invisible Hand of Planning: Capitalism, Social Science, and the State in the 1920s* (Princeton: Princeton University Press, 1985); Don S. Kirschner, *The Paradox of Professionalism: Reform and Public Service in Urban America, 1900–1940* (Westport, Conn.: Greenwood Press, 1986), pp. 53–57.

90. Report to the Christamore Board of Directors, April 1915, quoted in Clark, "First Fifty Years at Christamore House," p. 16. The movement toward federation of charities in Indianapolis is traced in Ruth Hutchinson Crocker, "Making Charity Modern: Business and the Reform of Charities in Indianapolis, 1879–1930," *Business and Economic History*, 2d Ser. (Urbana, Ill.: 1984): 158–70; Seeley, *Community Chest*, pp. 87–88; Indianapolis Charity Organization Society, *Report of the Businessmen's Committee of the Indianapolis COS for the Year 1890–1891* (Indianapolis), ISL; Oscar McCulloch, "The Opportunity of the Commercial Club," Address to the board of directors of the Commercial Club, July 8, 1890, ISL.

91. *The Leisure of a People: Report of a Recreation Survey of Indianapolis* (n.p., 1929), p. 386.

92. "Christamore," pamphlet (1925?) (Christamore House).

93. *The Leisure of a People*, p. 387; Judith A. Trolander, *Settlement Houses and the Great Depression* (Detroit: Wayne State University Press, 1975).

94. "Christamore" (1925). Social historians such as John Bodnar and Olivier Zunz have argued that in the early twentieth century, ethnic and even working-class subcultures, organized around the family and the community, enjoyed some independence within the hegemonic, dominant culture. Zunz believes that these separate, self-reliant cultures began to yield in the 1920s to the mass society. With the important exception of blacks, who experienced the opposite development, a solidifying of the ghetto, the working class including second-generation immigrants was being absorbed into the undifferentiated mass society. The settlements' Americanization work aided this process of absorption. John Bodnar, Roger Simon, and Michael P. Weber, *Lives of Their Own: Blacks, Italians and Poles in Pittsburgh, 1900–1960* (Urbana: University of Illinois Press, 1982); Olivier Zunz, *The Changing Face of Inequality: Urbanization, Industrial Development, and Immigrants in Detroit, 1880–1920* (Chicago: University of Chicago Press, 1982).

95. "Christamore Settlement House Is Big Achievement," Indianapolis *Star*, December 11, 1924; "Haughville: Irish Were First to Settle There; Then Came Others," newspaper clippings, December 2, 1961. Charities file, IPL. Interview with Mr. Ray Spencer, September 15, 1974. John H. Holliday, "The Life of Our Foreign Population," typescript, pp. 12–13. ISL.; Mary Ann Armborst, "Immi-

grant Groups in Indianapolis" (Honors thesis, Marian College, Indianapolis, 1963); Stammel and Parks, "The Slavic Peoples in Indianapolis" (M.S. thesis, Indiana University School of Social Service, 1930); Clark, "First Fifty Years at Christamore House," p. 21. See also James J. Divita, *Slaves to No One: A History of the Holy Trinity Catholic Community in Indianapolis . . .* (Indianapolis, 1981), pp. 9–10. On Americanization, see Edward G. Hartmann, *The Movement to Americanize the Immigrant* (New York: Columbia University Press, 1948); Thomas J. Archdeacon, *Becoming American* (New York: Free Press, 1983), pp. 167–68, 184–86.

96. Residency was only abandoned at Christamore in the 1950s. For the role of the volunteer in social work see Roy Lubove, *The Professional Altruist: The Emergence of Social Work as a Career* (Pittsburgh: University of Pittsburgh Press, 1965), pp. 49–54.

97. *The Leisure of a People,* pp. 385–86.

98. "Haughville: Irish Were First to Settle There, Then Came Others"; Spencer interview.

99. National Conference of Social Work, *Proceedings of the Fifty-Eighth Meeting of the National Conference of Social Work* (Minneapolis: June 1931), p. 289.

100. Admitting the state's responsibility for teaching housekeeping, the Indiana legislature passed a law in 1913 making instruction in domestic science compulsory for girls in all Indiana high schools. See "Domestic Science in the Public Schools of Indiana," State of Indiana Department of Public Instruction, *Biennial Report for 1915 and 1916,* pp. 634–46. For the improved standard of living see Robert S. and Helen M. Lynd, *Middletown: A Study in American Culture* (New York: Harcourt, Brace, 1929); Winifred D. Wandersee, *Women's Work and Family Values, 1920–1940* (Cambridge: Harvard University Press, 1981).

101. Historian Mary Ryan writes, "The bureaucratized new century had less use for creative humanitarians than for self-absorbed service workers, whom it rewarded with a paycheck." *Womanhood in America: From Colonial Times to the Present* (New York: New Viewpoints, 1975), p. 257; Nancy Cott, *The Grounding of Modern Feminism* (New Haven: Yale University Press, 1987).

102. Trolander, *Settlement Houses and the Great Depression.*

103. Report submitted by Elizabeth Kemper Adams to the standing committee of the Intercollegiate Community Service Association, February 1922. Van Kleek Papers, Box 79. Sophia Smith Collection.

Chapter 2: Foreign House/American Settlement

1. Allen F. Davis, *Spearheads for Reform: The Social Settlements and the Progressive Movement, 1890–1914* (New York: Oxford University Press, 1967), pp. 84–94. Davis estimated that 283 out of the 307 settlement houses listed in the *Handbook of Settlements* served mainly immigrants. Robert A. Woods and Albert J. Kennedy, *Handbook of Settlements* (New York: Charities Publication Committee, 1911); George Cary White, "Social Settlements and Immigrant Neighbors," *Social Service Review* 33 (March 1959): 55–66.

2. For the metaphor of settlement house as colonizer see Martha Vicinus, *Independent Women: Work and Community for Single Women, 1850–1920* (London: Virago Press, 1985), pp. 219–20. Visitors to settlements often remarked on the contrast between settlement residents and their surroundings. Of his visit to Graham Taylor's University of Chicago Settlement in its early years, charity expert Alexander Johnson wrote, "Missionaries in the heart of Africa would hardly present a greater contrast with their surroundings than did these cultured and refined people in such a neighborhood." Quoted in Louise G. Wade, *Graham Taylor: Pioneer for Social Justice* (Chicago: University of Chicago Press, 1964), p. 119. See also Robert A. Slayton, *Back of the Yards: The Making of a Local Democracy* (Chicago: University of Chicago Press, 1986), pp. 173–79.

3. Jane Addams, *Twenty Years at Hull House* (New York: Macmillan, 1910; Signet, 1960), pp. 169–85; Lillian Wald, *The House on Henry Street* (New York: Henry Holt, 1915); Vida Scudder, *On Journey* (New York: E. P. Dutton, 1937) and "Work with Italians in Boston," *Survey* 22 (April 3, 1909): 47–51. An example of the influence of settlement workers as intermediaries for immigrants is Grace Abbott's testimony against the literacy test (a measure to limit immigration) before the House Committee on Immigration and Naturalization. Her opposition helped defeat the bill in 1912 (though one was later passed). Lela B. Costin, *Two Sisters for Social Justice: A Biography of Grace and Edith Abbott* (Urbana: University of Illinois Press, 1983), pp. 85–86.

4. Philip Gleason, "American Identity and Americanization," *Harvard Encyclopedia of American Ethnic Groups* (Cambridge: Belknap Press of Harvard University Press, 1980), p. 40; John Higham, *Strangers in the Land: Patterns of American Nativism, 1860–1925* (New York: Atheneum, 1965), p. 236; Michael B. Katz, *Poverty and Policy in American History* (New York: Academic Press, 1983), p. 201; White, "Social Settlements and Immigrant Neighbors"; Alvin Kogut, "The Settlements and Ethnicity: 1890–1914," *Social Work* 17 (May 1972): 22–31. As a group, settlement workers "probably erred on the side of sentimentality rather than bigotry," Allen Davis wrote. *Spearheads for Reform*, p. 86.

5. See, for example, Raymond Mohl and Neil Betten, "Paternalism and Pluralism: Immigrants and Social Welfare in Gary, Indiana, 1906–1940," *American Studies* 15 (Spring 1974): 5–30; Rivka Lissak, "Myth and Reality: The Pattern of Relationship between the Hull House Circle and the 'New Immigrants' on Chicago's West Side, 1890–1919," *Journal of American Ethnic History*, 2 (Spring 1983): 21–50; and *Pluralism and Progressives: Hull House and the New Immigrants 1890–1919* (Chicago: University of Chicago Press, 1989); Paul McBride, *Culture Clash: Immigrants and Reformers, 1880–1920* (San Francisco: R & E Research Associates, 1975); Virginia Yans McLaughlin, *Family and Community: Italian Immigrants in Buffalo, 1880–1930* (Ithaca, N.Y.: Cornell University Press, 1977), pp. 133–56; Slayton, *Back of the Yards*, pp. 172–87. See also David Whisnant, *All That Is Native and Fine: The Politics of Culture in an American Region* (Chapel Hill: University of North Carolina Press, 1984) for discussion of settlement work, this time with Appalachian people rather than immigrants.

6. Jane Addams, *The Spirit of Youth and the City Streets* (New York: Macmillan, 1910); Edward G. Hartmann, *The Movement to Americanize the Immigrant* (New York: Columbia University Press, 1948); John F. McClymer, *War and Welfare: Social Engineering in America* (Westport, Conn.: Greenwood Press, 1980), pp. 105–52; David M. Kennedy, *Over Here: The First World War and American Society* (New York: Oxford University Press, 1980), pp. 45–92.

7. Kirk H. Porter and Donald Bruce Johnson, comps., *National Party Platforms, 1840–1956* (Urbana: University of Illinois Press, 1956), pp. 347–48. In 1912, 838,172 immigrants entered the United States. U.S. Department of Commerce, Bureau of the Census, *Historical Statistics of the United States*, 2 vols., 1:105; McClymer, *War and Welfare*, p. 106.

8. Hartmann, *Movement to Americanize the Immigrant*, pp. 164 ff; Higham, *Strangers in the Land*, pp. 234–63.

9. Interview with Vera Morgan of the Haughville branch of the Indianapolis Public Library. Quoted in James J. Divita, *Slaves to No One: A History of the Holy Trinity Catholic Community in Indianapolis* (Indianapolis, 1981), p. 43. The observer was identified only as a "prominent writer."

10. "Indianapolis of To-Day: As Viewed by the Commercial Club," in R. L. Polk & Company, *Indianapolis City Directory for 1910*, pp. 5–6.

11. U.S. Department of Commerce, Bureau of the Census, *Fifteenth Census of the United States, 1930*: vol. 2, *Population*, pp. 199–200.

12. U.S. Department of Commerce, Bureau of the Census, *Thirteenth Census of the United States, 1910*: vol. 1, *Population*, pp. 574, 1007–15; *Fifteenth Census of the United States, 1930*: vol. 2, *Population*, p. 200; Mary Ann Armborst, "Immigrant Groups in Indianapolis" (Honors thesis, Marian College, Indianapolis, 1963). Between 1850 and 1900, the Germans were by far the largest group entering Indiana. The total German immigration in these years was estimated at 413,291, Irish immigration at 128,846, and that from Great Britain at 58,563. John D. Barnhardt and Donald F. Carmony, *Indiana: From Frontier to Industrial Commonwealth*, 4 vols. (New York: Lewis Historical Publishing Company, 1954), 2:298–300; Emma Lou Thornbrough, *Indiana in the Civil War Era, 1850–1880* (Indianapolis: Indiana Historical Bureau and Indiana Historical Society, 1965), pp. 547–55; Theodore G. Probst, "The Germans in Indianapolis" (M.A. thesis, Indiana University, 1951).

13. U.S. Department of Commerce, Bureau of the Census, *Thirteenth Census of the United States, 1910*: vol. 2, *Population*, p. 574.

14. Leander M. C. Campbell Adams, *An Investigation of Housing and Living Conditions in Three Districts of Indianapolis*, Indiana University Studies, vol. 8, no. 8 (1910), p. 127. Indianapolis in 1910 contained 40,000 people born in the United States of foreign-born parents. At 17.7 percent of the city's population, they constituted a significant foreign population. Predominant among them were immigrants from Great Britain, especially from Ireland, and Germany. Although a study of immigration into Indianapolis should certainly consider these groups, those who founded the Immigrants' Aid Association were

interested in the recent immigrants from southern and eastern Europe; hence those of foreign or mixed parentage have been excluded from this discussion. A community center that served Jews is the subject of Myra Auerbach, "A Study of the Jewish Settlement in Indianapolis" (M.A. thesis, Indiana University, 1937).

15. U.S. Department of Commerce, Bureau of the Census, *Twelfth Census: 1900. Occupations in the Twelfth Census*, pp. 574–76; Elavina S. Stammel and Charles R. Parks, "The Slavic Peoples in Indianapolis" (M.S. thesis, Department of Economics and Sociology, Indiana University, 1930), p. 56; Adams, *Housing and Living Conditions*, pp. 124, 127.

16. U.S. Department of Commerce, Bureau of the Census, *Thirteenth Census of the United States, 1910*: vol. 4, *Population, Occupation Statistics*, pp. 557–58. For Kingan's see Thornbrough, *Indiana in the Civil War Era*, p. 419; Clifton Phillips, *Indiana in Transition, 1880–1920* (Indianapolis: Indiana Historical Bureau and Indiana Historical Society, 1968), p. 281. The huge packing plant made Indianapolis the fifth largest center for the packing industry in the nation. In 1925, out of 250 foreign male employees, 146 were employed either at Kingan's, Armour and Company, or the Abattoir Company; of the 35 women working for wages, 20 were in meat-packing. In 1908, wages averaged 15 cents an hour for unskilled labor. See John H. Holliday, "The Life of Our Foreign Population," typescript, n.d. [1908?], ISL, p. 9; Mary Rigg, "A Survey of the Foreigners in the American Settlement District of Indianapolis" (M.A. thesis, Indiana University, 1925), pp. 25–29; Stammel and Parks, "Slavic Peoples," pp. 104, 120 ff.

17. Stammel and Parks, "Slavic Peoples," pp. 4–5, 87–88. Elavina Stammel and Charles Parks, two teachers in the public schools, also taught night school for two years, then taught at the Presbyterian Cosmopolitan Chapel. They claimed to have made extended efforts to get to know their subjects, whether in school, on the street, or in coffeehouses—hence the authentic detail that enlivens these case studies. Unfortunately, they interviewed few women. Also, they erroneously included Greeks and Turks in their survey of 501 "Slavs." Racial stereotypes such as the following abound in their otherwise careful case studies: "Mary shows that she is a Slav woman by her slowness of movement and her unexcitable nature." The phlegmatic Mary was probably slow because she was exhausted from hours of toil and quiet only in English. Stammel and Parks, p. 81.

18. *Forward!* (Indianapolis) 1 (December 1909): 2–3.

19. See Davis, *Spearheads for Reform*, pp. 18–22, for a thoughtful comparison between the COS and the settlement movement. Although, as Davis shows, liberal settlement workers had a more enlightened (and more effective) approach to urban ills than their COS counterparts, the two movements probably cooperated closely in many cities, as they did in Indianapolis. The contrast is also drawn in Robert A. Bremner, *From the Depths: The Discovery of Poverty in the United States* (New York: New York University Press, 1956), pp. 50–66.

20. Phillips, *Indiana in Transition*, p. 528; "Genuine Tribute Comes from Hearts at Holliday Memorial," clipping in Kingan Scrapbook, n.p., n.d.

(1921), IHS; Jacob Piatt Dunn, *Greater Indianapolis: The History, the Industries, the Institutions of a City of Homes*, 2 vols. (Chicago: Lewis, 1910), 1:75–80; 2:1006–8. Born in Indianapolis, Holliday attended Butler and Hanover colleges. Collins was born in 1870 in Massachusetts and did YMCA work in New York before coming to Indianapolis to read law in 1895. The juvenile court that he instituted in 1903 was one of the first in the country. He was decorated with the Order of St. Sava by the Jugoslav Consul General in Chicago in 1939 for his service to Indianapolis immigrants. Indianapolis *News* (December 4, 1946); Indianapolis *Star* (December 5, 1946); Dunn, *Greater Indianapolis*, 2:1162.

21. Charity Organization Society of Indianapolis, *Yearbook*, 1902–3, p. 14; 1904–5, pp. 3, 16; 1905–6, p. 16. See also *Charities and the Commons* 24 (December 19, 1908): 467; Roy Lubove, *The Progressives and the Slums: Tenement House Reform in New York City, 1890–1917* (Pittsburgh: University of Pittsburgh Press, 1962); Robert Barrows, " 'The Homes of Indiana': Albion Fellows Bacon and Housing Reform Legislation, 1907–1917," *Indiana Magazine of History*, 81 (December 1985): 309–50.

22. Adams, *Housing and Living Conditions*, p. 127. A separate ethnic neighborhood of Slovenes had developed west of the river in Haughville. Their history has been told by James Divita in *Slaves to No One*.

23. Adams, *Housing and Living Conditions*, pp. 128–32. This population profile, with its predominance of males, was typical of immigrant communities at the time, and in fact typical of an early stage of urbanization in general. See, for example, Michael Anderson, "Family, Household and the Industrial Revolution" and John Modell and Tamara K. Hareven, "Urbanization and the Malleable Household: An Examination of Boarding and Lodging in American Families," in Michael Gordon, ed., *The American Family in Social-Historical Perspective*, 2d ed. (New York: St. Martin's Press, 1978), pp. 38–68; Donna Gabaccia, *From Sicily to Elizabeth Street: Housing and Social Change Among Italian Immigrants, 1880–1920* (Albany, N.Y.: SUNY Press, 1983), p. 75. See also Josef Barton, *Peasants and Strangers: Italians, Roumanians, and Slovaks in an American City* (Cambridge: Harvard University Press, 1975).

24. Adams, *Housing and Living Conditions*, p. 132. The new social historians were much more impressed with immigrant housing strategies than were early twentieth-century reformers. John Bodnar argues that immigrants only departed from the nuclear-family form (taking in paying boarders or lodgers) when the family economy demanded it. *The Transplanted: A History of Immigrants in Urban America* (Bloomington: Indiana University Press, 1985), pp. 82–83; Gabaccia, *From Sicily to Elizabeth Street*, p. 75; Olivier Zunz, *The Changing Face of Inequality: Urbanization, Industrial Development, and Immigrants in Detroit, 1880 to 1920* (Chicago: University of Chicago Press, 1982), pp. 62–63, 70–71.

25. Robert A. Woods and Albert J. Kennedy, *The Settlement Horizon: A National Estimate* (New York: Russell Sage Foundation, 1922), p. 326. The quotation is from an anonymous settlement worker.

26. Holliday, "Our Foreign Population," p. 11.

27. "Constitution of the Immigrants' Aid Association," in Holliday, "Our Foreign Population," p. 17. Cf. George Creel's statement that the primary goal

of Americanization was to end "the tendency toward segregation" of ethnic communities. Quoted in Kennedy, *Over Here*, p. 66.

28. Holliday, "Our Foreign Population," p. 2.

29. Ibid., p. 13; McClymer, *War and Welfare*, pp. 83–100.

30. Holliday, "Our Foreign Population," pp. 3, 16. My analysis here relies on Paul Boyer, who convincingly identifies two strands in turn-of-the-century urban moral reform: the "coercive crusades" and "positive environmentalism." Boyer, *Urban Masses and Moral Order in America, 1810–1920* (Cambridge: Harvard University Press, 1978), pp. 220–33.

31. Constitution of the Immigrants' Aid Association in Holliday, "Our Foreign Population," p. 17; "Foreign Colony Students Active," Indianapolis *Sunday Star* (February 21, 1915), p. 3; Adams, *Housing and Living Conditions*, p. 122; Milton Gordon, *Assimilation in American Life* (New York: Oxford University Press, 1964). For settlement leaders' views that the American standard of living would act as an Americanizer, see "An Experimental Definition of the American Standard of Living," "Note X," Woods and Kennedy, *Settlement Horizon*, pp. 419–20. See also Francis G. Couvares, *The Re-Making of Pittsburgh: Class and Culture in an Industrializing City, 1877–1919* (Albany, N.Y.: SUNY Press, 1984), p. 120. There were exceptions to the dominant Americanization theory: for contemporary expressions of what later came to be called "cultural pluralism," see Horace M. Kallen, "Democracy versus the Melting-Pot," *The Nation* (February 1915): 190–94, 217–20, and Randolph S. Bourne, "Trans-National America," *Atlantic Monthly* 118 (July 1916): 86–97. For the rise of new forms of ethnicity in modern America, see Will Heberg, *Protestant, Catholic, Jew: An Essay in American Religious Sociology*, 2d ed. (New York: Doubleday, 1955; Anchor, 1960), and Nathan Glazer and Daniel Patrick Moynihan, *Beyond the Melting Pot: The Negroes, Puerto Ricans, Jew, Italians, and Irish of New York City* (Cambridge: MIT Press and Harvard University Press, 1964).

32. Adams, *Housing and Living Conditions*, p. 122. It is fascinating to contrast the Americanizers' account of immigrant culture with discussions by present-day social historians. Where the former saw a tangle of pathology, historians today see functioning, even admirable, social and familial systems. For a sophisticated analysis of the spatial and cultural meanings of ethnic neighborhoods see Zunz, *Changing Face of Inequality*, pp. 178–95 and passim.

33. Adams, *Housing and Living Conditions*, p. 132.

34. Ibid., p. 133.

35. *First Annual Report of the Immigrants' Aid Association of Indianapolis, Indiana, 1911–1912*, pp. 1, 3; "Foreign Quarters in City to be Improved," Indianapolis *News* (July 29, 1911), p. 16; Holliday, "Our Foreign Population," p. 17.

36. *First Annual Report of the Immigrants' Aid Association of Indianapolis, Indiana, 1911–1912*, p. 3; "Prepares Clubhouse for City's Foreigners. Improvement Is Its Aim," Indianapolis *News* (August 25, 1911), p. 11. The building had been constructed by the Free Kindergarten Society in 1886 for a teacher-training school. They sold it to the Immigrants' Aid Association in 1910. In 1908, a kindergarten was being carried on there, and the building was called the "Pearl Street Settlement." Indianapolis Free Kindergarten and Children's

Aid Society, *Superintendent's Report*, March 31, 1908. Blaker Collection, Box 1527, IHS. See also *Leisure of a People*, p. 368.

The names of the settlement house and its locations are as follows:

1911–23, Immigrants' Aid Association, 617 West Pearl Street, Indianapolis
1923–39, American Settlement, same address.
1939–61, Southwest Social Center, 1917 West Morris Street, Indianapolis
1961– Mary Rigg Center, same address.

37. "Foreign Quarters in City to be Improved." Immigrants' Aid Association, *First Annual Report*, pp. 4–5; *Second Annual Report*, pp. 6–7. For the free floor discussion at Graham Taylor's settlement see Wade, *Graham Taylor: Pioneer for Social Justice*.

38. "Foreign Colony Students Active"; Ora Ellen Cox, "The Socialist Party in Indiana Since 1896," *Indiana Magazine of History*, 12 (1916): 95–130.

39. For Hurty's role in the housing reform campaign, see Dunn, *Greater Indianapolis* 2: 741–44; Adams, *Housing and Living Conditions*, p. 130; Barrows, " 'The Homes of Indiana' "; Phillips, *Indiana in Transition*, pp. 471, 487; *Second Annual Report*, p. 8; Indianapolis Board of Health, *Report for 1902*, p. 245. Despite the reformers' efforts, Mary Rigg reported in 1925 that many immigrant women still had to haul all their water a block or more. Mary Rigg, "Survey of the Foreigners," p. 55.

40. *First Annual Report*, p. 3; *Second Annual Report*, p. 7; "Foreign Quarters in City to Be Improved."

41. *Second Annual Report*, p. 8.

42. Stammel and Parks, "Slavic Peoples," pp. 10–11.

43. *Annual Report*, p. 5; "The Dream and the Reality," Indianapolis *News* (June 1, 1913), Supplement, p. 1.

44. *Second Annual Report*, pp. 4, 9. Kingan's ran a school for its employees, but no details of its programs remain.

45. Woods and Kennedy, *Settlement Horizon*, p. 331.

46. "Dream and the Reality"; *First Annual Report*, p. 4; "Indianapolis City Missions," *Missionary Tidings* 33 (November 1915), 285; Foreign House Ledger, p. 51. At Mary Rigg Center. Nationally, estimates of rates of return to the homeland range from 64 percent for Magyars to about 35 to 40 percent for Germans, and 40 percent for Greeks. Bodnar, *The Transplanted*, pp. 53–54, summarizes the literature on return migration.

47. Stammel and Parks, "Slavic Peoples," pp. 92–93.

48. *First Annual Report*, p. 4; Holliday, "Our Foreign Population," p. 16.

49. Dunn, *Greater Indianapolis*, 1:438; *The American Home Missionary, Yearbook of the Churches of Christ* (1914), p. 68. UCMS; *American Home Missionary* (1909), p. 21; Charles H. Hopkins, *The Rise of the Social Gospel in American Protestantism, 1865–1915* (New Haven: Yale University Press, 1940); Henry F. May, *Protestant Churches and Industrial America* (New York: Harper, 1949); Theodore Abel, *Protestant Home Missions to Catholic Immigrants* (New York: Institute of Social and Religious Research, 1933). For the religious activities of the settlements, see Chapter 4.

50. "Indianapolis City Missions," p. 284.

51. "Sunday School Collections and Attendances, 1914" and "Sunday School Expenses for the Year, 1916" show expenditures for "Slovenian literature" and for Croatian hymnbooks. Mary Rigg Collection, ISL. "Each teacher is assigned to five foreign students, so that the maximum of intensive practice may be secured," it explained. "The men have manifested deep enthusiasm in the classes, and have not failed to recognize the teaching as a Christian service." *Missionary Tidings* (November 1916), p. 279.

52. "Indianapolis City Missions," pp. 284–85.

53. Stammel and Parks, "Slavic Peoples," pp. 85–86. A recent study of the Polish experience in America is John J. Bucowczyk, *And My Children Did Not Know Me: A History of the Polish-Americans* (Bloomington: Indiana University Press, 1987).

54. Stammel and Parks, "Slavic Peoples," pp. 81–82. Barton, *Peasants and Strangers*, analyzes patterns of assimilation among the Romanians.

55. Stammel and Parks, "Slavic Peoples," p. 78.

56. In contrast to Oscar Handlin's portrait of immigrant disorientation and loss in *The Uprooted* (Boston: Little, Brown, 1951), recent historiography has stressed immigrants' success in maintaining aspects of their traditional culture while adopting new "survival strategies" in American cities. See Rudolph J. Vecoli, "Contadini in Chicago: A Critique of *The Uprooted*," *Journal of American History* 51 (December 1964): 404–17; John Bodnar, "Immigration and Modernization: The Case of the Slavic Peasants in Industrial America," *Journal of Social History* 10 (1976): 44–71; Timothy L. Smith, "Lay Initiative in the Religious Life of American Immigrants, 1880–1950," in Tamara K. Hareven, ed., *Anonymous Americans* (Englewood Cliffs, N.J.: Prentice-Hall, 1971), pp. 214–49 and "Religion and Ethnicity in America," *American Historical Review* 83 (December 1978): 1153–81, present the challenging view that immigrants modified their religious practices as befitted "aspiring modernizers."

57. Foreign House Yearbook, p. 60. At Mary Rigg Center; *First Annual Report*, p. 5; *Second Annual Report*, p. 6; Mary Rigg, "Survey of the Foreigners," p. 59.

58. "Foreign Colony Students Active."

59. Foreign House Yearbook, p. 53.

60. "Foreign Colony Students Active"; Holliday, "Our Foreign Population," p. 8. Lissak argued that because settlement workers mistrusted and misunderstood the culture of the new immigrants, the settlement "remained a marginal institution" in the ethnic neighborhood. *Pluralism and Progressives*, p. 122.

61. Foreign House Yearbook, p. 60. In 1919, attendances as follows were recorded in the settlement's yearbook:

Clinic (mothers and babies)—4
Night School—8 to 13
Girls' Club—15 to 30
Library day—40 to 50
Christmas Entertainment—193

Foreign House Yearbook, p. 101.

62. American Settlement, *Annual Report,* 1928–1929; Indianapolis *Sunday Star,* (March 14, 1937), pt. 5, 4.

63. When the College Settlement in Boston first offered clubs for Italian women, "jealous husbands waited across the street to observe and draw conclusions as to the propriety of what went on within." Scudder, *On Journey,* p. 255. Quoted in Woods and Kennedy, *Settlement Horizon,* p. 333. See also Gabaccia, *From Sicily to Elizabeth Street,* pp. 113–14.

64. Herbert G. Gans, *The Urban Villagers: Group and Class in the Life of Italian Americans* (New York: Free Press, 1962), p. 148–49; William F. Whyte, *Street Corner Society: The Social Structure of an Italian Slum* (Chicago: University of Chicago Press, 1943, 1955). The National Federation of Settlements concluded after a survey, *Young Working Girls,* that the main barrier to settlements' attempts to reach immigrant families was the near-tyrannical control exercised in such families by the father. "Every effort should be made to appeal to his (the father's) pride in his womenfolk and to induce him to individualize them." Robert Woods and Albert J. Kennedy, *Young Working Girls: A Summary of Evidence from Two Thousand Social Workers* (Boston, 1913), quoted in McLaughlin, *Family and Community,* p. 149; "Syrian Women in Chicago: New Responsibilities, New Skills," in Maxine Seller, ed., *Immigrant Women* (Philadelphia: Temple University Press, 1981), pp. 137–38; Paul S. Taylor, *Mexican Labor in the United States. Chicago and the Calumet Region* (Berkeley: University of California Press, 1932), pp. 202–3. Donna Gabaccia in " 'The Transplanted': Women and Family in Immigrant America," *Social Science History* 12 (Fall 1988): 243–53, calls for more attention to gender as a category of analysis in immigration history. She points to a certain romanticism in Bodnar's treatment of the immigrant family and household—romanticism that has obscured questions about power relations within the family.

65. *Missionary Tidings,* November 1916, p. 279.

66. National Bureau of Municipal Research, "Survey of Social Agencies in Indianapolis, 1918," typescript, mimeographed, IUPUI, p. 237.

67. Ibid., pp. 238–39.

68. Phillips, *Indiana in Transition,* p. 611; John R. Seeley et al., *Community Chest* (Toronto: University of Toronto Press, 1957), pp. 87–88. Judith A. Trolander, *Professionalism and Social Change: From the Settlement House Movement to Neighborhood Centers, 1886 to the Present* (New York: Columbia University Press, 1987); Don S. Kirschner, *The Paradox of Professionalism: Reform and Public Service in Urban America, 1900–1940* (Westport, Conn.: Greenwood Press, 1986); Roy Lubove, *The Professional Altruist: The Emergence of Social Work as a Career* (Pittsburgh: University of Pittsburgh Press, 1965).

69. Ibid., p. 92. Indianapolis Council of Social Agencies, *The Leisure of a People. Report of a Recreation Survey of Indianapolis* (Indianapolis, 1929), p. 368.

70. Mary Rigg, "Southwest Social Center," typescript, attached to a letter to Frank O. Wilking, Wilking Music Company, April 15, 1959. Mary Rigg Center.

71. Mary Rigg, "My Own Record," typescript, Mary Rigg Center. Among her other positions, she was executive director of the Social Service Department of the Indianapolis Church Federation, a leader in the AAUW, and president of

Indiana University's Women's Club. She served three times as chair of the Indianapolis Federation of Settlements. She was also on the board of the National Federation of Settlements. She was the director of the American Settlement (then Southwest Social Center) from 1924–61, a total of thirty-seven years.

72. *Leisure of a People*, p. 371.

73. Kate Milner Rabb and William Herschell, eds., *An Account of Indianapolis and Marion County* (Dayton, Ohio: Dayton Historical Publishing Co., 1924), p. 120. In Indiana, the state had to provide a public night school upon the petition of a sufficient number of its citizens. John McClymer, "The Americanization Movement and the Education of the Foreign Born Adults, 1919–1925," in Bernard J. Weiss, ed., *American Education and the European Immigrant, 1840–1940* (Urbana: University of Illinois Press, 1982), pp. 96–111.

74. Stammel and Parks, "Slavic Peoples," p. 86.

75. Ibid., p. 86; Maxine Seller, "The Education of the Immigrant Woman, 1900–1915," *Journal of Urban History*, 4 (May 1978): 307–30. A brief but suggestive essay by Donna Gabaccia faults many historians of immigrants for leaving out women and the family in a specious "genderless history." "*The Transplanted*: Women and Family in Immigrant America."

76. *Leisure of a People*, p. 369. Roy Rosenzweig, in a study of workers' leisure in Worcester, Mass., characterizes the middle-class reformers' campaigns for parks and playgrounds as "concerted campaigns to thwart working-class efforts at carving out and maintaining distinctive and autonomous spheres of leisure time and space." Rosenzweig, *Eight Hours for What We Will: Workers and Leisure in an Industrial City, 1870–1920* (Cambridge: New York, 1983, paperback ed. 1985), pp. 4–5. See also Couvares, *The Re-Making of Pittsburgh*, pp. 112–16; Stephen Hardy and Alan G. Ingham, "Games, Structure and Agency: Historians on the American Play Movement," *Journal of Social History* 17 (Winter 1983): 285–301; Dominic Cavallo, *Muscles and Morals: Organized Playgrounds and Urban Reform, 1880–1920* (Philadelphia: University of Pittsburgh Press, 1981).

77. *American Settlement Annual Report, 1928–1929*, p. 4; Mary Rigg, "Survey of the Foreigners," p. 56; "Report of the Public Health Nursing Association Clinic at the American Settlement," typewritten, dated March 24, 1932. ISL. For Sheppard-Towner see Sheila Rothman, *Woman's Proper Place: A History of Changing Ideals and Practices, 1870 to the Present* (New York: Basic Books, 1978), pp. 136–53; Clarke A. Chambers, *Seedtime of Reform: American Social Service and Social Action* (Ann Arbor: University of Michigan Press, 1967), p. 125; Costin, *Two Sisters for Social Justice*, pp. 175–76.

78. Quoted in Hartmann, *Movement to Americanize the Immigrant*, p. 214. See also William Preston, Jr., *Aliens and Dissenters: Federal Suppression of Radicals, 1903–1933* (New York: Harper Torchbooks, 1963); Kennedy, *Over Here*, pp. 63–75.

79. "Greek Community in Haughville," undated clipping (1925?), Mary Rigg Center.

80. "Gay Roumanian Colony Here Proud of Native Costumes, Roman Lineage," Indianapolis *Star*, August 9, 1929; "Bulgarian Colony Thriving in City," undated clipping, IPL. "Greek Community in Haughville."

81. Mary Rigg, "Survey of the Foreigners," pp. 55–56, 57, 60.

82. Ibid., pp. 41, 59.

83. Bernard Fall, "The Foreigner in Indianapolis," n.p.; Mary Rigg, "Survey of the Foreigners," p. 50; Stammel and Parks, "Slavic Peoples," p. 51. An example of a custom frowned on by the settlement but dear to immigrants was this Bulgarian betrothal ceremony, described by Mary Rigg as follows:

> Wedding invitations were sent out as follows: A friend of the bride and groom would give out the invitations. Equipped with a large wooden jug, . . . filled with the finest of wine, the friend goes to different houses and invites the household by asking each member to take a drink from the jug. The bride pins a flower on the lapel of the friend's coat before he starts on his journey of invitation. The women who receive invitations tie handkerchiefs on the handle of the jug or pin flowers on the friend's coat as the bride had done. . . . These are all taken to the bride.

Ibid., pp. 45–46.

84. *American Settlement, Annual Report, 1928–1929*, p. 5.

85. Stammel and Parks, "Slavic Peoples," p. 160; Mary Rigg, "Survey of the Foreigners," pp. 27–28; *American Settlement, Annual Report, 1928–1929*, p. 4. This recalls Emma Goldman's remark that settlements were places where the poor learned to eat with forks.

86. *American Settlement, Annual Report, 1928–1929*, p. 4.

87. Mary Rigg, "Survey of the Foreigners," p. 161. Settlement workers in the Calumet Region found as late as the 1930s that Mexican fathers regarded the use of the settlement gymnasium by girls as immoral. Taylor, *Mexican Labor in the United States*, p. 202.

88. Stammel and Parks, "Slavic Peoples," p. 132. One hundred and three out of 501 of the immigrant group studied had tried independent businesses. Of these 15 had failed and had become wage-workers. The figures were higher for some groups: 63 percent of the Greeks and 45 percent of Bulgarians had started businesses by 1928. Stammel and Parks, "Slavic Peoples," pp. 129, 143, 150. Joseph Barton found significant differences in the enthusiasm with which different groups embraced mobility: "The Italians expected to grasp at new opportunities without interrupting ties to their village origins. And the Rumanians enthusiastically embraced the promise of mobility. Their secular values and mobile leaders gave them a head start in making it [in Cleveland.]" *Peasants and Strangers*, pp. 89, 90.

89. *American Settlement, Annual Report 1928–1929*, pp. 3–4. Luther Gulick, a leader of the early-twentieth-century folk-dancing movement, advocated folk-dancing as a way to create unity, not as a celebration of ethnic distinctiveness. Folk dancing was "a positive moral force, a social agency . . . that is destined to have in the future a great function in welding together a unified whole from those whose conditions and occupations are exceedingly diverse." Quoted in Patricia Mooney Melvin, "Building Muscles and Civics: Folk Dancing, Ethnic Diversity, and the Playground Association of America," *American Studies* 24 (Spring 1983): 89–99.

90. "Settlement House Center of Life of Stockyard Workers," undated clipping (1928?), IPL. Couvares asserts that the Americanization campaign failed in its goal of remaking the American working class. Faced with the apparent paradox that Americanization happened anyway, he paraphrases E. P. Thompson to say that immigrants weren't Americanized—they Americanized themselves. Couvares, *The Remaking of Pittsburgh*, pp. 118–19. "Commerce also contributed to this transformation: "Commerce overmatched reform and contributed to the re-making of working-class culture." p. 120. I leave to others the question of who or what made the new mass culture, with its blurring of both class and ethnic lines.

Chapter 3: Flanner House

1. Allen F. Davis, *Spearheads for Reform: The Social Settlements and the Progressive Movement, 1890–1912* (New York: Oxford University Press, 1967), p. 94; Introduction to the 1984 Edition (New Brunswick, N.J.: Rutgers University Press, 1984). A critical study of Chicago settlements for blacks is Thomas A. Philpott, *The Slum and the Ghetto: Neighborhood Deterioration and Middle Class Reform, Chicago, 1880–1930* (New York: Oxford University Press, 1978).

2. Robert A. Woods and Albert J. Kennedy, *Handbook of Settlements* (New York: Charities Publication Committee, 1911), p. v.

3. Walter I. Trattner, *From Poor Law to Welfare State: A History of Social Welfare in America*, 2d ed. (New York: Free Press, 1979), pp. 145–46. Michael B. Katz's study, *Poverty and Policy in American History* (New York: Academic Press, 1983), though not focusing centrally on the settlement workers, describes them as "the most humane and progressive reformers" and as "more sympathetic to cultural diversity than other reformers, more critical of economic, social, and political relations," p. 201, n. 10.

4. Steven J. Diner, "Chicago Social Workers and Blacks in the Progressive Era," *Social Service Review* 44 (December 1970): 398–99. Jane Addams's wit and wisdom can be sampled in "The Subtle Problems of Charity," *Atlantic Monthly* 83 (1899): 165–78, and "Charity and Social Justice," *Survey* 24 (June 11, 1910).

5. Diner, "Chicago Social Workers and Blacks," p. 400–401; Alvin B. Kogut, "The Negro and the Charity Organization Society in the Progressive Era," *Social Service Review* 44 (March 1970): 11. For Taylor, see Louise G. Wade, *Graham Taylor, Pioneer for Social Justice* (Chicago: University of Chicago Press, 1964). Social-work historian Judith Ann Trolander is excellent on the relationship of the settlements to blacks since 1945 but sketchy on the earlier period, though she correctly states that "settlements tended to give in to the prejudices of their white neighbors during this period [1886–1945] rather than impose more racially enlightened views." Judith Ann Trolander, *Professionalism and Social Change: From the Settlement House Movement to Neighborhood Centers, 1886 to the Present* (New York: Columbia University Press, 1987), p. 22.

6. John Daniels, *In Freedom's Birthplace: A Study of the Boston Negroes* (New York: Negro Universities Press, 1914, 1968); Mary White Ovington, *Half a*

Man: The Status of the Negro in New York (New York: Negro Universities Press, 1911, 1969); W. E. B. Du Bois, *The Philadelphia Negro—A Social Study* (New York: Schocken Books, 1899, 1967), was sponsored by Susan Wharton of the College Settlement, Philadelphia. The study of Negro domestic workers appended to Du Bois's work was by Isabel Eaton, a settlement worker. For "scientific social work" among blacks, Jesse Thomas Moore, *A Search for Equality: The National Urban League, 1910–1961* (University Park: Pennsylvania State University Press, 1981), pp. 47–55; Arvarh E. Strickland, *History of the Chicago Urban League* (Urbana: University of Illinois Press, 1966), pp. 41–44. Davis, *Spearheads for Reform*, pp. 99–102; Gilbert Osofsky, *Harlem: The Making of a Ghetto* (New York: Harper and Row, Harper Torchbooks, 1968), pp. 53–67.

7. Elting Morison, ed., *The Letters of Theodore Roosevelt*, 8 vols. (Cambridge: Harvard University Press, 1951–54), 7:801.

8. Rayford Logan, *The Negro in American Life and Thought: The Nadir, 1877–1901* (New York: Dial Press, 1954), later revised as *The Betrayal of the Negro: From Rutherford B. Hayes to Woodrow Wilson* (London: Collier Books, 1965); I. A. Newby, ed., *The Development of Segregationist Thought* (Homewood, Ill.: Dorsey Press, 1968). The "nadir" is variously defined as stretching from 1877 to 1901, 1915, or even to 1924.

9. Jack Temple Kirby, *Darkness at the Dawning: Race and Reform in the Progressive South* (Philadelphia: J. B. Lippincott, 1972), p. 4.

10. Robert A. Woods and Albert J. Kennedy, *The Settlement Horizon: A National Estimate* (New York: Russell Sage Foundation, 1922), p. 337.

11. David A. Gerber, *Black Ohio and the Color Line, 1860–1915* (Urbana: University of Illinois Press, 1976), p. 282. The Ohio settlement houses are the subjects of Judith Trolander, "Twenty Years at Hiram House," *Ohio History* 78 (Winter 1969), and Jon A. Peterson, "From Social Settlement to Social Agency: Settlement Work in Columbus, Ohio, 1898–1958," *Social Service Review* 39 (1965): 191–208. Cleveland's Karamu Settlement, the Playhouse Settlement, a black settlement founded and run by white Progressives, became a center for the celebration of black folk culture. Kenneth Kusmer describes it as "a unique social institution." Kenneth L. Kusmer, *A Ghetto Takes Shape: Black Cleveland, 1870–1930* (Urbana: University of Illinois Press, 1976), pp. 216–18.

12. Woods and Kennedy, *Handbook of Settlements*, p. 150.

13. "It is the belief of the managers of Christamore that the color line is not drawn closely enough in the district," wrote sociologist Leander M. C. Campbell Adams in 1910. "Hence, they, as part of their plan of action, have decided to exclude negroes. The settlement is open only to white people." Leander M. C. Campbell Adams, *An Investigation of Housing and Living Conditions in Three Districts of Indianapolis*, Indiana University Studies, no. 8 (Bloomington: Indiana University Press, 1910), p. 134. See Chapter 1.

14. A similar pattern can be seen in several cities. Pittsburgh's Kingsley House moved in 1919 to a white neighborhood in order to avoid serving blacks. Chicago's Abraham Lincoln Center attempted to serve blacks as well as whites, but white attendance declined. Ronald J. Butera, "A Settlement House and the Urban Challenge: Kingsley House in Pittsburgh, Pennsylvania, 1893–1920,"

Western Pennsylvania Historical Magazine 66 (January 1983): 36; Trolander, *Professionalism and Social Change,* p. 22; Philpott, *The Slum and the Ghetto.*

15. Neil Betten, "The Evolution of Racism in an Industrial City," *Journal of Negro History,* 59 (1974): 51–64; Raymond A. Mohl and Neil Betten, *Steel City: Urban and Ethnic Patterns in Gary, Indiana, 1906–1950* (New York: Holmes and Meier: 1986); pp. 48–90. Gary's two white Protestant settlement houses, Campbell House and Neighborhood House, became racially integrated as early as the 1920s. See Chapters 4, 5, and 7.

16. Woods and Kennedy, *Handbook of Settlements,* pp. 30–31, 39–40, 47, 50, 77, 97–98, 121–22, 171, 178–79, 259, 271–72, 298; W. E. B. Du Bois, *Efforts for Social Betterment among Negro Americans,* Atlanta University Publications, no. 14 (Atlanta: Atlanta University Press, 1909), pp. 121–26; Philpott, *Slum and the Ghetto;* Jeffrey A. Hess, "Black Settlement House, East Greenwich, 1902–1914," *Rhode Island History* 29 (1970): 113–27; Mary White Ovington, "The Color Line in Social Work," *Charities* 14 (April 11, 1905); Cynthia Neverdon Morton, *Afro-American Women of the South and the Advancement of the Race, 1895–1925* (Knoxville: University of Tennessee Press, 1989), surveys racial-advancement institutions founded by blacks in the South. See also Julius Franklin Nimmons, Jr., "Social Reform and Moral Uplift in the Black Community, 1890–1930: Social Settlements, Temperance, and Social Purity" (Ph.D. dissertation, Howard University, 1981), pp. 83–129.

17. Neverdon Morton, *Afro-American Women,* pp. 145–63. For the urban black experience, see Kenneth L. Kusmer, "The Black Urban Experience in American History," in *The State of Afro-American History, Past, Present, and Future,* ed. Darlene Clark Hine (Baton Rouge: Louisiana State University Press, 1986); Zane L. Miller, "The Black Experience in the Modern American City," in *The Urban Experience: Themes in American History,* ed. Raymond A. Mohl and James F. Richardson (Belmont, Calif: Wadsworth, 1973), pp. 44–60; Thomas C. Holt, "Afro-Americans," in *Harvard Encyclopedia of American Ethnic Groups,* ed. Stephan Thernstrom (Cambridge: Belknap Press, 1980), pp. 15–16; Du Bois, *Efforts for Social Betterment;* Moore, *Search for Equality,* pp. 24–35.

18. Jacqueline Rouse, *Lugenia Burns Hope: A Black Southern Reformer* (Athens: University of Georgia Press, 1989).

19. Neverdon Morton, *Afro-American Women,* pp. 105–9.

20. Nimmons, "Social Reform and Moral Uplift," pp. 99–103; Bishop Reverdy C. Ransom, *The Pilgrimage of Harriet Ransom's Son* (Nashville, Tenn.: Sunday School Union, 1949); Woods and Kennedy, *Handbook of Settlements,* pp. 77–78. Ransom went on to be a founder of the Niagara Movement.

21. Nimmons, "Social Reform and Moral Uplift," pp. 103–8; Evelyn Brooks, "The Women's Movement in the Black Baptist Church, 1880–1920" (Ph.D. dissertation, University of Rochester, 1984).

22. According to Nimmons, Ransom received financial support from Mrs. George M. Pullman, Mrs. Victoria Lawson (wife of the publisher of the Chicago *Daily News*), and Robert T. Lincoln, president of the Pullman Company; Richard Wright had the support of Mrs. Potter Palmer, Mrs. Louise Swift, and Mrs. George Webster of the Armour Company; both the Frederick Douglass Center

and the Wendell Phillips Center received financial help from Julius Rosenwald. Nimmons, "Social Reform and Moral Uplift," p. 100.

23. Philpott, *Slum and the Ghetto*, p. 315. For the institutional response to migration in one Upper South city, see George C. Wright, *Life behind a Veil: Blacks in Louisville, Kentucky, 1865–1930* (Baton Rouge: Louisiana State University Press, 1985). Most of the Louisville settlements for blacks did not last long because they lacked "workers, funding, and well-developed programs," pp. 123–55.

24. Nimmons, "Social Reform and Moral Uplift," pp. 110–16; Woods and Kennedy, *Handbook of Settlements*, pp. 50–51; *Who's Who in Colored America*, 1: 231; Celia Parker Woolley, "The Frederick Douglass Center," *Commons* 9 (July 1904): 328–29; Diner, "Chicago Social Workers and Blacks," p. 404; Du Bois, *Efforts for Social Betterment*, p. 122.

25. Nimmons, "Social Reform and Moral Uplift," pp. 117–18; Diner, "Chicago Social Workers and Blacks," pp. 405–6.

26. Linda Marie Perkins, "Quaker Beneficence and Black Control: The Institute for Colored Youth, 1852–1903," in *New Perspectives on Black Educational History*, ed. Vincent P. Franklin and James D. Anderson (Boston: G. K. Hall, 1978), pp. 19–43; Vincent P. Franklin, "In Pursuit of Freedom: The Educational Activities of Black Social Organizations in Philadelphia, 1900–1930," in ibid., pp. 117–18. See also Benjamin S. Phillip, *The Philadelphia Quakers in the Industrial Age, 1865–1920* (Philadelphia: Temple University Press, 1976); Margaret H. Bacon, *The Quiet Rebels: The Story of the Quakers in America* (New York: Basic Books, 1969); Daisey Newman, *A Procession of Friends: Quakers in America* (Garden City, N.Y.: Doubleday, 1972); William C. Braithwaite, *The Beginnings of Quakerism* (Cambridge: Cambridge University Press, 1961).

27. Historian Allen Davis summarized the differences between settlement workers and charity workers as follows: "The philosophy of the charity organization movement led to philanthropy, and the philosophy of the settlement movement, to reform." *Spearheads for Reform*, p. 19. For Oscar McCulloch, see Genevieve C. Weeks, *Oscar Carleton McCulloch, 1843–1891: Preacher and Practitioner of Applied Christianity* (Indianapolis: Indiana Historical Society, 1976), pp. 129–30. The settlement developed out of the secular work of McCulloch's Plymouth Congregational Church. Weeks put the date of its founding as 1899. See also Woods and Kennedy, *Handbook of Settlements*, p. 83. Charity Organization Society of Indianapolis, *Report of the Charity Organization Society of Indianapolis, 1898–1899*, p. 8; Frank Dekker Watson, *The Charity Organization Movement in the United States* (New York: Macmillan, 1922); Bremner, *From the Depths: The Discovery of Poverty in the United States* (New York: New York University Press, 1956), pp. 46–57. A useful article identifying different strands in the charity-organization movement is Kenneth L. Kusmer, "Organized Charity in the Progressive Era: Chicago as a Case Study," *Journal of American History* 60 (December 1973): 657–78.

28. Oscar C. McCulloch, "The Opportunity of the Commercial Club," Address to the board of directors of the Indianapolis Commercial Club, July 8, 1890, ISL. McCulloch's sermons often contained comments on the industrial

situation; in 1886 he condemned the verdict in the Haymarket trial. Weeks, *Oscar McCulloch,* pp. 144–45. The organic philosophy underlying late-nineteenth-century thinking about self and community that helped shape the settlement movement is discussed in Jean B. Quandt, *From the Small Town to the Great Community: The Social Thought of Progressive Intellectuals* (New Brunswick, N.J.: Rutgers University Press, 1970), and Patricia Mooney Melvin, *The Organic City: Urban Definition and Neighborhood Organization, 1880–1920* (Lexington: University of Kentucky Press, 1987).

29. "History of Flanner House," typescript, n.d., p. 3, FHP; Sarah Colton Smith, obituary, Indianapolis *Star* (May 2, 1939); Ray Stannard Baker, "The Negro Struggle for Survival in the North," *American Magazine* 65 (November 1907): 481.

30. Charity Organization Society of Indianapolis, *Report of the Charity Organization Society of Indianapolis, 1898–1899,* p. 8. Flanner, whose business was in the black community, was an active participant in many schemes of civic improvement and reform. His more famous daughter was the expatriate writer Janet Flanner. Jacob Piatt Dunn, *Representative Citizens of Indiana* (Indianapolis: B. F. Bowen, 1912), p. 467; Woods and Kennedy, *Handbook of Settlements,* p. 83. "Charities Yearbook," ISL.

31. Woods and Kennedy, *Handbook of Settlements,* pp. 121–22, 178–79; Osofsky, *Harlem,* pp. 53–54, 67; Howard Jacob Karger, "Phyllis Wheatley House: A History of the Minneapolis Black Settlement House, 1924 to 1940," *Phylon* 47 (March 1986): 79–90; Trolander, *Professionalism and Social Change,* p. 22.

32. Woods and Kennedy, *The Settlement Horizon,* p. 337; Diner, "Chicago Social Workers and Blacks in the Progressive Era," p. 393.

33. Frederick Doyle Kershner, Jr., "A Social and Cultural History of Indianapolis, 1860–1914" (Ph.D. dissertation, University of Wisconsin, 1950), p. 166; James H. Madison, *The Indiana Way: A State History* (Bloomington: Indiana University Press and Indiana Historical Society, 1986), pp. 169–73.

34. Jacob Piatt Dunn, *Greater Indianapolis: The History, the Industries, the Institutions, the People of a City of Homes,* 2 vols. (Chicago: Lewes, 1910), 1:252–53; Emma Lou Thornbrough, *The Negro in Indiana: A Study of a Minority* (Indianapolis: Indiana Historical Bureau, 1957), pp. 219–20, 258; Kershner, "History of Indianapolis," p. 168.

35. U.S., Dept. of Commerce, Bureau of the Census, *Negroes in the United States, 1920–1932* (Washington, D.C., 1935); *Thirteenth Census of the United States, 1910: Population* 2, 574; *Fourteenth Census, 1920: Population* 3, 308; *Fifteenth Census of the United States, 1930: Population* 3, 744; Emma Lou Thornbrough, "Segregation in Indiana during the Klan Era of the 1920s," *Mississippi Valley Historical Review* 47 (March 1961): 597–98; Emma Lou Thornbrough, *Since Emancipation: A Short History of Indiana Negroes, 1863–1963* (Indianapolis: American Negro Emancipation Centennial Authority, 1963), pp. 22–23; T. J. Woofter, Jr., *Negro Problems in Cities* (New York: Negro Universities Press, 1928, 1969), pp. 136–38; Adams, *Housing and Living Conditions,* p. 134.

36. Most donations were between $1 and $10. "The Good Work of the Flanner Guild," Indianapolis *News* (May 31, 1902), p. 1; *Freeman* (Indianapolis),

April 12, 1902, p. 3, June 28, 1902. Ray Stannard Baker, who described Flanner House as "maintained largely by white contributions, but . . . controlled wholly by colored people," seems to have been not quite right on either account. Baker, "Struggle for Survival," p. 481.

37. "History of Flanner House," p. 3.

38. *Second Annual Report, Flanner Guild Industrial Neighborhood House* (1904), p. 5; "The Good Work of the Flanner Guild"; "Working for the Salvation of the Negro by Training Young Members of the Race," Indianapolis *News*, August 24, 1903.

39. The largest employer in the Flanner House district, Atlas Engine Works, hired only whites. See Adams, *Housing and Living Conditions*, pp. 134–35. See also W. E. B. Du Bois and Augustus Granville Dill, eds., *The Negro American Artisan*, Atlanta University Publications, no. 17 (Atlanta, Ga., 1912), pp. 57, 84, 99, 130; "The Industrial Color Line in the North," *Century Magazine* 60 (July 1900): 477–78; "Our Relations to Labor," *Freeman* (Indianapolis), August 21, 1897. For black labor unions in Indianapolis, see Kershner, "History of Indianapolis," p. 169, "Struggle for Survival," p. 479; Philip Foner, *Organized Labor and the Black Worker, 1619–1973* (New York: Praeger, 1974); Philip Foner, ed., *The Black Worker: A Documentary History*, vol. 3, *The Black Worker during the Era of the Knights of Labor* (Philadelphia: Temple University Press, 1978); U.S. Dept. of Commerce, Bureau of the Census, *Twelfth Census of the United States, 1900: Occupations at the Twelfth Census*, pp. 574–76. Included in the census category "domestic and personal service" was a range of occupations including barbers, janitors, saloon keepers, servants, and waiters. Of 3,906 black males in this category in 1900, 57 percent were "laborers not specified," 27 percent were servants and waiters. Of 2,410 black woman in "domestic and personal service," 33 percent were laundresses, and 58 percent servants and waitresses. Twenty-seven nurses and midwives were also in this category. Ibid, pp. 574–76. For blacks in the northern economy before the Great Migration, Joe William Trotter, Jr., *Black Milwaukee: The Making of an Industrial Proletariat, 1915–1945* (Urbana: University of Illinois Press, 1985), pp. 3–33; Lorenzo J. Greene and Carter G. Woodson, *The Negro Wage Earner* (New York: Russell and Russell, 1930); Theodore Hershberg et al., "A Tale of Three Cities: Blacks, Immigrants, and Opportunity in Philadelphia, 1850–1880, 1930, 1970," in Hershberg, ed., *Philadelphia: Work, Space, Family, and Group Experience in the Nineteenth Century: Essays Towards an Interdisciplinary History of the City* (New York: Oxford University Press, 1981).

40. *Third Annual Report, Flanner Guild* (1905), p. 5; "Free Cooking School to Aid Colored People," Indianapolis *News*, July 18, 1914, p. 5.

41. Indianapolis *News*, August 24, 1903, p. 8.

42. Du Bois, *Efforts for Social Betterment*, p. 61. Lillian T. Fox was employed by the Indianapolis *News* in 1900 to write a regular column on African-American affairs. She was active in numerous reform initiatives. Earline Ray Ferguson, "The Woman's Improvement Club of Indianapolis: Black Women Pioneers in Tuberculosis Work, 1903–1938," *Indiana Magazine of History* 84 (September 1988): 240. Gerda Lerner writes, "Unlike their white counterparts,

black club women frequently successfully bridged the class barrier and concerned themselves with issues of importance to poor women . . . " Lerner, "Community Work of Black Club Women," p. 167.

43. Twenty-seven speakers participated in these forums during 1905 alone. *Third Annual Report* (1905), p. 3. For George Knox, see Willard Gatewood, Jr., *Slave and Freemen: The Autobiography of George L. Knox* (Lexington: The University Press of Kentucky, 1979).

44. Baker wrote," For so long a time, the Negro has been driven, or forced to work, as in the South, that he learns only slowly, in an intense, impersonal, competitive life like that of the North, where work is at a premium, that he himself, not the white man, must do the driving. It is the lesson that raises many from slavery into freedom." "Struggle for Survival," p. 483. See also Moore, *A Search for Equality*, p. 39. In a new and controversial hypothesis that recalls Baker's argument, historian Roger Lane cites blacks' exclusion from the "discipline" of industrial labor as contributing to the development of a "criminal subculture" among blacks in the twentieth century. Roger Lane, *Roots of Violence in Black Philadelphia, 1860–1900* (Cambridge: Harvard University Press, 1986). "The most important fact about the structure of black opportunity, both blue collar and white, was that it was almost wholly unaffected by the contemporary industrial revolution," Lane, pp. 37, 173.

Historians have generally been much more critical of the moral and social revolution that industrial discipline ushered in. See, especially, E. P. Thompson, "Time, Work Discipline, and Industrial Capitalism," *Past and Present* 38 (December 1967): 56–97. See also Daniel T. Rodgers, *The Work Ethic in Industrial America, 1850–1920* (Chicago: University of Chicago Press, 1978).

45. Flanner Guild Industrial Neighborhood House, *Second Annual Report* (1904), pp. 5, 9; *Third Annual Report* (1905), p. 5; Du Bois, *Efforts for Social Betterment*, p. 125.

46. A similar program in Cleveland, the black YWCA, helped black women adjust to urban life, provided services for them, and acted as a domestic-work agency. See Adrienne Lash Jones, "Jane Edna Hunter and the Phyllis Wheatley House of Cleveland" (Ph.D. dissertation, Case Western Reserve University, 1983). For the Progressives and "Educated Motherhood," see "The Ideology of Educated Motherhood," in Sheila M. Rothman, *Woman's Proper Place* (New York: Basic Books, 1978), pp. 97–127.

47. *Freeman* (Indianapolis), November 26, 1898, p. 4. The "History of Flanner House" says that, in its early years, Flanner House was "fought and criticised by the small minds of both races" p. 2. Historian Ralph Luker notes opposition from blacks to segregated agencies in other cities. Letter to the author, May 28, 1984. The black press expressed fears that "Southern ways were coming North." Divisions within the black elites in various cities of the North are analyzed in Gerber, *Black Ohio and the Color Line*, pp. 417–18, 433–34; Kusmer, *A Ghetto Takes Shape*, pp. 113–54; Allan H. Spear, *Black Chicago: The Making of a Negro Ghetto, 1890–1920* (Chicago: University of Chicago Press, 1967); David Katzman, *Before the Ghetto: Black Detroit in the Nineteenth Century*

(Urbana: University of Illinois Press, 1973); James D. Anderson, *The Education of Blacks in the South, 1860–1935* (Chapel Hill: University of North Carolina Press, 1988), pp. 105–9.

48. The whole quotation reads: "[Washington] spoke for the segment of blacks who somehow succeeded despite these odds in advocating accommodation, at least for the time, to what blacks could not change, and gathering strength through education, economic struggle, and black solidarity as a surer foundation for progress." Louis R. Harlan, *Booker T. Washington: The Wizard of Tuskegee, 1901–1915* (New York: Oxford University Press, 1983), p. 33. See also Harlan, "Booker T. Washington and the Politics of Accommodation," in John Hope Franklin and August Meier, *Black Leaders of the Twentieth Century* (Urbana: University of Illinois Press, 1982), pp. 1–18.

49. *Freeman* (Indianapolis), August 4, 1888.

50. Ibid. April 22, 1916.

51. "History of Flanner House," p. 3.

52. Flanner Guild Industrial Neighborhood House, *Second Annual Report*, p. 9; Woods and Kennedy, *Handbook of Settlements*, p. 83. This "History" is apparently in error in listing 1889 as the date when B. J. Morgan became head resident; Woods and Kennedy reproduced this error in the 1911 *Handbook of Settlements*. Dr. Morgan was leader of the Colored Young Men's Prayer Band, which later developed into the Senate Avenue branch of the YMCA. Indianapolis Council of Social Agencies, *Leisure of a People (Report of a Recreation Survey of Indianapolis)*, pp. 335 ff. By 1909, he was field agent of the Slater Fund. Du Bois, *Efforts for Social Betterment*, pp. 31, 35.

53. Brokenburr was general manager for the Indianapolis-based Madame C. J. Walker Company, one of the largest black-owned businesses in the nation. He was elected to the state senate in 1941 as a Republican. His association with Flanner House seems to have been short-lived. John W. Lyda, *The Negro in the History of Indiana* (Terre Haute, Ind., 1953), p. 70. Robert Lee Brokenburr Papers, IHS.

54. "The Good Work of the Flanner Guild," *Freeman* (Indianapolis), June 21, 1902, p. 1; *Third Annual Report, Flanner Guild* (1905), p. 5. For the black-clubwomen's movement, Gerda Lerner, "Community Work of Black Club Women," *Journal of Negro History* 59 (April 1974): 158–67, and Lerner, ed., *Black Women in White America: A Documentary History* (New York: Vintage Books, 1972), pp. 435–58; Darlene Clark Hine, *When the Truth is Told: A History of Black Women's Culture and Community in Indiana, 1875–1950* (Indianapolis: National Council of Negro Women, 1981).

55. *Annual Report of the Flanner Guild* (1910). A settlement report mentioned that the board tried first to secure a male director from Hampton or Tuskegee. We do not know what became of this attempt.

56. "The Good Work of the Flanner Guild," p. 1; *Annual Report of the Flanner Guild* (1910).

57. *Flanner Guild Report* (1905), n.p.; Dunn, *Greater Indianapolis* 2:1162; Dunn, *Representative Citizens of Indiana*, p. 467. Also on the board of trustees

were two members of the Indianapolis school board, including Charles W. Moores, a faculty member of the Indiana Law School. Dunn, *Greater Indianapolis*, 1:278, 408, 565.

58. Flanner Guild Industrial Neighborhood House, *Second Annual Report* (1904), p. 9; Baker, "Struggle for Survival," p. 481. "Once with a bank book, they are on the road to genuine improvement," Baker commented.

59. *Annual Report of the Flanner Guild* (1910); Du Bois, *Efforts for Social Betterment*, pp. 124–25. For the Indianapolis Juvenile Court see George W. Stubbs, "The Mission of the Juvenile Courts," in *National Conference of Charities and Corrections*, Proceedings, 1904, pp. 350–57; Helen Worthington Rogers, "The Probation System of the Juvenile Court of Indianapolis," ibid., pp. 369–79.

60. Baker, "Struggle for Survival," p. 481; *Third Annual Report* (1905), p. 6.

61. Baker, "The Color Line in the North," *American Magazine* 65 (February 1908): 348. Sumner Furniss was born in Mississippi in 1874 and graduated from Indiana University Medical College in 1894. *Freeman* (Indianapolis), February 10, 1900, p. 1; Joseph J. Boris, ed., *Who's Who in Colored America 1928–29*, p. 139; Thornbrough, *Since Emancipation*, p. 72; Dunn, *Greater Indianapolis* 1: 253.

62. *Third Annual Report* (1905), p. 11.

63. Diner, "Chicago Social Workers and Blacks," p. 396.

64. For the Missionary Training School, see Dunn, *Greater Indianapolis* 1:436; *Flanner House Annual Report: Twenty-First Year, 1919*, pp. 8–9; "History of Flanner House," p. 5; *Indianapolis Study* (Indianapolis: Flanner House, 1939), p. 2; "Flanner House," vertical files, United Christian Missionary Society, Indianapolis, UCMS.

65. Nimmons, "Social Reform and Moral Uplift," p. 107. The Louisville settlement houses again provide parallels: in 1910, the Presbyterian church U.S.A. and the Reformed church agreed to take over John Little's missions for blacks in that city. Wright, *Life behind a Veil*, pp. 147–49.

66. *Missionary Tidings*, August 31, 1913, p. 139; "Flanner House," UCMS. The *Indianapolis Study* stated that blacks made some of the decisions at the agency. *Indianapolis Study*, p. 2. In contrast, in Nashville, important work was being done to train black social workers at Fisk University's Department of Social Science under the direction of Dr. George Haynes. Neverdon Morton, *Afro-American Women*, pp. 166–69.

67. "Flanner house," synopses of CWBM executive-committee minutes, vertical files, UCMS.

68. National Bureau of Municipal Research, "Survey of Social Agencies in Indianapolis," 1918, p. 229, typescript, mimeo, IUPUI.

69. Charles O. Lee, "New Aspects of the Negro in the Industrial World," *Missionary Tidings*, November 1918, pp. 239–41; "Indianapolis City Missions," *Missionary Tidings*, November 1917, p. 281.

70. Lee, "New Aspects," p. 240.

71. Ibid., pp. 241, 242.

72. Lee, "New Aspects of the Negro in the Industrial World" p. 241. For blacks in the northern economy in the early twentieth century, see Sterling D.

Spero and Abram L. Harris, *The Black Worker* (New York: Columbia University Press, 1931), p. 257; U.S. Dept. of Labor, Division of Negro Economics, *Negro Migration, 1916–1917* (Washington, D.C.: Government Printing Office, 1919); Joseph A. Hill, "Recent Northward Migration of the Negro," *Monthly Labor Review* 18 (March 1924); William H. Harris, *The Harder We Run: Black Workers since the Civil War* (New York: Oxford University Press, 1982), pp. 61–62.

73. National Bureau of Municipal Research, "Survey of Social Agencies in Indianapolis," p. 26. On the Great Migration, see Louise Venable Kennedy, *The Negro Peasant Turns Cityward* (College Park; Md.: McGrath, 1930, 1969); Florette Henri, *Black Migration: Movement North 1900–1920* (Garden City, N.Y.: Doubleday, 1975); Daniel M. Johnson and Rex R. Campbell, *Black Migration in America: A Social Demographic History* (Durham, N.C.: Duke University Press, 1981).

74. National Bureau of Municipal Research, "Survey of Social Agencies in Indianapolis," p. 136.

75. Ibid., p. 221. The conservative effects of this dependent relationship remained mostly implicit. However, much later, in 1947, an open breach between conservative board members and more activist blacks occurred when Wilson Head, a staff member of Flanner House, led a Civil Rights Committee campaign against segregated eating places in Indianapolis. When Head was fired from Flanner house it was widely believed to be through the influence of a white department-store owner who was a settlement board member. Emma Lou Thornbrough, "Breaking Racial Barriers to Accommodations in Indiana, 1935–1963," *Indiana Magazine of History* 83 (December 1987): 317–19.

76. National Bureau of Municipal Research, "Survey of Social Agencies in Indianapolis," p. 222. The move is documented in "History of Flanner House," p. 6; "Flanner House Gets New Site," unidentified clipping, October 20, 1918, IPL; *Missionary Tidings*, November 1918, p. 230. The new Flanner House complex, consisting of a double house, two cottages, and an office building, were at 802–814 North West Street. At first considered temporary, the buildings were still in use in 1939.

77. *Annual Report* (1922–23), n.p.; John Seeley et al., *Community Chest* (Community Surveys, Inc., Toronto: University of Toronto Press, 1957), pp. 90–94. For the significance of community chests, see Roy Lubove, *The Professional Altruist: The Emergence of Social Work as a Career* (Pittsburgh: University of Pittsburgh Press, 1965), pp. 182–219; Judith Ann Trolander, *Settlement Houses and the Great Depression* (Detroit: Wayne State University Press, 1975), pp. 141–43 and passim; Trolander, *Professionalism and Social Change*.

78. For the National Urban League, Strickland, *History of the Chicago Urban League*; Moore, *A Search for Equality*; Nancy J. Weiss, *The National Urban League, 1910–1940* (New York: Oxford University Press, 1974). In some cities, the YWCA played a similar role in the 1920s to Flanner House. For example, Cleveland's Phyllis Wheatley House, founded by black leader Jane Edna Hunter and controlled by an interracial board, provided services, including an employment agency, to black women new to the city. Hunter was fiercely criticized by some members of the black middle class, however. Jones, "Jane Edna Hunter."

79. _Flanner House Annual Report, Twenty-First Year_ (1919); _Flanner House, Report_ (1920–21); _Annual Report_ (1922–23); "The Flanner House, Indianapolis," _World Call_ (Indianapolis), May 1921.

80. "Flanner House Head's Report Covers New Negro Problem," August 1923, newspaper clipping, IPL; _Indianapolis Study_, pp. 10, 16.

81. For the housing situation, see Woofter, _Negro Problems_, pp. 87, 260; Albion Fellows Bacon, "The Housing Problem in Indiana," _Charities and the Commons_ 21 (December 1908): 378–79; James H. Madison, _Indiana through Tradition and Change: A History of the Hoosier State and Its People, 1920–1945_ (Indianapolis: Indiana Historical Society, 1982), pp. 45 ff.; Thornbrough, "Segregation in Indiana," pp. 596–606. For the segregation of schools, see Judy Jolley Mohraz, _The Separate Problem: Case Studies of Black Education in the North, 1900–1930_ (Westport, Conn: Greenwood Press, 1979). For the development of segregated recreation, Walter Jarvis, "Indianapolis Provides for Its Colored Citizens," _Playground_ 16 (February 1923).

82. Baker, "Color Line in the North," p. 348. Baker quoted figures given him by Dr. Furniss that among blacks deaths outnumbered births in the city for each year between 1901 and 1905. Indianapolis Board of Health, _Report of the Indianapolis Board of Health for 1911_, p. 460; John S. Haller, "Race, Mortality, and Life Insurance: Negro Vital Statistics in the Late Nineteenth Century," _Journal of the History of Medicine_ 25 (July 1970): 247–61; U.S. Dept. of Commerce, Bureau of the Census, _Negroes in the United States, 1920–1932_, p. 327. Ferguson, "The Woman's Improvement Club of Indianapolis," pp. 245–47; Thornbrough, _Since Emancipation_, p. 89. Black physician Dr. Joseph Ward treated TB patients in his private hospital. _Annual Report of the Flanner Guild_ (1910).

83. Hine, _When the Truth Is Told_, p. 39; National Bureau of Municipal Research, "Survey," p. 227; "Statement of the Herman G. Morgan Health Center," FHP. A complete account of the tuberculosis work of the WIC is in Ferguson, "The Woman's Improvement Club of Indianapolis."

84. Lee, "The Flanner House, Indianapolis," p. 13; _Annual Report, Flanner House, from October 1, 1920 to June 30, 1921_, p. 2; Ferguson, "The Woman's Improvement Club of Indianapolis," pp. 256–60.

85. Lee, "New Aspects of the Negro in the Industrial World," p. 241.

86. Ibid.

87. National Bureau of Municipal Research, "Survey of Social Agencies in Indianapolis," pp. 31, 226.

88. Charles O. Lee, "The Flanner House, Indianapolis, _World Call_ (Indianapolis), May 1921, p. 13; _Annual Report, Flanner House, From October 1, 1920 to June 30, 1921_, p. 2.

89. TB prevention work at Flanner House is described in _Flanner House Annual Report_ (1919), n.p.

90. Hine, _When the Truth Is Told_, p. 39. A Flanner House memo dated 1931 estimated that blacks, with 12 percent of the population, had 7 percent of the hospital beds. FHP.

91. U.S. Dept. of Commerce, Bureau of the Census, *Fifteenth Census of the United States, 1930: Population,* vol. 4, *Occupations by States,* p. 510. In 1900, 92 percent of black women listed by the census as working for wages in Indianapolis were in domestic work. U.S. Dept. of Commerce, Bureau of the Census, *Occupations at the Twelfth Census, 1904,* p. 576. In the U.S. as a whole, David Katzman estimated that between 1890 and 1920, "the number of white female servants declined by one third, while black female domestics increased in number by forty-three percent . . . In 1920, black women comprised forty percent of all domestic servants." Katzman, *Seven Days a Week: Women and Domestic Service in Industrializing America* (New York: Oxford University Press, 1978), p. 72. See also Joseph A. Hill, *Women in Gainful Occupations, 1870–1920,* Census Monographs 9 (Washington, D.C. Government Printing Office, 1929); Trotter, *Black Milwaukee,* pp. 46–47, 159.

92. Elizabeth Clark-Lewis, "'This Work Had an End,' African-American Domestic Workers in Washington, D.C., 1910–1940," in Carol Groneman and Mary Beth Norton, eds. *"To Toil The Livelong Day": America's Women at Work, 1780–1980* (Ithaca, N.Y.: Cornell University Press, 1987), pp. 196–212. See also Katzman, *Seven Days a Week,* pp. 35–36, 93. Whites may have been willing to accept this change to day work when the servant was of a different race.

93. Flanner House, *Report* (1920–21), n.p.; *Indianapolis Study,* p. 16. Workforce participation was much higher among black than among native-born white or immigrant women. For example, among black women describing themselves as widowed or divorced, 63 percent were in paid employment compared to 39 percent of native-born whites and 17 percent of immigrants. U.S. Dept. of Commerce, Bureau of the Census, *Fifteenth Census of the United States, 1930: Population,* vol. 4, *Occupation by States,* p. 510. See also Leslie Woodcock Tentler, *Wage-Earning Women: Industrial Work and Family Life in the United States, 1900–1030* (New York: Oxford University Press, 1979).

94. Some less-than-successful attempts to persuade white employers to use model contracts for household workers are described in Phyllis Palmer, "Housewife and Household Worker: Employer-Employee Relationships in the Home, 1928–1941," in Groneman and Norton, eds., *To Toil the Livelong Day,* pp. 179–95. See also Susan Strasser, "Mistress and Maid, Employer and Employee: Domestic Service Reform in the United States," *Marxist Perspectives* (Winter 1978), 52–67.

95. Called the "Door of Hope" program, it is described in Flanner Guild Industrial Neighborhood House, *Second Annual Report* (1904), p. 5; Du Bois, *Efforts for Social Betterment,* p. 125; "Indianapolis City Missions," *Missionary Tidings,* November 1916, p. 279; November 1918, p. 273.

96. *Flanner House Report (1920–21); Flanner House Annual Report (1919),* pp. 11–12; *Indianapolis Study,* p. 16; Lee, "The Flanner House, Indianapolis," p. 11; Flanner House Employment Department, "Circular of Information Concerning Day Workers," n.p., n.d. (1922?).

97. Charles O. Lee, "Where Washing Is a Science," *World Call* (Indianapolis), July 1924, p. 367.

98. "Flanner House Service Girls' Club Answers Demand for Efficient Maids," Indianapolis *Sunday Star*, April 21, 1929, which begins, "Everybody knows how hard it is to get a good maid, but not everybody knows about the work that the [Flanner House] Service Girls' Club is doing in order to train good maids for the community."

99. Jacqueline Jones, *Labor of Love, Labor of Sorrow: Black Women, Work, and the Family from Slavery to the Present* (New York: Basic Books, 1984), pp. 184–85. For an overview of changes in household technology see Ruth Schwarz Cowan, *More Work for Mother: The Ironies of Household Technology, From the Open Hearth to the Microwave* (New York: Basic Books, 1983); Susan Strasser, *Never Done: A History of American Housework* (New York: Pantheon Books, 1982); Susan J. Kleinburg, "Technology and Woman's Work: The Lives of Working Women in Pittsburgh, 1870–1900," *Labor History* 17 (Winter 1976): 58–72; Strasser, "Mistress and Maid."

100. Lee, "Where Washing Is a Science"; "Flanner House Trains for Service"; Lee, "Flanner House, Indianapolis."

101. Lee, "Where Washing Is a Science," p.36.

102. "Flanner House Trains for Service"; "Flanner House Service Girls' Club Answers Demand for Efficient Maids."

103. "Flanner House Trains for Service." For the idea of household service as vocation, I am indebted to Phyllis Palmer, "Housework and Domestic Labor: Racial and Technological Change," in Karen Brodkin Sacks and Dorothy Remy, eds., *My Troubles Are Going to Have Trouble with Me: Everyday Trials and Triumphs of Women Workers* (New Brunswick, N.J.: Rutgers University Press, 1984), p. 81. See also Evelyn Brooks Barnett, "Nannie Burroughs and the Education of Black Women," in *The Afro-American Woman: Struggles and Images*, ed. Sharon Harley and Rosalyn Terborg-Penn (Port Washington, N.Y.: Kennikat Press, 1978), pp. 99–105. Nannie Burroughs made domestic work part of racial uplift at her National Training School for black women and girls in Washington, D.C. Its motto was "Bible, Bath, and Broom." Barnett, "Nannie Burroughs," p. 99. See also Jones, "Jane Edna Hunter." Middle-class black women joined white reformers in urging poor black women not to look down on domestic work, but to seize it as an opportunity for self-help and advancement. Both the white-run Presbyterian missions and the black settlement of black minister Reverend Harris in Louisville had similar employment departments; Harris even provided dormitory rooms at the settlement for the domestic workers. Wright described Little as "paternalistic, at worst, a racist," and implied that these settlements offered blacks little of value. However, he noted that the black-run settlement of Rev. E. G. Harris was no better: it, too, only trained blacks to be better servants. Wright, *Life behind A Veil*, pp. 149, 151.

104. "Flanner House, Indianapolis," p.11.

105. Palmer, "Housework and Domestic Labor," p. 84.

106. *Flanner House Annual Report* (1922–23), n.p.

107. Davis, "Introduction" to the 1984 edition, *Spearheads for Reform*, "The settlement workers tried to promote both social justice and social control, and they saw no contradiction between the two," pp. xxi–xxii.

Part 2: Gary

1. Address of the president, Twelfth Annual General Meeting of the Iron and Steel Institute, American Iron and Steel Institute, *Bulletin*, 5 (May–June): 79.

2. Charles R. Walker, *Steel: The Diary of a Furnace Worker* (Boston: Atlantic Monthly Press, 1922: repr. ed., New York: Arno Press, 1977), p. 28; Charles P. Neill, *Report on Conditions of Employment in the Iron and Steel Industry*, 62 Congress, 1 Session, Senate Document no. 110 (Washington, 1913), 3:112–16, 121; John Fitch, *The Steel Workers*, vol. 3 of *The Pittsburgh Survey* (New York: Charities Publication Committee, 1911); John A. Garraty, "The United States Steel Corporation Versus Labor: The Early Years," *Labor History* 1 (Winter 1960): 23; David Brody, *Steelworkers in America: The Nonunion Era* (New York: Harper and Row, Harper Torchbooks, 1969), pp. 96–111. On return migration, see Thomas J. Archdeacon, *Becoming American: An Ethnic History* (New York: Free Press, 1983), p. 139.

3. In 1910, the foreign-born numbered 8,242 out of a population of 16,802. U.S. Department of Commerce, Bureau of the Census, *Thirteenth Census of the United States, 1910: Abstract*, p. 618. Edna Hatfield Edmondson, *Juvenile Delinquency and Adult Crime in Gary, Indiana, with Special Reference to the Immigrant Population*, Indiana University Studies, vol. 8 (Bloomington: Indiana University Press, June 1921), p. 17. Edmondson was a juvenile-court officer in Gary for two years.

4. Graham Romeyn Taylor, *Satellite Cities: A Study of Industrial Suburbs* (New York: Appleton, 1915); Taylor, "Creating the Newest Steel City," *Survey* 22 (April 3, 1909): 20–36; Powell A. Moore, *The Calumet Region* (Indianapolis: Indiana Historical Bureau, 1959), pp. 258–59; Arthur Shumway, "Gary, Shrine of the Steel God," *American Parade* 3 (1929): 2; Isaac J. Quillen, "Industrial City: A History of Gary, Indiana" (Ph.D. dissertation, Yale University, 1942), p. 52; Raymond A. Mohl and Neil Betten, *Steel City: Urban and Ethnic Patterns in Gary, Indiana, 1906–1950* (New York: Holmes and Meier, 1985), pp. 10–25.

5. U.S. Department of Commerce, Bureau of the Census, *Fourteenth Census of the United States, 1920*: vol. 2, *Population*, pp. 63, 760–61; *Fifteenth Census, 1930*: vol. 3, pt. 1, *Population*, p. 715; U.S. Department of Commerce, Bureau of the Census, *Fourteenth Census of the United States, 1920*: vol. 4, *Population, Occupations*, pp. 265–69.

6. Eugene J. Buffington, "Making Cities for Workmen," *Harper's Weekly* 53 (May 8, 1909); Quillen, "Industrial City," pp. 116 ff; Edward Greer, "Monopoly and Competitive Capital in the Making of Gary, Indiana," *Science and Society* 40 (Winter 1976–77): 465–78; Stanley Buder, *Pullman* (New York: Oxford University Press, 1967).

7. Raymond A. Mohl and Neil Betten, "The Failure of Industrial City Planning: Gary, Indiana, 1906–1910," *Journal of the American Institute of Planners* 38 (July 1972): 203–15. Greer described Gary as a manufacturing city "typical of American monopoly capital, in which some of the contours of urban life have been set by the priorities of the U.S. Steel Corporation, while others have been

determined by free enterprise market forces," "Monopoly and Competitive Capital," p. 465; Edmondson, *Juvenile Delinquency and Adult Crime*, p. 17; Taylor, *Satellite Cities*, pp. 169–89.

8. Mohl and Betten, "Failure of Industrial City Planning," pp. 203–6; Edmondson, *Juvenile Delinquency and Adult Crime*, pp. 17–18; Quillen, "Industrial City," pp. 126 ff; U.S. Department of Labor, Children's Bureau, *Children of Preschool Age in Gary, Indiana*, by Elizabeth Hughes, bureau report no. 122, pp. 16–19; James B. Lane, *City of the Century: A History of Gary, Indiana* (Bloomington: Indiana University Press, 1978), pp. 34–37.

9. Edmondson, *Juvenile Delinquency and Adult Crime*, p. 16

10. Hughes, *Children of Preschool Age*, pp. 1–2, 103; 151; Katherine Stone, "The Origins of Job Structures in the Steel Industry," in Richard Edwards, Michael Reich, David Gordon, eds., *Labor Market Segmentation* (Lexington, Mass.: D.C. Heath, 1975). The families of 3,991 preschool children were studied. See also Peter R. Shergold, *Working-Class Life: The American Standard in Comparative Perspective* (Pittsburgh: University of Pittsburgh Press, 1982).

11. Interchurch World Movement, *Report on the Steel Strike of 1919* (New York: Harcourt, Brace and Howe, 1922), p. 25; Brody, *Steelworkers in America*, pp. 148–49; David Brody, *Labor in Crisis: The Great Steel Strike of 1919* (New York: Lippincott, 1965), pp. 19–27; Gerald G. Eggert, *Steelmasters and Labor Reform, 1886–1923* (Pittsburgh: University of Pittsburgh Press, 1981), pp. 33–41, 67–69.

12. Elbert Gary, Address, May 29, 1911, *Addresses and Statements of Elbert H. Gary* (compiled by the Business History Society, November 1927); *Interchurch Report*, p. 25; Charles Adams Gulick, Jr., *Labor Policy of the United States Steel Corporation*, vol. 116, Columbia Studies in History, Economics and Public Law (New York: Columbia University Press, 1924); Ida Tarbell, *The Life of Elbert H. Gary* (New York: D. Appleton, 1925), pp. 163–77. The evolution of this policy can also be followed in the iron-and-steel trade journal, the *Iron Age*. See, for example, "The Betterment of Labor Conditions in the Steel Industry," *Iron Age*, 86 (November 1910): 1030; Brody, *Steelworkers in America*, pp. 87–93, 148–49; Eggert, *Steelmasters and Labor Reform*, p. 46.

13. Gulick, *Labor Policy*, pp. 138–55. For activities of welfare workers in southern mill towns, see American Iron and Steel Institute, *Bulletin* 5, 1 and 2 (January–February 1917, March–April 1917); Marlene Hunt Rikard, "An Experiment in Welfare Capitalism: The Health Care Services of the Tennessee Coal, Iron, and Railroad Company" (Ph.D. dissertation, University of Alabama, 1983).

14. Quillen, "Industrial City," pp. 178–79; Brody, *Steelworkers in America*, pp. 118–19; Shumway, "Shrine of the Steel God," p. 27; Moore, *Calumet Region*, p. 328.

15. Lane, *City of the Century*, p. 47; Quillen, "Industrial City," p. 269; Moore, *Calumet Region*, pp. 273–74, 288–89.

16. Quillen, "Industrial City," pp. 458–61.

17. *Interchurch Report*, pp. 155, 243; "To Boycott Clergy in Gary. Strikers Contend They Are Aiding Forces to Weaken Tie-Up," *New York Times*, Octo-

ber 1, 1919. The *Interchurch Report*, which focused on the Pittsburgh region, found some clergy on both sides of the strike issue. For an analysis of forces arrayed against the strike in Gary, see Mohl and Betten, *Steel City*, pp. 33–43. Dennis C. Dickerson, "The Black Church in Industrializing Western Pennsylvania, 1870–1950," *Western Pennsylvania Historical Magazine*, 64 (October 1981), 329–44, describes a situation in that region also where black ministers were dependent on the companies for philanthropy and for employment.

18. David Montgomery, *The Fall of the House of Labor: The Workplace, the State and American Labor Activism* (New York: Cambridge University Press, 1987, paperback ed., 1989), p. 244.

19. *Report of the Old Settlers Association for 1911*, quoted in Quillen, "Industrial City," p. 152.

20. Gary *Daily Tribune*, May 9, 1910, p. 1.

21. United States Steel Corporation, *Fifteenth Annual Report for the Fiscal Year Ending December 21, 1916*, p. 25; U.S. Department of Commerce, Bureau of the Census, *Fourteenth Census of the United States, 1920:* vol. 2, *Population*, p. 120.

22. Mrs. Frank J. Sheehan, comp., "Gary in the World War," 2 vols. "Civilian History" (1923), 2:35. Typescript, GPL.

23. Sheehan, "Gary in the World War," 2:122, 261; Robert K. Murray, *Red Scare: A Study in National Hysteria, 1919–1920* (Minneapolis: University of Minnesota Press, 1955); David Kennedy, *Over Here: The First World War and American Society* (New York: Oxford University Press, 1980); William Preston, Jr., *Aliens and Dissenters: Federal Suppression of Radicals, 1903–1933* (New York: Harper and Row, Harper Torchbook, 1966), pp. 11–34.

24. David Farner, "Indiana, the Press, and the Red Scare of 1919–1920" (M.A. thesis, Purdue University, 1979), p. 25; Stanley Coben, "A Study in Nativism: The American Red Scare of 1919–1920," *Political Science Quarterly* 79 (March 1964): 52; Mrs. J. H. Eppler, "War Mothers," in Sheehan, "Gary in the World War," 2:128.

25. Mrs. I. Miltimore, "Calumet Township Council of Defense," in Sheehan, "Gary in the World War," 2:5–8.

26. Illinois Steel Company, *Gary Works Circle*, 3 (September–October 1918): 14; *Gary Works Circle*, 3 (November–December 1918): 21.

27. "United War Work, or 'Seven in One Drive'," in Sheehan, "Gary in the World War," 2:122; G. M. McGinnis, "Gary Tin Mill," in ibid. 2:227.

28. In August 1919, 69,284 employees of U.S. Steel Corporation were working a twelve-hour day. However, the Interchurch Commission exaggerated when it claimed that over half the U.S. Steel work force was doing so. For a detailed if inconclusive discussion of wages see Gulick, *Labor Policy*, pp. 56–92.

20. Ibid., p. 86.

30. Brody, *Labor in Crisis*, p. 74.

31. Ibid. See also Raymond A. Mohl, "The Great Steel Strike of 1919 in Gary, Indiana: Working-Class Radicalism or Trade Union Militancy?" *Mid-America* 63 (January 1981): 36–52. Mohl disproves the employers' claims that "radicals" instigated the strike.

32. David Brody, *Labor in Crisis: The Steel Strike of 1919* with a new Bibliographical Afterword (Urbana: University of Illinois Press, Illini Book, 1987); Mohl and Betten, *Steel City*, pp. 26–47.

33. *Gary Works Circle* 4 (February 1919):1.

34. Quoted in Montgomery, *Fall of the House of Labor*, p. 244.

35. For wages in steelmaking, Paul H. Douglas, *Real Wages in the United States, 1890–1926* (Boston: Houghton Mifflin, 1930), p. 272. For the ending of the twelve-hour day, Brody, *Steelworkers in America*, pp. 273–74; *Labor in Crisis*, p. 178.

36. Shumway, "Shrine of the Steel God," p. 23.

37. A paid announcement by the Loyal American League in the Gary *Daily Tribune*, September 15, 1919, announced, "The parasite with nothing to lose except the other fellow's belongings and with everything to gain is here— whether you call him Bolsheviki, I.W.W., Agitator, or Enemy." Quoted in Quillen, "Industrial City," p. 349.

38. Quoted in Brody, *Labor in Crisis*, p. 78.

39. John Foster Potts, "Growth of the Negro Population of Gary, Indiana" (M.A. thesis, Cornell University, 1937), p. 7; U.S. Department of Commerce, Bureau of the Census, *Fifteenth Census of the U.S., 1930:* vol. 2, *Population*, p. 202.

40. "H. S. Norton Predicts Year of Prosperity Ahead in Steel City. Shows Benefit Land Company Has Been to Gary," Gary *Post Tribune*, May 8, 1923, p. 1; Moore, *Calumet Region*, pp. 325–26.

41. Gary, Indiana Chamber of Commerce, "Report of the Commercial Club Committee of the Chamber of Commerce," November 1926. GPL.

Chapter 4: Campbell Friendship House

1. Caroline Williamson Montgomery, Introduction to Montgomery, comp., *Bibliography of College, Social, University and Church Settlements* (New York: College Settlements Association, 1900).

2. Jane Addams, *Twenty Years at Hull House* (New York: Macmillan, 1910; Signet, 1960), pp. 307–8; "The Objective Value of a Social Settlement," in Addams et al., *Philanthropy and Social Progress* (New York: Thomas Y. Crowell, 1893), pp. 27–56. Settlement leaders in this discussion are loosely defined as those active in the National Federation of Settlements, those who wrote about the settlement movement, or those who were thought by contemporaries to speak for the movement. The intellectual background is brilliantly discussed in James T. Kloppenberg, *Uncertain Victory: Social Democracy and Progressivism in European and American Thought, 1870–1920* (New York: Oxford University Press, 1986), pp. 113–14 and passim.

3. Mary E. Richmond, *Friendly Visiting among the Poor: A Handbook for Charity Visitors* (Montclair, N.J.: Paterson Smith, 1899, 1969), p. 173. For the professionalization of social work, see Roy Lubove, *The Professional Altruist: The Emergence of Social Work as a Career* (Pittsburgh: University of Pittsburgh Press,

1965); Robert A. Bremner, *From the Depths: The Discovery of Poverty in the United States* (New York: New York University Press, 1956), pp. 131–39; and Judith A. Trolander, *Professionalism and Social Change: From the Settlement House Movement to Neighborhood Centers, 1886 to the Present* (New York: Columbia University Press, 1987); Paul Boyer, *Urban Masses and Moral Order in America, 1820–1920* (Cambridge: Harvard University Press, 1978), pp. 148–49, 156–57.

4. Aaron I. Abell, *The Urban Impact on American Protestantism, 1865–1900* (Cambridge: Harvard University Press, 1943), p. 246. See also Robert D. Cross, ed., *The Church and the City* (Indianapolis: Bobbs-Merrill, 1967), and *The Emergence of Liberal Catholicism in America* (Cambridge: Harvard University Press, 1958); Henry F. May, *Protestant Churches and Industrial America* (New York: Harper, 1949); Charles Howard Hopkins, *The Rise of the Social Gospel in American Protestantism, 1865–1915* (New Haven: Yale University Press, 1940). Historians disagree about whether the churches were actually losing ground in this period. The estimated membership of the Protestant churches rose from 4.5 million in 1860 to 12.5 million in 1890. But some historians remain unimpressed. The rise in membership, Paul Boyer writes, "only threw into sharper relief the church's failure in the crucial urban area." Boyer, *Urban Masses and Moral Order*, p. 132.

5. *North End Mission Magazine* (January 1, 1872), quoted in Abell, *Urban Impact*, p. 36. For missions, see Bremner, *From the Depths*, pp. 32–35; Boyer, *Urban Masses and Moral Order*, pp. 134–35; Norris A. Magnuson, "Salvation in the Slums: Evangelical Social Welfare Work, 1865–1920" (Ph.D. dissertation, University of Minnesota, 1968). Mina Carson, *Settlement Folk: Social Thought and the American Settlement Movement, 1885–1930* (Chicago: University of Chicago Press, 1990), has an excellent discussion of the settlements' origins in Liberal Christianity.

6. Historian Allen F. Davis compiled a list of 389 "relatively prominent settlement workers." For 274 of these he obtained biographical information. Of 174 whose religious affiliation could be determined, 53 were Congregationalist; 42 Presbyterian; 31 Episcopalian; 22 Jewish; 13 Unitarian; 9 Methodist; and 4 Baptist. *Spearheads for Reform: The Social Settlements and the Progressive Movement, 1890–1914* (New York: Oxford University Press, 1967), p. 265, n. 4. See also Allen F. Davis, "Spearheads for Reform: The Social Settlements and the Progressive Movement, 1890–1914" (Ph.D. dissertation, University of Wisconsin, 1959), pp. 66–75. A survey conducted by the American Institute of Social Service in 1905 found that three-fourths of social workers were church members. See W. D. P. Bliss, "The Church and Social Method," *Outlook* (January 20, 1906), 122–25. This survey revealed that 88 percent of settlement workers were communicants of a church, as compared with 92 percent of charity workers and 71 percent of those who were classified as "other reform organization workers." Ibid., p. 122. See also Bremner, *From the Depths*, p. 65.

7. Alice Hamilton, *Exploring the Dangerous Trades* (Boston: Little, Brown, 1943), p. 61; Rev. J. D. Davis, "Foreign Missions at Home," *Charities and the Commons* 1 (July 4, 1896), 3–5; Mina Carson, "Agnes Hamilton of Fort

Wayne: The Education of a Christian Settlement Worker," *Indiana Magazine of History* 80 (March 1984), 1–34.

8. Robert A. Woods and Albert J. Kennedy, *The Settlement Horizon: A National Estimate* (New York: Russell Sage Foundation, 1922), p. 326; Robert A. Woods, "The University Settlement Idea," in Addams, *Philanthropy and Social Progress,* pp. 80–81, and "Neutrality in Religion," in Stanton Coit, ed., *Neighborhood Guilds: An Instrument of Social Reform* (New York: 1891, Arno Press, 1974), pp. 36–39; Davis, *Spearheads for Reform,* p. 15.

9. Julia Lathrop, "Hull House as a Sociological Laboratory," NCCC, *Proceedings of the Twenty-First Meeting of the NCCC* (Nashville, Tenn., 1894), p. 319.

10. John Gavit, "Missions and Settlements," *Commons* 2 (February 1898), 1. Italics in the original.

11. "Report of the Social Settlement Committee," NCCC, *Proceedings of the Twenty-Third Annual Meeting of the NCCC* (Grand Rapids, Mich., 1896), pp. 167, 172–73.

12. Dean George Hodges, "Religion in the Settlement," NCCC, *Proceedings of the Twenty-Third Annual Meeting of the NCCC* (Grand Rapids, Mich, 1896), pp. 150–53.

13. Walter Rauschenbusch, *Christianizing the Social Order* (New York: Macmillan, 1912), p. 116; Mary K. Simkhovitch, *The Settlement Primer* (Boston: National Federation of Settlements, 1926), p. 56. Jane Addams had started from a position close to Christian Socialism. She "thought of Hull House as a religious institution," wrote Allen F. Davis, *American Heroine: The Life and Legend of Jane Addams* (New York: Oxford University Press, 1976), pp. 73–74.

14. "As a seedbed of values and a generator of reform zeal, Protestantism would remain a potent force in the urban moral control movement. As a formal institutional factor, its day had passed." Boyer, *Urban Masses and Moral Order,* pp. ix, 142; Timothy L. Smith, Introduction to Lyman Abbott, *Christianity and Social Problems* (New York: Johnson Reprint Corporation, 1970); David Reimers, "Protestantism's Response to Social Change, 1890–1930," in Frederick Cople Jaher, ed., *The Age of Industrialism in America* (New York: Free Press, 1968), pp. 364–83; William S. Rainsford, "What Can We Do for the Poor?" *Forum* 11 (April 1891).

15. Addams, *Twenty Years at Hull House,* pp. 307–8. Generalizations about the evolution of the settlement movement are based on a reading of NCCC Conference Proceedings, *Charities and the Commons,* and *Commons,* which followed it. See also Frank J. Bruno, *Trends in Social Work as Reflected in the Proceedings of the National Conference of Social Work, 1874–1946* (New York: Columbia University Press, 1948).

16. Robert A. Woods and Albert J. Kennedy, *Handbook of Settlements* (New York: Russell Sage Foundation, 1911), p. v. Their own evidence showed that the typical settlement was far from their ideal of neutrality. See also the interview with Albert J. Kennedy quoted in Allen F. Davis, "Spearheads for Reform" (1959), pp. 72–73.

17. John Herrick, "A Holy Discontent: The History of the New York City Social Settlements, 1919–1941" (Ph.D. dissertation, University of Minnesota, 1970), p. 6.

18. Simkhovitch, *Settlement Primer,* p. 56.

19. Anna Stover, "A Reminiscent History of Christamore, the College Settlement," typescript, 1911, in the possession of the author; Anna Stover and Edith Surbey, "Remembrances," typescript, n.d., pp. 13–14. See Chapter 1.

20. Allen F. Davis, in his study of the connection between the settlements and progressive reform, tended to rule the small conservative and religious settlements out of the movement. Noting "the nonsectarian nature of the most important American settlements," he mentioned that there were also religious settlements, for example hundreds, even thousands of Catholic settlements. Yet "these were more like missions than settlement houses and contributed little to reform." Davis, *Spearheads for Reform,* pp. 14–15.

21. Since Campbell House was a Methodist settlement, this chapter emphasizes the role of Methodism in Gary. Other Protestant denominations were of course active in the Americanization drive as well. Sometimes friction among the denominations was avoided by tacit or open division of the territory for evangelism. "Methodism probably does not need to feel a sense of responsibility for Tolleston [an area west of Gary annexed in 1910]," wrote Reverend Seaman in 1920, "The Christian denomination has made a beginning there and the Presbyterians have a work pretty well established." First Methodist Episcopal Church, Gary, Indiana, "Types of Ministry," Box Mc 60, DePauw.

22. The settlement was variously called "Campbell House," "Friendship House," or "Campbell Friendship House." WPA Writers' Project, *Calumet Region Historical Guide* (Gary, Ind.: Gary Board of Education, 1939), p. 54; Jack Detzler, *History of the Northwest Indiana Conference of the Methodist Church* (Nashville, Tenn.: Parthenon Press, 1953), p. 124.

23. Mrs. C. Claude Travis, *Campbell Settlement, Gary, Indiana* (Cincinnati, Ohio: WHMS, 1929?), GPL.

24. Mrs. Bess Sheehan, Mrs. Clinton G. Clark, and Mrs. George Hulbert, *History of Campbell Friendship House, Gary, Indiana, 1912–1940,* pp. 5–6.

25. First Methodist Church, Gary, Ind., "Official Board Minutes," handwritten, Box Mc 115, October 25, 1911, p. 2, DePauw. However, the company had just donated over $200,000 to the YMCA. Powell A. Moore, *The Calumet Region* (Indianapolis: Indiana Historical Bureau, 1959), p. 332.

26. Sheehan et al., *History of Campbell Friendship House,* p. 2.

27. Lawrence B. Davis, *Immigrants, Baptists and the Protestant Mind in America* (Urbana: University of Illinois Press, 1973), p. 45, 193.

28. Joseph B. Clark, D.D., *Leavening the Nation: The Story of American Home Missions* (New York: Baker and Taylor, 1903), p. 277.

29. Sheehan, *History of Campbell Friendship House,* p. 7. First Methodist Episcopal Church, Gary, Ind., "Official Board Minutes," October 16, 1913, handwritten, Mc 115, DePauw. For women as founders of cultural and reform societies, see Mary P. Ryan, *Cradle of the Middle Class: The Family in Oneida County, New York, 1790–1865* (New York: Cambridge University Press, 1981),

pp. 186–229; Gerda Lerner, *The Female Experience: An American Documentary* (Indianapolis: Bobbs-Merrill, 1977), p. 190.

30. Sheehan, *History of Campbell Friendship House.* Bess Sheehan came to Gary in 1908 as a teacher and became active in civic work. A graduate of the University of Michigan in history, she edited and collected the accounts that made up the two-volume collection, "Gary in the World War." She was also a leader in the movement to establish the Dunes Park. See Moore, *Calumet Region*, p. 598 n.

31. Sheehan, *History of Campbell Friendship House*, p. 4.

32. Ibid., pp. 8–10, 15–16.

33. Ibid., p. 20.

34. Quoted in Robert T. Handy, *A Christian America: Protestant Hopes and Historical Realities* (New York: Oxford University Press, 1971), pp. 170–71.

35. General Conference of the Methodist Church, *Journal* (1896), quoted in Abell, *Urban Impact*, p. 167. The language of industrialism and engineering was not at all uncommon among church writers at this time. An undated survey, "The Calumet Region," refers to the efforts of Gary's churches as "religious engineering." "Letters Pertaining to the Building of City Methodist Church," CRA. Similarly, an account of Christamore, Indianapolis, in the 1920s refers to it as a "plant turning out little Americans." See Chapter 1.

36. "City Methodist Church (First Methodist Church), Gary, Indiana, 1906–1956."

37. Detzler, *Northwest Conference*, p. 124.

38. Beatrice Lewis, "City Methodist Church," "Gary," in Church History File, DePauw. See also James B. Lane, *City of the Century: A History of Gary, Indiana* (Bloomington: Indiana University Press, 1978), pp. 112–17; Quillen, "Industrial City," p. 451.

39. Rev. W. G. Seaman to Dr. D. D. Forsythe, December 1916, Box Dc 58, "Building Fund 1920," DePauw.

40. Ibid.

41. William Grant Seaman, "The Calumet Region" (1921), MS History of the Calumet Region, CRA.

42. "Building Fund 1920," Box Dc 58, DePauw. In 1910, there were an estimated 369 males to every 100 females in the foreign-born population; by 1920, the ratio had improved to 188 males to 100 females. U.S. Department of Commerce, Bureau of the Census, *Fourteenth Census of the United States: 1920*, vol. 2, *Population*, p. 120; vol. 3, *Population*, p. 307; Edna Hatfield Edmondson, *Juvenile Delinquency and Adult Crime*, vol. 8, Indiana University Studies (Bloomington: June 1921), "proved" a correlation between delinquency and absence of church affiliation, p. 60. Historians have tended to focus on the migration of entire families since they are interested in how families aided immigrant adaptation to America, but the immigrant stream contained more individuals than families at some stages. A large proportion of individual immigrants returned to their homelands. Archdeacon found a strong correlation between the predominance of males in an immigrant group and its remigration rate. Thomas Archdeacon, *Becoming American: An Ethnic History* (New York:

Free Press, 1983), p. 139; John Bodnar, *The Transplanted: A History of Immigrants in Urban America* (Bloomington: Indiana University Press, 1985), pp. 53–54; John Bodnar, Roger Simon, and Michael P. Weber, *Lives of Their Own: Blacks, Italians, and Poles in Pittsburgh, 1900–1960* (Urbana: University of Illinois Press, 1982).

43. Timothy L. Smith, "Religion and Ethnicity in America," *American Historical Review* 83 (December 1978), 1175; Oscar Handlin, *The Uprooted* (Boston: Houghton Mifflin, 1951); Rudolph J. Vecoli, "'Contadini' in Chicago: A Critique of *The Uprooted*," *Journal of American History* 51 (December 1964), 404–17. Leonard Dinnerstein and David M. Reimers, *Ethnic Americans: A History of Immigration and Assimilation* (New York: Dodd Mead, 1975); Leonard Dinnerstein, David M. Reimers, and Roger L. Nichols, *Natives and Strangers: Ethnic Groups and the Building of America* (New York: Oxford University Press, 1979); Thomas Kessner, *The Golden Door: Italian and Jewish Immigrant Mobility in New York City, 1880–1915* (New York: Oxford University Press, 1977). The vast secondary literature on immigration can be sampled in the 350-plus-item bibliography attached to Bodnar's *The Transplanted*, pp. 267–85.

44. "First Episcopal Methodist Church. Types of Ministry," n.p.

45. Ibid. See also Charles Loring Brace, *The Dangerous Classes of New York and Twenty Years' Work among Them* (New York: Wynkoop and Hallenbeck, 1872), pp. 34–35.

46. Smith, "Religion and Ethnicity"; Milton Gordon, *Assimilation in American Life* (New York: Oxford University Press, 1964).

47. Northwest Conference of the Methodist Episcopal Church, *Minutes* (1917), pp. 165–66.

48. Northwest Conference of the Methodist Episcopal Church, *Minutes* (1919), p. 471. For the expansion of the U.S. Steel work force during World War I, see United States Steel Corporation, *Thirteenth Annual Report of the U.S. Steel Corporation*, p. 23; *Fourteenth Annual Report of the U.S. Steel Corporation*, p. 23; *Fifteenth Annual Report of the U.S. Steel Corporation*, p. 25.

49. The findings of this study were summarized as follows: "Gary—Population, 50,000. 7,000 Croatians, 4,600 Poles,

     3,500 Bohemians, 3,000 Slavonians, 2,000 Swedes
     2,000 Roumanians, 1,000 Ruthenians, 500 Greeks
     5,000 Colored, scores of small groups.

U.S. Steel Corporation—investment, $75,000,000. They employ 18,000 men." American Baptist Home Mission Society, "The Foreign Problem in Northwest Indiana" (1918), Pamphlet, GPL.

50. H. R. DeBra, Calumet Missionary Society, Report in Northwest Conference, *Minutes* (1919), p. 456, *Minutes* (1944), p. 101.

51. Northwest Conference, *Minutes* (1919), p. 456.

52. "The Calumet Region, Our Greatest Missionary Field," in Ibid. (1917), p. 165; H. R. DeBra, "Report of the Calumet Missionary Society to the Northwest Indiana Conference, 1918," in Ibid. (1918), pp. 321–22.

53. Except among blacks and Slovaks, Margaret Byington wrote in her study of Homestead, Pa., "The contributions for church were pitifully small, rarely

more than a few cents for Sunday School." *Homestead: The Households of a Mill Town* (Pittsburgh: 1910, University Center for International Studies, University of Pittsburgh, 1974), p. 89; Rudolph J. Vecoli, "Prelates and Peasants: Italian Immigrants and the Catholic Church," *Journal of Social History* 2 (Spring 1969), p. 237; Neil Betten and Raymond A. Mohl, "From Discrimination to Repatriation: Mexican Life in Gary, Indiana," *Pacific Historical Review* 42 (August 1973), 370–88; Paul S. Taylor, *Mexican Labor in the United States, Chicago and the Calumet Region* (Berkeley: University of California Press, 1932), p. 210. Yet some immigrant groups built huge, expensive churches and community buildings: one congregation of Poles in Pittsburgh in the 1890s built a $100,000 church, a $41,000 school building, and a $70,000 parish house. Bodnar, *Lives of Their Own*, p. 76.

54. Sheehan, *History of Campbell Friendship House*, p. 12.

55. "Report of the Women's Home Missionary Society," Northwest Indiana Conference, *Minutes* (1918), p. 337; "Report of the Calumet Missionary Society," in Ibid. (1921), p. 181.

56. David Farner, "Indiana, the Press and the Red Scare of 1920" (M.A. thesis, Purdue University, 1979); David Kennedy, *Over Here: The First World War and American Society* (New York: Oxford University Press, 1980), pp. 45–92: Robert K. Murray, *Red Scare: A Study in National Hysteria, 1919–1920* (Minneapolis: University of Minnesota Press, 1955); John Higham, *Strangers in the Land: Patterns of American Nativism, 1860–1925* (New York: Atheneum, 1965); David Brody, *Labor in Crisis: the Great Steel Strike of 1919* (Philadelphia: J. Lippincott, 1965).

57. Reverend DeBra was the author. *Calumet Federation Messenger,* October 1, 1919, GPL.

58. "Report of the Calumet Missionary Society," Northwest Indiana Conference, *Minutes* (1919), p. 457. Woods and Kennedy warned that excessive sympathy of settlement workers for their immigrant clients could result in the settlement workers becoming too cosmopolitan in outlook. The influence should not be allowed to flow the "wrong" way. "Nationality, even a foreign one, is vastly to be preferred to cosmopolitanism," they wrote. Woods and Kennedy, *Settlement Horizon,* p. 331. See also McBride, *Culture Clash*, p. 27. According to Taylor, however, the foreign workers at settlement houses frequently showed "the zeal of converts," being more intolerant toward Catholicism than native-born Americans. Taylor, *Mexican Labor,* p. 213.

59. Campbell Settlement, *Report*, 1922, GPL.

60. Moore, *Calumet Region*, p. 332; Quillen, "Industrial City," p. 377; Charles Adams Gulick, Jr., *Labor Policy of the United States Steel Corporation*, vol. 116, Columbia Studies in History, Economics, and Public Law (New York: Columbia University Press, 1924).

61. Gary *Evening Post*, June 16, 1922.

62. Ibid. See also Quillen, "Industrial City," p. 459; Lane, *City of the Century*, p. 39.

63. Interchurch World Movement, *Report on the Steel Strike of 1919* (New York: Harcourt, Brace, and Howe, 1920), p. 84. The seven-day week was an

affront to Sabbatarians, of course. U.S. Steel did not allow absenteeism for religious observance on Sundays or other days, and a foreman who remonstrated with William Gleason that the seven-day week prevented his attendance at church was reportedly fired on the spot. Lane, *City of the Century*, p. 41. For the campaign against Sunday labor, see Gerald G. Eggert, *Steelmasters and Labor Reform, 1886–1923* (Pittsburgh: University of Pittsburgh Press, 1981), 47–55. For the ending of the twelve-hour day, see Brody, *Steelworkers in America*, p. 274.

64. Moore, *Calumet Region*, pp. 273–74 n, 288–89; Lane, *City of the Century*, pp. 39–44; "The Program of Methodism in Gary," Box Dc 58, DePauw.

65. Ida M. Tarbell, *The Life of Elbert H. Gary* (New York: D. Appleton, 1925), pp. 30, 63; Lane, *City of the Century*, pp. 37–39. See also Donald Wilhelm, "The 'Big Business' Man as Social Worker. Part 1. Judge Gary of the Steel Trust," *Outlook*, August 22, 1914, pp. 1005–9.

66. Seaman to Norton, n.d. (1920), Box Mc 115; Norton to Seaman, July 1, 1920, Box Mc 115, DePauw.

67. Seaman to Norton, n.d. (1920), Box Mc 115, DePauw. "We should have a churchly auditorium housed in a building of distinctly ecclesiastical architecture," Seaman wrote.

68. Beatrice Lewis (Mrs. Arthur J. Lewis), "Methodism in Gary," p. 6, typescript, in "Church History" file, DePauw.

69. Seaman to Judge Gary, July 1, 1920, Box Mc 115, DePauw.

70. Seaman, "The Calumet Region," CRA.; William Z. Foster, *The Great Steel Strike and Its Lessons* (New York: Huebsch, 1920), pp. 100–101. Foster claimed that the steel company had imported 30,000 to 40,000 black workers to Gary, Cleveland, and other steel centers in 1919. Neil Betten and Raymond A. Mohl, "The Evolution of Racism in an Industrial City," *Journal of Negro History* 59 (1974): 52. John Foster Potts, "A History of the Growth of the Negro Population of Gary, Indiana" (M.A. thesis, Cornell University, 1937). Blacks formed 9.6 percent of Gary's population in 1920, 18 percent by 1930. Ninety-three percent of them had been born in other states.

71. "First Methodist Episcopal Church, Gary, Indiana. Types of Ministry."

72. R. R. DeBra, "A Personal Note," in ibid.

73. "Program of the Methodist Episcopal Church, Gary, Indiana. Proposed First Church," p. 13, Box Mc 60, DePauw.

74. Lewis, "Methodism in Gary," p. 7.

75. *Annual Report of Campbell Settlement* (1922–23), n.p. See also Campbell House, *Report* (1922), pamphlet.

76. Campbell House, *Report* (1922). This was despite the fierce opposition of the Methodist church at this time to commercial movies which, by the 1920s, were attracting a national audience of over fifty million weekly. For early opposition to the growth of the movies in one community, see Roy Rosenzweig, *Eight Hours for What We Will: Workers and Leisure in an Industrial City, 1870–1920* (New York: Cambridge University Press, 1983), pp. 208–21.

77. Travis, *Campbell Settlement*, n.p.

78. In many parts of Central Europe, quilts and bedding are aired from balconies and windows each day.

79. Moore, *Calumet Region*, p. 545; Official Board, Gary First Methodist Episcopal Church, "Minutes," handwritten (October 16, 1913), p. 22, Box Mc 115, DePauw; Joseph R. Gusfield, *Symbolic Crusade: Status Politics and the American Temperance Movement* (Urbana: University of Illinois Press, 1969).

80. "Program of the Methodist Episcopal Church, Gary, Indiana. Proposed First Church," p. 12, Box Mc 60, DePauw.

81. Gary *Post Tribune*, January 23, 1926; Quillen, "Industrial City," p. 434.

82. Taylor, *Mexican Labor*, pp. 124–25.

83. Ibid., p. 212. See also "The Story of an Immigrant Minister," in Theodore Abel, *Protestant Home Missions to Catholic Immigrants* (New York: Institute of Social and Religious Research, 1933), pp. 111–43, a heartbreaking firsthand account of a home missionary's struggles. For a different view of what the urban missionaries were doing, see Herbert J. Gans, *The Urban Villagers: Group and Class in the Life of Italian-Americans* (New York: Free Press, 1962). In the case of a Baptist-run settlement house in the North End of Boston, Gans found that the opposition of the priest did not significantly deter Catholic users, ibid., p. 147.

84. Taylor, *Mexican Labor*, p. 212.

85. Travis, *Campbell Settlement*, n.p.

86. Taylor, *Mexican Labor*, p. 211. According to Herbert Gans, this is typical of a "client-caretaker" relationship. Settlement workers, in his view, were "external caretakers" even though they lived in the neighborhood, because they were middle class and represented white, Protestant, middle-class culture. *Urban Villagers*, pp. 144–45.

87. Gerald Shaughnessy, *Has the Immigrant Kept the Faith?* (New York: Macmillan, 1925); Henry J. Browne, "Catholicism in the United States," in James Ward Smith and A. Leland, eds., *The Shaping of America: Religion*, 4 vols. Princeton N.J.: Princeton University Press, 1961), pp. 1, 63. See also Vecoli, "Prelates and Peasants," pp. 217 ff.

88. Taylor, *Mexican Labor*, p. 210; Raymond A. Mohl and Neil Betten, "The Immigrant Church in Gary, Indiana: Religious Adjustment and Cultural Defense," *Ethnicity* (1981), 5–6; Archdeacon, *Becoming American*, p. 155; Bodnar, *The Transplanted*, p. 154.

89. Vecoli, "Prelates and Peasants," p. 268.

90. Blacks and whites lived in proximity early in Gary's history. See Thyra Edwards, "The Gary Interracial Project," *Southern Workman* 54 (December 1925), 545–53; U.S. Department of Labor, Children's Bureau, *Children of Preschool Age in Gary, Indiana*, by Elizabeth Hughes, Bureau publication no. 122 (Washington, D.C.: Government Printing Office, 1922), pp. 19–23. "The clannishness of these groups and language differences were early barriers to the Negroes against establishing satisfactory community relations with their neighbors." Quoted in Mohl and Betten, "Evolution of Racism," p. 52.

91. Taylor, *Mexican Labor*, p. 234. Mohl and Betten argue that the Americanization of Gary's immigrants involved teaching them race prejudice. Raymond A. Mohl and Neil Betten, *Steel City: Urban and Ethnic Patterns in Gary, Indiana, 1906–1950* (New York: Holmes and Meier, 1986), p. 54. See also Chapter 7.

92. Campbell Settlement, Gary, Ind. (October 1931), p. 2.

93. Travis, *Campbell Settlement,* n.p. In 1940, the enrollment at the house was reported to be about 60 percent black and 40 percent white. "Enrolls 3,081 in Friendship House Service. Director Collins says Settlement Welds Racial Groups" (April 1, 1940), unidentified clipping, Settlements File, GPL. By 1944, attendance was all black, according to an Urban League report. J. Harvey Kerns, "A Study of the Social and Economic Conditions of the Negro Population of Gary, Indiana," Mimeo (Urban League, 1944), pp. 31–32, GPL.

94. Woods and Kennedy, *Settlement Horizon,* p. 364.

Chapter 5: Neighborhood House

1. Quintin Hoare and Geoffrey Nowell Smith, trans. and eds., *Selections from the Prison Notebooks of Antonio Gramsci* (New York: International Publishers, 1971), p. 304. The quotation reads in full,

[the new industrialism] wants the man as worker not to squander his nervous energies in the disorderly and stimulating pursuit of occasional sexual satisfaction. The employee who goes to work after a night of 'excess' is no good for his work. The exaltation of passion cannot be reconciled with the timed movements of productive motions connected with the most perfected automatism. pp. 304–5

2. Details about the steel corporation's welfare policies can be found in the trade journal, the *Iron Age,* in the *Bulletins* of the U.S. Steel Bureau of Safety, Sanitation, and Welfare, and in Charles Gulick, Jr., *Labor Policy of the United States Steel Corporation,* Columbia Studies in History, Economics and Public Law, vol. 116 (New York: Columbia University Press, 1924); Ida M. Tarbell, *The Life of Elbert H. Gary* (New York: D. Appleton, 1925), pp. 226 ff; Interchurch World Movement, Commission of Inquiry, *Report on the Steel Strike of 1919* (New York: Harcourt, Brace and Howe, 1920); John Garraty, "The United States Steel Corporation *versus* Labor: The Early Years," *Labor History* 1 (Winter 1960): 32; Gerald G. Eggert, *Steelmasters and Labor Reform, 1886–1923* (Pittsburgh: University of Pittsburgh Press, 1981).

3. Eugene J. Buffington, "Making Cities for Workmen," *Harper's Weekly* 53 (May 8, 1909): 15; Stanley Buder, *Pullman* (New York: Oxford University Press, 1967).

4. Graham Romeyn Taylor, *Satellite Cities* (New York: D. Appleton, 1915), pp. 182–83; Taylor, "Creating the Newest Steel City," *Survey* 22 (April 1909): 26; Edward Greer, "Monopoly and Competitive Capital in the Making of Gary, Indiana," *Science and Society* 40 (Winter 1976–77): 463–78; Raymond A. Mohl and Neil Betten, *Steel City: Urban and Ethnic Patterns in Gary, Indiana, 1906–1950* (London: Holmes and Meier, 1986), pp. 22–23, and "The Failure of Industrial City Planning: Gary, Indiana, 1906–1910," *Journal of the American Institute of Planners* 38 (July 1972): 203–215; Edna Hatfield Edmondson, *Juvenile Delinquency and Adult Crime in Gary, Indiana,* Indiana University Studies, no. 8

(Bloomington: Indiana University Press, June 1921), pp. 16–17 contains some vivid descriptions of Gary in its early years by a juvenile court officer.

5. "Civic Development at Gary," *Iron Age* (March 24, 1910): p. 673; James B. Lane, *City of the Century: A History of Gary, Indiana* (Bloomington: Indiana University Press, 1979), pp. 34–37.

6. U.S. Department of Labor, Children's Bureau, *Children of Preschool Age in Gary, Indiana,* by Elizabeth Hughes, report no. 122 (Washington, D.C.: Government Printing Office, 1922), p. 19. Gary had fewer problems of crowding than steel towns like Braddock, Pennsylvania. The houses "had at least the advantage of greater privacy" than the boardinghouses, but they were "of extremely makeshift, ramshackle construction," Elizabeth Hughes reported.

7. "Judge Gary, a devout Methodist, and Buffington, a Congregationalist, decided that only four should be permitted on Corporation property, and only two of these were built." Isaac J. Quillen, "Industrial City: A History of Gary: Indiana to 1929" (Ph.D. dissertation, Yale University, 1942), pp. 126–27.

8. "Four Months of Free Water," Gary *Daily Tribune,* May 9, 1910, p.1. In contrast, only 1.5 percent of homes in the First Subdivision were without indoor water supply. Hughes, *Children of Preschool Age,* p. 144. The families investigated in this Children's Bureau study comprised all those with children born in Gary between 1911 and 1915 and who were still living in Gary on March 1918—6,015 children in all, in 3,991 families.

9. The quote in full reads, "[Welfare work] served a more important purpose than to quiet public criticism. It added the measure of betterment needed to win the steelworker's consent to the terms of his employment. It ensured the stability of the labor system that had developed along with the industry." David Brody, *Steelworkers in America: The Nonunion Era* (New York: Harper Torchbook ed., 1969), p. 179. See also Gulick, *Labor Policy,* p. 156; Eggert, *Steelmasters and Labor Reform.*

10. Garraty, "U.S. Steel Corporation *versus* Labor," p. 32; Leifur Magnusson, *Housing by Employers in the United States,* U.S. Department of Labor, Bulletin of the Bureau of Labor Statistics, no. 263 (Washington, D.C., 1920); Daniel Nelson, *Managers and Workers: Origins of the New Factory System in the United States, 1880–1920* (Madison: University of Wisconsin Press, 1975), p. 111. See also Marlene Hunt Rikard, "The Welfare Work of the Tennessee Coal, Iron, and Railroad Company" (Ph.D. dissertation, University of Alabama, 1983). For welfare work among black steelworkers, see Dennis C. Dickerson, *Out of the Crucible: Black Steelworkers in Western Pennsylvania, 1875–1980* (Albany: N.Y.: SUNY Press, 1986), pp. 101–18.

11. U.S. Steel Corporation, Bureau of Safety, Sanitation, and Welfare, *Bulletin* no. 5 (1917), p. 56; Gulick, *Labor Policy,* pp. 170–71. H. S. Norton of the Gary Land Company denied the charge that the company had neglected the housing needs of its workers: the accusations of the Children's Bureau reports were false, he declared in 1923—the Gary Land Company had not prevented foreign-born workers from renting or buying company-owned housing. "H. S. Norton Predicts Year of Prosperity in Steel City. Shows Benefit Land Company Has Been to Gary," Gary *Post Tribune,* May 8, 1923, p. 1.

12. Nelson, *Managers and Workers*, pp. 79–100. For the problem in the iron-and-steel industry, see Magnus Alexander, "Waste in Hiring and Discharging Men," *Iron Age* 95 (October 29, 1914): 1032; David Montgomery, *The Fall of the House of Labor: The Workplace, the State, and American Labor Activism, 1865–1925* (Cambridge: Cambridge University Press, 1987 [1989]), pp. 238–39.

13. American Iron and Steel Institute, *Bulletin* 5 (July–August, 1917): 103; Brody, *Steelworkers in America*, pp. 90–91.

14. Edmondson, *Juvenile Delinquency and Adult Crime*, pp. 16–17; U.S. Department of Commerce, Bureau of the Census, *Fifteenth Census of the United States: 1930*, vol. 1, *Population,*, p. 330.

15. Described in U.S. Steel Corporation, Bureau of Safety, Sanitation, and Welfare, Bulletin, no. 7 (December 1918), pp. 5–6.

16. Gulick, *Labor Policy*, pp. 85–86; Peter R. Shergold, *Working-Class Life: The American Standard in Comparative Perspective, 1899–1913* (Pittsburgh: University of Pittsburgh Press, 1982).

17. Stephen J. Meyer, *The Five Dollar Day: Labor Management and Social Control in the Ford Motor Company, 1905–1921* (Albany, N.Y.: SUNY Press, 1981). See also Gerd Korman, *Industrialization, Immigrants, and Americanizers: The View From Milwaukee, 1866–1921* (Madison: University of Wisconsin Press, 1967). On nativism see Oscar Handlin, *Race and Nationality in American Life* (Boston: Little, Brown, Anchor Books, 1957), pp. 74–110; John Higham, *Strangers in the Land: Patterns of American Nativism, 1860–1925* (New York: Atheneum, 1966); John McClymer, "The Americanization Movement and the Education of the Foreign-Born Adults, 1915–1940," in Bernard J. Weiss, ed., *American Education and the European Immigrant, 1840–1940* (Urbana: University of Illinois Press, 1982), 96–116.

18. "The standards set by the Sociological Department to qualify for the five-dollar day pertained above all to the life-styles of the immigrants." Montgomery, *Fall of the House of Labor*, p. 236. The Welfare Department at the Wisconsin Steel Company, Chicago, reported that their industrial nurse "tries to be friend and helper, to advise and suggest where any abnormal condition prevails in the home of an employee." American Iron and Steel Institute, *Bulletin* 5 (1917). Gramsci described the attempts by American corporations to control the lives of their workers, though often unsuccessful, as "the biggest collective effort to date to create, with unprecedented speed and with a consciousness of purpose unmatched in history, a new type of worker and of man." *Prison Notebooks*, p. 302.

19. Because of the twelve-hour shifts, U.S. Steel could only offer Americanization classes every two weeks. The *Interchurch Report on the Steel Strike* concluded, "Americanization of the steel workers cannot take place while the twelve-hour day persists." *Interchurch Report on the Steel Strike*, p. 84.

20. "What Americanization Is," Illinois Steel Company, *Gary Works Circle* 3 (September-October 1918): 23.

21. Dr. Hugh Jack, "A Message to Mothers. Written Especially for the Mothers Who Have Recently Come with Their Husbands and Children from Foreign Lands, to Make Homes in America," *Gary Works Circle* 14 (August 1920): 6–7.

22. Estelle Sternberger, "Gary and the Foreigners' Opportunity," *Survey* 42 (June 18, 1918): 480–82.

23. Ronald D. Cohen and Raymond A. Mohl, *The Paradox of Progressive Education: The Gary Plan and Urban Schooling* (New York: Kennikat Press, 1979), pp. 95–97, 179. The Gary school board established night schools in 1908 to teach English to foreigners. Enrollment continued to rise during the 1920s to a peak of 16,763 in 1928–29. See also Raymond A. Mohl and Neil Betten, "Paternalism and Pluralism: Immigrants and Social Welfare in Gary, Indiana, 1906–1940," *American Studies* 15 (Spring 1974): 5–30.

24. "Kindergarten Spearheads Gary's First Social Work," pamphlet written for Gary Golden Jubilee, 1956, CRA. Descriptions of Gary in the early years are in Quillen, "Industrial City," pp. 163–68; Edmondson, *Juvenile Delinquency and Adult Crime,* pp. 7, 16–24; Taylor, "Building the Newest Steel City," pp. 30–33; Powell H. Moore, *The Calumet Region* (Indianapolis: Indiana Historical Bureau, 1959), pp. 257–303.

25. "Kindergarten Spearheads Gary's First Social Work."

26. The male-female ratio among foreign-born whites was 369 per hundred in 1910, 188 per hundred in 1920. Among all groups, it was 219 per hundred in 1910 and 135 per hundred in 1920. U.S. Department of Commerce, Bureau of the Census, *Fourteenth Census of the United States: 1920,* vol. 2, *Population,* p. 120; Edmondson, *Juvenile Delinquency and Adult Crime,* p. 19.

27. Netta Beppler to Miss Williams, Gary, Indiana, May 28, 1909, CRA; Henry David Jones, *Twenty Years of Neighborliness* (1929), pp. 2–4.

28. "Money Secured for Mission. Present One a Success," Gary *Daily Tribune,* October 31, 1911, p. 1; "South Side Mission to Begin Work. To be Gary's Hull House," Gary *Daily Tribune,* May 9, 1910, p. 1; Robert A. Woods and Albert J. Kennedy, *The Settlement Handbook* (New York: Charities Publication Committee, 1911), list it as "The Gary Settlement," set up "for the purpose of assisting the foreigners of the city to learn American ways, and to uplift them mentally, morally, and physically," p. 82.

29. "Americanizing the Foreign-Born," Gary *Daily Tribune,* February 14, 1910, p. 4; "South Side Mission to Begin Its Work," Gary *Daily Tribune,* May 9, 1910, p. 1; Editorial, "Gary Again in the Van of Progress," Gary *Daily Tribune,* November 1, 1911, p. 2. On settlement paternalism, see Mohl and Betten, "Paternalism and Pluralism".

30. Quoted in Jones, *Twenty Years of Neighborliness,* p. 4.

31. Ibid.

32. "Kindergarten Spearheads Gary's First Social Work."

33. Sternberger, "Gary and the Foreigners' Opportunity," p. 481.

34. Home Mission Committee, Synod of Indiana, *Annual Report of the Home Mission Committee, Synod of Indiana* (1912), p. 6, CRA. The report was quick to point out that these men, as immigrants and foreign-speakers themselves, were well suited for work in the home-mission field. Mr. Baligrodski, "whose fervor in the work languished at the last," spoke Polish and "other tongues and dialects." Mr. Backora spoke Hungarian.

35. Jones, *Twenty Years of Neighborliness,* p. 6.

36. "Neighborhood House Doing Its Share in the Great Melting Pot," undated newspaper clipping, 1916?, CRA.

37. "Gary Neighborhood House" [1914?], CRA. This was evidently the text for a talk, probably to a group of potential benefactors. Miss Warmington's detailed account of one day of her duties as a settlement worker has enabled me to reconstruct Neighborhood House programs in some detail. She described her work as entailing "an enormous number of visits to South Side homes," p. 25. See also Neighborhood House, "Minutes of Neighborhood House Staff" (subsequently referred to as Neighborhood House, "Minutes"), April 14, 1915, CRA.

38. "Neighborhood House Doing Its Share in the Great Melting Pot." The Minutes of the Neighborhood House staff meetings are full of the difficulties that the agency had in securing staff. To begin with, the settlement had a new director nearly every year, as follows:

1909 Miss Danford
1909–10 Miss Emma Flinn
1910 Rev. Baligrodski
1910–11 Rev. Backora
1913–14 L. V. West
1914–15 Miss Warmington and Rev. T. H. Owens
1916–22 Rev. Cummins
1922–27 Rev. Harold Martin
1927–29 Rev. Henry D. Jones

Gerda Lerner suggests that there has been a pattern of community building,

> whereby the early infrastructure is created and maintained through the voluntary association of women, who then proceed to institution building. Frequently, such institutions, once established, become "businesses," or are taken over by the community as public institutions. In either case, they are then headed by a man and led by corporate trustees, usually also men. Once institutions have reached that stage, they are noted as "existing" by historians. Thus, the community-sustaining initiative of women remains outside of history, while that of men is noticed and therefore validated. [Gerda Lerner, *The Female Experience, An American Documentary* (Indianapolis: Bobbs-Merrill, 1977), p. 190]

39. "History of the Gary Neighborhood House," ?1915, pamphlet, CRA; *Neighborhood House Visitor,* vol. 1, no. 3 (October 13, 1916), GPL.

40. Walter Albion Squires B.D., *The Gary Plan of Church Schools* (Philadelphia: Department of Religious Education, Presbyterian Board of Publication and Sabbath School Work), CRA.

41. Neighborhood House Doing Its Share in the Great Melting Pot"; "What Gary Neighborhood House Has Done in Four Years," Gary *Daily Tribune,* November 24, 1916, p. 1. Infant-mortality statistics showed a higher death rate among immigrants than among native-born. The U.S. average for 1917 was 100 deaths per 1,000 live births. In Gary, the figure averaged 133.5 among Gary's foreign-born. The high rate among some groups (such as the Poles, with

a rate of over 148 per thousand), showed the urgency of Americanization, the Children's Bureau Report author argued. Hughes, *Children of Preschool Age*, pp. 1–2, 41, 54, 57, 103; Dr. Lloyd Roberts, *Infant Mortality, Results of a Field Study in Gary, Indiana, Based on Births in One Year*, U.S. Department of Labor, Children's Bureau, Publication no. 112 (Washington, D.C.: Government Printing Office, 1923).

42. "The Gary Neighborhood House. A Statistical Statement of 1918 Accomplishments," pamphlet, CRA.

43. Gary Neighborhood House, *Eleventh Annual Report of the Superintendent*, April 1, 1920, p. 8. But Rivka Lissak, "The Pattern of Relationship between the Hull House Circle and the 'New Immigrants' on Chicago's West Side, 1890–1919" *Journal of American Ethnic History* (Spring 1983), found that those ethnic groups that were drawn to Hull House were all marginal to the immigrant community. For example, the Jews who came to Hull House were either "radicals or assimilationists," p. 30. Lissak was skeptical of the settlement's claim to be a real influence in the ethnic neighborhood. Although she found twenty-six different Italian societies (out of about two hundred) holding their meetings at Hull House by 1921, Lissak concluded that this "success was achieved only after Hull House became reconciled with its neutralized position as a center with no influence," pp. 37–38.

44. Minor incidents of friction were inevitable: when members of a Hungarian society using a room at the settlement made themselves at home by smoking and spitting on the floor, the settlement board drafted a letter of protest reminding the users of the rules. Neighborhood House, "Minutes," September 1, 1914, p. 22; October 4, 1918, p. 66, GNH.

45. "Features of the Week Day Work—A Day at Gary Neighborhood House," pamphlet; Mrs. Frank J. Sheehan, comp., "Gary in the World War," 2 vols., typescript, vol. 2, "Civilian History," GPL. For the Red Scare in Gary, see David Farner, "Indiana, the Press, and the Red Scare" (M.A. thesis, Purdue University, 1979).

46. "Statistical Statement of Attendance at Activities, April 1920 to April 1921," GPL. Adjusted for inflation, the increase is less dramatic. Neighborhood House, "Minutes," pp. 15, 71.

47. "History of the Gary Neighborhood House," ?1915, Pamphlet, CRA; *Eleventh Annual Report of the Superintendent*, April 1, 1920.

48. Neighborhood House, "Minutes," October 3, 1918, p. 60; November 23, 1920, p. 89; April 29, 1924, pp. 140–41.

49. Attendance at the Gleason Center by 1929 averaged 280 per week, mostly Mexicans. Illinois Steel Company, Gleason Center, *Report of the Gleason Center for the Year 1929*, GPL.

50. Jones, *Twenty Years of Neighborliness*, p. 6; "Changes in the Foreign Communities, Gary, Indiana," October 3, 1929; International Institute Memorandum, mimeographed, II Papers, CRA. The black population increased from 9.6 percent of Gary's population in 1920 to 17.8 percent in 1930, Mexicans from only 0.3 percent to 3.5 percent in the same years. U.S. Department of Commerce, Bureau of the Census, *Fourteenth Census of the United States, 1920:*

vol. 2, *Population,* pp. 63, 760–61; *Fifteenth Census of the United States, 1930: Population* 3 (pt. I):715, 720.

51. Neighborhood House, "Minutes," October 1, 1923. The writer blamed the migration for an alarming rise in the crime rate. "A survey of the Negro situation showed 11,000 negroes now in Gary—settling all about N.H.—At least a murder a month in the vicinity ," p. 128.

52. Rev. H. R. Martin, "The Gary Neighborhood House," 1924–25, GPL.; Neighborhood House, "Minutes," May 3, 1926.

53. Neighborhood House, "Minutes," April 29, 1924, p. 136; April 28, 1925, p. 148.

54. "Twenty Years of Neighborliness," n.p., ?1929; J. Harvey Kerns, "A Study of the Social and Economic Conditions of the Negro Population of Gary, Indiana," National Urban League, 1944, p. 39, mimeo, GPL.

55. Neighborhood House, "Minutes," November 17, 1925, p. 156. Sociologist Paul Taylor received the following answer when he inquired of a Chamber of Commerce official whether the Mexicans were "colored." "No, they are not regarded as colored: but they are regarded as an inferior class. Are the Mexicans regarded as white? Oh, no!" Paul Taylor, *Mexican Labor in the United States: Chicago and the Calumet Region,* p. 235. See also Ruth Hutchinson Crocker, "Gary Mexicans and 'Christian Americanization': A Study in Cultural Conflict," in *Forging a Community: The Latino Experience in Northwest Indiana, 1919–1975,* ed. James B. Lane and Edward J. Escobar (Chicago: Calumet Regional Studies Series, Cattails Press, 1987); Neil Betten and Raymond A. Mohl, "From Discrimination to Repatriation: Mexican Life in Gary, Indiana, During the Great Depression," *Pacific Historical Review* 42 (August 1973): 370–88; Mohl and Betten, *Steel City,* pp. 91–107; Francisco Arturo Rosales and Daniel T. Simon, "Mexican Immigrant Experience in the Urban Midwest: East Chicago, Indiana, 1919–1945," *Indiana Magazine of History* 77 (December 1981): 333–57.

56. Neighborhood House, "Minutes," November 1926, p. 175; "Mission Metodista Mexicana," May 4, 1929. I have attempted to assess the impact of the settlements' missionary efforts in Chapter 4.

57. Robert A. Woods and Albert J. Kennedy, "An Experimental Definition of the American Standard of Living," n.x., *The Settlement Horizon: A National Estate* (New York: Russell Sage Foundation, 1922), pp. 419–20.

58. U.S. Department of Commerce, Bureau of the Census, *Fourteenth Census of the U.S.: 1920,* vol. 4, *Population,* pp. 265–69; *Fifteenth Census: 1930,* vol. 4, *Occupations by States,* p. 510. A study of female employment in Gary conducted by the Civic Service Club in 1918 found only 255 women and girls employed in manufacturing. "Gary Study by the International Institute," January 8-17, 1919, p. 4. Typescript, International Institute Papers, CRA. The situation for women's employment was similar to that in Pittsburgh, where researcher Margaret Byington found that the majority of wives of steelworkers were not employed for wages. Margaret Byington, *Homestead, the Households of a Mill Town,* vol. 4 of *The Pittsburgh Survey,* ed. Paul U. Kellogg, 6 vols. (New York: Charities Publication Committee, 1909–14), p. 649.

59. Women workers were not hired in the Gary steel mills until World War II, according to Kerns, "Social and Economic Conditions," pp. 8–9. For the settlements' activities with working women, see Allen F. Davis, "The Women's Trade Union League: Origins and Organization," *Labor History* 5 (Winter 1964): 3–17; Nancy Schrom Dye, *As Equals and as Sisters: Feminism, the Labor Movement, and the Women's Trade Union League* (Columbia: University of Missouri Press, 1980); Elizabeth Anne Payne, *Reform, Labor, and Feminism: Margaret Dreier Robins and the Women's Trade Union League* (Urbana: University of Illinois Press, 1988). See also Alice Kessler-Harris, "Women, Work and the Social Order," in Berenice Carroll, ed., *Liberating Women's History, Theoretical and Critical Essays* (Urbana: University of Illinois Press, 1978), 310–43.

60. Hughes, *Children of Preschool Age*, p. 153.

61. Leslie Woodcock Tentler, *Wage-Earning Women: Industrial Work and Family Life in the United States, 1900–1930* (New York: Oxford University Press, 1979), esp. pp. 176–78. On prohibitions regarding immigrant women's wage-work, see Virginia Yans McLaughlin, *Family and Community: Italian Immigrants in Buffalo, 1880–1930* (Ithaca, N.Y.: Cornell University Press, 1977); Donna Gabaccia, *From Sicily to Elizabeth Street: Housing and Social Change among Italian Immigrants, 1880–1930* (Albany, N.Y.: SUNY Press, 1984), pp. 113–14.

62. Hughes, *Children of Preschool Age*, pp. 154–55.

63. Ibid., p. 151. Cost-of-living data are from Gulick, *Labor Policy*, pp. 85–86. Data on income of breadwinners are from Hughes, *Children of Preschool Age*, p. 151; U.S. Department of Commerce, Bureau of the Census, *Fifteenth Census, 1930, Population*, vol. 4, *Occupations by States* (Washington, D.C.: Government Printing Office, 1933), p. 514. Evidently most of the women who kept boarders were not entered as "gainfully employed" by census enumerators. Other declared their occupation as "lodging house keepers" and were included as gainfully employed; 96 percent of this group were either widowed or divorced. Mimi Abramowitz, *Regulating the Lives of Women: Social Welfare Policy from Colonial Times to the Present* (Boston: South End Press, 1988), pp. 181–206.

64. Hughes, *Children of Preschool Age*, pp. 18–19, 29; Warmington, "Gary Neighborhood House"; International Institute, "Foreign Language Groups in Gary," p. 8, n.d. (1920?), CRA. Mohl and Betten argue that the International Institute was more tolerant of immigrant cultures than the settlement houses, "Paternalism and Pluralism."

65. Tentler, *Wage-Earning Women*, pp. 117–18, 144–45. On networks of migration see John Bodnar, *The Transplanted: A History of Immigrants in Urban America* (Bloomington: Indiana University Press, 1985), pp. 57–84; See also John Modell and Tamara K. Hareven, "Urbanization and the Malleable Household: An Examination of Boarding and Lodging in American Families," *Journal of Marriage and the Family* 35 (August 1973): 467–79; Michael Anderson, "Family, Household, and the Industrial Revolution," in Michael Gordon, ed., *The American Family in Social Historical Perspective*, 2d ed. (New York: St. Martin's Press, 1978), pp. 38–50; Gabaccia, *From Sicily to Elizabeth Street*; Olivier Zunz, *The Changing Face of Inequality: Urbanization, Industrial Development, and Immigrants in Detroit, 1880–1920* (Chicago: University of Chicago Press, 1982), pp.

239, 240; Tamara Hareven, *Family Time and Industrial Time: The Relationship between the Family and Work in a New England Industrial Community* (New York: Cambridge University Press, 1982).

66. International Institute, "Materials Relating to 1929 Survey of the Needs of the Foreign Population of Gary," II, Misc. Papers.

67. U.S. Department of Labor, Children's Bureau, *Infant Mortality*, by Elizabeth Hughes, Bureau Publication no. 112 (Washington, D.C.: Government Printing Office, 1923), p. 67; Warmington, "Gary Neighborhood House," n.p.; Hughes, *Children of Preschool Age*, pp. 18–19. Data on living space also confirm the importance of boarding in immigrant households: one-third of immigrant children lived in houses where there were two or more persons per room, but only 7 percent of children in native-born American households did so. Hughes, *Children of Preschool Age*, pp. 18–19, 29.

68. Warmington, "Gary Neighborhood House."

69. Robert A. Woods and Albert J. Kennedy, eds., *Young Working Girls: A Summary of Evidence from Two Thousand Social Workers* (Boston: Houghton Mifflin, 1913), pp. 13–14, 43–44; Beverly Warner, "Social Settlements and Charity Organization Problems," National Conference on Charities and Corrections, *Proceedings of the Thirteenth Conference, Atlanta, May 1903*, p. 311. Kathy Peiss, *Cheap Amusements: Working Women and Leisure in New York City, 1880–1920* (Philadelphia: Temple University Press, 1985). On household technology, see Susan J. Kleinburg, "Technology and Women's Work: The Lives of Working Class Women in Pittsburgh, 1870–1900," *Labor History* 17 (Winter 1976): 58–72. The Lynds found striking differences in Muncie, Indiana, in the late 1920s between the households with modern conveniences and those with "1890 habits." Some families with an automobile, electric washer, iron, and vacuum cleaner were still without city water or sewage connections. Robert S. Lynd and Helen Lynd, *Middletown: A Study in American Culture* (New York: Harcourt Brace, 1929), pp. 97–98.

70. *Young Working Girls*, p. 101. Grace Warmington inquired about a girl who was absent from the Neighborhood House girls' club. "Oh, her cousin wouldn't let her come. She is so pretty, he wants her to stay in his saloon, then lots of people come in. If she learned English, she wouldn't want to stay," she was told. "I cannot begin to tell you the temptations these girls have, and how important it is that they learn English," Warmington commented. Warmington, "Gary Neighborhood House." See also Jane Addams, *The Spirit of Youth and the City Streets* (New York: Macmillan, 1909; Urbana: University of Illinois Press, 1972). See also Elisabeth Israels Perry, "The General Motherhood of the Commonwealth: Dance Hall Reform in the Progressive Era," *American Quarterly* 37 (Winter 1985): 719–33.

71. International Institute, "Foreign Language Groups in Gary" (1920?), p. 7. II Misc. Papers, CRA.

72. Two-thirds of working-class wives interviewed by the Lynds had not baked bread that day—and 82 percent of "business-class wives." *Middletown*, pp. 154–55. A writer in the *Central Labor Union News* poured scorn on the idea of social workers teaching immigrant women to cook: Americanization meant

nothing more than learning to use a can opener, he scoffed. See also Cowan, *More Work for Mother*, pp. 71–73.

73. "The number of restaurants and hotels in Gary suggests that the population does not live in normal family groups," Edmondson, *Juvenile Delinquency and Adult Crime*, p. 19.

74. Jane Addams, *Twenty Years at Hull House* (New York: Macmillan, 1912, Signet Classics, 1960), p. 301. For the settlements and standards in the home, see Warner, "Social Settlements and Charity Organization Problems," p. 313. For a radically different view of domesticity, see Charlotte Perkins Gilman, *The Home: Its Work and Influence* (New York: McClure, Phillips and Co., 1903). Gilman, who favored commercializing household labor, reserved her most barbed comments for home cooking.

75. Neighborhood House, "Minutes," October 1, 1923, p. 134. This recalls Emma Goldman's remark that settlement houses were places where the poor learned to eat with forks.

76. Jones, *Twenty Years of Neighborliness* (1929). See also Mary E. Richmond, *Friendly Visiting among the Poor* (Montclair, N.J.: Paterson Smith, 1899, 1969), pp. 66–67; Corinne Krause, "Urbanization without Breakdown: Italian, Jewish, and Slavic Immigrant Women in Pittsburgh, 1900–1945," *Journal of Urban History* 4 (May 1978): 291–306.

77. U.S. Department of Labor, Children's Bureau, *Children of Preschool Age in Gary, Indiana, Part II, Diet of the Children*, by Lydia Roberts, M.D. Bureau publication no. 122 (Washington, D.C.: Government Printing Office, 1922), p. 55.

78. Ibid., pp. 64–71. Eighty-five percent of foreign-born children surveyed drank tea or coffee, but only 37 percent of native-born whites, and 33 percent of blacks.

79. Ibid., pp. 75, 84.

80. Ibid., pp. 59–61, 118. The diets of Americans also left a lot to be desired. The Children's Bureau investigators rated 42.5 percent of white Americans and 72.4 percent of black children as having type "D or E," that is, inadequate diets, p. 61.

81. This was defined as "Milk, cereals, and simply cooked foods, potatoes, meat, vegetables, and fruit—and instead of pie . . . fruits or simple puddings," p. 89–90.

82. Warmington, "Gary Neighborhood House"; Hughes, *Infant Mortality*, pp. 71–73. In 1918, there was one food-and-milk inspector in Gary, who was both a city and a state official. He was charged with inspecting the 126 farms that supplied Gary's milk and the 13 licensed dairies that processed and distributed it. His reports on the dairies were published weekly in the Gary newspapers, with the milk of each dairy being described as either "clean," "slightly dirty," or "dirty."

83. Woods and Kennedy, "An Experimental Definition of the American Standard of Living."

84. *Fifty Years in Christian Fellowship. The Story of Katherine House* (1969), ECHS; Hughes, *Children of Preschool Age*, pp. 26, 41, 159. In Muncie, Indiana,

in 1925, one in four houses still lacked running water. Lynd and Lynd, *Middletown*, p. 97. I have relied in this section on the sympathetic portrayal of the world of working-class housewives in Cowan, *More Work for Mother*, pp. 165–68.

85. Davis, *Spearheads for Reform*, pp. 153 ff; Howard E. Wilson, *Mary McDowell, Neighbor* (Chicago: University of Chicago Press, 1928).

86. *Eleventh Annual Report of the Superintendent, Gary Neighborhood House.*

87. Katherine House, Minutes of Staff, Box 1. ECHS; "What the Neighborhood House Has Done in Four Years," Gary *Daily Tribune*, November 24, 1916, p. 1; "Neighborhood House Doing Its Share in the Great Melting Pot."

88. Helen Hart, "The Changing Function of the Settlement under Changing Conditions," *Proceedings of the Fifty-Eighth National Conference of Social Work* (Minneapolis, June 1931), p. 289. Yet the Governor's Commission on Unemployment Relief, *Recovery in Indiana*, August 1936–37, reported the results of a WPA survey which showed that at least 25 percent of homes in Gary still had no baths, toilet facilities, or running water. Mohl and Betten, *Steel City*, p. 28, n. 9.

89. Woods and Kennedy, *The Settlement Horizon*, p. 237.

90. Dolores Hayden, *The Grand Domestic Revolution: A History of Feminist Designs for American Homes, Neighborhoods, and Cities* (Cambridge: MIT Press, 1982), esp. pp. 150–79, and Dolores Hayden, "Two Utopian Feminists and Their Campaigns for Kitchenless Houses," *Signs* 4 (Winter 1978): 274–90, for contemporary feminist schemes for revolutionizing the household and its work. For a description of the demonstration kitchens at Hull House see Addams, *Twenty Years*, p. 102. One reason for the failure of these kitchens, Jane Addams recalled, was that their sponsors underestimated the strength of "the wide diversity of nationality and inherited tastes." Despite the scientific correctness of food preparation in the Hull House kitchens, it was unappealing. One woman told Jane Addams that "the food was certainly nutritious, but that she didn't like to eat what was nutritious, that she liked to eat 'what she'd ruther.'" See also Cecilia Baxter, "Sicilian Family Life," *Family*, 14 (May 1933): 85; Lynd and Lynd, *Middletown*, pp. 153–58. A witty but impressionistic essay on the "new woman" in the twenties is "The Sexy Saleslady," in Mary Ryan, *Womanhood in America from Colonial Times to the Present* (New York: New Viewpoints, 2d rev. ed. 1979 [1975]).

91. Seller, *Immigrant Woman*, p. 56.

92. Edmondson, *Juvenile Delinquency and Adult Crime*, pp. 7–8.

93. Ibid., p. 23. On the other hand, some social workers judged young working women *too* quick to adopt American dress. "In their eagerness to adopt American fashions of dress, some ludicrous effects are achieved—such, for example, as the wearing of white or gay-colored satin party dresses on the streets in broad daylight," Edmondson wrote. See also Mary E. Richmond, *Friendly Visiting among the Poor.* Charity visitors were warned not to be too exasperated by the "cheap finery" of immigrant women. "Our own example is far more likely to be followed in the long run," p. 68. See also Mary Simkhovitch, *The City Worker's World in America* (New York: Macmillan, 1917), p. 131.

94. Warmington, "Gary Neighborhood House," p. 4. Hull House Labor Museum was an attempt to keep traditional crafts alive. It is the lone example. See Addams, Twenty Years, pp. 172–77; and Allen F. Davis, American Heroine: The Life and Legend of Jane Addams (New York: Oxford University Press, 1973), pp. 128–29. Bruce R. Kahler, "Art and Life: The Arts and Crafts Movement in Chicago, 1897–1910" (Ph.D. dissertation, Purdue University, 1986).

95. "Attendance at Sewing School for Tuesday was forty-five," Miss Beppler, evidently the Sunday-school teacher, wrote. "It was so large that we have divided the school into divisions . . . "; Netta Beppler to Miss Williams, Gary, Indiana, May 28, 1909, handwritten, CRA; Warmington, "Gary Neighborhood House"; Neighborhood House Visitor (October 13, 1916).

96. Netta Beppler to Miss Williams, May 28, 1909.

97. Woods and Kennedy, "Experimental Definition of the American Standard of Living."

98. Molly Ladd-Taylor, ed., Raising a Baby the Government Way: Mothers' Letters to the Children's Bureau, 1915–1932 (New Brunswick, N.J.: Rutgers University Press, 1986). The other side of the rise of home economics as a "science" was the disparagement of the "amateur" housewife and her traditional knowledge. Glenna Matthews, "Just a Housewife": The Rise and Fall of Domesticity in America (New York: Oxford University Press, 1987), pp. 145–71. See also Barbara Ehrenreich and Deirdre English, For Her Own Good: One Hundred Years of the Experts' Advice to Women (Garden City, N.Y.: Doubleday Anchor, 1978). Judith Ann Trolander, Professionalism and Social Change: From the Settlement House Movement to Neighborhood Centers, 1886 to the Present (New York: Columbia University Press, 1987), traces the efforts of settlement workers to remain "friendly neighbors" while becoming professionals as well. See also Don S. Kirschner, The Paradox of Professionalism: Reform and Public Service in Urban America, 1900–1940 (Westport, Conn.: Greenwood Press, 1986).

99. Enrico Sartorio, Social and Religious Life of Italians in America (Boston: Christopher, 1918), quoted in Maxine Seller, ed., Immigrant Women (Philadelphia: Temple University Press, 1981), p. 164.

100. "What the Gary Neighborhood House Has Done in Four Years," Gary Daily Tribune, November 24, 1916, p. 1; Eleventh Annual Report of the Superintendent, Gary Neighborhood House; Rev. H. R. Martin, "The Gary Neighborhood House" (1924–25); Hughes, Children of Preschool Age, p. 156.

101. Jones, Twenty Years of Neighborliness, pp. 7–8.

102. Ibid., pp. 8–9.

103. Ibid., p. 8.

104. Eleventh Annual Report of the Superintendent, pp. 3–4.

105. Jones, Twenty Years of Neighborliness, p. 8.

106. Hughes, Children of Preschool Age, p. 157. Sheila Rothman writes of such day nurseries, "The clientele was generally made up of destitute and deserted wives who were unable to turn to friends or relatives for aid. Lacking all choice, they were forced to accept the charity of the middle class." Sheila Rothman, Woman's Proper Place: A History of Changing Ideals and Practices, 1870 to the Present (New York: Basic Books, 1978), pp. 90–91. See also Tentler, Wage-

Earning Women. Tentler writes, "Many nursery directors were apparently as interested in the control and reformation of working-class family life as they were in providing low-cost care to the children of working mothers," pp. 163–64.

107. *Eleventh Annual Report of the Superintendent, Gary Neighborhood House,* pp. 2, 4; Rev. H. R. Martin, "The Gary Neighborhood House."

108. Martin, "The Gary Neighborhood House." For domestic work see David Katzman, *Seven Days a Week: Women and Domestic Service in Industrializing America* (New York: Oxford University Press, 1978); Phyllis Palmer, "Housework and Domestic Labor: Racial and Technological Change," in Karen Brodkin Sacks and Dorothy Remy, eds., *My Troubles Are Going to Have Trouble With Me* (New Brunswick, N.J.: Rutgers University Press, 1984), pp. 80–91; and "Housewife and Household Worker: Employer-Employee Relationships in the Home, 1928–1941," in Carol Groneman and Mary Beth Norton, eds., *"To Toil the Livelong Day": America's Women at Work, 1780–1980* (Ithaca, N.Y.: Cornell University Press, 1987), pp. 179–95. See also Chapter 3.

109. International Institute, "Material Relating to 1929 Survey of the Needs of the Foreign Population of Gary," II Misc. Papers. (Handwritten transcripts of interviews with prominent nationality leaders in Gary. Schedule of questions asked in the Survey), CRA. The author can vouch for the fact that immigration—even from one English-speaking country to another—is traumatic, soothing notions about adaptation to the contrary.

110. II, "Materials Relating to 1929 Survey." For a sophisticated study comparing living-space arrangements of immigrants before immigration and in the United States, see Gabaccia, *From Sicily to Elizabeth Street.*

111. II, "Materials Relating to 1929 Survey," CRA.

112. Sternberger, "Gary and the Foreigners' Opportunity," p. 482.

113. Gary Neighborhood House, *Annual Report of the Gary Neighborhood House,* April 1, 1938–April 1, 1939, CRA. Linda Gordon criticizes the assumption that welfare bureaucracies have necessarily had an undifferentiated impact on working-class families. By exploring the dynamics of the working-class family in its confrontation with welfare agencies, Gordon posits a dynamic relationship between agency and family, with women negotiating to improve their lot within the family. Gordon's focus is different from that of the present study; however, using her analysis at least allows us to speculate that although the settlements' aim was "social control," their influence could be brought to bear to help working-class women, while curbing the power of their husbands. Linda Gordon, "Family Violence, Feminism, and Social Control," *Feminist Studies* 12 (Fall 1986): 453–78. See also Donna Gabaccia, *"The Transplanted:* Women and Family in Immigrant America," *Social Science History* 12, 3 (Fall 1988): 243–53, which persuasively argues the need for more attention to gender in immigration history.

114. Quoted in Paul S. Taylor, *Mexican Labor in the United States: Chicago and the Calumet Region,* University of California Publications in Economics, vol. 7 (Berkeley: University of California Press, 1932), p. vii.

115. The use of leisure varied, of course, among immigrant groups. For the Italians, see Baxter, "Sicilian Family Life," and Yans McLaughlin, *Family and*

Community. For Buffalo Italians, McLaughlin writes, recreation was a "highly personal, family or religious matter." In Buffalo, "as in Italy, the independent female leisure activities, sewing and talking, took place within the home." She concludes, "The Italian immigrant perceived all social workers as intruders into his [sic] private world, more offensive than politicians or employers whose demands, after all, did not penetrate so immediately into his intimate life" pp. 135–38. For the rise of commercial leisure and workers' struggle to use it on their own terms, see Roy Rosenzweig, *Eight Hours for What We Will: Workers and Leisure in an Industrial City, 1870–1920* (New York: Cambridge University Press, 1983), and Francis G. Couvares, *The Remaking of Pittsburgh: Class and Culture in an Industrializing City, 1877–1919* (Albany, N.Y.: SUNY Press, 1984). Peiss, *Cheap Amusements*, concentrates on working-class women's confrontation with commercial leisure. Along with the rise of the consumer culture went the triumph of heterosexuality. For its double-edged implications for women and feminism see Nancy Cott, *The Grounding of Modern Feminism* (New Haven: Yale University Press, 1987), pp. 148–52 and passim.

116. French historian Karen Offen, in "Defining Feminism: A Comparative Historical Approach," *Signs* 14 (Autumn 1988): 119–57, argues that we must admit to the feminist historical tradition not only those movements that sought to enhance women's individuality and aimed for equality with men, but also all movements that stressed improvement for women *as women*, which she calls "relational feminism." Grace Mary Warmington and her sisters and co-workers at Neighborhood House, and all the other female settlement workers of this study, many of them nameless, were feminists of this latter kind. To collapse Chafe's category, "social feminists" with NWP feminists would certainly allow the Progressive-era settlement workers back into the category of feminists—but it would disturb the elegant analyses of early-twentieth-century feminism by Cott and others. See Nancy F. Cott, "What's in a Name? The Limits of 'Social Feminism,' or Expanding the Vocabulary of Women's History," *Journal of American History* 76 (December 1989): 809–29.

117. Edmondson, *Juvenile Delinquency and Adult Crime*, p. 23.

118. Warmington, "Gary Neighborhood House."

119. Of Gary families surveyed by the Children's Bureau in 1917, 45 percent either owned or were buying their home. This breaks down as 35 percent of native-born whites, 11 percent of blacks, and a remarkable 52 percent of foreign-born. How to interpret this high level of homeownership among immigrants is disputed, however. James R. Barrett, echoing Bodnar, calls immigrant homeownership "the product of a defensive, security-conscious mentality shaped by workers' experiences in a volatile labor system, a sign neither of the primitive peasant still attached to the land nor of the acquisitive, upwardly mobile nascent capitalist." See Barrett, "John Bodnar's *The Transplanted:* Roundtable and Debate," *Social Science History* 12 (Fall 1988): 224. See also Bodnar, *The Transplanted*, pp. 193–94, and "Immigration and Modernization: The Case of Slavic Peasants in Industrial America," *Journal of Social History* 10 (1976): 44–71.

120. On the changing nature of patriarchal power, see Eileen Boris and Peter Bardaglio, "Gender, Race, and Class: The Impact of the State on the Family

and the Economy, 1790–1945," in Naomi Gerstel and Harriet Gross, eds., *Families and Work: Toward Reconceptualization* (Philadelphia: Temple University Press, 1987), pp. 132–51, and, generally critical of it, Frances Fox Piven, "Ideology, Power and the Welfare State," in ibid., pp. 512–19; Abramowitz, *Regulating the Lives of Women.*

Chapter 6: Gary-Alerding Settlement House

1. Foreign-born whites numbered 16, 294 in 1920 and 19,345 in 1930. Mexicans were counted separately. U.S. Department of Commerce, Bureau of the Census, *Fourteenth Census of the United States: 1920*, vol. 2, *Population*, pp. 63, 760–61; *Fifteenth Census, 1930*: vol. 3, (pt. 1), *Population*, pp. 715–20.

2. "United War Work, or 'Seven in One Drive'," in Mrs. Frank J. Sheehan, comp., "Gary in the World War," 2: 22; "Civilian History" (1923), 122, GPL; Ronald D. Cohen and Raymond A. Mohl, *The Paradox of Progressive Education: The Gary Plan and Urban Schooling* (Port Washington, N.Y.: Kennikat Press, 1979), pp. 83–109; Raymond A. Mohl and Neil Betten, *Steel City: Urban and Ethnic Patterns in Gary, Indiana, 1906–1950* (New York: Holmes and Meier, 1986), pp. 129–47.

3. James B. Lane, *City of the Century: A History of Gary, Indiana* (Bloomington: Indiana University Press, 1978), p. 47; Powell A. Moore, *The Calumet Region* (Indianapolis: Indiana Historical Bureau, 1959), pp. 323–26; Isaac J. Quillen, "Industrial City: A History of Gary, Indiana to 1929" (Ph.D. dissertation, Yale University, 1942), pp. 249–54.

4. There were 43,403 Catholics in Lake County out of a total church membership of 68,137. U.S. Department of Commerce, Bureau of the Census, *Religious Bodies, 1916* (Washington, D.C.: Government Printing Office, 1919), 1: 258–59.

5. This was the gist of findings of the U.S. Children's Bureau Reports on Gary, published in 1923. For an attempt to combat these accusations, see Captain Norton's speech to the Gary Board of Realtors, "H. S. Norton Predicts Year of Prosperity," Gary *Post Tribune*, May 8, 1923, p. 1. Steel-corporation officials complained that they were as often accused of "neglect" of the city's social problems as blamed for paternalistic intervention in them. See also Edward Greer, "Monopoly and Competitive Capital in the Making of Gary, Indiana," *Science and Society* 40 (Winter 1976–77): 465–78.

6. Moore, *Calumet Region*, p. 329.

7. Bishop John Noll, *The Diocese of Fort Wayne* (Fort Wayne, Ind. 1941), 2:395. See also "Gary-Alerding House Met Needs of Many," Gary *Post Tribune*, Jubilee Edition, June 10, 1956, which states, "The settlement house really started back in 1913 when William P. Gleason, then general superintendent of Gary Steel Works, first proposed it."

8. Raymond A. Mohl and Neil Betten, "The Immigrant Church in Gary, Indiana: Religious Adjustment and Cultural Defense," *Ethnicity* 8 (1981): 1–17; Timothy L. Smith, "Lay Initiative in the Religious Life of American

Immigrants, 1880–1950," in Tamara Hareven, ed., *Anonymous Americans* (Englewood Cliffs, N.J.: Prentice Hall, 1971), pp. 214–49; Milton Gordon, *Assimilation in American Life* (New York: Oxford University Press, 1964), pp. 197–99. See also W. L. Warner and L. Srole, *The Social Systems of American Ethnic Groups* (New Haven, Conn.: Yale University Press, 1943). Mohl and Betten claim that "All of Gary's immigrant Catholic parishes were lay founded and were generally bodies closely reflecting the needs and aspirations of their members." Ibid., p. 3. While convincing, their account fails to consider the part played by the steel company—also a "lay" effort—in founding immigrant churches.

9. Mohl and Betten, "Immigrant Church," p. 3; Noll, *Diocese of Fort Wayne* 2:387; Cohen and Mohl, *Paradox of Progressive Education*, p. 105.

10. Alerding, "Memorandum," October 3, 1920. Bishop Alerding Letters, Chancery, Diocese of Fort Wayne, Ind. (hereafter AL).

11. Alerding to His Eminence, Cardinal Gasparri, March 4, 1923. The growth of Gary together with that of neighboring East Chicago and Indiana Harbor created the greatest problems of Alerding's career, according to his successor, Bishop John Noll. The most difficult task was to find priests "to shepherd these flocks." Noll, *Diocese of Fort Wayne*, p. 145. See also Henry J. Browne, "The 'Italian Problem' in the Catholic Church of the United States, 1880–1900," *United States Catholic Historical Society, Records and Studies* 35 (New York, 1946): 46–72; Rudolph J. Vecoli, "Prelates and Peasants: Italian Immigrants and the Catholic Church," *Journal of Social History* 2 (Spring 1969): 217–68.

12. Alerding to de Ville, February 25, 1913, AL.

13. Alerding to Elbert Gary, March 10, 1913, AL.

14. Alerding to de Ville, June 3, 1913, AL.

15. Alerding to E. J. Buffington, president, Illinois Steel Company, Chicago, April 5, 1913, AL.

16. E. H. Gary to Bishop Alerding, March 17, 1913, AL. The role of the immigrant church as Americanizer has been the subject of extended historical debate. In Gary, the immigrant churches seem to have functioned simultaneously as an expression of cultural autonomy and social control.

17. Alerding to Elbert Gary, March 21, 1913, April 28, 1913, AL.

18. Alerding to Elbert Gary, March 10, 1913, AL. The national parish, Milton Gordon writes, was "an inspired middle ground position which met the needs of the immigrants themselves without compromising the future needs of their descendants." Gordon, *Assimilation in American Life*, p. 217.

19. Mohl and Betten, "Immigrant Church"; Cohen and Mohl, *Paradox of Progressive Education*, p. 105. In 1919, 1,440 children were enrolled in parochial schools in Gary. The major schools, with their enrollments, were as follows:

Holy Angels 375   Sacred Heart 51
St. Hedwig's 91   St. Luke's 91
Holy Trinity 253

International Institute, "Gary (Gary Study)," January 8–17, 1919, p. 2. Typescript. II Papers, CRA.

20. "Historical Sketch of the Lithuanians in Gary," p. 6, pamphlet, GPL. Many Czech workers at Gary had been steel workers prior to immigration. Telephone conversation with Dr. William Clark, 1981. The Immigration Commission, in a study of a midwestern steel town, found that most of the steel workers had previously been engaged in agriculture. The figures were dramatically different for some immigrant groups: of the 104 Welsh immigrant steelworkers surveyed, over 87 percent had previously been employed in iron and steel, but only 5 percent of Poles and 3 percent of Lithuanians. Immigration Commission, *Immigrants in Industries*, pt. 2, *Iron and Steel* 2:605.

21. William M. Leiserson, *Adjusting Immigrant and Industry* (New York: Arno Press, 1969); Gerd Korman, "Americanization at the Factory Gate," *Industrial and Labor Relations Review* 18 (April 1965): 396–419. Leading officials at two Youngstown-area steel plants reported it was necessary to keep 25 percent more men on the payrolls than would be necessary, "were the men to report regularly for work instead of intermittently as they do now." *Iron Age* (September 12, 1918), p. 670. Was such a phenomenon evidence of the preindustrial *mentalité* of the peasant-turned-steel-worker (see Herbert Gutman, "Work, Culture, and Society in Industrializing America, 1815–1919," *American Historical Review* 78 [June 1, 1973]: 531–88) or was it simply that the wartime labor shortage allowed workers to work on their own terms? As a writer editorialized in *La Parola dei Socialisti* in December 1915, "No more does one see in Chicago the long queues of foreigners who a year ago waited patiently for a call in front of unemployment agencies. . . . The Italians, Greeks and Poles, to whom any compensation might be offered have disappeared." The few who were left were no longer "humbly submissive to factory owners and foremen." "The Scarcity of Labor Due to the War," *La Parola dei Socialisti*, December 4, 1915, Chicago Foreign Language Press Survey, Reel #30 ID 2c, p. 3, Chicago Public Library (CPL).

22. For a description of in-plant Americanization classes, see Illinois Steel Company, *Gary Works Circle* 3 (September-October 1918): 2-3; George Quimby, comp., *Proceedings of the National Conference on Americanization in Industries* (Nantucket Beach, Mass., 1919). For a summary of community efforts at Americanization in Gary, see Estelle M. Sternberger, "Gary and the Foreigners' Opportunity," *Survey* 42 (June 18, 1919): 480–82.

23. Quimby, *Americanization in Industries*; "Breaking Down the Language Barrier," *Iron Age* 97 (February 3, 1916): 293–94; "Educating Illiterate Employees," *Iron Age* 94 (October 16, 1913): 862. The Conference on Americanization in Industries resolved in June 1919 that such instruction should not be compulsory, but in the employee's own time, and without compensation.

24. "Teaching the Foreign Laborer to Speak English"; Frances Kellor, "Americanization: A Conservation Policy for Industry," *Annals of the American Academy of Political and Social Science* 65 (May 1916): 240–44.

25. "Welfare Work in the Steel Industry," *Iron Age* 105 (June 3, 1920): 1600–1601; Gulick, *Labor Policy*, pp. 138–40; Quimby, *Americanization in Industries*, pp. 36–39, 78.

26. A. H. Wyman, in Quimby, *Americanization in Industries*, pp. 13–19; "Educating Foreign Employees," *Iron Age* 94 (November 13, 1913): 1119; "Educating Illiterate Employees," *Iron Age* 94 (October 16, 1913): 863.

27. "English to Foreigners in Shop Hours," *Iron Age* 95 (May 21, 1914): 1286.

28. "Americanization and Research," *Iron Age* 103 (December 26, 1918): 1593.

29. "Americanization Schools at Mid-West Plants," *Iron Age* 103 (February 6, 1919): 406; Walter Gordon Merritt, "Anti-Social Militant Methods Condemned," *Iron Age* 104 (July 3, 1919): 11.

30. "Waste in Hiring and Discharging Men," *Iron Age* 95 (October 29, 1914): 1032.

31. Bishop Noll, *Diocese of Fort Wayne*, p. 382; "Gary-Alerding House Met Needs of Many," Gary *Post Tribune* Jubilee Edition, June 10, 1956, p. 15; H. J. Alerding, memorandum, May 25, 1917, AL, describes the visit. See also "The Judge Gary-Bishop Alerding Settlement House," p. 1, pamphlet, GPL.

32. Alerding, memorandum, May 25, 1917, AL.

33. Ibid.

34. Campbell Settlement, *Report*, 1922, GPL (see Chapters 4 and 5).

35. Alerding to the Reverend J. E. Burke, C.S.P., March 14, 1920, AL. For the work of the Catholic Welfare Council and developments in national Catholicism at this time, see Aaron I. Abell, *American Catholicism and Social Action: A Search for Social Justice, 1865–1950* (South Bend, Ind.: University of Notre Dame Press, 1963).

36. Gary *Daily Tribune*, November 5, 1919; "New Association Organized Here for Welfare Work," Gary *Evening Post and Daily Tribune*, June 13, 1922. "The Judge Gary-Bishop Alerding Settlement House," p. 8; Sheehan, "Gary in the World War." See also John McClymer, *War and Welfare: Social Engineering in America, 1890–1925* (Westport, Conn.: Greenwood Press, 1980).

37. Sheehan, "The Red Cross Chapter," in "Gary in the World War," 2: 97; "Second Red Cross Campaign," in ibid., p. 87. "Open Headquarters for Settlement House Fund Drive in Gary Hotel," Gary *Post Tribune*, October 18, 1922, p. 5; John Higham, *Strangers in the Land: Patterns of American Nativism, 1860–1925* (New York: Atheneum, 1965); William Preston, Jr., *Aliens and Dissenters: Federal Suppression of Radicals, 1903–1933* (New York: Harper and Row, Harper Torchbook ed., 1966); David Kennedy, *Over There: The First World War and American Society* (New York: Oxford University Press, 1980).

38. David Brody, *Labor in Crisis: The Great Steel Strike of 1919* (Philadelphia: J. Lippincott, 1965); Raymond A. Mohl, "The Great Steel Strike of 1919 in Gary, Indiana: Working-Class Radicalism or Trade Union Militancy?" *Mid-America* 63 (January 1981): 36–52; William Z. Foster, *The Great Steel Strike and Its Lessons* (New York: B. W. Huebsch, 1920); Marshall Olds, *Analysis of the Interchurch World Movement Report on the Steel Strike* (New York: Putnam's, 1923).

39. Graham Taylor, "At Gary: Some Impressions and Interviews," *Survey*, November 8, 1919, p. 66; Moore, *Calumet Region*, pp. 512–19; Farner, "Indiana, the Press and the Red Scare," pp. 82 ff. The Loyal American League bought full-page advertisements in the two Gary newspapers every day from September 15 to October 8, 1919.

40. "The Americanization Movement in Gary," *Gary Works Circle* 4 (1919–20): 4–6; John de Ville, "Biographical Notes," de Ville papers, Chancery, Fort Wayne Diocese; "De Ville Founded Settlement," Gary *Post Tribune*, June 10, 1956, D. 15; Richard Ginder, *With Cross and Crozier: A Biography of John Francis Noll, Fifth Bishop of Fort Wayne and Founder of Our Sunday Visitor* (Huntington, Ind., 1952).

41. De Ville, "Biographical Notes"; "War Relief Work," in Sheehan, "Gary in the World War," tells of de Ville's activities on behalf of Liberty Bonds. Ibid., pp. 146–48.

42. "The Judge Gary-Bishop Alerding Settlement House," pp. 1–3; Noll, *The Fort Wayne Diocese,* p. 395. See also "Catholic Work for Better Citizenship," *Indiana Catholic and Record,* March 7, 1919, p. 4. The paper advocated Catholic Americanization work such as that sponsored by the National Catholic War Council (later National Catholic Welfare Council). The council published textbooks for civics and Americanization classes and rented out movies for use with foreigners learning English. De Ville used their materials in Gary. During 1920, movies such as "Forging the Links of Americanization" were shown every Monday and announced regularly in the newspapers. See Gary *Daily Tribune,* January 25, 1921, p. 2.

43. "The Judge Gary-Bishop Alerding Settlement House," p. 1.

44. "Great Move for Loyalty under Way," Gary *Daily Tribune,* December 1, 1919, p. 1. See also "Rev. De Ville to Help Aliens in Michigan," Gary *Daily Tribune,* January 18, 1921, p. 6. The bishop of Detroit heard of de Ville's methods of Americanization, "whereby each nationality conducts their own classes in English and citizenship in their own neighborhoods . . . ," and invited the Gary leader to start a similar program in Detroit. Gary *Evening Post and Daily Tribune,* January 19, 1922, p. 2. De Ville initiated a program of Americanization in New Chicago also.

45. "Americanization Movement in Gary," *Gary Works Circle* (January 4, 1920), p. 4; "Great Move for Loyalty under Way." Mexicans who tried to attend other immigrant Catholic churches were sometimes turned away and told to attend "their own" church. Paul S. Taylor, *Mexican Labor in the United States: The Calumet Region,* University of California Publications in Economics, vol. 7 (Berkeley: University of California Press, 1932), p. 213.

46. "Americanization Movement in Gary," pp. 4–5.

47. Ibid.

48. Alerding to Rev. John B. de Ville, director, March 6, 1920, AL.

49. Alerding to Elbert Gary, March 14, 1920, AL.

50. "The Bolsheviki, the Socialist and the Remedy," *Indiana Catholic and Record,* April 25, 1919, p. 4. See also John Fitzpatrick, "The Bishops' Labor Programme," *National Catholic War Council Bulletin* 1 (July 1919). For the attitude of churches toward the steel strike, see Interchurch World Movement, *Report on the Steel Strike,* esp. p. 84. See also "To Boycott Clergy in Gary," *New York Times,* October 1, 1919, p. 2. "Churches Make Appeal to Steel Corporation," *Iron Age* 105 (March 18, 1920): 821, contains details of Edward T. Devine's appeal to Elbert Gary on behalf of the Federal Council of Churches

of Christ. In "Anti-Foreign Fanatical Agitation," February 21, 1919, the *Indiana Catholic and Record* deplored the "frenzied fanaticism" that was sweeping the country and denied that America's foreign immigrants were fomenting "radicalism."

51. For the "Flurry of welfare efforts," see Brody, *Steelworkers in America*, p. 264.

52. "Reduction in Steel Corporation Wages," *Iron Age* 108 (August 25, 1921): 501. By one estimate, the steel mills were operating at between 40 and 50 percent capacity in 1920 and 1921. Moore, *Calumet Region*, pp. 329–30, 389.

53. H. J. Alerding, memorandum, October 3, 1920, AL.

54. Alerding to de Ville, February 16, 1921, AL.

55. "Judge Gary-Bishop Alerding Settlement House," p. 4.

56. "Open Headquarters for Settlement House Fund Drive in Gary Hotel," Gary *Post Tribune*, October 18, 1922, p. 5.

57. Ibid. For the International Institute, see Raymond A. Mohl, "The International Institute Movement and Ethnic Pluralism," *Social Science* 56 (Winter 1981): 14–21; Raymond A. Mohl and Neil Betten, "Ethnic Adjustment in the Industrial City: The International Institute of Gary, 1919–1940," *International Migration Review* 6 (Winter 1972): 361–76.

58. Gary *Post Tribune*, July 13, 1923; Gary *Evening Post*, June 16, 1922.

59. "New $75,000 Settlement House Plan," Gary *Evening Post and Daily Tribune*, March 18, 1922, p. 3.

60. Alerding to His Eminence, Cardinal Gasparri, March 14, 1923, p. 2. Late in 1922 or early in 1923, de Ville wrote to Cardinal Gasparri in Rome, requesting that the papacy confer a knighthood on Elbert Gary for his "deserving and generosity towards the Catholic Church in Gary." The bishop shrewdly informed the cardinal, "This generosity may not be a desire to help the Catholic Church as such, but rather to prevent as much as possible strikes and other labor troubles in the Steel Works." However, should the papacy confer this honor on Gary, it might "dispose him still more favorably, and to still greater generosity." There is no record of the steel chairman's reaction to this suggestion or whether the honor was ever given. Meanwhile, the ending of the twelve-hour day in steel-making in 1923 promised a surer guarantee of labor peace than these exotic proposals.

61. Brody, *Steelworkers in America*, p. 73; Moore, *Calumet Region*, pp. 330–31; "Business Conditions Improving," *Iron Age* 109 (June 1, 1922): 1493.

62. U.S. Department of Commerce, Bureau of the Census, *Fourteenth Census: 1920*, vol. 2, *Population*, pp. 63, 760–61; *Fifteenth Census: 1930, Population*, vol. 3 (pt. 1): 715–20. Taylor, *Mexican Labor in the United States: The Calumet Region*, pp. 36–37, 46; Lane, *City of the Century*, pp. 71–74; Francisco Arturo Rosales and Daniel T. Simon, "Mexican Immigrant Experience in the Urban Midwest: East Chicago, Indiana, 1919–1945," *Indiana Magazine of History* 77 (December 1981): 333–57; Neil Betten and Raymond A. Mohl, "From Discrimination to Repatriation: Mexican Life in Gary, Indiana, during the Great Depression," *Pacific Historical Review* 42 (August 1973): 370–88; Brody,

Steelworkers in America, p. 254; Mohl and Betten, *Steel City*, pp. 91–93; Mark Reisler, *By the Sweat of Their Brow: Mexican Immigrant Labor in the United States 1900–1940* (Westport, Conn.: Greenwood Press, 1976), pp. 102–3. Seventy-nine percent of the Mexicans were classified as unskilled workers, 19 percent as semiskilled, only 1.8 percent as skilled.

63. Taylor, *Mexican Labor*, pp. 213, 234–35; "De Ville, O'Hay Rouse Two Gary Audiences by Frank Addresses," Gary *Post Tribune*, January 28, 1927, pp. 1, 12; Ruth Hutchinson Crocker, "Gary Mexicans and 'Christian Americanization': A Study in Cultural Conflict," in *Forging a Community: The Latino Experience in Northwest Indiana, 1919–1975*, ed. James B. Lane and Edward J. Escobar (Chicago: Calumet Regional Studies Series, Cattails Press, 1987).

64. The gift was acknowledged when the settlement house was dedicated, "Thousands Pay Tribute to de Ville and Donors of Settlement House," Gary *Post Tribune*, May 19, 1924, p. 1, and "Judge Gary-Bishop Alerding Settlement House," p. 10. According to "Gary-Alerding Settlement Met the Needs of Many," Gary *Post Tribune*, June 10, 1954, D 15, the Gary Land Company gave land valued at $29,000, and the steel company gave $100,000 for the settlement building.

65. "Judge Gary-Bishop Alerding Settlement House," pp. 4–5; De Ville, "Biographical Notes"; Noll, *Diocese of Fort Wayne*, p. 395. For the Italians, see Browne, " 'Italian Problem' in the Catholic Church," and Vecoli, "Prelates and Peasants."

66. Letter entitled *"Ave, Amice, Moriturus te Salutat"* ("Greetings, Friends! He who is about to Die Salutes You"), de Ville Papers. He went on, "However, it was probably only a subconscious effort to justify myself to myself and gratify my own craving for them. Later on . . . when sorely in need of money—a condition I was continuously subject to—I was compelled to dispose of them in a hurry, piece by piece, at ruinous prices." Arthur Shumway described de Ville as "Bibliophile, art collector, writer and gentleman of culture," "Shrine of the Steel God," p. 29. See also "New $75,000 Settlement House Plan."

67. Jane Addams, *Twenty Years at Hull House* (New York: Macmillan, 1910; Signet Classic, 1960), esp. pp. 78, 257–75. When an exhibition opened at University Settlement in New York City in the 1890s, the *average* daily attendance for four weeks was 3,200. Charles R. Henderson, *Social Settlements* (New York: Lentilhon, 1899), p. 47. For English origins, see Henrietta Barnett, "Pictures for the People," in *Practicable Socialism: Essays on Social Reform* (London: Longmans, Green, 1888), pp. 109–25; Mina Carson, *Settlement Folk: Social Thought and the American Settlement House Movement, 1885–1930* (Chicago: University of Chicago Press, 1990), pp. 115–16.

68. Gary *Daily Tribune*, December 11, 1923, p. 1; "Open Settlement House and Circus Tonight," and "Settlement House, 25th and Van Buren, Formally Opened," Gary *Post Tribune*, December 12, 1923, p. 2.

69. Tom Cannon, "Thousands Pay Tribute to de Ville and Donors of Settlement House," Gary *Post Tribune*, May 19, 1924, p. 1. See also "Judge Gary-Bishop Alerding Settlement House," pp. 6–10. The accounts are essentially identical.

70. Ibid.

71. Ibid. For Seidenberg, see Abell, *American Catholicism and Social Action,* p. 182.

72. Brody, *Steelworkers in America,* pp. 267–68. "Mobility among the un-skilled, dependence in the upper ranks, the repressive power of the steel com-panies—all served to reinforce the acquiescence of the steelworkers," David Brody writes. *Steelworkers in America,* p. 278. Greer, "Racism at U.S. Steel," p. 52. In 1918, over half of the families of foreigners surveyed were buying their homes or already owned their homes, as compared to 35 percent of white Amer-icans. Hughes, *Children of Preschool Age,* p. 22.

73. Gary, Ind., Chamber of Commerce, "Report of the Community Chest Committee," typescript, pp. 5–6, GPL. My thanks to Prof. Lance E. Trusty for this reference. For the development of community chests see Lubove, *Profes-sional Altruist,* pp. 183–219; Judith Trolander, *Professionalism and Social Change: From the Settlement House Movement to Neighborhood Centers, 1886 to the Present* (New York: Columbia University Press, 1987).

74. Quillen, "Industrial City," p. 377.

75. "Is Welfare Work Overdone?" *Iron Age* 110 (September 21, 1922): 737–38; "Employers Are Blamed for Radicalism," *Iron Age* 105 (May 27, 1920): 1532.

76. "Employers Are Blamed for Radicalism." See also "Welfare Work Is Cur-tailed at Youngstown," *Iron Age* 105 (June 17, 1920): 1735; and "What Thoughts Guide Executives To-Day," by Don F. Kennedy, *Iron Age* 106 (May 5, 1921): 1172–73.

77. Rev. James Cis, letter to the author, November 23, 1981. Reverend Cis was director of the Gary-Alerding Settlement between 1943 and 1953.

78. Bishop Alerding died in Fort Wayne in November 1924 at the age of seventy-nine. Noll, his successor, described him as "tender-hearted, affable and appreciative." Noll, *Diocese of Fort Wayne,* pp. 145–46; Ginder, *With Cross and Crozier,* pp. 188–89. There had been frequent borrowings for maintenance of the buildings. Rev. James Cis, letter to the author.

79. "Introduce New Boys' Worker," Gary *Daily Tribune,* February 6, 1926, p. 13. As a measure of the increasing professionalism of settlement workers, this young man had a B.A. from Marquette and further training in "boy guidance" from Notre Dame. "New Sewing Class for Mexican Women Opens at Settle-ment House," Gary *Daily Tribune,* December 29, 1926, p. 13; "Mexicans Ob-serve Feast. Bishop is Speaker at Meet. Noll Urges Loyalty to the United States," Gary *Daily Tribune,* December 13, 1926, p. 13.

80. "Check Crime by More Religion in Home, Father de Ville Pleads Here," Gary *Post Tribune,* June 19, 1924, p. 1.

81. Gary *Post Tribune,* January 23, 1926.

82. "De Ville, O'Hay Rouse Two Gary Audiences by Frank Addresses," Gary *Post Tribune,* January 28, 1927, pp. 1, 12.

83. The de Ville papers contain several introspective and pathetic letters from this period at the end of his life.

84. James Cis, *Gary-Alerding Settlement House, Silver Jubilee of Community Service* (1949). Rev. James Cis, letter to the author, November 23, 1981.

Chapter 7: Stewart House

1. This exchange took place early in 1919. The Tennessee Coal, Iron, and Railroad Company and the Illinois Steel Company were major subsidiaries of the U.S. Steel Corporation. United States Steel Corporation, *Addresses and Statements of Elbert H. Gary*, 8 vols. Compiled by the Business History Society (November 1927), 4:32–33.

2. "Stewart House to Observe Anniversary This Weekend," Gary *Post Tribune*, November 24, 1926, p. 6.

3. The Commercial Club, founded in 1907 by "Captain" Norton, moved in 1928 into new quarters in the Gary Hotel which a contemporary report described as "princely." Arthur Shumway, "Gary, Shrine of the Steel God," *American Parade* 3 (1929): 27; Isaac J. Quillen, "Industrial City: A History of Gary, Indiana to 1929" (Ph.D. dissertation, Yale University, 1942), pp. 178–79. The club was periodically denounced as a tool of U.S. Steel by small businessmen and others who wanted a more diversified economy in Gary. Powell A. Moore, *The Calumet Region* (Indianapolis: Indiana Historical Bureau, 1959), pp. 328–29.

4. Both C. Oliver Holmes and Floyd Williams were said to be Klansmen although both denied membership. Both were candidates for the Republican nomination for mayor in 1925. "Holmes admitted the receipt of a telegram from Klan leaders urging him to withdraw in favor of Williams because the latter was the Klan's candidate. Holmes refused, but Williams won the nomination anyway." Moore, *Calumet Region*, pp. 557–58. See also Neil Betten and James B. Lane, "Nativism and the Klan in Town and City: Valparaiso and Gary, Indiana," *Studies in History and Society* 6 (Summer 1973): 3–16. C. O. Holmes aided in incorporating the city of Gary in 1906. He was president of the school board, founded the Gary *Times* in 1906, was a prominent banker and a nationally known Methodist lay leader. The sardonic Arthur Shumway says of him, "[He] shoved a busy finger into every available pie." Shumway, "Gary, Shrine of the Steel God," p. 24.

5. Moore, *Calumet Region*, pp. 434–36. By 1940, Snyder was said to be the most powerful man in Gary. Raymond A. Mohl and Neil Betten, *Steel City: Urban and Ethnic Patterns in Gary, Indiana, 1906–1950* (New York: Holmes and Meier, 1986), p. 83. Norton was president of the Commercial Club until his retirement in 1940. Quillen, "Industrial City," p. 178. See also Edward Greer, "Monopoly and Competitive Capital in the Making of Gary, Indiana," *Science and Society* 40 (Winter 1976–77), 465–78; Raymond A. Mohl and Neil Betten, "The Failure of Industrial City Planning: Gary, Indiana, 1906–1910," *Journal of the American Institute of Planners* 38 (July 1972): 203–15.

6. Thyra Edwards, "The Gary Interracial Project," *Southern Workman* 54 (December 1925): 545–53. Hueston later received a national position in the

Post Office Department for his support of the Republican party. Mohl and Betten, *Steel City*, p. 85. On "clientage politics," see Ira Katznelson, *Black Men, White Cities: Race, Politics, and Patronage in the United States, 1900–1930, and Britain, 1948–1968* (London: Oxford University Press, 1973), pp. 105–19.

7. The best overview and analysis of race relations in Gary in this period is Mohl and Betten, *Steel City*, pp. 48–90, and their earlier "Evolution of Racism in an Industrial City, 1906–1940: A Case Study of Gary, Indiana," *Journal of Negro History* 59 (1974): 51–64. For Garveyism, Amy Jacques-Garvey, comp., *Philosophy and Opinions of Marcus Garvey*, 2 vols. (New York: Universal Publishing House, 1925; Arno Press, 1969); Lawrence W. Levine, "Marcus Garvey and the Politics of Revitalization," in John Hope Franklin and August Meier, eds., *Black Leaders of the Twentieth Century* (Urbana: University of Illinois Press, 1982), pp. 105–39; Tony Martin, *Race First: The Ideological and Organizational Struggles of Marcus Garvey and the Universal Negro Improvement Association* (Westport, Conn: Greenwood Press, 1976); E. David Cronon, *Black Moses: The Story of Marcus Garvey and the Universal Negro Improvement Association* (Madison: University of Wisconsin Press, 1965, 1969). See also J. Harvey Kerns, "A Study of the Social and Economic Conditions of the Negro Population of Gary, Indiana" (Gary: National Urban League, 1944), pp. 37–38. GPL.

8. Quoted in E. Digby Baltzell, Introduction to *The Philadelphia Negro: A Social Study*, by William E. Burghardt Du Bois (New York: 1899, Schocken Books, 1967), p. xix.

9. Ibid., pp. xviii. See also Herman F. Hegner, "The Scientific Value of the Social Settlement," *American Journal of Sociology* 3 (September 1897): 171–82; Robert Bremner, *From the Depths: The Discovery of Poverty in the United States* (New York: New York University Press, 1956), pp. 140–63; Paul Boyer, *Urban Masses and Moral Order in Urban America, 1820–1920* (Cambridge: Harvard University Press, 1978), pp. 198–99; John F. McClymer, *War and Welfare: Social Engineering in America, 1890–1925* (Westport, Conn.: Greenwood Press, 1980). The National Urban League's Department of Research and Investigations continued this emphasis on quantitative research and surveys. See Nancy J. Weiss, *The National Urban League, 1910–1940* (New York: Oxford University Press, 1974), pp. 216–33; Arvarh E. Strickland, *History of the Chicago Urban League* (Chicago: University of Chicago Press, 1966), pp. 1–44; Jesse Thomas Moore, *A Search for Equality: The National Urban League, 1910–1961* (University Park: Pennsylvania State University Press, 1981), pp. 47–55.

10. Ellen Fitzpatrick, *Endless Crusade: Woman Social Scientists and Progressive Reform* (New York: Oxford University Press, 1990). The most famous study was, of course, the Pittsburgh Survey. Paul U. Kellogg, ed., *The Pittsburgh Survey*, 6 vols. (New York: Russell Sage Foundation, 1909–14). For the reform activities of the settlements, Allen F. Davis, *Spearheads for Reform: The Social Settlements and the Progressive Movement, 1890–1914* (New York: Oxford University Press, 1967); Clarke A. Chambers, *Seedtime of Reform: American Social Service and Social Action* (Ann Arbor: University of Michigan Press, 1967); Clarke A. Chambers, *Paul U. Kellogg and the Survey: Voices for Social Welfare and Social Justice* (Minneapolis: University of Minnesota Press, 1971).

11. Horace R. Cayton and George S. Mitchell, *Black Workers and the New Unions* (Chapel Hill: University of North Carolina Press, 1939), p. 3; Sterling D. Spero and Abram L. Harris, *The Black Worker* (New York: Columbia University Press, 1931), p. 246; U.S. Congress, Senate, Reports of the Immigration Commission, *Immigrants in Industries, Iron and Steel Manufacturing*, pt 2, vol. 1, p. 17. However, at the same date (1907), blacks formed 39 percent of steelworkers in the South.

12. John Foster Potts, "A History of the Growth of the Negro Population of Gary, Indiana" (M.A. thesis, Cornell University, 1937), p. 7; Dolly Millender, *Yesterday in Gary: A Brief History of the Negro in Gary, 1906–1967* (Gary, Ind: 1967), p. 23; U.S. Department of Labor, Division of Negro Economics, *Negro Migration in 1916–1917*, pp. 27–28, 118–22; Spero and Harris, *Black Worker*, p. 257; Edward Greer, "Racism and U.S. Steel, 1906–1974," *Radical America* 10 (September-October 1976): 49; William Gleason, "The Illinois Steel Company's Part in the War," in Mrs. Frank J. Sheehan, comp., "Gary in the World War," vol. 2, "Civilian History" (1923), p. 217, GPL.

13. *Negro Migration in 1916–1917*, pp. 21–36, 86–89, 118–22; George Haynes, comp., "Letters of Negro Migrants of 1916–1918," *Journal of Negro History* 4 (January 1919): 290–340; Louise Venable Kennedy, *The Negro Peasant Turns Cityward* (College Park, Md.: McGrath Publishing Co., 1969), pp. 41–57; Cayton and Mitchell, *Black Workers and the New Unions*, pp. 16–28; Greer, "Racism and U.S. Steel," pp. 46–47; Katherine Stone, "The Origins of Job Structures in the Steel Industry," *Radical America* (November-December 1973), pp. 3–34; John Fitch, *The Steel Workers* (New York: 1911, Arno Press, 1969), pp. 150–65.

14. John A. Fitch, "Old Age at Forty," *American Magazine* 71 (March 1911): 655–64; Charles A. Gulick, Jr., *Labor Policy of the United States Steel Corporation*, Columbia Studies in History, Economics and Public Law no. 116 (New York: Columbia University Press, 1924), p. 86; David Brody, *Steelworkers in America: The Nonunion Era* (New York: Harper and Row, 1969, Torchbooks edn., 1969), pp. 93–94; Gerald G. Eggert, *Steelmasters and Labor Reform, 1886–1923* (Pittsburgh: University of Pittsburgh Press, 1981).

15. "Statement of Significance," typewritten history of Stewart House, n.p., n.d. CRA.

16. Millender, *Yesterday in Gary*, p. 23; William Z. Foster, *The Great Steel Strike and Its Lessons* (New York: Huebsch, 1920), pp. 100–101.

17. Potts, "Growth of the Negro Population," pp. 7–8; Spero and Harris, *Black Worker*, p. 250; Dennis C. Dickerson, *Out of the Crucible: Black Steelworkers in Western Pennsylvania, 1875–1980* (Albany, N.Y.: SUNY Press, 1986), pp. 27–53.

18. Potts, "Growth of the Negro Population," p. 7. In the same decade, the percentage of foreign-born whites in Gary fell from 29.4 percent to 19.3 percent. U.S. Department of Commerce, Bureau of the Census, *Negroes in the United States, 1920–1932* (Washington, D.C.: Government Printing Office, 1935), p. 55; *Fourteenth Census of the United States, 1920*: vol. 2, *Population*, pp. 63, 760–61; *Fifteenth Census of the United States, 1930*: vol. 3 (pt. 1) *Population*, pp. 715, 720.

19. Jane Addams, *Second Twenty Years at Hull House* (New York: Macmillan, 1930), p. 396. For a discussion of social control, see James Leiby, "Social Control and Historical Explanation," in Walter I. Trattner, ed., *Social Welfare or Social Control? Some Historical Reflections on 'Regulating the Poor'* (Knoxville: University of Tennessee Press, 1983). Leiby points out that the term "social control" had a favorable connotation from the time it first came into use in the early twentieth century until the 1950s, when it took on its present invidious meaning, pp. 97–98.

20. Vincent P. Franklin, *Black Self-Determination: A Cultural History of the Faith of the Fathers* (Westport, Conn: Greenwood Press, 1984), pp. 203–4.

21. "Negroes Lured from South by Higher Wages, Take Foreigners' Jobs," Gary *Daily Tribune*, July 25, 1916; "Uplift of the Colored Race," Gary *Daily Tribune*, July 22, 1916, pp. 4, 8; "Neighborhood House for the Colored," Gary *Daily Tribune*, July 20, 1916, p. 4.

22. "Uplift of the Colored Race."

23. "Strong Appeal to Aid Colored People of Gary," Gary *Daily Tribune*, July 20, 1916, p. 1; "Neighborhood House for the Colored"; "A YMCA for Colored People," Gary *Tribune*, August 8, 1916, p. 4. Segregation was gradually being introduced into YMCAs in northern cities; the newer YWCAs established separate black branches from the beginning. See Adrienne Lash Jones, *Jane Edna Hunter: A Case Study of Black Leadership* (Brooklyn: Carson Publishers, 1990).

24. "Judge Gary Donates $250 to the African Methodist Church," Clipping File, GPL; Cayton and Mitchell, *Black Workers and the New Unions*, p. 390.

25. "The Most Contemptible Act," Gary *Evening Post*, August 23, 1917, p. 4. The title referred to the accusations of a newspaper in neighboring Hammond that the scheme smacked of segregation. Millender believed that the subdivision was planned to house skilled black steel workers from Pittsburgh. *Yesterday in Gary*, p. 29.

26. During the war, the average length of employment for blacks in steelmaking was one month. By 1924, it had risen to only three and one-half months, according to John T. Clark, "The Negro in Steel," *Opportunity* 4 (March 1926). See also Dickerson, *Out of the Crucible*, p. 102; Potts, "Growth of the Negro Population," p. 8; Elizabeth Balanoff, "A History of the Black Community of Gary, Indiana, 1906–1940" (Ph.D. dissertation, University of Chicago, 1974), p. 28; United States Steel Corporation, Bureau of Safety, Sanitation, and Welfare, *Bulletin*, no. 8 (1910), p. 78. "From the viewpoint of northern industry the outstanding problem of the Negro migration is that of the labor turnover," *Negro Migration in 1916–1917*, p. 122; J. W. Knapp, "An Experiment with Negro Labor," *Opportunity* 1 (February 1923): 19–20. For a different interpretation of high turnover rates see labor historians David Montgomery and Herbert Gutman who suggest that the behaviors condemned by employers as "shiftlessness" meant that workers were exerting their control by choosing where and when to work. David Montgomery, *Workers' Control in America: Studies in the History of Work, Technology, and Labor Struggles* (Cambridge: Cambridge University Press, 1979); Herbert G. Gutman, "Work, Cul-

ture and Society in Industrializing America, 1815–1919," *American Historical Review* 78 (June 1973), 531–88.

27. Black minister quoted in Cayton and Mitchell, *Black Workers and the New Unions*, p. 391. For Captain Norton's explanation of the company's plan see "The Most Contemptible Act."

28. Balanoff, "Black Community," p. 28. Advocates of the segregated black neighborhood like Thyra Edwards pointed out that it contained model housing at low rents. Edwards, "Interracial Project," p. 550; "Need Church, Amusement for Negroes," Gary *Daily Tribune*, June 20, 1919, p. 8.

29. "Survey Problems of Colored Race in Calumet Region," Gary *Daily Tribune*, May 16, 1919, p. 2; "Colored Minister to Help Solve Big Problems in Gary," Gary *Daily Tribune*, May 8, 1919, p. 2. Because blacks were being turned away by more and more places of amusement—parks, beaches, theaters, dance halls, YMCAs—there was a genuine problem of where they could spend their leisure time. "The institutions of wholesome recreation are beginning to close their doors to Negroes when the need is most dire," concluded a Pennsylvania study of 1917. Kennedy, *Negro Peasant Turns Cityward*, p. 210.

30. "Need Church, Amusement for Negroes." Many of these institutions are described in Elizabeth Balanoff's monumental "History of the Black Community of Gary, Indiana." Church membership figures are notoriously unreliable as a guide to church attendance or commitment, anyway, 50 percent seems high.

31. William Grant Seaman to Captain Norton, July 6, 1920, City Church Collection, CRA.

32. Ibid.

33. Ibid. Seaman was referring to L. I. H. Caldwell's support of the striking steelworkers in 1919. According to the Gary *Daily Tribune*, Caldwell addressed a meeting of strikers in October 1919 and accused ministers of supplying the mills with strikebreakers. "Ministers and Churches Attacked," Gary *Daily Tribune*, October 1, 1919, p. 8.

34. Seaman to Norton. Alumni clubs of Fisk, Meharry, and other black colleges were active in Gary in the twenties; "Askings," in "The Program of Methodism in Gary," City Church Collection, CRA. See also Balanoff, "Black Community," pp. 407 ff. On Meharry, see Darlene Clark Hine, "The Pursuit of Professional Equality: Meharry Medical College, 1921–1938," in Vincent P. Franklin and James D. Anderson, eds., *New Perspectives on Black Educational History* (Boston: G. K. Hall, 1978), pp. 173–92.

35. According to Captain Norton. "Presents Deed to Settlement House," Gary *Post Tribune*, January 16, 1928, p. 4.

36. Brody, *Steelworkers in America*, pp. 96–111, 273. The lives of immigrant steel workers are described in Fitch, *Steel Workers*, pp. 144–47; Margaret F. Byington, *Homestead: The Households of a Mill Town*, vol. 4 of *The Pittsburgh Survey*, ed. Paul Kellogg (New York: Russell Sage Foundation, 1909–14), pp. 131–33. See also John Bodnar, Roger Simon, and Michael P. Weber, *Lives of Their Own: Blacks, Italians and Poles in Pittsburgh, 1900–1960* (Urbana: University of Illinois Press, 1982).

37. Greer, "Racism and U.S. Steel," p. 48; Clark, "Negro in Steel," pp. 87–88; Spero and Harris, *Black Worker*, p. 145.

38. The welfare worker "gave us an insight into the peculiarities of their race," wrote John Knapp, "An Experiment with Negro Labor," pp. 19–20; Clark, "The Negro in Steel"; Cayton and Mitchell, *Black Workers and the New Unions*, p. 383; Dickerson, *Out of the Crucible*, pp. 104 ff; Gulick, *Labor Policy of the United States Steel Corporation*; Ida Tarbell, *The Life of Elbert H. Gary* (New York: D. Appleton, 1925), pp. 163–77. Welfare work in the iron-and-steel industry can be followed in the trade journal, the *Iron Age*. See, for example, "The Betterment of Labor Conditions in the Steel Industry," *Iron Age*, 86 (November 1910): 1030; Brody, *Steelworkers in America*, pp. 87–93; Eggert, *Steelmasters and Labor Reform*. For the rise of welfare work in other industries, see William H. Tolman, *Social Engineering: A Record of Things Done by American Industrialists Employing Upwards of One and One-Half Million of People* (New York: McGraw, 1909); Stephen J. Meyer, *The Five Dollar Day: Labor Management and Social Control in the Ford Motor Company, 1908–1921* (Albany, N.Y.: SUNY Press, 1981); Stuart Brandes, *American Welfare Capitalism, 1880–1940* (Chicago: University of Chicago Press, 1976); David Brody, "The Rise and Decline of Welfare Capitalism," in John Braeman, ed., *Change and Continuity in Twentieth Century America: The 1920s* (Columbus: Ohio State University Press, 1968); Daniel Nelson, *Managers and Workers: Origins of the New Factory System in the United States 1880–1920* (Madison: University of Wisconsin Press, 1975), pp. 101–21; Gerald Zahavi, *Workers, Managers, and Welfare Capitalism: The Shoeworkers and Tanners of Endicott Johnson, 1890–1950* (Urbana: University of Illinois Press, 1988); Robert Ozanne, *A Century of Labor-Management Relations at McCormick and International Harvester* (Madison: University of Wisconsin Press, 1967).

39. *Addresses and Statements of Elbert H. Gary*, 4:32–33. See also Dennis C. Dickerson, "The Black Church in Industrializing Western Pennsylvania, 1870–1950," *Western Pennsylvania Historical Magazine* 64 (October 1981), 329–44.

40. The first minister was Rev. John Whitlock; he died in 1917 and was replaced by a ministerial student. At the time of Delaney's appointment the minister was the J. W. V. Hutchinson, a graduate of Boston University School of Theology. Delaney wrote of his predecessor, "his intelligence challenged the respect of many of the leading people of this community." Learned and popular, Hutchinson did not match Seaman's pejorative stereotype of black preachers: it is interesting to speculate why Seaman and Norton agreed he had to be replaced. F. S. Delaney, "History of Trinity Methodist Episcopal Church and the John Stewart Memorial Settlement House by Rev. F. S. Delaney" (undated, probably written in 1935), pp. 1–4, CRA; "Statement of Significance," p. 2; "Trinity M.E. Church and Stewart House" (1925?).

41. Delaney, "History," pp. 2–3; "Opening of New Stewart House Home Tomorrow," *Gary Evening Post and Daily Tribune*, December 9, 1921, p. 4; Lane, *City of the Century*, pp. 194–95.

42. *Sixth Annual Report of the Activities of the John Stewart Memorial Settlement House*, 1926; *Stewart House at Trinity Methodist Episcopal Church* (March 1935).

43. Delaney, "History," p. 4; "Rev. Delaney Built Stewart House," Gary *Post Tribune*, September 21, 1974, by James B. Lane.

44. "Statement of Significance," n.p.

45. "Stewart House Pays Debts in New Program of Service," Gary *Colored American*, January 19, 1928, p. 2.

46. "Our Mendicant Priests," Gary *Colored American*, January 11, 1929, p. 4.

47. "Ministers and Churches Attacked," Gary *Daily Tribune*, October 1, 1919, p. 8. For the apology see Seaman to Norton, July 6, 1920, p. 3.

48. "Opening of New Stewart House Home Tomorrow." For Thyra Edwards see "Autobiographical Sketch" and "Professional History" (typescript), Thyra Edwards Papers, Box 1, Ch. H. S. Edwards was playground director for the Gary public schools, 1920–21; Lake County Juvenile Court probation officer, 1921–25; child-placing officer, Lake County Board of Children's Guardians, 1926–28; director, Lake County Children's Home, 1928–31. Edwards, "The Gary Interracial Project."

49. "The negro laborer is more accustomed to work for persons than for wages. When he gets a job, therefore, he is inclined to consider the source from which it comes." Spero and Harris, *Black Worker*, p. 129. Employers of Negro Labor might consciously have sought southern precedents. The *Iron Age*, in a discussion of the poor work habits of black migrants, suggested that "shiftless" workers could best be handled " by a man from the South who is familiar with their habits and characteristics." Quoted in Brody, *Steelworkers in America*, p. 186.

50. "Unveil Stone to Memory of John Stewart," Gary *Post Tribune*, November 30, 1925. p. 4.

51. T. J. Woofter, Jr., *Negro Problems in Cities* (New York: New York University Press, 1928).

52. "Stewart House Served Many in the Depression," by James B. Lane, Gary *Post Tribune*, September 22, 1974, usefully summarizes the settlement's relief work. Clipping File, GPL. Interviews with steelworkers are published in Cayton and Mitchell, *Black Workers and the New Unions*, p. 391. For the employment work of the Urban League, Weiss, *National Urban League*; Strickland, *History of the Chicago Urban League*; Balanoff, "Black Community," p. 317; Katznelson, *Black Men, White Cities*, pp. 105–19.

53. "John Stewart Settlement House at Trinity Methodist Episcopal Church" (Tenth Annual Report), November 11, 1930, n.p.

54. Balanoff, "Black Community," p. 263.

55. Gary *Sun*, August 26, 1927.

56. Mohl and Betten, *Steel City*, p. 50.

57. "Brief History of the Gary Branch NAACP" (n.p., n.d.), GPL.; Balanoff, "Black Community," pp. 411 ff; Betten and Mohl, "Evolution of Racism," p. 51; Mohl and Betten, *Steel City*, pp. 52, 55–56.

58. Franklin, *Black Self-Determination*. James D. Anderson, *The Education of Blacks in the South, 1860–1935* (Chapel Hill: University of North Carolina Press, 1988), contains much evidence about the determination of blacks, against overwhelming odds, to seek education.

59. The writer of the "Brief History of the Gary Branch NAACP" claimed that "everyone of any importance" in the black community in Gary in the 1920s supported the UNIA.

60. Editorial, "Stewart House," Gary *Colored American*, January 19, 1928; Millender, *Yesterday in Gary*, p. 36; Mohl and Betten, *Steel City*, p. 85; "Brief History of the Gary Branch NAACP."

61. For example, "Presents Deed to Settlement House," Gary *Post Tribune*, January 16, 1928, p. 4. Henry Burgess Snyder was editor of the Gary *Evening Post*; J. Ralph Snyder was business manager. The senior Snyder and another brother were also involved in the management of the *Evening Post and Daily Tribune*. Ralph Snyder was still actively supporting Stewart House in 1936. See, Gary *American*, March 13, 1936, p. 1; Mohl and Betten, *Steel City*, p. 83.

62. "Stewart House Head Ends Ninth Year Here Sunday," Gary *Post Tribune*, April 5, 1929, p. 29.

63. "Negro Cannot Win Promoting External Opposition" July 27, 1928, p. 1; "Negro Should Absorb White Culture," August 3, 1928; "Fate of Race in Its Own Hands," July 13, 1928, p. 2; "Debt," January 26, 1928, p. 8; "The Truth of Our Prejudices"; "Dying Woman Is Turned Away from D.C. Hospital. 'We Do Not Take Colored Patients,' says Doctor to Mother Dying of Gunshot Wounds," Gary *Colored American*, January 5, 1928.

64. U.S. Department of Labor, Children's Bureau, *Children of Preschool Age in Gary, Indiana*, by Elizabeth Hughes, Bureau Publication no. 122 (Washington, D.C.: Government Printing Office, 1922), pp. 19–23. "Europeans, Negroes, and Mexicans frequently occupy apartments in the same buildings, the Negroes, perhaps, being the only ones aware that there is anything unusual in such an arrangement," Edwards, "Gary Interracial Project," p. 546. "Blacks and immigrants arrived together and lived together in the city's early period to a degree not found in many other cities," Balanoff, "Black Community," p. ii.

65. This process is clearly delineated in Mohl and Betten, *Steel City*, pp. 65–73. See also Emma Lou Thornbrough, "Segregation in Indiana during the Klan Era of the 1920s," *Mississippi Valley Historical Review* 47 (March 1961): 594–618; Woofter, *Negro Problems in Cities*, p. 38.

66. Woofter, *Negro Problems in Cities*, pp. 122, 127, 137; *Negroes in the Unites States*, pp. 278, 285; Hughes, *Children of Preschool Age*, p. 22; U.S. Department of Commerce, Bureau of the Census, *Sixteenth Census of the United States: 1940, Housing, II, General Characteristics*, pt. 2 (Washington, D.C.: Government Printing Office, 1943), p. 925. The black population of Gary experienced a 238 percent increase between 1920 and 1930, causing increased pressure on available housing.

67. A study comparing homeowning among Poles, Germans, blacks, and Italians in Pittsburgh, concluded that the lower rate of ownership of blacks "resulted from a combination of job discrimination, greater independence of the children who might otherwise have contributed to savings, and perhaps more interest in career than property acquisition." Bodnar, Simon, and Weber, *Lives of Their Own: Blacks, Italians, and Poles in Pittsburgh*, p. 158. Olivier Zunz in his study of Detroit found that homeownership was "more an ethnocultural phe-

nomenon than one of class." But he ascribed blacks' failure to buy homes to "the brutal facts of segregation." Olivier Zunz, *The Changing Face of Inequality: Urbanization, Industrial Development, and Immigrants in Detroit, 1880–1920* (Chicago: University of Chicago Press, 1982), pp. 153, 397–98. Hughes, *Children of Preschool Age in Gary, Indiana,* shows that 35 percent of immigrant families owned their homes, but only 2 percent of black families, p. 22. Hughes's study was of families with preschool children; we should expect homeownership to be higher for such families than for those without children or for all families. However, the wide differences among the groups, native-born, foreign-born, and black, remain.

68. Kerns, "Social-Economic Conditions," pp. 16–17.

69. "Need Church, Amusement for Negroes," Gary *Daily Tribune,* June 20, 1919, p. 8.

70. Balanoff, "Black Community," pp. 245 ff; *Negroes in the United States,* pp. 374, 454. See also *Negro Migration, 1916–1917,* pp. 143–45; Edwards, "Gary Interracial Project," pp. 550–52. For evidence of protests by blacks against the insertion of restrictive clauses in real-estate deeds, see Quillen, "Industrial City," p. 416, n. 3.

71. *Negroes in the United States,* pp. 374, 454; *Negro Migration, 1916–1917,* pp. 143–45; Mohl and Betten, *Steel City,* p. 74.

72. "Brief History of the Gary Branch NAACP"; Balanoff, "Black Community," pp. 245, 350; Millender, *Yesterday in Gary,* p. 38; Mohl and Betten, *Steel City,* p. 63.

73. Delaney, "History," p. 6; *Sixth Annual Report of the Activities of the John Stewart Memorial Settlement House;* "Statement of Significance," p. 5; *Tenth Annual Report of John Stewart Settlement House, November 11, 1930,* n.p.

74. Ronald D. Cohen and Raymond A. Mohl, *The Paradox of Progressive Education: The Gary Plan and Urban Schooling* (Port Washington, N.Y.: Kennikat Press, 1979), pp. 110–22; Mohl and Betten, *Steel City,* pp. 55–60; Kennedy, *Negro Peasant Moves Cityward,* pp. 50–51.

75. Quoted in Mohl and Betten, *Steel City,* p. 82.

76. Ibid., p. 56.

77. Gary *Colored American,* November 10, 1927, p. 2.

78. Gary *American,* August 2, 1930. But by 1931 the same newspaper called the opening of Roosevelt School "an epoch in the history of Negroes in this state" and took pride in the fact that the million-dollar school was at least as good as any of the white schools. Cohen and Mohl, *Paradox of Progressive Education,* p. 140.

79. Letter from Ronald D. Cohen to the author, October 26, 1981.

80. Vincent P. Franklin, *The Education of Black Philadelphia* (Philadelphia: University of Pennsylvania Press, 1979), warns against drawing too sharp a difference between middle-class cultural and social organizations and organizations like the NAACP that were interested in the advancement of the race as a group—between "race-conscious" and "status-conscious" organizations. Both had an impact on the black community and both helped race advancement, Franklin argues, pp. 98–99. For Stewart House educational activities see *Sixth*

Annual Report; Eighth Annual Report, Stewart House; Delaney, "History," p. 6; Delaney, *Tenth Annual Report, John Stewart Memorial Settlement House,* November 11, 1930.

81. *Eighth Annual Report;* Kerns, "Social-Economic Conditions," p. 40.

82. Editorial, "We Speak of Parks," *Gary American,* June 14, 1935, p. 6; Betten and Mohl, "Evolution of Racism," p. 56; Mohl and Betten, *Steel City,* p. 60. U.S. Steel reserved a small stretch of beach for blacks on Lake Michigan, but after 1935, it no longer allowed them access—perhaps a punitive reaction to NAACP-led pressure for desegregation of parks and beaches. Balanoff, "Black Community," p. 462.

83. "Brief History of the Gary Branch NAACP"; Balanoff, "Black Community," pp. 459–60; Cayton and Mitchell, *Black Workers and the New Unions,* p. 140. Cayton and Mitchell transcribe the interview as follows: "The men were ultimately made to understand that if they or their children were found there, they would—of course, you understand—(lose their jobs) . . . "

84. Cayton and Mitchell, *Black Workers and the New Unions,* p. 140.

85. Gutman, "Work, Culture, and Society in Industrializing America," pp. 531–88; Weiss, *National Urban League.*

86. Greer, "Racism and U.S. Steel," p. 53; Delaney, "History"; *Sixth Annual Report; Stewart House at Trinity Methodist Episcopal Church;* "Eleven Thousand Poor People Fed in Gary," *Gary Colored American,* December 15, 1927; Weiss, *National Urban League;* Strickland, *History of the Chicago Urban League.*

87. "Brief History of the Gary Branch NAACP." A survey of women's employment reported in J. Harvey Kerns, "A Study of the Social Economic Conditions of the Negro Population, Gary, Indiana in 1944," showed that of 6,208 white women gainfully employed in 1940, 15 percent were in domestic work. Of 836 employed black women, 44 percent were in domestic work. Thirty-eight percent of whites but a negligible percentage of blacks were engaged in clerical and sales positions at that date, p. 9.

88. Balanoff, "Black Community," p. 504.

89. Brody, *Steelworkers in America,* pp. 267–70; Potts, "History of the Growth of the Black Population," p. 7; Greer, "Racism and U.S. Steel," p. 51; Cayton and Mitchell, *Black Workers and the New Unions,* pp. 17–28.

90. Paul S. Taylor, *Mexican Labor in the United States: The Calumet Region,* University of California Publications in Economics, vol. 7 (Berkeley: University of California Press, 1932), p. 190.

91. Ibid.

92. Ibid; *Gary Sun,* April 11, 1928.

93. "Brief History of the Gary Branch NAACP." For comments on Gleason, see interview with Reverend Hawkins in Quillen, "Industrial City," p. 421.

94. Kerns, "Social-Economic Conditions," p. 8. On the pay differential between black and white workers, Cayton and Mitchell, *Black Workers and the New Unions,* p. 29; Greer, "Racism and U.S. Steel," p. 52.

95. Franklin, *Black Self-Determination.*

96. "Local Pastor Dons Overalls in War on Present Day Evils," *Gary American,* February 13, 1932, p. 1. Overalls, that badge of working-class status,

made a dramatic statement of Delaney's appeal to poor blacks. In that pre-designer-jeans era, the effect must have been theatrical.

97. "He is the only colored man that can go into Mr.___ (a steel company official) office at any time." Presumably, the unnamed official was Mr. Norton. Cayton and Mitchell, *Black Workers and the New Unions*, p. 391.

98. Ibid., p. 391. Attendance at these meetings during 1925 and 1926 was over one hundred each week. *Sixth Annual Report of the John Stewart Memorial Settlement House, Gary, Indiana, 1926*; and *Eighth Annual Report of the . . . John Stewart Memorial Settlement House, 1928*.

99. Cayton and Mitchell, *Black Workers and the New Unions*, p. 390. Punctuation as in the original.

100. Ibid.

101. "Report of Frank S. Delaney, Pastor-Superintendent, to Board of Directors of Stewart Home, at Annual Meeting, Stewart House, January 20, 1938," pp. 3–4, GPL.

102. "Stewart House Drive Off to a Good Start," Gary *Colored American*, March 13, 1926, p. 1. Other speakers at this occasion were Captain Norton and Ralph Snyder. Blacks were deeply divided on their attitude to labor unions; their bitterness about the racism of the AFL unions predisposed them to distrust the new movement for industrial unionism. Balanoff, "Black Community," p. 222.

103. "The Job at Stewart House," Gary *American*, February 17, 1939.

104. Ibid. Elizabeth Balanoff does not discuss Delaney specifically, but she is sympathetic to the role of intermediaries like him. "Power brokers were always needed who could, on varying occasions, either appease or prod the white community." She sees the alternative, the separatism of the UNIA and others, as good for morale but ultimately impractical. Balanoff, "Black Community," pp. 225, 503.

105. Interview quoted in Cayton and Mitchell, *Black Workers and the New Unions*, August 29, 1934, p. 391.

Conclusion

1. For the settlements in the 1920s, see Clarke A. Chambers, *Seedtime of Reform: American Social Service and Social Action, 1918–1933* (Minneapolis: University of Minnesota Press, 1963). The social-unit plan, an example of experimental, neighborhood-based social reform, and its failure in the 1920s is described in Patricia Mooney Melvin, *The Organic City: Urban Definition and Neighborhood Organization, 1880–1920* (Lexington: University Press of Kentucky, 1987). The reaction against the maternal-and-child health system set up by the Sheppard-Towner Act is described in Sheila Rothman, *Woman's Proper Place: A History of Changing Ideals and Practices, 1870 to the Present* (New York: Harper Colophon Books, 1978), pp. 135–52. See also Molly Ladd-Taylor, *Raising a Baby the Government Way: Mothers' Letters to the Children's Bureau, 1915–1932* (New Brunswick, N.J.: Rutgers University Press, 1986), pp. 1–46.

2. For the English settlements, see Mrs. S. A. Barnett, *Canon Barnett: His Life, Work, and Friends. By His Wife*, 2 vols. (London: John Murray, 1921); Emily K. Abel, "Middle Class Culture for the Urban Poor: The Educational Thought of Samuel Barnett," *Social Service Review* 52 (1978), 596–620, and "Toynbee Hall, 1884–1914," *Social Service Review* 53 (1979), 606–32; Asa Briggs and Ann Macartney, *Toynbee Hall: The First Hundred Years* (London: Routledge and Kegan Paul, 1984); Standish Meacham, *Toynbee Hall and Social Reform, 1880–1914* (New Haven: Yale University Press, 1987). For the argument that the American settlements originated with the missions to freedmen, Ralph E. Luker, "Missions, Institutional Churches, and Settlement Houses: The Black Experience, 1885–1910," *Journal of Negro History* 69 (Summer-Fall 1984), 101–13; "The Social Gospel and the Failure of Racial Reform, 1877–1898," *Church History* 46 (March 1977), 176–246.

3. Aaron I. Abell, *American Catholicism and Social Action: A Search for Social Justice, 1865–1950* (South Bend, Ind.: University of Notre Dame Press, 1963).

4. Julia Lathrop, "Hull House as a Sociological Laboratory," *Proceedings of the National Conference on Charities and Corrections, Nashville, Tennessee, May 1894*, pp. 313–19; Allen F. Davis, *Spearheads for Reform: The Social Settlements and the Progressive Movement, 1890–1914*, 2d ed. (New Brunswick, N.J.: Rutgers University Press, 1984). See also Ellen Fitzpatrick, *Endless Crusade: Women Social Scientists and Progressive Reform* (New York: Oxford University Press, 1990).

5. This was the conclusion reached by Raymond A. Mohl and Neil Betten, "Paternalism and Pluralism: Immigrants and Social Welfare in Gary, Indiana, 1906–1940," *American Studies* 15 (Spring 1974), 5–30. In a recent revisionist study of Hull House, historian Rivka Lissak analyzed the relationship between Hull House workers and the immigrant communities surrounding the settlement. She found that the immigrants were very little influenced by Hull House, and that the Hull House relationship with the immigrants was characterized by the settlement workers' misunderstandings about immigrant cultures, misjudgment of immigrant values, and unrealistic assessment of the influence of Hull House on the neighborhood. Rivka Lissak, "Myth and Reality: The Patterns of Relationship Between the Hull House Circle and the 'New Immigrants' on Chicago's West Side, 1890–1919," *Journal of American Ethnic History* 2 (1983): 21–50.

6. John H. Holliday, "The Life of Our Foreign Population" (1908?), typescript, ISL.

7. Rivka Lissak, *Pluralism and Progressives: Hull House and the New Immigrants* (Chicago: University of Chicago Press, 1989); Raymond A. Mohl and Neil Betten, "The Immigrant Church in Gary, Indiana: Religious Adjustment and Cultural Defense," *Ethnicity* 8 (1981), 1–17. Hilda Satt Polacheck, *"I Came a Stranger": The Story of a Hull-House Girl* (Urbana: University of Illinois Press, 1989), is the story of an immigrant who embraced Hull House Americanization.

8. Davis, *Spearheads for Reform*; Cynthia Neverdon-Morton, *Afro-American Women of the South and the Advancement of the Race, 1895–1905* (Knoxville: University of Tennessee Press, 1989); Sharon Harley and Rosalyn Terborg-

Penn, eds., *The Afro-American Woman: Struggles and Images* (Port Washington, N.Y.: National University Publications, 1978); Jacqueline A. Rouse, *Lugenia Burns Hope: Black Southern Reformer* (Athens: University of Georgia Press, 1989).

9. For example, Linda M. Perkins, "Quaker Beneficence and Black Control: The Institute for Colored Youth, 1852–1903," in *New Perspectives on Black Educational History*, ed. Vincent P. Franklin and James D. Anderson (Boston: G. K. Hall, 1978).

10. For the importance of self-help organizations among African-Americans, see James O. and Lois E. Horton, *Black Bostonians: Family Life and Community Struggle in the Antebellum North* (New York, 1979); Howard Rabinowitz, *Race Relations in the Urban South, 1865–1890* (New York, 1978); Darlene Clark Hine, *When the Truth Is Told: A History of Black Women's Culture and Community in Indiana, 1875–1950* (Indianapolis: National Council of Negro Women, 1981).

11. Helen Horowitz, "Hull House as a Women's Space," *Chicago History*, 12 (Winter 1983–84), 40–55; Kathryn Kish Sklar, "Hull House in the 1890s: A Community of Women Reformers," *Signs* 10 (Summer 1985), 658–77; Blanche Wiesen Cook, "Female Support Networks and Political Activism: Lillian Wald, Crystal Eastman, Emma Goldman," in Nancy Cott and Elizabeth H. Pleck, eds., *A Heritage of Her Own: Toward a New Social History of American Women* (New York: Simon and Schuster, 1979), pp. 412–44; Estelle Freedman, "Separatism as Strategy: Female Institution Building, 1870–1930," *Feminist Studies* 5 (Fall 1979), 512–29. For material feminism, see Dolores Hayden, *The Grand Domestic Revolution: A History of Feminist Designs for American Homes, Neighborhoods, and Cities* (Cambridge: MIT Press, 1981).

12. Joanne Meyerowitz, *Women Adrift: Independent Wage-Earners in Chicago, 1880–1930* (Chicago: University of Chicago Press, 1988).

13. Most recently, Fitzpatrick, *Endless Crusade*. See also Barbara Sicherman, *Alice Hamilton: A Life in Letters* (Cambridge: Harvard University Press, 1984); Lela Costin, *Two Sisters for Social Justice: A Biography of Grace and Edith Abbott* (Urbana: University of Illinois Press, 1983); Allen F. Davis, *American Heroine: The Life and Legend of Jane Addams* (New York: Oxford University Press, 1973); Doris Groshen Daniels, *Always a Sister: The Feminism of Lillian D. Wald* (New York: Feminist Press, 1989). See also Mina Carson, "Agnes Hamilton of Fort Wayne: The Education of a Christian Settlement Worker," *Indiana Magazine of History* 80 (March 1984), 1–34.

14. Mrs. Bess Sheehan, Mrs. Clinton G. Clark, Mrs. George Hulbert, *History of Campbell Friendship House, Gary, Indiana, 1912–1940*, p. 7.

15. It would be rash to enter into the debate on the meaning(s) of "feminism" here. Readers should consult Nancy Cott, *The Grounding of Modern Feminism* (New Haven: Yale University Press, 1987), and "What's in a Name? The Limits of 'Social Feminism', or, Expanding the Vocabulary of Women's History," *Journal of American History* 76 (December 1989), 809–29.

16. This is "relational feminism" as defined by Karen Offen, "Defining Feminism: A Comparative Historical Approach," *Signs* 14, 1 (Autumn 1988), 119–57.

17. Phyllis Palmer, "Housework and Domestic Labor: Racial and Technological Change," in Karen Brodkin Sacks and Dorothy Remy, eds., *My Troubles Are Going to Have Trouble with Me: Everyday Trials and Triumphs of Women Workers* (New Brunswick, N.J.: Rutgers University Press, 1984), pp. 80–91.

18. Alice Kessler-Harris,"Women, Work, and the Social Order," in Berenice Carroll, ed., *Liberating Women's History* (Urbana: University of Illinois Press, 1976), p. 331; Mimi Abramowitz, *Regulating the Lives of Women: Social Welfare Policy from Colonial Times to the Present* (Boston: South End Press, 1988).

19. Mina Carson, *Settlement Folk: Social Thought and the American Settlement Movement, 1885–1930* (Chicago: University of Chicago Press, 1990), pp. 105–8; Eileen Boris, *Art and Labor: Ruskin, Morris, and the Craftsman Ideal in America* (Philadelphia: Temple University Press, 1986). See also Harry Braverman, *Labor and Monopoly Capital: The Degradation of Work in the Twentieth Century* (New York: Monthly Review Press, 1974).

20. Quoted in Davis, *Spearheads for Reform*, p. 103.

21. Ibid, p. 122.

22. Robert Wiebe, *Businessmen and Reform: A Study of the Progressive Movement* (Cambridge: Harvard University Press, 1962); Gabriel Kolko, *Railroads and Regulation, 1877–1916* (New York: W. W. Norton, 1965); James Weinstein, *The Corporate Ideal in the Liberal State* (Boston: Beacon Press, 1968); Judith Sealander, *Grand Plans: Business Progressivism and Social Change in Ohio's Miami Valley, 1890–1929* (Lexington: University Press of Kentucky, 1988). See also Larry G. Gerber, *The Limits of Liberalism: Josephus Daniels, Henry Stimson, Bernard Baruch, Donald Richberg, Felix Frankfurter and the Development of the Modern American Political Economy* (New York: New York University Press, 1983).

23. Roy Rosenzweig, *Eight Hours for What We Will: Workers and Leisure in an Industrial City, 1870–1920* (New York: Cambridge University Press, 1983), makes the argument that the community, no less than the workplace, was a battleground between workers and employers.

24. Judith A. Trolander, *Settlement Houses and the Great Depression* (Detroit: Wayne State University Press, 1975); *Professionalism and Social Change: From the Settlement House Movement to Neighborhood Centers, 1886 to the Present* (New York: Columbia University Press, 1987).

25. Charlotte Perkins Gilman, *The Living of Charlotte Perkins Gilman: An Autobiography* (New York: Harper and Row, 1975, first pub., 1935), pp. 184–85.

26. Quoted in Eric Foner, *Women and the American Labor Movement* (New York: Free Press, 1979), p. 290.

27. Robert Wiebe, *The Search for Order, 1877–1920* (New York: Hill and Wang, 1967).

28. Elbert Gary, public address, Gary, Ind., June 1922.

29. David Brody, *Steelworkers in America: The Nonunion Era* (New York: Harper and Row, 1960, Torchbooks ed., 1969), p. 107.

30. Christopher Lasch, *The New Radicalism in America, 1889–1963* (New York: Knopf, 1965); Don Kirschner, "The Ambiguous Legacy: Social Justice in the Progressive Era," *Historical Reflections* 2 (Summer 1975): 69–88.

31. Ralph E. Pumphrey, "Compassion and Protection: Dual Motivations in Social Welfare," *Social Service Review* 33 (March 1959): 21–29.

Bibliography

Settlement House Reports and Pamphlets

American Settlement, Indianapolis. *Annual Report of American Settlement,* 1928–29.
Butler College Settlement Association, Indianapolis, Indiana, 1905.
Campbell House, Gary, *Report.* 1922.
Campbell Settlement, Gary, Indiana. October 1931.
Cis, Rev. James. *Gary-Alerding Settlement House. Silver Jubilee of Community Service.* Pamphlet. 1949.
Christamore, The College Settlement of Indianapolis. 1906–07.
Christamore House Report. Over A Period of Twenty-Five Years. 1907–32.
Christamore, The College Settlement Association of Indianapolis. 1911.
———— . *The College Settlement Association. Christamore.* 1912.
The College Settlement in Indianapolis. Christamore. 1907.
Davis, Arthur W. "History of Stewart House." n.d. Typescript.
Delaney, Rev. Frank S. "History of Trinity Methodist Episcopal Church and the John Stewart Memorial Settlement House, by Rev. F. S. Delaney." 1935?
———— . "Report of Frank S. Delaney, Pastor-Superintendent, to Board of Directors of Stewart House, at Annual Meeting, Stewart House, 20 January 1938."
"Features of the Week-Day Work—A Day at Gary Neighborhood House." Pamphlet. 1920?
Fifty Years in Christian Fellowship. The Story of Katherine House. (East Chicago) 1957.
Flanner Guild, Industrial Neighborhood House. *Second Annual Report of the Flanner Guild Industrial Neighborhood House.* 1904.
———— . *Third Annual Report, Flanner Guild.* 1905.
———— . *Annual Report of the Flanner Guild.* 1910.
Flanner House. *Flanner House Annual Report. Twenty-First Year.* 1919.
———— . *Flanner House Report.* 1920–21.
———— . *Annual Report, Flanner House, From October 1, 1920 to June 30, 1921.* January 1922.
———— . *Flanner House Annual Report, July 1, 1922 to June 30, 1923.*
Flanner House Employment Department. "Circulation of Information Concerning Day Workers." n.d. 1922?
Foreign House Yearbook. At Mary Rigg Center.
The Gary Neighborhood House. A Statistical Statement of 1918 Accomplishments. Pamphlet.

Gary Neighborhood House. *Eleventh Annual Report of the Superintendent*. April 1, 1920.

———. "Minutes." October 22, 1913 to August 8, 1936. Handwritten.

———. *Annual Report of the Gary Neighborhood House*. April 1, 1938 to April 1, 1939.

———. *Statistical Statement of Attendance at Activities*, April 1920 - April 1921.

"History of Flanner House." n.d. Typescript.

"History of the Gary Neighborhood House." 1915.

Illinois Steel Company Gleason Center. *Report of the Gleason Center for the Year 1929*. Typescript. Bound in "History of Gary Organizations by Members."

Immigrants' Aid Association (Indianapolis). *First Annual Report of the Immigrants' Aid Association of Indianapolis, Indiana*. 1911–12. Pamphlet.

———. *Second Annual Report of the Immigrants' Aid Association*. 1912–13. Pamphlet.

Jones, Henry David. *Twenty Years of Neighborliness*. Pamphlet. 1929.

The Judge Gary-Bishop Alerding Settlement House. Pamphlet.

Martin. Rev. H. R. "The Gary Neighborhood House." 1924–25.

Neighborhood House Visitor. 1916.

Sheehan, Mrs. Bess; Clark, Mrs. Clinton G.; and Hulbert, Mrs. George. *History of Campbell Friendship House, Gary, Indiana, 1912-1940*.

Stewart House, Gary. *Sixth Annual Report of the John Stewart Memorial Settlement House, Gary, Indiana*. 1926.

———. *Eighth Annual Report of the John Stewart Memorial Settlement House, Gary, Indiana*. 1928.

———. *Tenth Annual Report of John Stewart Settlement House*. November 11, 1930.

———. *Eleventh Annual Report, Stewart House*. November 1930.

Stover, Anna. "Reminiscent History of Christamore the College Settlement." 1911. Typescript. Original in the possession of Mr. Ray Spencer, director of Christamore from 1955–65.

Stover, Anna, and Edith Surbey. "Remembrances." n.d. Typescript. Original in possession of Mr. Ray Spencer.

Travis, Mrs. C. Claude. *Campbell Settlement, Gary, Indiana*. Cincinnati, Ohio: Women's Home Missionary Society, 1929?

Warmington, Grace Mary. "Gary Neighborhood House."

Unpublished Materials

American Baptist Home Mission Society. "The Foreign Problem in Northwest Indiana." 1918. Pamphlet. GPL.

"Brief History of the Gary Branch NAACP" n.p., n.d. GPL.

City Methodist Church. "City Methodist Church (First Methodist Church), Gary, Indiana, 1906–1956."

———. "Building Fund 1920." Box Dc 58, DePauw.

———. "First Methodist Episcopal Church, Gary, Indiana. Types of Ministry."

———— . First Methodist Church, Gary, Indiana. Official Board Minutes. Box
Mc 115. Handwritten. DePauw.

———— . "Program of the Methodist Episcopal Church, Gary, Indiana. Proposed First Church." P. 13. Box Mc 60. DePauw.

Gary, Indiana Chamber of Commerce. "Report of the Commercial Club Committee of the Chamber of Commerce." November 1925. GPL.

"Historical Sketch of the Lithuanians in Gary." Pamphlet. GPL.

Indianapolis Free Kindergarten Society. "History of the Indianapolis Free Kindergarten Society, 1930–1931." Box 166, Typescript. Blaker Papers. IHS.

Holliday, John H. "The Life of Our Foreign Population." n.d. 1908? Typescript.
ISL.

Indianapolis Charity Organization Society. "Report of the Businessmen's Committee of the Indianapolis COS for the Year 1890–1891." Indianapolis,
1891. ISL.

International Institute. "Survey, 1929." II Miscellaneous Papers. CRA.

International Institute. "Changes in the Foreign Communities, Gary, Indiana."
October 3, 1929. Hernandez Folder, II Papers. CRA.

Kerns, J. Harvey. "A Study of the Social and Economic Conditions of the Negro Population of Gary, Indiana." Urban League, 1944. Mimeographed. GPL.

"Kindergarten Spearheads Gary's First Social Work." Pamphlet written for Gary
Golden Jubilee, 1956. CRA.

Leming, Bertha. "Indianapolis Chapter, American Association of Social Workers, 1923–1946." June 1946. Pamphlet. IUPUI.

Lewis, Beatrice. "City Methodist Church." n.d. Church History File, DePauw.

McCulloch, Oscar C. "The Opportunity of the Commercial Club." Address to
the Board of Directors of the Indianapolis Commercial Club, July 8, 1890.
ISL.

Mead, George Herbert. "The Functions of the Settlement." In "Minutes, National Conference of Settlements, St. Louis, June 1910." In National Federation of Settlements, "Minutes." Bound together. UNH.

National Bureau of Municipal Research. "Survey of Social Agencies in Indianapolis, 1918." Mimeographed. IUPUI.

National Federation of Settlements. Conference Reports, 1910–22. Bound together. UNH.

Public Health Nursing Association. "Report of the Public Health Nursing Association Clinic at the American Settlement." March 24, 1932. Typescript.
ISL.

Rigg, Mary. "My Own Record." Typescript. Mary Rigg Center.

———— . "Southwest Social Center." n.d. (1959?). Mary Rigg Center.

Rowlinson, Carlos. Rev. "The Neighborhood House." Address to the Local
Council of Women's Clubs, Indianapolis, January 2, 1901. ISL.

Seaman, Rev. William Grant. "The Calumet Region." 1921.

Sheehan, Mrs. Frank J., comp., "Gary in the World War." 2 vols. 1923. Typescript. GPL.

"Training School for Social Workers, Indianapolis, Indiana." 1912. Pamphlet.
ISL.

Theses and Dissertations

Balanoff, Elizabeth. "A History of the Black Community of Gary, Indiana, 1906–1940." Ph.D. dissertation, University of Chicago, 1974.

Barrows, Robert. "A Demographic Analysis of Indianapolis, 1870–1920." Ph.D. dissertation, Indiana University, 1977.

Clark, James O. "The First Fifty Years at Christamore House, 1905–1955." M.A. thesis, Indiana University, 1955.

Davis, Allen F. "Spearheads for Reform: The Social Settlements and the Progressive Movement, 1890–1914." PhD. dissertation, University of Wisconsin, 1959.

Farner, David. "Indiana, The Press, and the Red Scare of 1920." M.A. thesis, Purdue University, 1979.

Herrick, John. "A Holy Discontent: The History of the New York City Social Settlements, 1919–1941." Ph.D. dissertation, University of Minnesota, 1970.

Jones, Adrienne Lash. "Jane Edna Hunter: A Case Study of Black Leadership, 1910–1950." Ph.D. dissertation, Case Western Reserve University, 1983.

Karger, Howard J. "The Sentinels of Order: A Case Study of Social Control and the Minneapolis Settlement House Movement, 1897–1950." Ph.D. dissertation, University of Illinois, 1984.

Kershner, Frederick Doyle, Jr. "A Social and Cultural History of Indianapolis, 1860–1914." Ph.D. dissertation, University of Wisconsin, 1950.

Magnuson, Norris A. "Salvation in the Slums: Evangelical Social Welfare Work, 1865–1920." Ph.D. dissertation, University of Minnesota, 1968.

Nimmons, Julius Francis, Jr. "Social Reform and Moral Uplift in the Black Community 1890–1910: Social Settlements, Temperance, and Social Purity." Ph.D. dissertation, Howard University, 1981.

Piepho, Lois Ann. "The History of the Social Service Department of the Indiana University Medical Center, 1911–1932." M.A. thesis, Indiana University School of Social Service, June 1950.

Potts, John Foster. "A History of the Growth of the Negro Population of Gary, Indiana." M.A. thesis, Cornell University, 1937.

Probst, Theodore G. "The Germans in Indianapolis, 1850–1914." M.A. thesis, Indiana University, 1951.

Quillen, Isaac J. "Industrial City. A History of Gary, Indiana, to 1929." Ph.D. dissertation, Yale University, 1942.

Rigg, Mary, "A Survey of the Foreigners in the American Settlement District of Indianapolis." M.A. thesis, Indiana University, 1925.

Rikard, Marlene Hunt. "An Experiment in Welfare Capitalism: The Health Care Services of the Tennessee Coal, Iron and Railroad Company." Ph.D. dissertation, University of Alabama, 1983.

Stammel, Elavina S., and Parks, Charles R. "The Slavic Peoples in Indianapolis." M.S. thesis, Department of Economics and Sociology, Indiana University, 1930.

Newspapers

Freeman (Indianapolis), 1888–1904
Gary *American*, 1926–39
Gary *Colored American*, 1928–29
Gary *Daily Tribune*, 1910–26
Gary *Evening Post*, 1917–22
Gary *Evening Post and Daily Tribune*, 1921–22
Gary *Post Tribune*, 1922–28
Indiana Catholic and Record, 1919
Indianapolis *News*, 1902–25
Indianapolis *Star*, 1907–29
New York Times, 1919
WPA *Chicago Foreign Language Press Survey*, selected reels

Miscellaneous Serial Publications

American Iron and Steel Institute. *Bulletin of the American Iron and Steel Institute.* 1917.
Christian Women's Board of Missions, *Missionary Tidings* (Indianapolis). Selected issues, 1913–20.
Indiana University Bulletin. Selected issues, 1911–18.
Indianapolis Board of Health. *Report of the Indianapolis Board of Health.* 1902, 1911.
Indianapolis Charity Organization Society. *Yearbook of the Indianapolis Charity Organization Society,* 1898–99, 1902–3, 1914–15.
Indianapolis Free Kindergarten Association. *Superintendent's Reports, Indianapolis Free Kindergarten Association.* 1889–1911.
Iron Age, 1902–22.
Northwest Conference of the Methodist Episcopal Church. *Minutes of the Northwest Conference of the Methodist Episcopal Church.*
United States Steel Corporation, Bureau of Safety, Sanitation, and Welfare. *Bulletins of the U.S. Steel Corporation Bureau of Safety, Sanitation, and Welfare.* 1911–19.
——— . *Reports of the United States Steel Corporation.*
World Call. (Indianapolis). Selected issues, 1920–29.

Government Publications

U.S. Congress. Senate. *Report on Conditions of Employment in the Iron and Steel Industry.* S. Doc. 110, 62d Cong., 1st sess., 1913.
U.S. Department of Commerce. Bureau of the Census. *Tenth Census of the United States, 1880: Population.*

————— . *Twelfth Census of the United States, 1900: Population*, vol. 1.

————— . *Twelfth Census of the United States, 1900: Occupations at the Twelfth Census.*

————— . *Thirteenth Census of the United States, 1910:* vol. 4, *Population, Occupation Statistics.*

————— . *Thirteenth Census of the United States, 1910:* vol. 9, *Manufactures.*

————— . *Fourteenth Census of the United States, 1920:* vol. 2, *Population.*

————— . *Fourteenth Census of the United States, 1920:* vol. 3, *Population.*

————— . *Fourteenth Census of the United States, 1920:* vol. 4, *Population, Occupations.*

————— . *Fourteenth Census of the United States, 1920:* vol. 5, *Agriculture.*

————— . *Fourteenth Census of the United States, 1920:* vol. 9, *Manufactures.*

————— . *Fifteenth Census of the United States, 1930:* vol. 1, *Population.*

————— . *Fifteenth Census of the United States, 1930:* vol. 2, *Population.*

————— . *Fifteenth Census of the United States, 1930:* vol. 3, pt. 1, *Population.*

————— . *Fifteenth Census of the United States, 1930:* vol. 4, *Population, Occupations by States.*

————— . *Negroes in the United States, 1920–1932.*

————— . *Religious Bodies, 1906,* 2 vols.

————— . *Religious Bodies, 1916,* 2 vols.

U.S. Department of Labor, Bureau of Labor Statistics. *Wages and Hours of Labor in the Iron and Steel Industry.* Washington, D.C., 1922.

U.S. Department of Labor, Children's Bureau. *Children of Preschool Age in Gary, Indiana.* Pt. 1, *General Conditions Affecting Child Welfare,* by Elizabeth Hughes. Pt. 2, *Diet of the Children,* by Dr. Lydia Roberts. Bureau publication no. 122. 1922.

U.S. Department of Labor. Children's Bureau. *Infant Mortality, Results of a Field Study in Gary, Indiana, Based on Births in One Year,* by Elizabeth Hughes. Bureau publication no. 112. 1923.

U.S. Immigration Commission. *Reports, Immigrants in Industries, Iron and Steel Manufacturing,* pt. 2, vols. 1, 2.

Books and Articles

Abel, Emily K. "Middle Class Culture for the Urban Poor: The Educational Thought of Samuel Barnett." *Social Service Review* 52 (1978): 596–620.

————— . "Toynbee Hall, 1884–1914." *Social Service Review* 53 (1979): 606–32.

Abel, Theodore. *Protestant Home Missions to Catholic Immigrants.* New York: Institute of Social and Religious Research, 1933.

Abell, Aaron I. *The Urban Impact on American Protestantism, 1865–1900.* Cambridge: Harvard University Press, 1943.

————— . *American Catholicism and Social Action: A Search for Social Justice, 1865–1950.* South Bend, Ind.: University of Notre Dame Press, 1963.

Abramowitz, Mimi. *Regulating the Lives of Women: Social Welfare Policy from Colonial Times to the Present.* Boston: South End Press, 1988.

Adams, Leander M. Campbell. *An Investigation of Housing and Living Conditions in Three Districts of Indianapolis.* Indiana University Studies, vol. 8, no. 8. Bloomington: Indiana University Press, 1910.

Addams, Jane. "The Subjective Necessity for Social Settlements." In Jane Addams et al., *Philanthropy and Social Progress.* New York: Thomas A. Crowell, 1893, pp. 1–26.

———. "The College Woman and the Family Claim." *Commons* 3 (September 5, 1898): 3–5.

———. "The Subtle Problems of Charity." *Atlantic Monthly* 83 (1899): 165–78.

———. *The Spirit of Youth and the City Streets.* New York: Macmillan, 1910.

———. *Second Twenty Years at Hull House.* New York: Macmillan, 1930.

———. *My Friend, Julia Lathrop.* New York: Macmillan, 1935.

———. *Twenty Years at Hull House.* New York: Macmillan, 1910, Signet ed. 1960.

"An Appeal for a New Work." February 12, 1889, n.p. In College Settlements Association, *Annual Reports,* vols. 1–7.

Archdeacon, Thomas J. *Becoming American: An Ethnic History.* New York: Free Press, 1983.

Arnove, Robert F., ed. *Philanthropy and Cultural Imperialism: The Foundations at Home and Abroad.* Bloomington: Indiana University Press, 1980.

Bacon, Albion Fellows. "The Awakening of a State, Indiana." *Survey* 25 (1910–11): 467–73.

———. "The Housing Problem in Indiana." *Charities and the Commons* 21 (December 1908): 376–83.

Baker, Ray Stannard. "The Color Line in the North." *American Magazine* 65 (February 1908): 345–57.

———. "The Negro's Struggle for Survival in the North." *American Magazine* 65 (November 1907): 473–84.

Barnett, Canon Samuel. "Education by Permeation." *Charities and the Commons* 16 (May 5, 1906): 186–88.

———, and Barnett, Henrietta. *Practicable Socialism.* London: Longmans, Green, 1915.

Barnhardt, John D., and Carmony, Donald F. *Indiana. From Frontier to Industrial Commonwealth.* 4 vols. New York: Lewis Historical Publishing Company, 1954.

Barrows, Robert. "The Homes of Indiana: Albion Fellows Bacon and Housing Reform Legislation, 1907–1917." *Indiana Magazine of History* 8 (December 1985): 309–50.

Bender, Thomas. *Community and Social Change in America.* Baltimore: The Johns Hopkins University Press, 1978.

Betten, Neil, and Mohl, A. Raymond. "From Discrimination to Repatriation: Mexican Life in Gary, Indiana, during the Great Depression." *Pacific Historical Review* 42 (August 1973): 370–88.

———. "The Evolution of Racism in an Industrial City." *Journal of Negro History* 59 (1974): 51–64.

Bliss, W. D. P. "The Church and Social Method." *Outlook* (January 20, 1906): 122–25.

Bodnar, John. *The Transplanted: A History of Immigrants in Urban America.* Bloomington: Indiana University Press, 1985.

———; Simon, Roger; and Weber, Michael P. *Lives of Their Own: Blacks, Italians, and Poles in Pittsburgh, 1900–1960.* Urbana: University of Illinois Press, 1982.

Borchert, James. *Alley Life in Washington: Family, Community, Religion, and Folklife in the City, 1850–1970.* Urbana: University of Illinois Press, 1980.

Boris, Eileen, and Bardaglio, Peter, "Gender, Race, and Class: The Impact of the State on the Family and the Economy, 1790–1945." In Gerstel, Naomi, and Gross, Harriet Engel, eds. *Families and Work: Towards Reconceptualization.* Philadelphia: Temple University Press, 1987: pp. 132–51.

Bourne, Randolph S. "Trans-National America." *Atlantic Monthly* 118 (July 1916): 86–97.

Boyer, Paul. *Urban Masses and Moral Order in America, 1820–1920.* Cambridge: Harvard University Press, 1978.

Brandes, Stuart D. *American Welfare Capitalism, 1880–1940.* Chicago: University of Chicago Press, 1970.

Brody, David. *Labor in Crisis: The Great Steel Strike of 1919.* Philadelphia: J. Lippincott, 1965.

———. *Steelworkers in America: The Nonunion Era.* New York: Harper and Row, 1960, Torchbooks ed. 1969.

———. "The Rise and Decline of Welfare Capitalism." In Brody, *Workers in Industrial America: Essays on the Twentieth Century Struggle.* New York: Oxford University Press, 1980.

Browne, Henry J. "The 'Italian Problem' in the Catholic Church of the United States, 1880–1900." *United States Catholic Historical Society, Records and Studies* 35 (New York, 1946): 46–72.

Bruno, Frank. *Trends in Social Work as Reflected in the Proceedings of the National Conference of Social Work, 1874–1946.* New York: Columbia University Press, 1948.

Buffington, Eugene J. "Making Cities for Workmen." *Harper's Weekly* 53 (May 8, 1909).

Buroker, Robert L. "From Voluntary Association to Welfare State: The Illinois Immigrants' Protective League, 1908–1926." *Journal of American History* 58 (December 1971): 643–60.

Butera, Ronald J. "A Settlement House and the Urban Challenge: Kingsley House in Pittsburgh, Pennsylvania, 1893–1920." *Western Pennsylvania Historical Magazine* 66 (January 1983): 25–47.

Byington, Margaret. *Homestead, the Households of a Mill Town.* Vol. 4 of *The Pittsburgh Survey*, ed. Paul U. Kellogg, 6 vols. New York: Charities Publication Committee, 1909–14.

Carson, Mina. "Agnes Hamilton of Fort Wayne: The Education of a Christian Settlement Worker." *Indiana Magazine of History* 80 (March 1984): 1–34.

———. *Settlement Folk: Social Thought and the American Settlement Movement 1885–1930.* Chicago: University of Chicago Press, 1990.

Cavallo, Dominick. *Muscles and Morals: Organized Playgrounds and Urban Reform, 1880–1920.* Philadelphia: University of Pennsylvania Press, 1981.

Cayton, Horace R., and Mitchell, George S. *Black Workers and the New Unions.* Chapel Hill: University of North Carolina Press, 1939.

Chambers, Clarke A. *Paul U. Kellogg and the Survey.* Minneapolis: University of Minnesota Press, 1971.

———. *Seedtime of Reform: American Social Service and Social Action.* Ann Arbor: University of Michigan Press, 1967.

———. "Toward a Redefinition of Welfare History." *Journal of American History* 73 (September 1986): 407–33.

Clark, John T. "Negro in Steel." *Opportunity* 4 (March 1926): 87–88.

Clark, Joseph B., D.D. *Leavening the Nation: The Story of American Home Missions.* New York: Baker and Taylor, 1903.

Coben, Stanley. "A Study in Nativism: The American Red Scare of 1919–1920." *Political Science Quarterly* 79 (March 1964): 52–75.

Cohen, Ronald D., and Mohl, Raymond A. *The Paradox of Progressive Education: The Gary Plan and Urban Schooling.* Port Washington, N.Y.: Kennikat Press, 1979.

Coleman, C. B. "The College Settlement in Indianapolis." *Indiana Bulletin of Charities and Corrections* 79 (December 1909): 432–33.

Conway, Jill. "Women Reformers and American Culture, 1870–1930." *Journal of Social History* 5 (Winter 1971–72): 164–77.

Cook, Blanche Wiesen. "Female Support Networks and Political Activism: Lillian Wald, Crystal Eastman, Emma Goldman." In Cott, Nancy F., and Pleck, Elizabeth H., eds. *A Heritage of Her Own: Toward a New Social History of American Women.* New York: Simon and Schuster, 1979. pp. 412–44.

Costin, Lela. *Two Sisters for Social Justice: A Biography of Grace and Edith Abbott.* Urbana: University of Illinois Press, 1983.

Couvares, Francis G. *The Remaking of Pittsburgh: Class and Culture in an Industrializing City, 1877–1919.* Albany: SUNY Press, 1984.

———. "The Triumph of Commerce: Class Culture and Mass Culture in Pittsburgh." In Frisch, Michael H., and Walkowitz, Daniel J., eds. *Working-Class America: Essays on Labor, Community, and American Society.* Urbana: University of Illinois Press, 1983. pp. 122–52.

Cremin, Lawrence. *The Transformation of the School: Progressivism in American Education, 1876–1957.* New York: Knopf, 1961.

Crenik, Mary White. "The Color Line In Social Work." *Charities* 14 (April 8, 1905): 645–46.

Crocker, Ruth Hutchinson. "Making Charity Modern: Business and the Reform of Charities in Indianapolis, 1879–1930." *Business and Economic History,* 2d ser., 12 (1984): 158–70.

———. "Christamore: An Indiana Settlement House from Private Dream to Public Agency." *Indiana Magazine of History* 88 (June 1987): 113–40.

Cronon, E. David. *Black Moses—The Story of Marcus Garvey and the Universal Negro Improvement Association.* Madison: University of Wisconsin Press, 1969 [1965].

Cross, Robert D., ed. *The Church and the City.* Indianapolis: Bobbs-Merrill, 1967.

Daniels, John. *America via the Neighborhood.* Boston: Harper Bros., 1920.

——— . *In Freedom's Birthplace: A Study of the Boston Negroes.* New York: Negro Universities Press, 1914, repr. ed. 1968.

Davis, Allen F. *American Heroine: The Life and Legend of Jane Addams.* New York: Oxford University Press, 1973.

——— , and McCree, Mary Lynn. *Eighty Years at Hull House.* Chicago: Quadrangle Books, 1969.

——— . *Spearheads for Reform: The Social Settlements and the Progressive Movement 1890–1914.* New York: Oxford University Press, 1967, 2d ed. New Brunswick, N.J.: Rutgers University Press, 1984. With a new introduction by the author.

——— . "The Women's Trade Union League: Origins and Organization." *Labor History* 5 (Winter 1964): 3–17.

Davis, Rev. J. D. "Foreign Missions at Home." *Charities and the Commons* 1 (July 4, 1896): 3–5.

Davis, Lawrence B. *Immigrants, Baptists and the Protestant Mind in America.* Urbana: University of Illinois Press, 1973.

Detzler, Jack. *History of the Northwest Conference of the Methodist Episcopal Church.* Nashville, Tenn.: Parthenon Press, 1953.

Devine, Edward T. *The Practice of Charity.* New York: Lentilhon, 1901.

Dickerson, Dennis C. *Out of the Crucible: Black Steelworkers in Western Pennsylvania, 1875–1980.* Albany: State University of New York Press, 1986.

——— . "The Black Church in Industrializing Western Pennsylvania, 1870–1950." *Western Pennsylvania Historical Magazine,* 64 (October 1981): 329–44.

Diner, Steven J. "Chicago Social Workers and Blacks in the Progressive Era." *Social Service Review* 44 (December 1970): 379–92.

Divita, James J. *Slaves to No One: A History of the Holy Trinity Catholic Community in Indianapolis, . . .* Indianapolis, 1981.

Dolan, Jay. *The Immigrant Church: New York's Irish and German Catholics, 1815–1865.* Baltimore, Md.: The Johns Hopkins University Press, 1975.

Drake, St. Clair, and Cayton, Horace R. *Black Metropolis: A Study of Negro Life in a Northern City.* New York: Harcourt Brace, 1945.

Du Bois, William E. Burghardt, ed. *Efforts for Social Betterment among Negro Americans: Report of a Study Made by Atlanta University.* Atlanta University Publications, no. 14. Atlanta: Atlanta University Press, 1909.

——— . *The Philadelphia Negro—A Social Study.* New York: Schocken Books, 1899, repr. ed. 1967.

——— and Dill, Augustus Granville, eds. *The Negro American Artisan.* Atlanta University Publications, no. 17. Atlanta, Ga., 1912.

Duffus, Robert L. *Lillian Wald: Neighbor and Crusader.* New York: Macmillan, 1938.

Dunn, Jacob Piatt. *Representative Citizens of Indiana.* Indianapolis: B. F. Bowen, 1912.

———. *Greater Indianapolis: The History, the Industries, the Institutions, the People of a City of Homes.* 2 vols. Chicago: Lewis, 1910.

Edmondson, Edna Hatfield. *Juvenile Delinquency and Adult Crime in Gary, Indiana, with Special Reference to the Immigrant Population.* Indiana University Studies, vol. 8. Bloomington: Indiana University Press, June 1921.

Edwards, Thyra. "The Gary Interracial Project." *Southern Workman* 54 (December 1925): 545–53.

Eggert, Gerald G. *Steelmasters and Labor Reform, 1886–1923.* Pittsburgh: University of Pittsburgh Press, 1981.

Encyclopedia of Social Work. "Professional Organization," by David W. French. New York: National Association of Social Workers, 1965.

Ewen, Elizabeth. *Immigrant Women in the Land of Dollars: Life and Culture on the Lower East Side, 1890–1925.* New York: Monthly Review Press, 1985.

Faulkner, Harold U. *The Quest for Social Justice, 1898–1914.* New York: Macmillan, 1931.

Ferguson, Earline Ray. "The Woman's Improvement Club of Indianapolis: Black Women Pioneers in Tuberculosis Work, 1903–1938." *Indiana Magazine of History* 84 (September 1988): 237–61.

Fitch, John A. "Old Age at Forty." *American Magazine* 71 (March 1911): 655–64.

———. *The Steel Workers.* Vol. 3 of *The Pittsburgh Survey,* ed. Paul U. Kellogg. 6 vols. New York: Charities Publication Committee, 1909–14.

Fitzpatrick, Ellen. *Endless Crusade: Women Social Scientists and Progressive Reform.* New York: Oxford University Press, 1990.

Flexner, Abraham. "Is Social Work a Profession?" NCCC, *Proceedings of the 42nd Meeting of the NCCC.* Baltimore, Md., pp. 576–90.

Foner, Eric. "Why Is There No Socialism in the United States?" *History Workshop* 17 (Spring 1984): 57–80.

Foster, William Z. *The Great Steel Strike and Its Lessons.* New York: B. W. Huebsch, 1920.

Fox-Genovese, Elizabeth. "The Political Crisis of Social History." In Fox-Genovese, Elizabeth, and Genovese, Eugene D., *Fruits of Merchant Capital: Slavery and Bourgeois Property in the Rise and Expansion of Capitalism.* New York: Oxford University Press, 1983. pp. 179–212.

Franklin, John Hope, and Meier, August, eds. *Black Leaders of the Twentieth Century.* Urbana: University of Illinois Press, 1982.

Franklin, Vincent P. *The Education of Black Philadelphia. The Social and Educational History of a Minority Community, 1900–1950.* Philadelphia: University of Pennsylvania Press, 1978.

Gabaccia, Donna. "'The Transplanted': Women and Family in Immigrant America." *Social Science History* 12 (Fall 1988): 243–53.

Gans, Herbert J. *The Urban Villagers: Group and Class in the Life of Italian Americans.* New York: Free Press, 1962.

Garraty, John A. "The United States Steel Corporation versus Labor: The Early Years." *Labor History* 1 (Winter 1960): 3–38.

Gavit, John. "Missions and Settlements." *Commons* 2 (February 1898): 3–4.

Gerber, David A. *Black Ohio and the Color Line, 1860–1915*. Urbana: University of Illinois Press, 1976.

Gettleman, Marvin L. "Philanthropy and Social Control in Late Nineteenth-Century America: Some Hypotheses and Data on the Rise of Social Work." *Societas* 5 (Winter 1975): 49–59.

Ginder, Richard. *With Cross and Crozier: A Biography of John Francis Noll, Fifth Bishop of Fort Wayne and Founder of Our Sunday Visitor.* Huntington, Ind., 1952.

Goldmark, Josephine. *Impatient Crusader: Florence Kelley's Life Story.* Urbana: University of Illinois Press, 1953.

Gordon, Linda. "Family Violence, Feminism, and Social Control." *Feminist Studies* 12 (Fall 1986): 453–78.

Gordon, Milton. *Assimilation in American Life.* New York: Oxford University Press, 1964.

Greer, Edward. "Monopoly and Competitive Capital in the Making of Gary, Indiana." *Science and Society* 40 (Winter 1976–77): 463–78.

———. "Racism and U.S. Steel, 1906–1974." *Radical America* 10 (September-October 1976): 45–68.

Groneman, Carol, and Norton, Mary Beth, eds. *To Toil the Livelong Day: America's Women at Work, 1780–1980.* Ithaca, N.Y.: Cornell University Press, 1987.

Gulick, Charles Adams, Jr. *Labor Policy of the United States Steel Corporation.* Vol. 116, Columbia Studies in History, Economics and Public Law. New York: Columbia University Press, 1924.

Gutman, Herbert. "Work, Culture, and Society in Industrializing America, 1815–1919." *American Historical Review* 78 (June 1973): 531–88.

Hamilton, Alice. *Exploring the Dangerous Trades.* Boston: Little, Brown, 1943.

Handlin, Oscar. *The Uprooted.* Boston: Little, Brown, 1951.

Handy, Robert T. *A Christian America: Protestant Hopes and Historical Realities.* New York: Oxford University Press, 1971.

Harlan, Louis R. "Booker T. Washington and the Politics of Accommodation." In Franklin, John Hope, and Meier, August, eds., *Black Leaders of the Twentieth Century.* Urbana: University of Illinois Press, 1982. pp. 1–18.

Hart, Helen. "The Changing Function of the Settlement under Changing Conditions." *Proceedings of the Fifty-Eighth National Conference of Social Work.* Minneapolis, June 1931.

Hartmann, Edward G. *The Movement to Americanize the Immigrant.* New York: Columbia University Press, 1948.

Harvard Encyclopedia of American Ethnic Groups. "American Identity and Americanization," by Philip Gleason.

Haskell, Thomas L. *The Emergence of Professional Social Science: The American Social Science Association and the Nineteenth Century Crisis of Authority.* Urbana: University of Illinois Press, 1977.

Hayden, Dolores. *The Grand Domestic Revolution: A History of Feminist Designs for American Homes, Neighborhoods, and Cities.* Cambridge: MIT Press, 1981.

Haynes, George, comp. "Letters of Negro Migrants of 1916–1918." *Journal of Negro History* 4 (January 1919): 290–340.

Hegner, Herman F. "The Scientific Value of the Social Settlement." *American Journal of Sociology* 3 (September 1897): 171–82.

Henderson, Charles. *Social Settlements.* New York: Lentilhon, 1895.

Hess, Jeffrey A. "Black Settlement House, East Greenwich, 1902–1914." *Rhode Island History* 29 (1970): 113–27.

Higham, John. *Strangers in the Land: Patterns of American Nativism, 1860–1925.* New York: Atheneum, 1965.

Hine, Darlene Clark. *When the Truth Is Told: A History of Black Women's Culture and Community in Indiana, 1875–1950.* Indianapolis: National Council of Negro Women, Indianapolis Section, 1981.

Hodges, Dean George. "Religion in the Settlement." NCCC, *Proceedings of the Twenty-Third Annual Meeting of the NCCC.* Grand Rapids, Mich., 1896: 150–53.

Holden, Arthur C. *The Settlement Idea: A Vision of Social Justice.* New York: 1922, Arno Press, 1970.

Holloway, W. R. *Indianapolis: A Historical and Statistical Sketch of the Railway City.* Indianapolis: Indianapolis Journal Printing Company, 1870.

Hopkins, Charles Howard. *The Rise of the Social Gospel in American Protestantism, 1865–1915.* New Haven, Conn.: Yale University Press, 1940.

Interchurch World Movement. *Report on the Steel Strike of 1919.* New York: Harcourt, Brace and Howe, 1920.

Jackson, Kenneth T. *The Ku Klux Klan in the City.* New York: Oxford University Press, 1967.

Jackson, Philip. "Black Charity in Progressive Era Chicago." *Social Service Review* 52 (September 1978): 400–417.

Jarvis, Walter, "Indianapolis Provides for Its Colored Citizens." *Playground* 16 (February 1923).

Kallen, Horace M. "Democracy Versus the Melting-Pot." *Nation* 100 (February 1915): 190–94, 217–20.

Karger, Howard Jacob. *The Sentinels of Order: A Study of Social Control and the Minneapolis Settlement House Movement, 1915–1950.* Lanham, Md.: University Press of America, 1987.

Katz, Michael B. *Poverty and Policy in American History.* New York: Academic Press, 1983.

Katzman, David. *Seven Days a Week: Women and Domestic Service in Industrializing America.* New York: Oxford University Press, 1978.

Katznelson, Ira. *Black Men, White Cities: Race, Politics, and Patronage in the United States, 1900–1930, and Britain, 1948–1968.* London: Oxford University Press, 1973.

Kellogg, Paul U. *The Pittsburgh Survey.* 6 vols. New York: Charities Publication Committee, 1909–14.

Kellor, Frances. "Americanization: A Conservation Policy for Industry." *Annals of the American Academy of Political and Social Science* 65 (May 1916): 240–44.

Kennedy, David. *Over Here: The First World War and American Society.* New York: Oxford University Press, 1980.

Kessler-Harris, Alice. *Out to Work: A History of Wage-Earning Women in the United States.* New York: Oxford University Press, 1982.

———. "Women, Work and the Social Order," In Carroll, Berenice, ed. *Liberating Women's History: Theoretical and Critical Essays.* Urbana: University of Illinois Press, 1978.

Kessner, Thomas. *The Golden Door: Italian and Jewish Immigrant Mobility in New York City, 1880–1915.* New York: Oxford University Press, 1977.

Kirschner, Don. "The Ambiguous Legacy: Social Justice and Social Control in the Progressive Era." *Historical Reflections* 2 (Summer 1975): 69–88.

———. *The Paradox of Professionalism: Reform and Public Service in Urban America, 1900–1940.* New York: Greenwood Press, 1986.

Kleinburg, Susan J. "Technology and Women's Work: The Lives of Working-Class Women in Pittsburgh, 1870–1900." *Labor History* 17 (Winter 1976): 58–72.

Knapp, J. W. "An Experiment with Negro Labor." *Opportunity* 1 (February 1921): 19–23.

Knapp, John M., ed. *The Universities and the Social Problem.* London: Rivington, Percival, 1895.

Kogut, Alvin. "The Negro and the Charity Organization Society in the Progressive Era." *Social Service Review* 44 (March 1970): 11–21.

———. "The Settlements and Ethnicity: 1890–1914." *Social Work* 17 (May 1972): 22–31.

Korman, Gerd A. *Industrialization, Immigrants, and Americanizers: The View from Milwaukee, 1865–1925.* Madison: State Historical Society of Wisconsin, 1967.

Lane, James B. *City of the Century: A History of Gary, Indiana.* Bloomington: Indiana University Press, 1978.

Lathrop, Julia. "Hull House as a Sociological Laboratory." NCCC *Proceedings of the Twenty-First Meeting of the NCCC.* Nashville, Tenn., 1894: 313–19.

Lerner, Gerda. "Early Community Work of Black Club Women." *Journal of Negro History* 59 (April 1974): 158–67.

Levine, Daniel. *Jane Addams and the Liberal Tradition.* Madison: University of Wisconsin Press, 1971.

Levine, Lawrence W. "Marcus Garvey and the Politics of Revitalization." In Franklin, John Hope, and Meier, August, eds. *Black Leaders of the Twentieth Century.* Urbana: University of Illinois Press, 1982. pp. 105–37.

Lissak, Rivka. "Myth and Reality: The Pattern of Relationship between the Hull House Circle and the 'New Immigrants' on Chicago's West Side, 1890–1919." *Journal of American Ethnic History* 2 (Spring 1983): 21–50.

———. *Pluralism and Progressives: Hull House and the New Immigrants, 1890–1919.* Chicago: University of Chicago Press, 1989.

Lubove, Roy. *The Professional Altruist: The Emergence of Social Work as a Career.* Pittsburgh: University of Pittsburgh Press, 1965.

———. *The Progressives and the Slums: Tenement House Reform in New York City, 1890–1917.* Pittsburgh: University of Pittsburgh Press, 1962.

Luker, Ralph E. "The Social Gospel and the Failure of Racial Reform, 1877–1898." *Church History* 46 (March 1977): 176–246.

―――― . "Missions, Institutional Churches, and Settlement Houses: The Black Experience, 1885–1910." *Journal of Negro History* 69 (Summer-Fall 1984): 101–13.

Lyda, John W. *The Negro in the History of Indiana.* Terre Haute, Ind.: Hathaway Printery, 1953.

McBride, Paul. *Culture Clash: Immigrants and Reformers, 1880–1920.* San Francisco: R&E Research Associates, 1975.

McCarthy, Kathleen D. *Noblesse Oblige: Charity and Cultural Philanthropy in Chicago, 1849–1929.* Chicago: University of Chicago Press, 1982.

McClymer, John F. "The Federal Government and the Americanization Movement, 1915–1924." *Prologue. The Journal of the National Archives* 10 (Spring 1978): 22–41.

―――― . "The Pittsburgh Survey, 1907–1914: Forging an Ideology in the Steel District." *Pennsylvania History* 41 (April 1974): 169–86.

―――― . *War and Welfare: Social Engineering in America, 1890–1925.* Westport, Conn.: Greenwood Press, 1980.

McLaughlin, Virginia Yans. *Family and Community: Italian Immigrants in Buffalo, 1880–1930.* Ithaca, N.Y.: Cornell University Press, 1977.

Madison, James H. *Indiana through Tradition and Change: A History of the Hoosier State and Its People, 1920–1945.* The History of Indiana, vol. 5. Indianapolis: Indiana Historical Society, 1982.

May, Henry F. *Protestant Churches and Industrial America.* New York: Harper, 1949.

Meyer, Stephen J. *The Five Dollar Day: Labor Management and Social Control in the Ford Motor Company, 1905–1921.* Albany: State University of New York Press, 1981.

Millender, Dolly. *Yesterday in Gary: A Brief History of the Negro in Gary, 1906–1967.* Published by Dolly Millender: Gary, Ind., 1967.

Modell, John, and Hareven, Tamara K. "Urbanization and the Malleable Household: An Examination of Boarding and Lodging in American Families." *Journal of Marriage and the Family* 35 (August 1973): 467–79.

Mohl, Raymond A. "The Great Steel Strike of 1919 in Gary, Indiana: Working-Class Radicalism or Trade Union Militancy?" *MidAmerica* 63 (January 1981): 36–52.

―――― . "The International Institute Movement and Ethnic Pluralism." *Social Science* 56 (Winter 1981): 14–21.

―――― . "The Failure of Industrial City Planning: Gary, Indiana, 1906–1910." *Journal of the American Institute of Planners* 38 (July 1972): 203–15.

―――― . "The Immigrant Church in Gary, Indiana: Religious Adjustment and Cultural Defense." *Ethnicity* 8 (1981): 1–17.

―――― . "Paternalism and Pluralism: Immigrants and Social Welfare in Gary, Indiana, 1906–1940." *American Studies* 15 (Spring 1974): 5–30.

Mohl, Raymond A., and Betten, Neil. "Ethnic Adjustment in the Industrial City: The International Institute of Gary, 1919–1940." *International Migration Review* 6 (Winter 1972): 361–76.

————, and Betten, Neil. *Steel City: Urban and Ethnic Patterns in Gary, Indiana, 1906–1950.* New York: Holmes and Meier, 1986.

Mohraz, Judy Jolley. *The Separate Problem: Case Studies of Black Education in the North, 1900–1930.* Westport, Conn.: Greenwood Press, 1979.

Montgomery, Caroline Williamson, comp. *Bibliography of College, Social, University and Church Settlements.* New York: College Settlements Association, 1900.

Montgomery, David. *Workers' Control in America: Studies in the History of Work, Technology, and Labor Struggle.* New York: Cambridge University Press, 1979.

Moore, Powell A. *The Calumet Region.* Indianapolis: Indiana Historical Bureau, 1959.

Murray, Robert K. *Red Scare: A Study in National Hysteria, 1919–1920.* Minneapolis: University of Minnesota Press, 1955.

Nelson, Daniel. *Managers and Workers: Origins of the New Factory System in the United States, 1880–1920.* Madison: University of Wisconsin Press, 1975.

Neverdon Morton, Cynthia. *Afro-American Women of the South and the Advancement of the Race, 1895–1925.* Knoxville: University of Tennessee Press, 1989.

Noll, Bishop John. *The Diocese of Fort Wayne.* 2 vols. Fort Wayne, Ind., 1941.

Olds, Marshall. *Analysis of the Interchurch World Movement Report on the Steel Strike.* New York: G. P. Putnam's, 1923.

Pacey, Lorene M., ed. *Readings in the Development of Settlement Work.* New York: Association Press, 1950.

Patterson, James T. *America's Struggle against Poverty, 1900–1980.* Cambridge: Harvard University Press, 1981.

Perry, Elisabeth Israels. "'The General Motherhood of the Commonwealth': Dance Hall Reform in the Progressive Era." *American Quarterly* 37 (Winter 1985): 719–33.

Peiss, Kathy. *Cheap Amusements: Working Women and Leisure in Turn of the Century New York.* Philadelphia: Temple University Press, 1985.

Peterson, Jon A. "From Social Settlement to Social Agency: Settlement Work in Columbus, Ohio, 1898–1958." *Social Service Review* 39 (1965): 191–208.

Phillips, Clifton. *Indiana in Transition, 1880–1920.* Indianapolis: Indiana Historical Bureau and Indiana Historical Society, 1968.

Philpott, Thomas Lee. *The Slum and the Ghetto: Neighborhood Deterioration and Middle Class Reform, Chicago, 1880–1930.* New York: Oxford University Press, 1978.

Picht, Werner. *Toynbee Hall and the English Settlement Movement,* rev. ed., trans. Lilian A. Cowell. London: G. Bell, 1914.

Piven, Frances Fox. "Women and the State: Ideology, Power, and the Welfare State." In Gerstel, Naomi, and Gross, Harriet Engel, eds., *Families and Work: Towards Reconceptualization.* Philadelphia: Temple University Press, 1987. pp. 512–19.

Pleck, Hafkin Elizabeth. "A Mother's Wages: Income Earning among Married Italian and Black Women, 1896–1911." In Gordon, Michael, ed. *The American Family in Social Historical Perspective.* New York: St. Martin's Press, 1978. pp. 490–510.

————. *Black Migration and Poverty: Boston 1865–1900.* New York: Academic Press, 1979.

Preston, William, Jr. *Aliens and Dissenters: Federal Suppression of Radicals, 1903–1933.* New York: Harper Torchbooks, 1963.

Pumphrey, Ralph E. "Compassion and Protection: Dual Motivations in Social Welfare." *Social Service Review* 33 (March 1959): 21–29.

Quandt, Jean B. *From the Small Town to the Great Community: The Social Thought of Progressive Intellectuals.* New Brunswick, N.J.: Rutgers University Press, 1970.

Quimby, George, comp. *Proceedings of the National Conference on Americanization in Industries.* Nantucket Beach, Mass., 1919.

Rabb, Kate Milner, and Herschell, William, eds. *An Account of Indianapolis and Marion County.* Dayton, Ohio: Dayton Historical Publishing Company, 1924.

Rainsford, William S. "What Can We Do for the Poor?" *Forum* 11 (April 1891): 115–26.

Rauschenbusch, Walter. *Christianizing the Social Order.* New York: Macmillan, 1912.

Reimers, David. "Protestantism's Response to Social Change, 1890–1930." In Jaher, Frederick Cople, ed. *The Age of Industrialism in America.* New York: Free Press, 1968.

"Report of the Social Settlement Committee." NCCC *Proceedings of the Twenty-Third Annual Meeting NCCC.* Grand Rapids, Mich., 1896.

Richmond, Mary E. *Friendly Visiting among the Poor: A Handbook for Charity Visitors.* Montclair, N.J.: Paterson Smith, 1899, repr. ed. 1969.

Robbins, Jane. "The First Year at the College Settlement." *Survey* 27 (February 24, 1912): 1800–1802.

Rochefort, David A. "Progressive and Social Control Perspectives on Social Welfare." *Social Service Review* 55 (December 1981): 568–92.

Rogers, Helen Worthington. "A Modest Experiment in Foster Motherhood: The Work of the Pure Milk Commission of the Children's Aid Association of Indianapolis." *Survey* 22 (May 1, 1909): 176–83.

Rosales, Francisco Arturo, and Simon, Daniel T. "Mexican Immigrant Experience in the Urban Midwest: East Chicago, Indiana, 1919–1945." *Indiana Magazine of History* 77 (December 1981): 333–57.

Rosenzweig, Roy. *Eight Hours for What We Will: Workers and Leisure in an Industrial City, 1870–1920.* New York: Cambridge University Press, 1983.

Rothman, Sheila. *Woman's Proper Place: A History of Changing Ideals and Practices, 1870 to the Present.* New York: Basic Books, 1978.

Rousmanière, John P. "Cultural Hybrid in the Slums: The College Woman and the Settlement House, 1889–1894." *American Quarterly* 22 (Spring 1970): 45–66.

Ryan, Mary P. *Cradle of the Middle Class: The Family in Oneida County, New York, 1790–1865.* New York: Cambridge University Press, 1981.

Sacks, Karen Brodkin, and Remy, Dorothy. *My Troubles Are Going to Have Trouble with Me: Everyday Trials and Triumphs of Women Workers.* New Brunswick, N.J.: Rutgers University Press, 1984.

Scudder, Vida. *On Journey*. New York: E. P. Dutton, 1937.

———. "Work with Italians in Boston." *Survey* 22 (April 3, 1909): 47–51.

Seeley, John R., et al. *Community Chest: A Case Study in Philanthropy.* Toronto: Toronto University Press, 1957.

Seller, Maxine Schwartz. "The Education of the Immigrant Woman, 1900–1935." *Journal of Urban History* 4 (May 1978): 307–30.

———, ed. *Immigrant Women*. Philadelphia: Temple University Press, 1981.

"Settlements and the Boy." *Survey* 47 (January 21, 1922): 630–31.

Settlements and Their Outlook: An Account of the First International Conference of Settlements, Toynbee Hall, London, July, 1922. London: P. S. King, 1922.

Shumway, Arthur. "Gary, Shrine of the Steel God." *American Parade* 3 (January-March 1929): 23–32.

Sicherman, Barbara. *Alice Hamilton: A Life in Letters.* Cambridge: Harvard University Press, 1984.

Simkhovitch, Mary K. *The Settlement Primer.* Boston: National Federation of Settlements, 1926.

Sklar, Kathryn Kish. "Hull House in the 1890s: A Community of Women Reformers." *Signs* 10 (Summer 1985): 658–77.

Smith, Timothy L. "Lay Initiative in the Religious Life of American Immigrants, 1880–1950." In Hareven, Tamara, ed. *Anonymous Americans.* Englewood Cliffs, N.J.: Prentice Hall, 1971. pp. 214–49.

———. "Religion and Ethnicity in America." *American Historical Review* 83 (December 1978): 1153–85.

Spero, Sterling D., and Harris, Abram L. *The Black Worker.* New York: Columbia University Press, 1931.

Squires, Walter Albion, B.D. *The Gary Plan of Church Schools.* Philadelphia: Department of Religious Education, Presbyterian Board of Publication and Sabbath School Work, n.d.

Sternberger, Estelle. "Gary and the Foreigners' Opportunity." *Survey* 42 (June 18, 1919): 480–82.

Stone, Katherine. "The Origins of Job Structures in the Steel Industry." In Edwards, Richard, Reich, Michael, and Gordon, David, eds., *Labor Market Segmentation.* Lexington, Mass.: D.C. Heath, 1975.

Strickland, Arvarh E. *History of the Chicago Urban League.* Urbana: University of Illinois Press, 1966.

Strong, Josiah. *Religious Movements for Social Betterment* New York: Baker and Taylor, 1900.

Szuberla, Guy. "Three Chicago Settlements: Their Architectural Form and Social Meaning." *Journal of the Illinois State Historical Society* 14 (1977): 114–29.

Tarbell, Ida M. *The Life of Elbert H. Gary.* New York: D. Appleton, 1925.

Taylor, Graham. "At Gary: Some Impressions and Interviews." *Survey* 43 (November 8, 1919): 65–66.

———. "Creating the Newest Steel City." *Survey* 22 (April 3, 1909): 20–36.

Taylor, Graham Romeyn. *Satellite Cities: A Study of Industrial Suburbs.* New York: D. Appleton, 1915.

Taylor, Paul S. *Mexican Labor in the United States. Chicago and the Calumet Region.* University of California Publications in Economics, vol. 7. Berkeley: University of California Press, 1932.

Tentler, Leslie Woodcock. *Industrial Work and Family Life in the United States, 1900–1930.* New York: Oxford University Press, 1979.

Thernstrom, Stephen. *The Other Bostonians: Poverty and Progress in the American Metropolis, 1880–1970.* Cambridge: Harvard University Press, 1973.

Thornbrough, Emma Lou. *Eliza B. Blaker: Her Life and Work.* Indianapolis: Eliza Blaker Club and Indiana Historical Society, 1965.

———. *Indiana in the Civil War Era, 1850–1880.* Indiana Historical Bureau and Indiana Historical Society, 1965.

———. *The Negro in Indiana: A Study of a Minority.* Indianapolis: Indiana Historical Bureau, 1957.

———. "Segregation in Indiana during the Klan Era of the 1920's." *Mississippi Valley Historical Review* 47 (March 1961): 594–618.

———. *Since Emancipation: A Short History of Indiana Negroes, 1863–1963.* Indianapolis: American Negro Emancipation Centennial Authority, 1963.

Trattner, Walter I., ed. *From Poor Law to Welfare State: A History of Social Welfare in America.* 4th. ed. New York: Free Press, 1989.

———. *Social Welfare or Social Control? Some Historical Reflections on Regulating the Poor.* Knoxville: University of Tennessee Press, 1983.

Trolander, Judith A. *Professionalism and Social Change: From the Settlement House Movement to Neighborhood Centers, 1886 to the Present.* New York: Columbia University Press, 1987.

———. *Settlement Houses and the Great Depression.* Detroit, Mich.: Wayne State University Press, 1975.

Trotter, Joe William. *Black Milwaukee: The Making of an Industrial Proletariat, 1915–1945.* Urbana: University of Illinois Press, 1985.

United States Steel Corporation. *Addresses and Statements of Elbert H. Gary.* 8 vols. Compiled by the Business History Society (November 1927).

Vecoli, Rudolph J. "'Contadini' in Chicago: A Critique of *The Uprooted.*" *Journal of American History* 51 (December 1964): 404–17.

———. "European Americans: From Immigrants to Ethnics." *International Migration Review* 6 (Winter 1972): 403–34.

———. "Prelates and Peasants: Italian Immigrants in the Catholic Church." *Journal of Social History* 2 (Spring 1969): 217–68.

Vicinus, Martha. *Independent Women: Work and Community for Single Women, 1850–1920.* London: Virago Press, 1985.

WPA Writers' Project. *Calumet Region Historical Guide.* Gary, Ind.: Gary Board of Education, 1939.

Wade, Louise. *Graham Taylor, Pioneer for Social Justice.* Chicago: University of Chicago Press, 1964.

Wald, Lillian. *The House on Henry Street.* New York: Henry Holt, 1915.

Warner, Beverly. "Social Settlements and Charity Organization Problems." NCCC, *Proceedings of the Thirteenth Conference, NCCC.* Atlanta, May 1903: 311.

Watson, Frank. *The Charity Organization Movement in the United States.* New York: Macmillan, 1922.

Weeks, Genevieve C. *Oscar Carleton McCulloch, 1843–1891: Preacher and Practitioner of Applied Christianity.* Indianapolis: Indiana Historical Society, 1976.

Weiss, Nancy. *The National Urban League, 1910–1940.* New York: Oxford University Press, 1974.

Whisnant, David. *All That Is Native and Fine: The Politics of Culture in an American Region.* Chapel Hill: University of North Carolina Press, 1984.

White, George Cary. "Social Settlements and Immigrant Neighbors." *Social Service Review* 33 (March 1959): 55–66.

White, Morton and Lucia. *The Intellectual versus the City.* Cambridge: Harvard University Press, 1962.

Whyte, William F. *Street Corner Society: The Social Structure of an Italian Slum.* Chicago: University of Chicago Press, 1943, 2d ed., 1955.

Wiebe, Robert H. *The Search for Order, 1879–1920.* New York: Hill and Wang, 1967.

Wilhelm, Donald. "The 'Big Business' Man as Social Worker. 1. Judge Gary of the Steel Trust." *Outlook* 22 (August 1914): 1005–9.

Wilson, Howard E. *Mary McDowell, Neighbor.* Chicago: University of Chicago Press, 1928.

Woods, Eleanor. *Robert A. Woods. Champion of Democracy.* Boston and New York: Houghton Mifflin and Company, 1929.

Woods, Robert. "Social Work: A New Profession." *Charities and the Commons* 15 (January 6, 1906): 469–76.

———. "The University Settlement Idea," in Addams et al. *Philanthropy and Social Progress.* New York: Thomas Y. Crowell, 1893, pp. 57–97.

———, and Kennedy, Albert J. *Handbook of Settlements.* New York: Charities Publication Committee, 1911.

———. *The Settlement Horizon: A National Estimate.* New York: Russell Sage Foundation, 1922.

———, eds. *Young Working Girls: A Summary of Evidence from Two Thousand Social Workers.* Boston: Houghton Mifflin, 1913.

Woofter, T. J., Jr. *Negro Problems in Cities.* New York: Negro Universities Press, 1928, repr. ed., 1969.

Wright, George C. *Life behind a Veil: Blacks in Louisville, Kentucky, 1865–1930.* Baton Rouge: Louisiana State University Press, 1985.

Zahavi, Gerald. "Negotiated Loyalty: Welfare Capitalism and the Shoemakers of Endicott Johnson, 1920–1940." *Journal of American History* 70 (December 1983): 602–20.

Zunz, Olivier. *The Changing Face of Inequality: Urbanization, Industrial Development, and Immigrants in Detroit, 1880–1920.* Chicago: University of Chicago Press, 1982.

Index

A Note on the Author

Ruth Hutchinson Crocker is assistant professor of history and chair of the Women's Studies Program at Auburn University. She has written and spoken widely on the settlement movement.